Corrections

Corrections

Second Edition

Alejandro del Carmen
University of Texas at Arlington

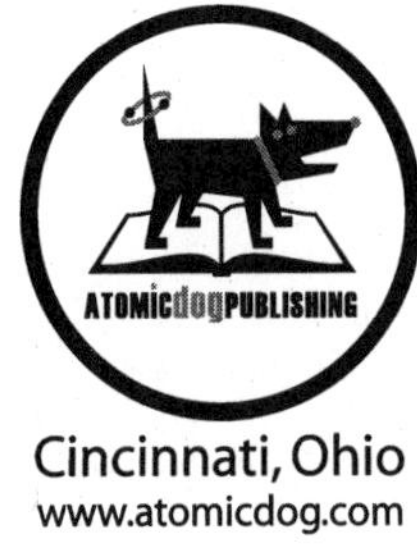

Cincinnati, Ohio
www.atomicdog.com

Cover: © Royalty-Free/CORBIS

Library of Congress Catalog Card Number: 2003107012

ISBN 1-59260-056-5

Printed in the United States of America by Atomic Dog Publishing, 1148 Main Street, Third Floor, Cincinnati, OH 45202.
10 9 8 7 6 5 4 3 2 1

To

Denise,
Gabriel and Gemma

and in memory of

Michael B. Paris, Joey Cushman, and Mel Thee

Brief Contents

Contents

Chapter 12

Chapter 13

Chapter 14

Chapter 15 

Chapter 16 

Preface

As we face uncertain economic and political times, social issues seem to be more relevant than ever before in the history of the United States. Violence has found a home in America's schools, public facilities, and some of the best-known national landmarks. The public believes that no one is safe anymore. Many ask why we never appreciated life before September 11, 2001.

Images of airplanes crashing into the World Trade Center and the Pentagon often reappear in our minds as we recall where we were when we first heard of the September 11 terrorist attacks against the United States. We often wonder about the motive terrorists and other violent offenders had when they considered engaging in violence. Why would an individual kill someone and deprive them from the benefit of life? Why do people kill without paying attention to the pain they will cause innocent bystanders?

Although it is important to consider the motives of offenders, it is not within the scope of this textbook. This book is primarily concerned with the reaction we invoke when a suspect is arrested and convicted. Once the suspect is apprehended, what are we to do with them? Is incarceration an effective method of punishment? Can we deter offenders from committing crimes again? This book attempts to address all of these important questions. I hope that, after reading this text, you will have an understanding of the historical significance of punishment, the alleged utility of punishment, and the social consequences that are a result of current penal practices.

The word "corrections" suggests that something must be fixed. Many view the correctional system as a component of the criminal justice system charged with the mission of correcting those who have violated social rules. Others feel that corrections involves nothing more than a jail cell, where the offender is housed until the completion of a sentence. This text will show you that corrections is a world that involves professionals from the correctional field and other disciplines who come together daily and carry out the provisions that the law mandates.

This text examines a number of issues affecting today's correctional system, such as probation, parole, female and male offenders, prisons, and jails. In the second edition, you will find new material that complements and strengthens the areas that were considered strong in the first edition of this text.

The publisher of this book, Atomic Dog, adheres to the philosophy of providing students with quality books at a reduced price. My wish is that this book gives merit to their important mission.

I sincerely hope that you enjoy reading this book as much as I have delighted in writing it. Have a wonderful journey in learning about the world of corrections.

Online and In Print

Corrections, Second edition, is available online as well as in print. The online chapters demonstrate how the interactive media components of the text enhance presentation and understanding. For example,

- Animated illustrations help clarify concepts.
- Clickable glossary terms provide immediate definitions of key concepts.
- The search function allows you to quickly locate discussions of specific topics throughout the text.
- Highlighting capabilities allow you to emphasize main ideas. You can also add personal notes in the margin.

You may choose to use just the online version of the text, or both the online and the print versions together. This gives you the flexibility to choose which combination of resources works best for you. To assist those who use the online and print versions together, the primary heads and subheads in each chapter are numbered the same. For example, the first primary head in Chapter 1 is labeled 1-1, the second primary head in this chapter is labeled 1-2, and so on. The subheads build from the designation of their corresponding primary head: 1-1a, 1-1b, etc. This numbering system is designed to make moving between the online and print versions as seamless as possible.

Finally, next to a number of figures and tables in the print version of the text, you will see icons similar to the ones on the left. These icons indicate that these figures or tables in the online version of the text are interactive in a way that applies, illustrates, or reinforces the concept.

Acknowledgements

Writing the second edition of this textbook would not have been possible without the love and support of several individuals. My wife, Denise, often provided the support and encouragement a writer needs to complete a manuscript. Her love and understanding were my constant companions in the process of writing the second edition of *Corrections.* My young children were amazed at the amount of time their dad would spend in front of a computer monitor without falling sleep. They reminded me in small ways that the most important task in my life is, and should always be, spending time with them.

My parents, Alejandro and Maria Cristina, have also provided much encouragement. Their courage in coming to the United States and beginning a new life, for the sake of their children's freedom, will never cease to inspire me. I hope that the publication of this second edition serves as evidence to them that their many sacrifices will not go unappreciated.

My sister Marcela, who is a remarkable human being, has truly been an inspiration. Her love and kindness towards others has inspired me to be a better human being. Marcela's dedication and passion in the medical field often reminds me that there is still hope for humanity. I am also grateful to my brother Mauricio who often refers to the important aspects of life.

This book could not have made it to its second edition without the assistance of my friend and editor Tom Romaniak. Tom made it all happen and fall together in ways I never thought possible. I know in my heart that every word I wrote in this manuscript would not have had the same meaning without Tom's assistance. Even at difficult times, he always took his time to guide my efforts in an effective manner. A "thank you" is also in order to Christine Abshire, developmental editor, who spent many long days and even longer nights working on this manuscript. I am amazed at Christine's unwavering determination to persevere and complete this book, even at times when I thought it would be impossible to finish it in a timely manner. Thank you Tom and Christine for your hard work and for making the second edition of this book a reality.

The second edition of this book is a result of the opportunity to write a corrections book that Sue Titus-Reid once provided. Thanks again Sue for continuing to be a good friend and mentor. The Atomic Dog team has worked diligently in the production of this book. Vickie Putman, vice president of production; along with Sydney Jones, content developmental editor; Kathy Davis, production coordinator; and Lesley Adams, copyeditor, held to a rigorous production schedule while always keeping sight of our goal. I also want to thank Rachael Erter for her assistance during this process.

I would like to express my sincere gratitude to my friend and mentor George C. Wright. His words of wisdom have truly had a positive effect in my life. Thank you George!

While I take full responsibility for any oversights in the final book, I want to express my gratitude to the following individuals for their reviews of the first manuscript:

First Edition
Mathew Kanjirathinkal, Texas A&M University-Commerce
Ronald Burns, Texas Christian University
Dennis J. Stevens, University of Massachusetts at Boston

Second Edition
Jerry C. Jolley, Lewis-Clark State College
Debra L. Stanley, Ph.D., Central Connecticut State University

Finally, I want to thank the individuals who have made a difference in my life—my late grandparents, Carlos, Alejandro and Aida. They each taught me in their special way the value of education and the importance of exploring and understanding my roots. Also, a special thanks to my grandmother Luisa for continuing to provide words of wisdom at times I most needed them.

I began to write the second edition of this book at a time when one of my students, Michael B. Paris, passed away in a car accident. I feel truly blessed that I had the opportunity of meeting and interacting with Michael. Upon hearing of his death, I realized that those of us in the academic world often learn from our students as much as we teach them. Thank you Michael for reminding me of the ideals that led me to this profession and for making me a more compassionate human being.

Alejandro del Carmen

About the Author

Alejandro del Carmen

Alejandro del Carmen was born in the small town of Jinotepe, 40 kilometers south of Managua, Nicaragua. His family fled to the United States in 1979, at the end of the most violent civil war that has ever taken place in Nicaragua. At the time of his arrival, Dr. del Carmen spoke very little English but was quick to grasp the language and learn about the customs of his adoptive nation. After living in several U.S. cities, the del Carmen family moved to Miami, Florida, where they resided for many years. It was in Miami that Dr. del Carmen attended both high school and college. Upon completion of his Bachelor's degree in criminal justice from Florida International University, he attended the Florida State University's School of Criminology and Criminal Justice, where he earned his master's and Ph.D. degrees.

Dr. del Carmen's childhood experiences in large part shaped his decision to become a criminologist. Having been exposed to the horrors of war and the dehumanizing experience of being an immigrant, he chose a profession that facilitates an environment conducive to ideological tolerance and academic freedom. He firmly believes that the hope of humanity rests on the shoulders of those commissioned to shape the minds of future leaders.

Currently, Dr. del Carmen lives with his wife and two children in Arlington, Texas. Aside from being an associate professor, he serves as graduate advisor and director of the Center for Criminal Justice Research and Training at the University of Texas at Arlington. As director, he has established a close working relationship with criminal justice agencies in Texas. Dr. del Carmen enjoys spending time with his family and listening to the immortal sounds of Frank Sinatra.

Chapter

Chapter 1

Overview of the Correctional System

Outline

A news report announced that a California woman was sentenced to three months in jail and five years of probation after being found guilty of endangering the lives of her children. Rosemarie Radovan, 31, pleaded no contest to two counts of felony child endangerment. Ms. Radovan, who worked at an electronics store in Santa Clara, locked her two children inside the trunk of her vehicle while she was at work.[1]

Key Terms

certiorari
corrections
"Three Strikes and You're Out" Law
writ of habeas corpus

Stories such as these are not hard to find in today's newspapers. Most people in our society consider harsh punishment appropriate for an act of cruelty against children. Social conditioning prompts society to contemplate punishment for acts considered offensive to social standards. Punishment is not a new phenomenon—it has been evident since the beginning of human existence. The form in which punishment is administered, however, has been subject to dramatic change throughout the years. Today, the administration of punishment as established by the court system is carried out by the institution called corrections. The objective of this textbook is to introduce the history, organization, management, and other dimensions of corrections in the United States.

When asked about a particular aspect of corrections, it has been found most people have formulated an opinion of the correctional system. Despite the many conclusions, most responses are not based on concrete evidence. They are often formulated from feelings or past experiences that have influenced a person's outlook of the correctional system.

One popular image of the correctional system is of inmates wearing denim clothes with tattooed bodies while holding metal cups, awaiting their daily serving of bread and water. This image continues to be popularized by Hollywood and other media. In reality, the world of corrections involves

much more. The main concern is the correctional client but it also includes personnel and equipment that support the existence of the incarcerated individual. The personnel are complex and vary in their goals and duties. The personnel include doctors, counselors, guards, cooks, pharmacists, nurses, chaplains, and administrators. They all have the same mission— custody and rehabilitation—although they seem to neglect or prefer one mission. In addition to the personnel, the correctional system relies heavily on the use of technology and equipment to accomplish its goal. These include computer systems, surveillance cameras, infrared equipment, and electronic gates. The incarcerated, the personnel, the equipment, and the technology are the foundation of the complex world of corrections. It is important to note that corrections is only one of three components of the criminal justice system (the other two are police and courts). This chapter presents a brief overview of the criminal justice system with special emphasis on two of its components—police and courts—as they relate, in later chapters, to the operation of the correctional system. This chapter also provides a brief look at today's correctional trends.

1-1 Criminal Justice: An Overview

Corrections
The component of the criminal justice system concerned with the investigation, confinement, supervision, and treatment of offenders.

The criminal justice system in the United States is a billion dollar business enterprise. According to the U.S. Department of Justice, federal, state, and local governments spent $130 billion for civil and criminal justice systems in fiscal 1997. This constitutes an 8 percent increase over 1996 expenditures. For every resident, the three levels of government together spent $368. The largest percentage increase of those funds, 381 percent, was from **corrections**, while the judicial branch and police agencies increased their budgets by 267 percent and 207 percent respectively.[2] These figures suggest that of the three components of the criminal justice system, corrections is growing the fastest although it seems to be the least understood by the public. It is the corrections component that is affected most by the actions of the police, prosecutors, defense attorneys, and judges.

1-1a The System Aspect of Criminal Justice: Effect on Corrections

The systematic aspect of criminal justice is often overlooked. Many people ignore how the criminal justice body operates as a system (see Figure 1-1 on pages 4 and 5). What takes place at one stage may have a tremendous impact on what happens at another stage or in another component.

As Figure 1-1 indicates, a person might be released from the system of criminal justice at any stage. Upon apprehension of a suspect, the police might decide not to arrest. After being arrested and after booking, the accused might be released because the prosecutor decides not to proceed with the case. After the initial appearance before a magistrate or after the preliminary hearing, the charges might be dropped or the case dismissed. If the case must go before a grand jury, the jury might refuse to return an indictment, thus ending the case before trial. Charges might also be dismissed at the arraignment stage. At any time before trial, the charges may be reduced. This is usually done in exchange for an agreement by the defense to plead guilty to lesser charges. This will also void the time and expense of a trial. A large percentage of criminal cases are processed out of the system at one of these stages, a fact that has raised considerable criticism among those who argue that this occurs because of socioeconomic status or other non-legal criteria. Figure 1-2 (on page 6) will help us visualize the theory that as the system progresses, the number of cases is reduced.

Figure 1-2 shows how the number of cases decreases as they proceed through the criminal justice system. This is significant because a few of the many cases that are processed result in incarceration. Some argue that processing some cases out of the system before trial is based on the legal seriousness of the offense and the time and resources necessary to accommodate the trial. Further, it is held that it is in the interest of society as well as the accused not to try all cases.

Even if a case is tried and the evidence suggests beyond a reasonable doubt that the accused is guilty, the jury or judge will decide what punishment the convicted offender will receive. In some circumstances, judges or juries may find the time served while the trial is taking place suffices and no additional prison time may be imposed. This occurs when the accused has been denied bail. In some cases, the convicted person will not spend additional time in prison.

It is also important to note that referrals of juveniles to law enforcement officials are often handled informally as this reduces the number of juveniles who enter the corrections phase of the adult criminal justice system.

The following discussion of the police and the courts illustrates how actions within each component affect corrections. The interrelationship of the various elements of the criminal justice system can be explained by the Gideon[3] case, which established a right to counsel in felony cases. Since the Supreme Court applied the ruling of that case retroactively, 4,000 prisoners in Florida who had been convicted in felony cases without representation had to be retried. The county jails were temporarily overcrowded as a result. Two thousand of these inmates were not reconvicted, and Florida, for the first time in years, had empty prison beds.

Another way in which one component of the criminal justice system affects corrections is represented in the use of probation and parole. If the judges begin imposing sentences instead of using probation, the prisons will be confronted with increasing populations. Likewise, if parole boards significantly decrease the number of cases in which parole is granted, it will increase the amount of time inmates spend in prison. This results in a rise of the inmate population.

1-1b Organization of State Criminal Justice Systems

The state system of criminal justice is generally disorganized. The fragmentation of the criminal justice system was noted by the President's Commission on Law Enforcement and Administration of Justice in 1967, the Advisory Commission on Intergovernmental Relations in 1971, the Committee for Economic Development in 1972, and the National Advisory Commission on Criminal Justice Standards and Goals in 1973. After the passage of the Omnibus Crime Control and Safe Streets Act of 1968, some states reorganized and established planning networks with federal funds dispensed[4]; however, only eight states have grouped together more than one major component of their respective criminal justice systems at the state level.[5]

The constitutional requirement of the separation of powers in the judiciary and the executive branches of government prohibits the courts' inclusion in executive reorganizations. The courts can be included in some functions of the reorganization, such as the training of court personnel. The major components of the criminal justice "superagency" would include the state police, the state prosecution, and the state adult and juvenile corrections system. Coordination of these components would reduce the serious gaps and overlaps of the various state systems that have grown— in most cases— because of political expediency rather than rational planning based on empirical evidence of what is effective.[6]

1-1c Components of the Criminal Justice System

The components of the criminal justice system include the police, courts, and corrections. Note the ways in which each of the first two components directly affects corrections.

The Police

In this section, the organization of police systems in the United States and the nature of policing are examined. The emphasis will be on the way policing impacts corrections.

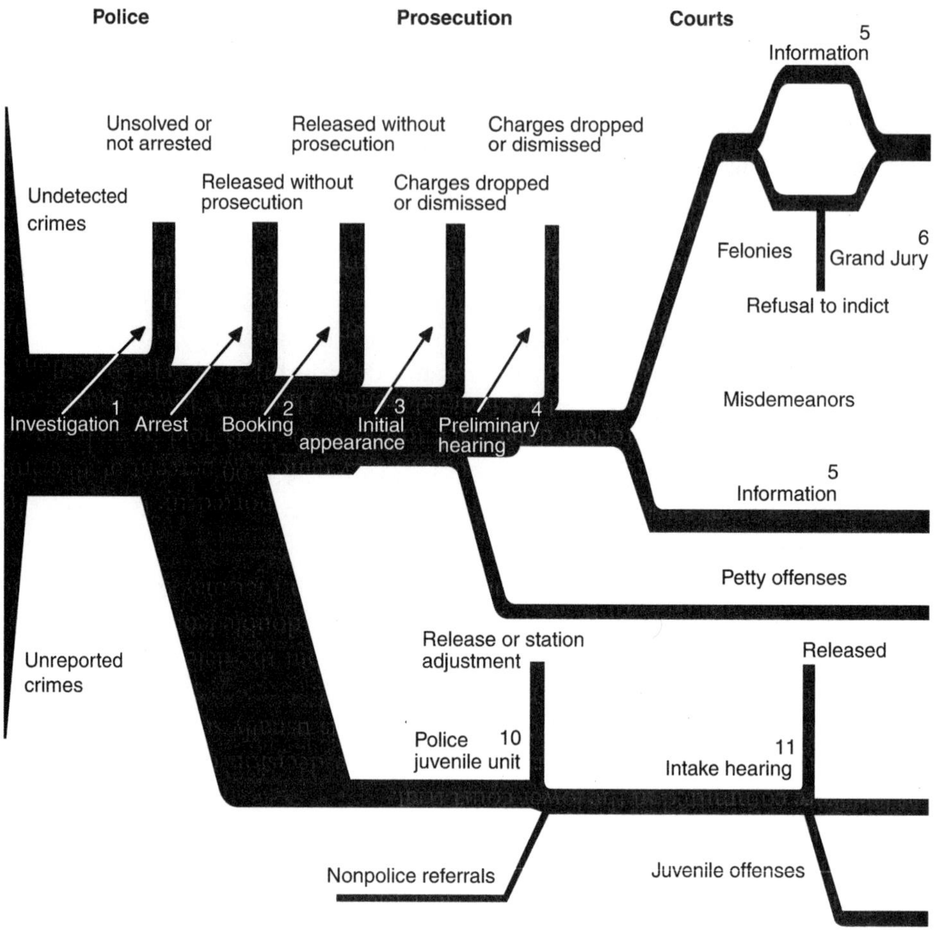

1. May continue until trial.
2. Administrative record of arrest. First step at which temporary release on bail may be available.
3. Before magistrate, commissioner, or justice of the peace. Formal notice of charge, advice of rights. Bail set. Summary trials for petty offenses usually conducted here without further processing.
4. Preliminary testing of evidence against defendant. Charge may be reduced. No separate preliminary hearing for misdemeanors in some systems.
5. Charge filed by prosecutor on basis of information submitted by police or citizens. Alternative to grand jury indictment; often used in felonies, almost always in misdemeanors.
6. Review whether government evidence sufficient to justify trial. Some states have no grand jury system; others seldom use it.

Figure 1-1
A General View of the Criminal Justice System.

Source: President's Commission on Law Enforcement and Administration of Justice, *The Challenge of Crime in a Free Society* (Washington, D.C.: U.S. Government Printing Office, 1967), pp. 8-9.

The Contemporary Police System in the United States

The police system in the United States is highly decentralized. It exists on three levels: local, state, and federal. The majority of law enforcement agencies are located in counties, cities, and towns.[7]

At the state level, the state patrol are the main law enforcers. They patrol the highways and regulate traffic. They are also primarily responsible for the enforcement of some state laws. They provide services such as criminal

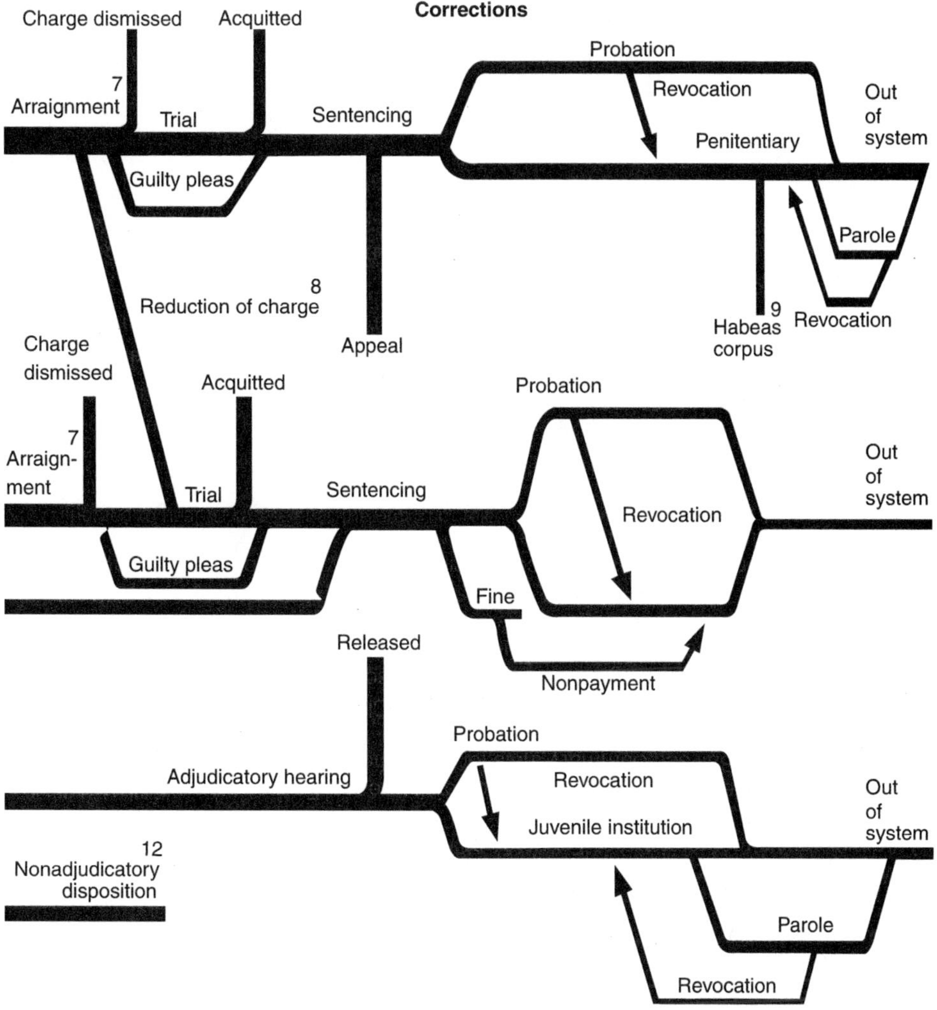

7. Appearance for plea; defendant elects trial by judge or jury (if available); counsel for indigent usually appointed here in felonies. Often not at all in other cases.
8. Charge may be reduced at any time prior to trial in return for plea of guilty or for other reasons.
9. Challenge on constitutional grounds to legality of detention. May be sought at any point in process.
10. Police often hold informal hearings, dismiss or adjust many cases without further processing.
11. Probation officer decides desirability of further court action.
12. Welfare agency, social services, counseling, medical care, etc, for cases where adjudicatory handling not needed.

identification systems, police training programs, and communications systems for local law officials.

Other state laws are enforced at the county and local level. The sheriff is the highest-ranking law enforcement officer at the county level of government. This person is selected for a term of two to four years. Their role is to keep the peace, preserve order and enforce court orders, execute civil and criminal processes, and patrol their jurisdiction. The chief law enforcers in suburban townships

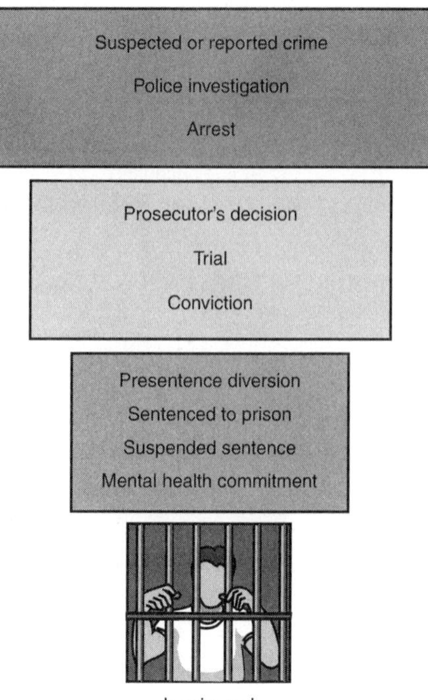

Figure 1-2
The Correctional Funnel

and municipalities are police officers. At all of these levels, jurisdiction (the territory of authority) is limited to the state, county, or municipality in which the person is a sworn officer of the law, unless the officer is chasing a felon across jurisdictional lines.

Federal law enforcement agents have a limited scope of responsibilities that are more specialized. Although federal law enforcement agencies carry a great deal of prestige in their work ethic and skill, they do not meet the public image created by movies and the media. FBI agents are often portrayed as individuals whose lives are constantly filled with glamour and danger. In the past few years, there has been public outrage and shock as news stories report that FBI crime labs are ill-equipped or are the subject of internal investigations.

Despite the level of enforcement, it is important to recognize that police agents have considerable control over the lives of citizens, and that directly affects corrections.

The Nature of Policing

If you watch television programs such as *Law and Order,* it is easy to understand why most people believe that police officers are constantly engaged in shoot-outs and drug busts. The reality of police work is quite different than this portrayal. Police work is reactive rather than proactive. The police spend most of their time responding to citizen calls—not detecting crime. James Q. Wilson, in his work Varieties of Police Behavior, found that most police work involves some sort of "fixing up." Specifically, Wilson found that most calls to the police were in regards to accidents or illnesses, animals, personal assistance, drunk persons, escort vehicles, fire, power lines or trees down, lost or found persons, or property damage. The second-highest percentage of police calls, according to Wilson, involved "order maintenance." This included gang disturbances, family problems, problems with neighbors, or fights. Only a very small percentage involved law enforcement-related calls.[8]

Case Study 1-1

Gideon v. Wainwright

CLARENCE EARL GIDEON v. LOUIE L. WAINWRIGHT
Date case was argued before the United States Supreme Court: January 15, 1963
Date case was decided by U.S. Supreme Court: March 18, 1963

Basis of the case:

The petitioner (Mr. Gideon) was charged in a Florida State Court with a noncapital felony. He did not have funds for an attorney and asked the State Court to appoint one to him. The court denied his request on the ground that the state law only permitted counsel to be appointed to indigent defendants in capital cases only. The petitioner defended himself at trial, was convicted, and sentenced to five years in state prison.

The petitioner applied to the Florida Supreme Court for a **writ of habeas corpus.** A writ of habeas corpus is often filed by inmates to challenge the legality of their confinement. After hearing the basis of the appeal, the Florida Supreme Court denied all relief. This prompted the petitioner to bring forth **certiorari,** requesting that the United States Supreme Court hear his case.

The United States Supreme Court heard the case January 15, 1963. When delivering his opinion on March 18, 1963, U.S. Supreme Court Justice Black held that the Sixth Amendment to the Federal Constitution—which states in all criminal prosecutions the accused shall have the right to counsel for his/her defense—is made obligatory in the states by the Fourteenth Amendment. He specified it is the right of the indigent defendant, when faced with a criminal charge, to enjoy the benefits of appointed counsel.[9]

Further Readings

Anthony Lewis, *Gideon's Trumpet,* (New York: Random House, 1964).

Police Impact on the Correctional System

The police have considerable discretion in their jobs. It is this decision-making power that closely connects the police to corrections. They have authority to determine to what extent an apprehended person will be processed through the stages of the criminal justice system. They decide who is arrested and who will be detained in jail. The evidence secured by the police influences whether charges are brought against an individual and whether they will be tried. What an officer reports about the conduct of a suspect upon arrest may influence the judge in sentencing. In all stages of the criminal justice system, the police have potentially more influence over the accused than any other component.

Writ of habeas corpus
A suit typically filed by inmates in order to challenge the legality of their imprisonment.

Certiorari
An appeal to a higher court to review a case.

Courts

The second major component of the criminal justice system is the courts. After a brief overview of the state and federal court system, the trial courts are examined.

The Dual Court System

The United States has a dual court system comprised of state and federal courts. State crimes are prosecuted in state courts and federal crimes are prosecuted in federal courts. State statutes define the crimes of the former and the latter are defined by acts of Congress. Most criminal cases are tried in state courts—approximately 85 percent of the total of all cases tried.

State Courts The court system differs from state to state. Lower trial courts exist to try the less serious offenses. Higher trial courts have general jurisdiction and try felonies and serious misdemeanors. All states have appeals courts. Some states have an intermediate appellate court. Others have only one court of appeals, which is often called the state supreme court. Table 1-1 represents the structure of the court systems at the state level.

TABLE 1-1 Structure of Court Systems at the State Level

State Supreme Court
Referred to as the "court of last resort" (state level)
Forty-eight states have only one state supreme court
Texas and Oklahoma have two state supreme courts—one for criminal cases and for civil cases
Intermediate Court of Appeals
Designed to alleviate some of the cases presented to the state supreme court
Hears all appeals introduced whether criminal or civil cases
Trial Courts of General Jurisdiction
Disposes of serious criminal cases (felonies) and major civil cases (torts, contracts, estates)
Authorized to hear all matters not specifically delegated to the lower courts
Also hears misdemeanor cases
Trial Courts of Limited Jurisdiction
Sometimes referred to as "inferior courts" or "lower courts"
Handles minor cases (traffic violations, petty criminal cases, and civil disputes under a set amount—usually $500-$1,000)
Authorized to impose fines, as high as $5,000, and to sentence defendants to up to five years in prison

Federal Courts The federal court system consists of three levels that exclude special courts, such as the United States Court of Military Appeals. These levels include district courts, appellate courts, and the United States Supreme Court. The United States district courts are trial courts. Cases may be appealed from the district courts to the appellate courts. There are eleven courts at this level and they are called circuit courts. The highest court is the Supreme Court which serves as an appeal court although it has jurisdiction to serve as a trial court in a few cases (see Table 1-2).

It is important to note that the lower federal courts and the state courts constitute separate systems. These systems operate under different organizational structures. A state court may be bound by the decisions of a lower federal court. All courts—federal and state—are subject to the decisions reached by the United States Supreme Court.

Trial and Appellate Courts

There is a distinction between trial and appellate courts. Trial courts hear the factual evidence of a case and determine the issues. The decisions may be made by a jury or by a judge. Appellate courts review the lower court trial but do not try the facts. The appellant (the party appealing the lower court decision) can ask for a new trial, alleging errors in the trial court proceeding. A few examples of errors are: the admission of hearsay evidence, illegal confessions, and minority exclusion from a jury. The appellee (the winning party in the lower court decision) argues that errors did not exist or did not constitute reversible errors—the errors did not prejudice the appellant—and therefore a new trial should not be granted.

When a trial court rules against the defendant, he or she has a right of appeal both in the state and the federal court systems. This right of appeal does not extend directly to the United States Supreme Court. The defendant may exhaust all possible appeals and then introduce the case to the Supreme Court. This does not mean the Supreme Court will hear the case. The U.S. Supreme Court only hears a small percentage of appeals cases.

TABLE 1-2 The Federal Court System

United States Supreme Court

Highest court in the nation

Comprised of nine justices (or judges)

Justices of the Supreme Court are nominated by the president, require confirmation by the Senate, and serve for life

Not mandated to hear all cases— has the option of rejecting a specific case

U.S. Court of Appeals

Created in 1891 to relieve the caseload of the U.S. Supreme Court

Staffed by judges who are nominated by the president, require confirmation by the Senate, and serve for life

The chief justice (the most senior judge in terms of service) of each circuit (region) has supervisory responsibilities for the circuit

U.S. District Courts

Federal trial courts

At least one per state

Staffed by judges who are nominated by the president, require confirmation by the Senate, and serve for life

During an appeal a judge or judges hear the case and the issues are confined to matters of law, not fact. The court looks at the trial court record and hears oral arguments from attorneys for both sides. It then determines whether any errors of law were committed in the lower court trial.

The appellate court can affirm or reverse the decision of the lower court. When a lower court decision is reversed, the case is usually sent back for a new trial. The case has then been "reversed and remanded."

Prosecutors can also appeal on basis of the law but the defendant cannot be retried because of the constitutional provision against double jeopardy. The prosecutor, if he or she wins on appeal, has won a decision that may be of benefit in future trials.

Lower courts The President's Crime Commission reported in 1967 that the most important courts are the lower courts, as they handle 90 percent of all criminal cases. Although this report dates back to the 1960s, it is held in high regard and considered applicable to today's judicial trends. The term "lower courts" can refer to two types of courts—general or limited jurisdiction. The President's Crime Commission refers to the trial court of general jurisdiction. As shown in Table 1-1, these courts serve an essential purpose in processing all types of cases including DWI, spousal abuse, fights, and other misdemeanors. Limited jurisdiction courts, in comparison, only oversee cases that carry a specific amount of jail/prison time and/or a specific amount of fines.

In some of the general and limited jurisdiction courts, defendants are not told their constitutional rights. Judges may have little time to obtain facts before determining whether to grant bail. An important decision may be based on the charge and the defendant's previous record. In courts of general jurisdiction, the trial may be brief and may not include all the procedural formalities required of a criminal trial. Rules of evidence are often ignored. The defendants usually receive sentences immediately. Pre-sentence reports and probation services rarely exist in many jurisdictions. Judges are often perturbed in presiding over petty offenses such as vagrancy, drunkenness, disorderly conduct, and prostitution. Often "defendants are treated with contempt, berated, laughed at, embarrassed . . ."[10]

Some improvements have been made since the 1967 Crime Commission report but lower courts are still plagued with many problems. One is a backlog resulting in delay of trial. An overworked court that decides cases quickly and with little individualized attention is causing injustices. In addition, there is little preparation time available to overworked prosecutors and defense attorneys. Crowded court dockets have created pressures that encourage plea-bargaining and mass handling of some cases. This can lead to unreasonable pressures on defendants to plead guilty. Such practices affect corrections extensively. For those not released on bail, defendants awaiting trial may be detained in correctional facilities with inhumane conditions. Continued court delays place strains on jails, especially in large metropolitan areas. Defendants who have court-appointed attorneys may not see them during this time because their attorneys are occupied with other cases. Such defendants are left with many questions and no answers, resulting in increased bitterness toward the criminal justice system. The attitudes are not conducive to treatment programs and may impede success upon release from incarceration. Long delays are also often characteristic of the appeals process. An inmate whose appeal to a higher court successfully reverses the conviction at the trial court may spend no less time imprisoned had the appeal been heard promptly.

Actions of trial courts affect corrections in another way. If the trial judge makes a decision based on inadequate information, the defendant may receive a longer sentence than is necessary or a shorter sentence than is reasonable. For example, trial judges who have the power to sentence a defendant to a particular institution may err in that decision. With comprehensive information acquired before sentencing, the judges' decisions are difficult—without such information they are impossible. Such problems might be avoided with extensive presentencing information.

Corrections

The final component of the criminal justice system is corrections, which is defined broadly as covering the ways society reacts to persons who have been accused of committing criminal acts as well as persons who are processed through the juvenile court. Many believe the main purpose of corrections is to administer punishment under the law. Others argue that corrections is nothing more than a mechanism in which people sentenced in a court are controlled in a highly restricted and secure environment. Although later chapters of this text discuss the history of the correctional system, it is important to become familiar with current corrections trends and past events that have made a significant impact on the American correctional system.

The Nature of Corrections

In October 1870, the National Prison Association met in Cincinnati, Ohio, and repudiated the concepts that characterized corrections of the time—the silent, lockstep system, rigid discipline, and hard labor. The conference called for a new approach to corrections advocating an emphasis on changing or rehabilitating rather than merely warehousing and punishing offenders. This resulted in the development and expansion of concepts such as parole during the twentieth century. Other concepts were a system of classifying inmates according to abilities and needs and the development of numerous types of rehabilitation programs. The 1970s and 1980s, however, were characterized by increasing crime rates and rising acts of violence within correctional institutions. These events led many to conclude that corrections had not met its goal of reducing crime and therefore a new approach should be taken. Others argued that the problem was not only in the correctional subsystem but also in the components characterized by discrimination against the poor and minorities. Coincidentally, these populations are over-represented in prison.

Some argue that the central focus of all correctional practices should be punishment. Others claim that the offenders should be embraced with love and compassion—also known as the rehabilitative approach. Despite these contrasting views, all agree that the future of corrections is a topic of debate and is in a state of transition. The field of corrections is attracting more attention today than it has in recent periods of our history.

Correctional Trends

The total number of individuals incarcerated at the federal and state levels by the end of 2000 was 1,381,892. This represented a 1.3 percent increase—less than the average increase of 6 percent since 1990. During the year 2000, the prison population was at its lowest level since 1972. The prison incarceration rate, by the end of 2000, was 478 sentenced inmates per 100,000 U.S. residents. This figure represents an increase from 292 in 1990. Overall, the United States experienced a decrease in the number of people incarcerated; however, the rate of incarceration increased when compared to earlier years. It is estimated that one in every 109 men and one in every 1,695 women were sentenced prisoners at the federal and state levels.[11]

The total number of individuals incarcerated in the United States by year-end 2000 was 2,071,686. The federal prison population grew by 9.4 percent in a twelve-month period. However, the state prison population only grew by 0.5 percent in the same twelve-month span. Despite the overwhelming criminal justice activity that took place at the state level, the federal prison population grew at a greater rate. Stated differently, in 2000, the federal prison system added 10,769 sentenced prisoners—this represents more than 200 new inmates per week.[12]

Of the thirteen states with the highest incarceration rates, nine were located in the South, two in the West, and two in the Midwest. This is consistent with past trends that have indicated the South has the highest prison incarceration rates in the U.S. The inmate population in state prisons has experienced a growth of 72 percent since 1990. An analysis of the ten-year period leading to 2000 reveals ten states doubled their sentenced inmate populations.[13] Four of these states merit further examination.

The Most Active States in Correctional Practices

Although most states' correctional systems have experienced growth in the past few years, the bulk of activity takes place in four states—New York, Florida, Texas, and California. These states oversee approximately 33 percent of all offenders under correctional supervision.

New York Historically, New York's correctional system was regarded by many as the innovator of correctional policy due to its role in creating the reformatory. Although this state is still involved with the national correctional platform, it is no longer regarded as the creator of correctional policy. Some of the characteristics of the New York correctional system are:

- Adult corrections operates under the supervision of the Department of Corrections.
- Juvenile corrections is supervised by the New York Division of Youth Services.

- The New York Correctional System is decentralized while maintaining strong state coordination efforts.
- The New York Division of Parole administers parole while probation is considered a county function.

One of the greatest predicaments affecting the New York correctional system is its present condition of inmate overcrowding. The number of inmates entering New York's correctional system is too great for the inadequate amount of correctional funding. After Governor George Pataki took office, he proposed more leniencies for minor repeat offenders with the hope of lessening pressures on the New York correctional system. Despite his efforts, many wonder how the state will continue to address the increasing number of inmates entering the system as it continues to be handicapped by an ill-funded budget.

Florida Florida is the newest member of the small group of states that oversee most of the correctional activity in the United States. Experts regard Florida as the state that represents where the nation's correctional activity will be by the year 2010. Changes in demographics of the correctional population coupled with the fast-changing social conditions are causing this growth in Florida's system. Some of the characteristics of Florida's correctional system are:

- All correctional services are administered under the executive branch (Office of the Governor).
- The Florida Department of Health and Rehabilitative Services oversees juvenile corrections.
- All community-based and institutional services are administered regionally.
- Regional directors have complete autonomy over their operations.

Florida, unlike New York, has a well-appropriated correctional budget. However, Florida legislators argue that a good portion of these funds should be applied to divert offenders from entering prison. This argument has prompted the state to start the Community Control Project in the past few years. This close supervision program targets offenders bound for prison. This project is the largest program of its kind in the United States and has diverted thousands of offenders from entering prison. In the recent past, Florida's prison admissions dropped significantly despite the fact that the prison population continues to grow. This phenomenon has taken place largely because of longer prison sentences issued in this state.

Texas The leading state in incarceration rates is Texas (157,997 incarcerated individuals by year-end 2000). More Americans are under correctional supervision in Texas than in any other state (730 prisoners sentenced to more than one year of incarceration per 100,000 U.S. residents). The state of Texas is known to be tough and punitive. Some of the features of the Texas correctional system are:

- All adult correctional activity takes place under the supervision of the Texas Department of Criminal Justice (which is supervised by a board made up of nine individuals who are appointed by the governor).
- The Texas correctional system is made up of three divisions—institutions, parole supervision, and probation.
- The Texas Parole Board reports directly to the Board of Criminal Justice.

Due to the state's aggressive correctional policy, Texas has recently been the subject of several legal suits. As a result, Texas has established a strict prison population cap. This policy has forced many jurisdictions to be cautious about incarceration, although the state continues to aggressively punish offenders by submitting them to a form of correctional supervision or by executing them. In 1999, Texas was responsible for executing 35 of the 98 total persons sentenced to capital punishment in the United States. Virginia followed with fourteen executions.[14]

California According to the Bureau of Justice Statistics (2002), California has the largest prison population in the United States and the second-highest increase in the number of prisoners. This rise is a result of California's tough sentencing policies. Some of the characteristics of the California system are:

- The Adult Authority supervises the operation of the California adult correctional system.
- The correctional system is part of the executive branch of government.
- The Youth Authority supervises juvenile correctional institutions.

Some of the recent legislation enacted in California such as the **"Three Strikes and You're Out" Law** (which requires mandatory sentences for third time felony offenders) will have a significant impact on the future of its correctional system. This legislation provides longer prison terms for third-time felons and increases the number of permanent correctional clients. This phenomenon, coupled with a struggling correctional budget, will lead to grave problems within California's correctional system in the near future. Experts argue that by the year 2010, California will have to resort to state funds not mandated by law to finance its correctional system.

"Three Strikes and You're Out" Law
A crime prevention tactic based on the notion that offenders who commit and are convicted of the same three serious violent offenses will be sentenced to life in prison without parole. The goal is to incarcerate repeat offenders while reducing the crime rate.

The corrections systems in New York, Florida, Texas, and California have several characteristics in common. Most have struggling budgets that barely pay for the construction and development of new correctional facilities. All have a firm commitment to continue their imprisonment trend and will be among the states that oversee the most correctional activity in the future. Unfortunately, other states are following closely with their own incarceration rates and correctional trends. More Americans are being imprisoned annually. CNN recently reported that the United States is close to becoming the nation that incarcerates the most citizens—a distinction that is presently held by Russia.[15]

Complexities in Correctional Management

In addition to the complexities mentioned previously, the management staffs of correctional facilities face numerous challenges daily. For example, correctional management staff is constantly under pressure by the public to be more punitive. They may receive this pressure via the news media reporting on stories in which an inmate is freed early due to his or her good behavior. The public is quick to criticize correctional staff for being too lenient on offenders. Additionally, correctional managers often feel isolated from the rest of society. They believe that most citizens do not understand the full scope of their jobs. This, and the stress of their jobs, makes their role as correctional managers extremely hard to fulfill. Finally, correctional managers must face legislators and other public figures who often regard the programs offered in prisons as not aggressive and unaccomplished in the mission of rehabilitating or punishing offenders. At times, the success or failure of these programs becomes the indicator of further funding. Although most states allocate a substantial amount of their budgets to corrections, state legislators and the public have unrealistic expectations that make the job of correctional managers almost impossible to bear.

Summary

This chapter is an overview of the three components of the criminal justice system. The activities of the police and the courts affect the correctional system directly and indirectly. This impact is particularly extensive at the beginning of the correctional system as the police enforce laws. The court system has a substantial influence on the system of corrections as it makes a determination of whether to commit an offender to correctional supervision. The actions taken by both law enforcement agencies and the courts constantly influence the welfare of the correctional system. The examination of the police and the courts illustrates some of the current correctional trends in New York, Florida, Texas, and California. The study of these states will also be helpful when reading about the theories of punishment in the next chapter.

Notes

1. APBNews.com, "Woman Receives Three Month Jail Sentence in Child Endangerment Case," August 1, 2001.
2. U.S Department of Justice (Bureau of Justice Statistics), *"The Justice System,"* Washington, D.C. (2001).
3. *Gideon v. Wainwright,* 372 U.S. 335 (1963).
4. Those states are Maryland, Kentucky, Montana, Virginia, New Mexico, Pennsylvania, North Carolina, and New Jersey. See National Institute of Law Enforcement, *Criminal Justice Organization,* p. 94.
5. *Criminal Justice Organization,* p. 94.
6. For additional information on reorganization of state criminal justice agencies, see *Criminal Justice Organization.*
7. The President's Commission on Law Enforcement and Administration of Justice, *Task Force Report: The Police* (Washington, D.C: U.S. Government Printing Office, 1967), pp. 7-8.
8. Wilson, James Q., *Varieties of Police Behavior: The Management of Law and Order in Eight Communities* (Cambridge, MA: Harvard University Press, 1968), p. 18.
9. *Gideon v. Wainwright,* 372 U.S. 335 (1963).
10. The President's Commission, *Courts,* pp. 30-31.
11. U.S. Department of Justice (Bureau of Justice Statistics), *"Expenditure and Employment Statistics,"* Washington, D.C. (2001).
12. U.S. Department of Justice (Bureau of Justice Statistics).
13. U.S. Department of Justice (Bureau of Justice Statistics).
14. U.S. Department of Justice (Bureau of Justice Statistics), "Capital Punishment Strategies—Survey Findings"
15. CNN.com, March 1, 1999.

Chapter 2

The Social Response to Crime

Societies react to criminal behavior in various ways— one of which is incarceration. Before the emergence of incarceration as a primary form of punishment, various forms of psychological and physical punishments were administered. Fines, restitution, and hard labor were common ways to punish an individual. Various theories and justifications supported specific and general forms of punishment. This chapter begins with a brief look at the main theories of punishment, thus setting the stage for a more detailed analysis of punishment in the proceeding chapters on sentencing and incarceration. Throughout the discussion of the history of punishment, there are justifications for the implementation of penal sanctions. A section of this chapter is devoted to considering the philosophies of incapacitation, reparation, maintenance of social solidarity, deterrence, reformation, rehabilitation, reintegration, retribution, and the Justice Model. Deterrence and crimes will be examined, placing specific emphasis on individual and general deterrence.

Key Terms

cultural consistency
social-structural theory
restitution
criminologists
criminal law
classical theorists
neoclassical theorists
deterrence
the wheel
hanging
classical school of criminology
social contract
utilitarianism
positive school of criminology
positivists
revenge
retribution
indeterminate sentence
reformation
scientific method
juries
just deserts
justice model
individual deterrence
general deterrence
reintegration
incapacitation
FBI Crime Index offenses

Outline

2-1 Theories of Punishment

Theories of punishment explain which individuals are punished in a particular society. Without the benefit of understanding the theories of punishment, individuals in society today share different and often uninformed opinions about why individuals who break laws should be punished. Many consider that punishment is issued in direct response to someone's illegal actions, while others believe it is intertwined with the economy and morality of a particular culture at a given time. The following sections on the main theories of punishment will provide better understanding on these two perspectives, including the cultural and sociological approaches to punishment.

2-1a Cultural Consistency

Cultural consistency
Theory that suggests that methods and severity of punishment will be consistent with other developments within the culture at a given time.

The theory of **cultural consistency** suggests that methods and severity of punishment are consistent with other developments within the culture at a given time. When physical suffering was regarded as the natural aspect of people, severe forms of corporal punishment were utilized. When greater emphasis was placed on the dignity of the individual and the equality of citizens, uniformity in sentencing was popularized. When the price system was developed, with fair prices set for various commodities, the system of letting the punishment fit the crime was practiced.[1] Individualization in the treatment of criminals occurred when individualization became important in medical treatment. When punishment was emphasized in the home and other social institutions, it was easier for the state to gain support for severe punishment. Finally, penalties increased in severity as the values that are threatened became more important.

Cultural consistency theory also suggests that as freedom of an individual becomes an important characteristic of a culture, imprisonment is considered a severe form of punishment because it deprives a person of that freedom.

2-1b Social Structure

Punishment has been related in theory to characteristics of the social structure. For example, some theorists argue that when labor is needed, punishment is light because prisoners are needed for the labor supply. When labor is in great supply, prisoners are punished severely or killed. The social structure holds that the economic need of a capitalistic society has often been the best predictor of the different methods of punishment implemented throughout history. Although this social structure perspective continues, it has been modified throughout history.

Social-structural theory
A theory that relates the methods and severity of punishment to the organization and traits of the social structure; includes the division of labor in a society at a given time.

A particular version of the **social-structural theory**, discussed by Edward Sutherland and Donald Cressey, is based on the relationship between the middle class and punishment. When the lower-middle class, which is composed of persons who most frequently repress their natural desires, is in control of punishment, severe and frequent punishment is inflicted. The literature suggests that if the lower-middle class is absent in a society, severe punishment is nonexistent. Sutherland and Cressey note, however, that one of the main problems with this approach is the absence of a precise definition of lower-middle class.[2]

Emile Durkheim proposed another version of the social-structural theory of punishment. His most important proposition was that punishment varies with the complexity of the division of labor in a society. In societies characterized by mechanical solidarity—in which the society is cohesive and deviation is a serious threat—people provide most of their own needs. While the division of labor is slight, punishment is punitive to repress deviant behavior. In societies characterized by a more complex division of labor, what Durkheim called "organic solidarity," the emphasis is on **restitution** and punishments are not as severe.[3] Restitution is defined as the compensation to victims for physical, financial, and emotional loss suffered because of a criminal incident. This compensation can be monetary or in the form of community service.

Restitution
The compensation to victims for the physical, financial, and emotional loss suffered as a result of a criminal incident. This compensation can be monetary or in the form of service to the community.

Although Durkheim's approach has been questioned since some have found it to be strictly social-based or not inclusive of other perspectives, Marxist theorists such as Steven Spitzer have concluded that Durkheim's model was a valuable one for studying punishment. "In linking the nature of control to the organization of society Durkheim makes explicit what too many investigators ignore—the fact that punishment is deeply rooted in the structure of society. Whether we determine that Durkheim's explanation must be specified or completely disregarded, one thing is clear; the investigation of punishment must be sensitive to the present political and economic dimensions of social life."[4]

Finally, the social-structural theory associates the frequency of punishment with the degree of social disorganization within a society. When a society is homogeneous, few people deviate and therefore non-punitive reactions are sufficient. As heterogeneity increases, often accompanied by increasing social disorganization, it becomes necessary to invoke more severe punishments.[5] Sutherland and Cressey cite examples of increasing punishments during periods of revolution when there is an accompanying increase in social disorganization. They conclude that none of these perspectives explain the process by which the culture, psychological conditions, or social structure create the change in punishment.[6] These perspectives are criticized due to the lack of supporting empirical evidence. In spite of these criticisms, the cultural and sociological theories of punishment can explain the history of punishment.

2-2 Historical Background of Punishment and Criminal Law

The formal development of criminology as a distinct discipline is recent, but we can historically trace the ideas of people who were early **criminologists**. Most of these people were lawyers, doctors, psychiatrists, or sociologists. All were reformers of **criminal law** and contributed important ideas to the philosophy of punishment.

Hermann Mannheim's compilation of essays on these early criminologists is an excellent source for the historical background of the punishment philosophies that have been most influential in the development of criminology.[7] Mannheim begins with the birth of Cesare Beccaria in 1738 and continues his discussions of these pioneers through the death of Gustave Aschaffendburg in 1944. He discusses their ideas about the causes of criminal behavior, as well as their philosophies of punishment. The works of these men are extremely important as most philosophies of punishment today can be traced to one or more of the early criminologists in the field.

The background against which the **classical** (late seventeenth century and early eighteenth century) and **neoclassical** (nineteenth century) **theorists** were writing should be examined. The efforts of these men were aimed at reform of the criminal law. The classical writers were rebelling against an arbitrary and corrupt system of law in which judges held an absolute and tyrannical power over those who came before them. Laws were often vague and judges took it upon themselves to interpret "the spirit of the law" to suit their purposes. Such widespread personal interpretation of the law led to a lack of consistency and impartiality which usually meant that the lower-class defendant received the blunt end of justice. Accusations were often secret and trials were a farce. The law was applied unequally to citizens and corruption was rampant. Confessions were obtained by the use of hideous torture and the death penalty was used for even trivial offenses. Due process and equality before the law were unknown. Once people were incarcerated, they were not classified. The old and the young, the hardened criminals and the first offenders, were all thrown into prison together. Two European countries, France and England, created a precedent as they used punitive methods.

Criminologists
Professionals who engage in the scientific study of crime, criminals, and criminal behavior.

Criminal law
The norms and statutes that, if violated, subject the accused individual to governmental prosecution.

Classical theorist
Writers and philosophers who promoted the principles set forth by the classical school of criminology.

Neoclassical theorist
Individual who holds that situations or circumstances that make it impossible to exercise free will are reasons to exempt the accused from being convicted.

2-2a The French Response to Crime

During the Middle Ages (900 AD–1453 AD) in France, decisions regarding sentencing of the accused were made in secret—judges could make decisions without any restrictions. The sentences were usually very severe, with the defendant having no right to defense at the trial. Secret tribunals decided punishments and defendants were punished "according to the authority of the secret bench."[8] Methods of torture differed from province to province within France. In some, the defendant would be tied to a chair that was moved closer and closer to a burning furnace. Another method was to shoe the defendant in high boots made of spongy leather, tie the defendant to a table, and pour boiling water into the boots. The water would eat away the flesh and sometimes dissolve the bones. A third method involved stripping a man half naked, tying his hands behind him with a ring between them, placing a weight of 180 pounds on his feet, and then raising him with sudden jerks by means of a rope on the ring. The weight was 250 pounds for more serious crimes. This process completely dislocated the individual's arms and legs.

The body of the defendant might be stretched, with a doctor and surgeon standing by to check his pulse. When they determined that he could no longer bear the pain, they would release him, revive him, and begin the method of torture again. Another form of punishment was execution by fire. If the accused died before the execution, the dead body would be burned. If it was discovered that a person was guilty of a crime after the person died and was buried, the body would be disinterred and the remains burned.

Possibly the most horrible torture was quartering. The offender was first put through preliminary torture, such as the burning of his or her limbs. Then the executioner would attach a rope to each of the four limbs and fasten each rope to a bar to which a strong horse was harnessed. First, the horses would be made to give short jerks, but as the offender cried out in agony, the horses would be suddenly urged on rapidly in different directions. If the limbs were not dismembered, the executioner would finish the job with a hatchet, put all of the limbs in front of the torso (which might still show some signs of life), and burn them.[9]

Philosophers were unsuccessful in changing the barbarous punishments of the Middle Ages in France. Most of these laws remained until the eve of the French Revolution.

2-2b The Response to Crime by England

The judicial system in England, before and during the time the classicists were writing about penal reform, was also severe and corrupt. According to a member of Parliament, a justice of the peace was "an animal who, for half-a-dozen chickens, would dispense with a dozen laws."[10] Graft and corruption were common among magistrates, watchmen, and constables, and lawyers did not always have good reputations. Dr. Johnson, referring to a man who had just left the room, said he "did not care to speak ill of any man behind his back, but he believed the gentleman was an attorney."[11] The popular belief was that laws were weak and punishments were severe. Criminal laws relied on **deterrence**, not on surveillance or detection. Capital punishment was provided for over 200 offenses.

Deterrence
A justification frequently used for punishing individuals. It is based on the concept that the punishment will prevent or discourage an individual from engaging in criminal behavior.

The wheel
A common form of execution which could be used in different ways. The most common was to tie a person to the outer rim of a wheel and then spike them down a hill to their death.

The English Code of the eighteenth century, often called the "bloody code," was one of the most severe in history. It barred torture and punishment by **the wheel,** (see chapter 15 for more discussion of the wheel), as well as cutting noses and ears, but it permitted other severe forms of punishment. It provided for capital punishment for such offenses as cutting down trees on an avenue or in a park, setting fire to a cornfield, taking part in a riot, shooting a rabbit, demolishing a turnpike gate, and escaping from jail. When the sentence was flogging in a cart drawn through town, spectators would often pay the executioner to whip more vigorously.

In 1790, Parliament repealed a law providing that a woman convicted of murdering her husband or of treason was to be burned alive. The humaneness of the people was demonstrated by the custom of strangling her before she was burned. Men hanged at the gallows for treason were cut down while still alive, their bowels removed and burned in front of them. They were then beheaded and quartered. Gallows existed in all districts in London and the victims were often left for the birds to eat. This also served as a deterrent to all who passed. Some victims would hang as long as thirty minutes before they died but they were given brandy to ease the pain. At times, the executioner would pull on victim's legs to hasten death. **Hanging** and other punishments were public and people lined the streets to see the victim on the way to the place of punishment. Peddlers sold food and drink and people sang ballads.

Hanging
Historically, the most popular method of execution. In a typical hanging, the noose fractured the individual's neck.

It was against that background of severe punishment and harsh laws that Cesare Beccaria initiated what has been termed the **classical school of criminology.**

Classical school of criminology
A school of thought that held that the punishment should fit the crime.

2-2c The Classical School

The only two members of the classical school recognized in most criminology texts are Cesare Beccaria and Jeremy Bentham. Their respective philosophies have influenced penal and legal development since the mid-eighteenth century. Also discussed is the influence of other thinkers of the day, including Francois Marie Arouep (pen name Voltaire), Charles Louis deSecondat, (pen name Montesquieu) and Jean-Jacques Rousseau.

Cesare Beccaria (1738-1794)

The leader of the classical school of thought was Beccaria, who was born in Milan, Italy, on March 15, 1738. Although his family was of aristocratic background, its political function had gradually ceased to be of any importance. After studying for eight years at the Jesuit College at Parma, Beccaria attended the University of Pavia, receiving his degree in 1758. He began as a mathematician and later became interested in economics and politics. In 1764, when he was only twenty-six years old, his influential essay, *Des delitti e delles pene*, was published in Italy. In 1767, the essay was published in England under the title *On Crimes and Punishments.*

The treatise drew the attention of the Paris intelligentsia. Beccaria's work was widely accepted as an important cry for change and reform, and was eventually translated into twenty-two languages. Beccaria's major contribution was the concept that the punishment should fit the crime, a philosophy that became the theme of the classical school of thought. He died in 1794, having produced only the one major work, which was a great impetus to the penal reform movement and served as a basis for the alteration of penal practices.[12]

Beccaria's words were accepted and put into practice to varying degrees by the enlightened monarchs. In Austria, Maria Teresa called for a reform of the penal code in 1768, and her son Joseph II abolished the death penalty in 1787. In 1772, King Gustavus III of Sweden abolished torture and reduced the infliction of the death penalty. The treatment of criminals improved greatly in the United States after 1776, especially in Pennsylvania under the guidance of the Quakers. Reform came under Frederick the Great of Prussia—around the same time, reform was introduced in England. Perhaps the most dramatic reforms came after the French Revolution of 1789, when the French Penal Code of 1791 was established.

Beccaria's work is extremely important today. "It is not an exaggeration to regard Beccaria's work as being of primary importance in paving the way for penal reform for approximately the last two centuries."[13] His short essay contains almost all the modern penal reforms. However, the greatest contribution of his work was "the foundation it laid for subsequent changes in criminal legislation."[14]

Social Contract Doctrine

Social contract
Doctrine that held that an individual was bound to society only by his or her consent and therefore society was responsible for the individual, and the individual was responsible for society.

At the time that Beccaria was writing, many philosophers and intellectuals were beginning to speak of the **social contract**. This concept held that an individual was bound to society only by his or her consent and, therefore, society was responsible to him or her as well. Such thinkers as Montesquieu, Voltaire, and Rousseau were making strong statements about the rights of people and the nature of society in general. Beccaria believed in the concept of the social contract and felt that each individual surrendered only enough liberty to the state to make society viable. Laws should merely be the necessary conditions of the social contract and punishments should exist only to defend the total sacrificed liberties against the usurpation of those liberties by other individuals. The basic principle that should guide legislation—and indeed form its backbone—is that the greatest happiness should be shared by the greatest number of people.[15]

Philosophy of Free Will

Another philosophy that strongly influenced Beccaria was that of free will. It was argued that human behavior is purposive and is based on hedonism (the pleasure-pain principle), meaning people choose those actions that give pleasure and avoid those that give pain. Punishment should be assigned to each crime in a degree that would result in more pain than pleasure for those who committed the forbidden act. This hedonistic view of human conduct prescribed that laws must be clearly written and not open to interpretation by judges. Only the legislature could specify punishment. The law must apply equally to all citizens, thus no defenses to criminal acts were permitted. The issue in court was whether a person committed the act; if so, a particular penalty prescribed by law for that act was imposed. The state made the laws but did not have the power to decide who violated the law; that was done by a third party—a judge or a group of the defendant's peers. Judges were mere instruments of the law, allowed only to determine innocence or guilt and then prescribe the set punishment. The law became rigid, structured, and impartial. The philosophy was to let the punishment fit the crime.

Punishment as a Deterrent

Beccaria did not believe in severe punishment. He felt the only reason to punish was to assure the continuance of society and to deter people from committing crimes. Deterrence would come, not from severe punishment, but from punishment that was appropriate, prompt, and inevitable. As for the death penalty, Beccaria believed that it did not deter crime and was an act of brutality and violence. He also believed "that capital punishment wasted human material, which was the principal asset of the state. . . . He further observed that capital punishment shocked general moral sentiment. . . . The reality of the shock . . . was illustrated by the popular detestation of executioners; and its result must be to weaken popular morality which the law ought instead to strengthen."[16]

Influence on Contemporary Criminal Law

The impact of Beccaria's arguments on modern American criminal law can be seen in this statement from Roscoe Pound: "Our substantive criminal law is based upon a theory of punishing the vicious will. It postulates a free moral agent, confronted with a choice between doing right and doing wrong, and choosing freely to do wrong."[17]

The major weaknesses in Beccaria's ideas on crimes and punishments were the rigidity of his concepts and the lack of provision for justifiable criminal acts. The classical school acknowledged these faults.

Jeremy Bentham

Jeremy Bentham (1748–1832), a contemporary of Beccaria, was a utilitarian hedonist. One critic, considering the "nature and importance of his work, its originality, its enormous extent, its many-sided character, its universal influence, its far-reaching practical results, and its potential virtues" concluded that he was tempted to "proclaim Bentham the greatest legal philosopher and reformer the world has ever seen."[18] Among Bentham's famous concepts is one advocating that the greatest good must go to the greatest number. One of his most important theories is felicific calculus—it assumed that people are rational creatures who would consciously choose pleasure and avoid pain. Therefore, a punishment must be assigned to each crime so that the pain would outweigh any pleasure derived from the commission of the crime. Thus, the philosophy of "let the punishment fit the crime" was further conceptualized. Today, both Beccaria and Bentham are accredited for their contributions to this philosophy.

Principle of Utilitarianism

Bentham was an armchair thinker who considered crime in the abstract. He failed "to consider criminals as human beings, as live, complicated, variegated personalities." Like Beccaria, he stood against the status quo and fought fiercely for reform in the criminal law. He saw a new ethical principle of social control, a "method of checking human behavior according to a general ethical principle." He called the principle **utilitarianism.** "An act is not to be judged by an irrational system of absolutes but by a supposedly verifiable principle . . . [which is] 'the greatest happiness for the greatest number' or simply 'the greatest happiness.'" Unfortunately, Bentham did not explain the theoretical basis for his principle, nor did he tell how the principle could be measured objectively and empirically.[19]

Utilitarianism
A theory that makes the happiness of the individual or society the criterion of the morally good and right.

Like Beccaria, Bentham also believed in the doctrine of free will, although he hinted at the theory of learned behavior as the explanation for criminal behavior. "He deserves considerable credit . . . for his adherence to a theory of social (that is, pleasure pursuit) causation of crime rather than a concept of biological, climatic, or other non-social causation."[20]

Bentham stated that the objectives of punishment are: to prevent all offenses, to keep down mischief, and to act as the least expense. He condoned severe punishment because of its reforming effect, but he acknowledged that the people must accept severity of punishment before it would be effective. He also felt criminal law was not be used as vengeance against the criminal but to prevent crime. His ideas on capital punishment were similar to Beccaria's. Capital punishment was carried out with extraordinary brutality, and was not to be regarded as satisfactory punishment since it created "more pain than is necessary for the purpose."[21]

2-2d Other Influences

Voltaire contributed indirectly and directly to the success of Beccaria's reform measures. Voltaire's indirect contribution was his work in laying the foundation for the Enlightenment. "By fighting religious intolerance and fanaticism, he contributed, more than any other, to the building of a more reasonable and humane society in which there was no longer any place for a criminal law based on superstition and cruelty." Without Voltaire's work, criminal reform would have been greatly delayed and Beccaria's essay on crime and punishment probably would

Profiles & Perspectives

Voltaire

Library of Congress, Prints and Photographs Division LC-USZ62-116230

Francois Marie Arouet
(pen name: Voltaire)
Author and Philosopher
November 21, 1694 – 1778
(Paris, France)

Voltaire was born in France in 1694. As a young adult, he was accepted in the sophisticated circles of France, which scholars argue was mostly due to his intellectual superiority and wit. In 1717, he was arrested for the first time due to his anti-governmental writings. Voltaire is also known for his exile which was caused because of an insult he provoked upon a noble man. To cause further controversy, upon his return to France, he wrote a book that placed the English at a superior stance when compared to the French. Consequently, he was once again sent away from Paris, to an estate named Ferney, near the French-Swiss borderwhere he spent the majority of his life. From Ferney, he wrote numerous manuscripts denouncing the contemporary governments in Europe. He was often visited by many of his friends who enjoyed his wit and counsel. He was finally allowed to return to Paris just before his death in 1778. Many attribute the excitement of returning to Paris as a factor in his death.

not have appeared. Voltaire contributed directly to the success of penal reform by publicizing Beccaria's work.[22]

Other philosophers, such as Montesquieu and Rousseau, were also sources of inspiration for Beccaria. It has been reported that Beccaria allowed some of the ideas introduced by these philosophers to shape the original argument made in *On Crimes and Punishments.* Montesquieu's work influenced Beccaria's notion of equal justice and punishment for all. Further, Rousseau's views on social agreements and the sense of community also influenced Beccaria's writings.

Another philosopher who influenced the classical period of criminology is German jurist Paul von Feuerbach (1775–1833). He thought punishment was not retributive. The purpose of punishment was to protect the rights of others and the penalties should be commensurate with the type of right violated. Von Feuerbach argued that the definitions of crimes and the punishments provided by the state should be clearly stated in the law. He is regarded as a forerunner of the most important principles of civil and Anglo-American law.

2-2e Neoclassical School

The neoclassical school of criminology flourished during the nineteenth century. It had the same basis as the classical school—a belief in free will. However, it also held that the penalties resulting from the classical doctrine were too severe and all encompassing for the humanitarian spirit of the time. In particular, the French Code of 1791 was found to be unduly severe and it was revised in 1810. The revisions provided for some judicial discretion, introducing minimum and maximum sentences, and it recognized the principle of extenuating circumstances, thus adhering to neoclassical penology. Further revisions in 1819 permitted more judicial discretion but only under objective circumstances. There were still no exceptions in the law from subjective circumstances—there was no consideration of the intent of the offender. The neoclassical criminologists, who were mainly from England, began complaining about the need for individualized treatment of some offenders.

Perhaps the most shocking aspect of the harsh penal codes of the classical period is that they made no provision for separate treatment of children who

Profiles & Perspectives
Montesquieu

Library of Congress Prints and Photographs Division LC-USZ62-104542

Charles Louis de Secondat de La Brede de Montesquieu
Philosopher
January 18, 1689 – February 10, 1755

Charles Louis de Secondat de La Brede de Montesquieu was born near Bordeaux at the Castle of La Brede in France. He was born on January 18, 1689. His parents were elevated to the aristocratic membership of France by Henry IV in the early 1600s. Historians point to the fact that Montesquieu's mother was closely related to the British nobility.

Montesquieu was educated in Paris by the Oratorians. During this period of his life, Montesquieu learned Latin, Geography, and History, among other subjects. He also learned dancing and fencing. However, his passion was modern sciences, particularly the study of Malebranche's philosophy.

Montesquieu was known as a philosopher and jurist. He studied the political writings of Locke. His main work, "The Spirit of Laws," which was written in 1748, elevated the British Constitution to a new level. Montesquieu's work prompted the world to admire the British Constitution. He was an advocate for the separation of powers, a principle adopted by the founding fathers and framers of the U.S. Constitution.

Profiles & Perspectives
Rousseau

© Archivo Iconografico, S.A./CORBIS

Jean-Jacques Rousseau
Philosopher
June 28, 1712 — 1778

Jean-Jacques Rousseau was born in Geneva, Switzerland,on June 28, 1712. As his mother died soon after his birth, Rousseau was raised by his father until the age of ten. It was then that Rousseau's father had to flee Geneva in order to avoid imprisonment due to a minor offense. As a result, an aunt and uncle raised Rousseau until he was sixteen.

When he turned sixteen, Rousseau moved often, working in many different jobs that supported his livelihood. His deep thoughts from this time can be traced to any aspect of modern philosophy. Although complex, his philosophy attempted to grasp the emotional and passionate side of man that he felt was ignored in most philosophical thought.

In the early stages of his writings, Rousseau argued that man was essentially a "noble savage" when he was in his state of nature and good people were often transformed into unhappy and corrupted individuals by their experiences in society. This presented the view that society, in general, was artificial and corrupt. His most important work was *The Social Contract,* in which Rousseau explained the relationship between man and society.

committed crimes. Although some argue that the Neoclassical period did not alter the legal responsibility age, others feel that the neoclassical period was responsible for introducing the concept that children under seven years of age were exempted from the law on the basis that they could not understand the difference between right and wrong. Mental disease was seen as a sufficient cause to impair responsibility and defense by reason of insanity crept into law. Any situation or circumstance that made it impossible to exercise free will was seen as reason to exempt the person involved from conviction.

Although the neoclassical school was not a scientific school of criminology, it did begin to deal with the problem of causation, which the classical school had not done. By making exceptions to the law, varied causation was implied, and the doctrine of free will could no longer stand alone as an explanation for criminal behavior.

2-2f The Positive School

Cesare Lombroso
Bettmann/CORBIS

Positive school of criminology
A school of thought that emphasizes the individual scientific treatment of the criminal.

Positivist
Theorists who believe in the positive school of thought and who hold that the punishment should fit the criminal and not the crime.

Retribution
A theory of punishment based on the premise that an offender should be punished for the crimes committed because he or she deserves it.

Revenge
A doctrine based on the concept that an individual who violates the law is punished in a way that replicates the victim's suffering.

Indeterminate sentence
A sentence whose length is not determined by legislators or the courts, but by professionals at an institution who determine when an offender is ready to return to society.

The classical school, defining crime in legal terms, emphasized the concept of free will and advocated that punishment gauged to fit the crime would be a deterrent to crime. The **positivists** rejected the harsh legalism of the classical school and substituted the doctrine of determinism for that of free will. They focused on the constitutional, not the legal, aspect of crime.

Cesare Lombroso, Rafaelle Garofalo, and Enrico Ferri were the three major figures in the **positive** (or Italian) **school of criminology**. Although their approaches differed, they all agreed that the emphasis in the study of crime should be on the scientific treatment of the criminal, not on the penalties to be imposed after the individual was convicted.

Cesare Lombroso

Cesare Lombroso (1835–1909) believed that the only justification for punishment was self-defense and that reforming the guilty rarely occurred. He believed that society had no right to impose any penalty on a criminal that was harsher than the degree of wrong done by that person to society. He excluded **retribution** and **revenge** as justifications for punishment. Unlike Beccaria, Lombroso believed that since different criminals had different needs, it was foolish to impose the same punishment on all who committed the same offense. He looked to Ferri, who argued that when a criminal could be rehabilitated in ten years, it was foolish to keep him or her in prison for twenty years when another person who needs to stay longer is released in five years. Lombroso became an early advocate of the **indeterminate sentence,** which is a sentence that includes a range of years individuals will spend in prison.

Lombroso was not in favor of short prison terms, which exposed criminals to other criminals and allowed no time for rehabilitation. He suggested that in these cases, alternatives such as "confinement at home, judicial admonition, fines, forced labor without imprisonment, local exile, corporal punishment, conditional sentence" should be imposed. He favored conditional sentencing or the probation system and advocated the death penalty only as a last resort.[23]

Rafaelle Garofalo

Baron Rafaelle Garofalo (1852–1934) was born in Naples, Italy, the son of a noble Spanish family. He studied law and criminal law reform, served as a professor of criminal law and procedure, and was a member of the magistracy. At the request of the Minister of Justice, Garofalo wrote a reform of the Italian criminal procedure used in the criminal courts. For political reasons, however, it was not adopted.

In 1885, Garofalo's most important work, titled *Criminology*, was published in Italian. In *Criminology*, Garofalo rejected most of the philosophies of the classical school such as the legal definition of crime, the belief that punishment should fit the crime (deterring criminal behavior), and the acceptance of the death penalty.

Garofalo believed that an offender's time in prison did not result in his or her moral **reformation.** Most prisons were too lenient; therefore, the offender did not suffer when incarcerated. Even if he or she suffered, that suffering was quickly forgotten. This did not mean that it was impossible to "transform the activity of the offender."[24] Garofalo had no doubts that "the manifestation of even the innate criminal propensities can often be repressed by 'a favorable concurrence' of external circumstances. The devising of appropriate measures of repression thus becomes the practical problem of central concern."[25] Garofalo warned that one could not expect too much from the attempt to change social conditions.

Reformation
A way in which the "prevention of crime" can be analyzed using Herbert Packer's conceptualization of behavioral prevention. In corrections, this term often refers to the idea that offenders can be changed or transformed into law-abiding citizens.

Enrico Ferri

Enrico Ferri (1856–1929) was the son of a poor shopkeeper. He was a problem student in his early life, became truant, and was almost expelled from school. Later, under the influence of Robert Ardigo, Ferri "found himself" and became interested in the scientific orientation. When he went to study with Lombroso for a year, Ferri had already become a positivist and had published some of his ideas. "While Ferri owed much of his system of ideas to the stimulation of Lombroso, he also became the catalyst who synthesized the latter's concepts with those of the sociologist and had no little influence on Lombroso's thinking."[26] Three years after he graduated, Ferri returned to his alma mater at Bologna as a professor of criminal law. There, in 1880, before he reached the age of twenty-five, he delivered a two-hour lecture on the new horizons in criminal law and procedure. This lecture became the basis for his best-known book, *Criminal Sociology.*

Ferri believed that the type of society from which the criminal came primarily produced crime. He postulated his *Law of Criminal Saturation,* which states, "in a given social environment with definite individual and physical conditions, a fixed number of [crimes], no more and no less, can be committed."[27] Crime can only be corrected by making changes in society. He called these changes penal substitutes (or equivalents) of punishment. Among them he listed changes in the tax structure (lower tax on necessities and increases on items such as alcohol), sanitary police regulations for dwellings in the city and the country, freedom of emigration, public improvements to supply work for the indigent, improved street lighting, substitution of metal for paper money to reduce counterfeiting, and cheap "workingmen's" houses. In addition to these economic reforms, he suggested electoral reforms, changes in marriage and divorce laws, an intelligent regulation of prostitution, and provisions for marriage of the clergy, which he believed would "avoid many infanticides, abortions, adulteries, and criminal assaults."[28]

Ferri strongly criticized legislators for their "blind worship of punishment," embodied in the philosophy of the classical school, which he believed resulted in an increase in punishment in an attempt to prevent crime. Consequently, the criminal was not reformed and the crime-producing elements of society were not corrected.

Emphasis on the Scientific Method

Ferri advocated the use of the **scientific method**, not only in the study of causation of criminal behavior, but also in the system of criminal justice. He felt decisions concerning the punishment and treatment of criminals should not be made by **juries** and untrained judges but by scientists. He advocated that the jury be abolished because sentencing decisions should be made by judges trained in the social and psychological sciences. Ferri worked actively for penal reform.

Scientific method
When applied to corrections, a positivist theory that holds that social scientists should decide the punishment and treatment of offenders (rather than allowing judges or juries to decide).

Juries
In a criminal case, a number of individuals summoned to court and sworn to hear a trial, determine certain facts, and issue a verdict of guilty or not guilty. In some jurisdictions, juries determine the offender's sentence.

TABLE **2-1** Comparison of Classical and Positive Schools

Classical School	Positive School
1. Accepted legal definition of crime	1. Rejected legal definition; Garofalo substituted "natural crime"
2. Let the punishment fit the crime	2. Let the punishment fit the criminal
3. Doctrine of free will	3. Doctrine of determinism
4. Support of the death penalty for some offenses	4. Abolition of the death penalty
5. Anecdotal method – No empirical research	5. Empirical research – use of inductive method
6. Mandatory sentence	6. Indeterminate sentence

Contributions of the Positive School of Thought

As indicated in the discussion of Lombroso, Garofalo, and Ferri, the contributions of the positive school toward the reform of the criminal law have been extensive. These individuals wrote in reaction to the classical school, emphasizing the importance of empirical research in their work. They believed that punishment should fit the criminal, not the crime, as advocated by the classical school. The positivists substituted the doctrine of determinism, some arguing that crime took place as a result of physical, psychological, social, or economic factors. As a result, the concept of the environment was introduced into criminology. The positivists spoke against the death penalty as an effective deterrent to crime and they advocated substituting the indeterminate sentence for the definite sentence. Their main contribution, however, was that they began the empirical study of the etiology of crime.

Methodological problems in the research of the positivists limited their explanations of criminal behavior but their attitudes on punishment and sentencing had a tremendous impact on developments in criminal law and corrections.

2-2g Comparison of the Classical and Positive Schools

Ferri, in comparing the positive and classical schools, said "we speak two different languages."[29] Table 2-1 gives a brief comparison of the main points of the two schools.

2-3 Justifications for Punishment

Just deserts
A principle based on the concept that an individual who commits a crime deserves to suffer for it.

In *The Limits of the Criminal Sanction (1968),* Herbert L. Packer took the position that punishment served only two basic purposes. First, the punishment is merited by the individual who committed the crime or the theory of **just deserts**. Because of his or her transgression, the evildoer deserves to suffer. The second purpose of punishment is to deter crime. Each of these purposes can be subdivided, an approach that is used in the discussion of justifications for punishment. Under the first purpose, retribution and revenge is analyzed. Under the second purpose, what Packer calls utilitarian prevention is analyzed. This involves general and specific deterrence and behavioral prevention, which involves rehabilitation, reintegration, and reformation.[30]

2-3a The Just Deserts Approach: A Philosophy of Retribution

Historically, one of the most common justifications for punishment has been that the wrongdoer deserves to be punished. The second theory, which has been urged as a basis for the imposition of penalties, is that of retribution. This may be regarded as the doctrine of legal revenge, or punishment merely for the sake of punishment. It is to make the criminal suffer by way of retaliation even if no benefit results to themselves or to others. This theory of punishment looks to the past and rests solely upon the foundation of vindictive justice. It is this idea of punishment that generally prevails, even though those who entertain it may not conscious of their decision. Historically, the origin of all legal punishments has its root in the natural impulse of revenge. This instinct prompted retaliatory measures by the individual who suffered because of the crime committed, or in the case of murder, by the victim's relatives. Later, the state took away the right of retaliation from individuals. Its own assumption of the function of revenge constituted the beginning of criminal law; however, the refinement and humanizing of society has been dispelling any such theory from penology. In classical times, moralists and philosophers rejected the idea as well.

Revenge

It is important to distinguish the concepts of retribution and revenge. Many who advocate that retribution is a valid justification for punishment are not looking at retribution as it has been used historically. The philosophy of just deserts is embraced under retribution today—the offender is punished based on what he or she deserves. In the past, retribution often meant revenge, which was manifested in the doctrine of *Lex Talionis* ("an eye for an eye and a tooth for a tooth") and can be traced back to the Bible and the Code of Hammurabi. Under this doctrine, a person who violates the laws of society should be treated in the same way that he or she treated the victim. In its extreme form, this position would advocate capital punishment for those who commit murder. Some argue that in the 1990s this position gained popularity as the citizenry frequently elected political figures who advertised themselves as having little or no sympathy for those who violated society's rules. This gave rise to higher incarceration rates, longer prison sentences, and a growing number of death-row inmates throughout the 1990s. Despite this, the most recent data provided by the Bureau of Justice Statistics suggests that the incarceration rate and number of death sentences issued per year may be slowing down.[31] Although it is too early to generalize from this particular phenomenon, it is possible that the concept of revenge is losing its popularity as a reason to incarcerate. There are other methods of revenge, such as posting the pictures of sex offenders on billboards, which are becoming more popular today. Notwithstanding the prison figures discussed, revenge will always play a significant role influencing the manner and frequency in which we punish.

Retribution

After years of disfavor, retribution has gained its position as a justification for punishment in the United States. Retribution has replaced rehabilitation as the basis for punishment. The acceptance of retribution can be seen in the capital punishment decisions of the U.S. Supreme Court, although not all of the justices agree. In the majority opinion of the 1972 Supreme Court Case of *Furman v. Georgia*[32] Justice Thurgood Marshall argued that retribution for its own sake was improper. However Justice Potter Stewart took the position that retribution might prevent private revenge. He argued that retribution is instinctual with humans and it is the purpose of the criminal justice system to divert that drive into the proper channels.[33] Even stronger support for the philosophy of retribution can be found in the dissenting opinion of Chief Justice Burger, who concluded. "It would be reading a great deal into the Eighth Amendment to hold that the punishments authorized by legislatures cannot constitutionally reflect a retributive purpose."[34]

In 1976, the Supreme Court recognized retribution as an appropriate reason for capital punishment. It is no longer the dominant objective, said the Court, "but neither is it a forbidden objective nor one inconsistent with our respect for the dignity of men . . . Indeed, the decision that capital punishment may be the appropriate sanction in extreme cases is an expression of the community's belief that certain crimes are themselves so grievous an affront to humanity that the only adequate response may be the penalty of death."[35] Referring to Justice Stewart's opinion in *Furman*, the Court noted that the instinct for retribution is a part of human nature and if the courts do not handle these situations, private individuals might take the law into their own hands. The Court concluded, "In part, capital punishment is an expression of society's moral outrage at particularly offensive conduct. This function may be unappealing to many, but it is essential in an ordered society that asks its citizens to rely on legal processes rather than self-help to vindicate wrongs."[36]

In an article on the death penalty, Jack P. Gibbs argued that in the past, the Supreme Court justices have given more support to the doctrine of retribution as a justification for capital punishment because they have realized that the evidence on deterrence is not strong and the public has become disillusioned with the doctrine of rehabilitation. Retribution is the only doctrine supporting punishment in general and the death penalty in particular, in which there is no question of effectiveness. The argument under retribution is that an individual is incarcerated because that is what he or she deserves. Retribution is not utilitarian. Since its goal is "'doing justice' rather than the prevention of crimes, it makes no instrumental claims." Its central defect, however, is that it "leaves so many questions about legal punishment unanswered that it cannot serve as a basis for a penal policy."[37]

Advocates do not give a clear, concise definition of retribution. They say one should be punished because that is what one deserves, but that precludes answers to some important questions. First, what is the appropriate punishment for a given type of crime? If we use the doctrine "let the punishment fit the crime," capital punishment is applicable only to murder, although people have been put to death for other offenses. Second, if one argues, as proponents of the retribution theory do, that punishment should be commensurate with the seriousness of the crime, how does one measure the latter? Is ten years in prison twice as severe as five years? How is imprisonment compared to the death penalty? Does the answer lie in what people perceive to be the severity of the crime (public opinion)? If so, how is public opinion determined? Finally, in past decisions on capital punishment, the Supreme Court has said that aggravating or mitigating circumstances must be considered, but the doctrine of retribution does not answer the question of how much and what kind of discretion. Gibbs concluded: "[T]he fundamental shortcoming of the retributive doctrine is not that it seeks to justify a legal punishment as an end in itself; rather, the doctrine offers no solutions to the specific problems that haunt the criminal justice system . . . the retributive doctrine is attractive precisely because it is little more than an empty formula."[38]

2-3b The Justice Model of Punishment: A Recent Approach

justice model
A philosophy based on the notion that justice is achieved when offenders receive punishments based on what is deserved for their offenses as specified in the law; the crime determines the punishment.

Retribution as a justification for punishment is seen in past cases on the issue of capital punishment. It also constitutes the framework for the **Justice Model** of punishment and sentencing. The focus of this discussion is the philosophy of punishment on which the Justice Model is based.

Andrew von Hirsch represented the position of the Committee for the Study of Incarceration in the book *Doing Justice: The Choice of Punishments.*[39] Indicating their basic mistrust of the power of the state, the committee members rejected rehabilitation and the indeterminate sentence. They believed in deterrence and just deserts as reasons for punishment. In its rejection of rehabilitation the committee, however, advocated shorter sentences and sparing use of incarceration.

Ernest van den Haag, who emphasized just deserts and the utilitarian aspect of punishment and concept of justice, also rejected the rehabilitation model.[40]

> Justice is done by distributing punishments to offenders according to what is deserved by their offenses as specified by law. Legal justice involves neither less nor more than honoring the obligation to enforce the laws, which the government undertook in the very act of making them. Benefits, such as the rehabilitation of offenders, the protection of society from them while they are incapacitated, or, even more, the deterrence of others, are welcome, of course. But they are not necessary—and never sufficient—for punishment, and they are altogether irrelevant to making punishment just.[41]

The person most responsible for the popularity of the Justice Model is David Fogel, who expressed his views in detail in his book "*. . . We Are the Living Proof . . .*" *The Justice Model for Corrections.*[42] Fogel formulated twelve propositions on which he believed the Justice Model could be operationalized.[43] He arugued that punishment is necessary for the implementation of criminal law—a law based on the theory that people act as a result of their own free will and must be held responsible for their actions. Prisoners should be considered and treated as "responsible, volitional and aspiring human beings . . . all of the processes of the agencies of the criminal justice system should be carried out in a milieu of justice." This precludes a correctional system that "becomes mired in the dismal swamp of preaching, exhorting, and treatment," a situation that, according to Fogel, results in a correctional system that is dysfunctional as an agency of justice. Discretion cannot be eliminated, but under the Justice Model, it will be controlled, narrowed, and subject to review.[44] The emphasis is shifted from the processor (the public or the administration) to the consumer of the criminal justice system (the offender). Fogel calls this the imperial or official perspective to the consumer or justice perspective. Justice for the offender cannot stop with the process of sentencing and must continue throughout the correctional process. "The justice perspective demands accountability from all processors, even the 'pure of heart.' Properly understood, the justice perspective is not so much concerned with administration of justice as it is with the justice of administration."[45]

Under Fogel's Justice Model, a person sentenced to serve time in a correctional facility should retain all of the rights "accorded free citizens consistent with mass living and the execution of a sentence restricting the freedom of movement."[46] The inmate should be allowed to choose whether he or she wishes to participate in rehabilitation programs. The purpose of the prison becomes confinement, not rehabilitation, of the criminal. The offender receives only the sentence he or she deserves and that sentence is implemented according to fair principles. "The entire case for a justice model rests upon the need to continue to engage the person in the quest for justice as he moves on the continuum from defendant to convict to free citizen."[47]

The influence of the classical school can be seen in this recent return to a theory of just deserts. Bentham and Beccaria argued that the punishment should fit the crime. The just and humane approach is to punish the criminal for what he or she has done, not to follow the treatment rehabilitation or so-called humanitarian approach. According to English theologian C. S. Lewis, the doctrine of humanitarianism "merciful though it appears, really means that each one of us, from the moment he breaks the law, is deprived of the rights of a human being . . . when we cease to consider what the criminal deserves and consider only what will cure him or deter others, we have tacitly removed him from the sphere of justice altogether; instead of a person, a subject of rights, we now have a mere object, a patient, a 'case.'"[48]

What are the problems with this justice view of retribution as a justification for punishment? The model emphasizes due process, but several criminologists have argued that although due process is important during the stages of the criminal justice system before incarceration, the model faces some problems after incarceration. "It's one thing to furnish safeguards against administrative abuse and to promote expanded offender rights, but yet another to introduce those rights and remedies into correctional programming."[49]

Critique of the Justice Model

The retribution or Justice Model leaves many questions unanswered. Previously, Jack P. Gibbs raised some of those questions. Essentially, the model is empty. It does not answer the important question "How much punishment is deserved?" Further, it has been argued that the new approach is characterized by "an absence of rationale, of cement or framework. Most of the recommendations are 'reactions' to past abuses, not prescriptions for future successes."[50] Finally, for those members of our society who already see themselves as victims of the social structure of power held by the middle and upper classes, will the retribution or Justice Model appear fair?

Prevention of Crime

In addition to the just deserts approach to punishment, Herbert L. Packer indicated that the second basic purpose of punishment is the prevention of crime. He divided this purpose into two categories: utilitarian prevention, in which he included **individual** and **general deterrence**, and behavioral prevention, which includes the goals of rehabilitation, reformation, and **reintegration.**

Individual deterrence
A philosophy of punishment based on the idea that the threat of punishment may prevent a specific individual from engaging in criminal activity.

General deterrence
A punitive philosophy based on the belief that punishment in a specific case will inhibit others from committing the same offense.

Reintegration
A punitive philosophy that emphasizes the return of the offender to the community with restored educational, employment, and family ties.

Incapacitation
A punitive theory based on the concept that an individual offender is incarcerated to prevent the commission of any other crimes.

Individual Deterrence

Individual deterrence refers to preventing the individual who is being punished from committing additional crimes. In the past, deterrence often took the form of **incapacitation**, usually corporal punishment, which would make it impossible for the individual to repeat the crime for which he or she had been apprehended. Incapacitation refers to the notion that an individual will be unable to commit a crime while he or she is in prison or under some form of correctional supervision. The person is incapacitated from engaging in illegal behavior. Historically, the hands of the thief would be cut off; the eye of the spy would be gouged; the rapist would be castrated. Less severe forms of punishment aimed at individual deterrence included such acts as branding the offender on the forehead with a letter representing the crime committed (e.g., a *T* for thief). The presumption was that public knowledge of the crime made it impossible for the offender to commit that crime again.

Today, it is assumed that individual or specific deterrence can be accomplished by the incarceration of the particular offender. It is true that most people can be restrained from criminal acts if they are incarcerated and closely guarded. They are prevented from committing criminal acts if a sentence of capital punishment is imposed and carried out. In some cases, incarceration is sufficient to prevent individuals from committing additional crimes after their release, although in those cases, such factors as the type of incarceration, treatment during incarceration, and the length of stay must be reviewed.[51]

Some very important questions remain unanswered with regard to individual or specific deterrence. How many convicted persons would be recidivists—repeat offenders—if they were not incarcerated or punished in other ways? How many people, especially those who are imprisoned, become more criminalistic because of the punishment they receive? Are most punishment efforts concentrated on those least likely to be deterred by such punishment—for example, the alcoholic, the drug addict, or the sex offender?

In the area of drug abuse, efforts have not been concentrated on the sellers (who might be deterred by strict law enforcement), but on the users (who are not likely to be deterred). White-collar criminals, middle-class people who shoplift, and traffic violators are probably more likely to be discouraged after some reaction from law enforcement officials. Unfortunately, criminal law efforts are not concentrated on these demographics.[52]

General Deterrence

General deterrence, which is based on the belief that punishment of one individual dissuades others from committing the same offense, can be seen in the writings of Beccaria, Bentham, and Feuerbach and Greek philosophy. The brief excerpt from *Regina v. Jones,*[53] in Case Study 2-1, shows this reliance on general deterrence, even at the risk of imposing a sentence that might be detrimental to the person convicted. The respondent had pleaded guilty to three charges of indecent assault on girls ages six, seven, and eight. He was fined $150 for each charge. The maximum penalty in that jurisdiction was five years in prison plus whipping. On appeal, the court changed the sentence to a prison term.

This reliance on general deterrence to justify punishment led Justice Holmes to remark: "If I were having a philosophical talk with a man I was going to have [executed] I should say, 'I don't doubt that your act was inevitable for you but to make it more avoidable by others we propose to sacrifice you to the common good. You may regard yourself as a soldier dying for your country. . . . But the law must keep its promises.'"[54] As an eighteenth-century judge told the accused: "You are to be hanged not because you have stolen a sheep but in order that others may not steal sheep.'"[55]

2-3c Deterrence of Types of Crimes and Types of People

The debate over deterrence should be narrowed to examine types of crime and types of people. This is often overlooked in the debate concerning punishment as a means to prevent others from committing crime. Perhaps punishment (or the threat of punishment) is effective in deterring a woman from shoplifting but not necessarily from poisoning her husband. Perhaps laws deter certain types of people.[56]

Discussions of the theory of deterrence often commit the fallacy of absolutism—since all behavior is not deterred by penalties, punishment does not deter. However, in order to justify the existence of punishment, the case is often made that without it more crime would exist and an increase in crime rates would occur.

Ernest van den Haag has argued that punishment deters all but "persons who have little to lose." He quoted Herbert L. Packer as saying "Deterrence does not threaten those whose lot in life is already miserable beyond the point of hope."[57] Van den Haag argues that the stigmatizing effect of punishment is a deterrent to many, but it is influenced by their social status—the higher the socioeconomic status, the greater the effect.[58]

Case Study 2-1

Regina v. Jones

Basis of the case:

For the respondent it is urged that a prison sentence is not appropriate in the circumstances in this case. The reasons urged by counsel for the respondent against imposing a term of imprisonment are that the respondent is suffering from a form of sex perversion, which Dr. McLarty, one of the psychiatrists, describes as sexual repression, that there is not much likelihood of a recurrence of the offense by the respondent, and that a prison term will be definitely detrimental to the respondent's condition. These are all considerations relating to the rehabilitation of the respondent and, in my opinion, entirely overlook the element of deterrence to others in the imposition of sentence for a criminal offense. It may be that this particular respondent, after continuation of psychiatric treatment, will not repeat the offense and there is a possibility of him being cured of his condition by such psychiatric treatment, but these are matters of grave uncertainty. I think I would agree that, so far as the condition of this particular respondent is concerned, a prison term may be detrimental to his recovery, but in my opinion the offense is too serious for punishment by a fine or by suspending sentence and placing the respondent upon probation. It is said that the prison term will not have any deterrent effect upon other persons who are truly sex perverts. That may be so, but I do not think it justifies disregarding the deterrent effect upon those persons whom sentence will deter and who might be disposed to commit an assault of this character. . .

2-3d Severity and Certainty of Punishment

Several scholars have argued that it is not the threat of punishment that is a significant deterrent, but rather the severity and certainty of that punishment. One argument is that the surety of punishment influences people's perceptions and they will be afraid to violate the law. This proposition has not, however, been examined explicitly and the conclusions of a few studies question its validity.[59]

Several studies conducted by Jack Gibbs and Charles Tittle are particularly relevant to this topic. Gibbs studied rates of homicide while Tittle analyzed crime rates for all **FBI Crime Index offenses**, considering both certainty and severity of punishment. They both found these themes to be inversely related to homicide—as the degree of certainty and severity of punishment increased, the homicide rates decreased. Gibbs found the relationship to be stronger for severity and Tittle found it to be more significant between certainty and punishment.[60] Later studies found no consistent support for the hypothesis that severe punishment deters crime.[61] Thus, the current state of knowledge regarding this particular topic is inconclusive.

FBI Crime Index Offenses Classification of offenses found in the Uniform Crime Report. These include homicide, arson, forcible rape, robbery, aggravated assault, burglary, larceny/theft, and auto theft.

2-3e Deterrence: The Need for Theory

Analysis of the issue of deterrence, both general and specific, is complicated by the fact that it is difficult to identify those persons who have been deterred by the threat of punishment. Other variables associated with deterrence are also difficult to measure, but Robert F. Meier argued that the basic need is for development that is more theoretical. He concluded that the "inability to formulate valid deterrence models is likely to continue to plague the development of this field until there is sufficient theoretical progress to permit specifying pertinent variables in addition to strictly legal factors, and to stipulate the manner in which their presumed relationship with behavior can be best tested."[62]

2-3f Behavioral Prevention

A second way in which the prevention of crime can be analyzed is in Packer's conceptualization of behavioral prevention, which is often referred to by the terms rehabilitation, reformation, and reintegration.

In the past century, the hallmark of progressive corrections in this country has been the belief that the purpose of punishment is to reform or rehabilitate the offender. This position has been strongly endorsed by social scientists and even acknowledged by the courts.[63] Rehabilitation has been described as the "rehabilitative ideal,"[64] characterized by the juvenile court, probation, parole, and individualized sentencing and treatment. The ideal is based on the premise that human behavior is the result of antecedent causes that may be known by objective analysis and that permit scientific control of human behavior. The assumption is, therefore, that the offender should be treated, not punished.

Recently the doctrine of rehabilitation has lost popularity. Some argue that it should no longer be the guiding purpose of punishment because it does not work or because it is ethically objectionable. As David L. Bazelon, Chief Judge of the United States Court of Appeals in Washington, D.C., concluded, "The guiding faith of corrections—rehabilitation—has been declared a false God."[65]

Judge Bazelon argued that the problem with rehabilitation as a justification for punishment is that it "should never have been sold on the promise that it would reduce crime. Recidivism rates cannot be the only measure of what is valuable in corrections. Simple decency must count too. It is amoral, if not immoral, to make cost-benefit equations a lodestar in corrections."[66] Others have argued that treatment programs, though they may not be effective in coerced situations, should be available in prisons for those inmates who want to be rehabilitated. It is noteworthy to mention that those who strongly support the doctrine of rehabilitation have not given up easily. Many have emphasized the importance of the reintegration of the offender into the community, resulting in a strong emphasis on community-based programs.

The argument that the doctrine of rehabilitation is unjust to the offender was raised in the early 1950s by C. S. Lewis, who argued that the rehabilitative ideal removes the concept of just deserts. Society is no longer interested in a "just" cure but only in a cure; not in a "just" deterrent but only in a deterrent.[67] It is this type of adversity to the rehabilitation model that has formed the basis for the return in the 1990s to an emphasis on retribution. The Justice Model appears to be the pervasive model of punishment today. The recent terrorist attack on The World Trade Center reminds us that revenge is an influential concept in the lives of many individuals whose goal is to "get back" at those they deem responsible for their failures.

Summary

This chapter provided instruction on the main theories of punishment, the historical background of punishment and criminal law, justifications for punishment, and the prevention of crime. The cultural consistency and social structure theories provide particular insights into the mechanisms that have provoked the implementation of different types of punishments throughout history. Some of these punishments were implemented in France and England, where torture and death became known concepts among the citizenry. Fortunately, individuals such as Cesare Beccaria and Jeremy Bentham contributed toward the reform of these punitive methods. Out of these reforms, the classical school of criminology was born. Although this school of thought was quite popular at the time, it dwindled and was followed by the works of Cesare Lombroso, Rafaelle Garofalo, and Enrico Ferri. The writings of these three individuals created the foundation for the positive school of criminology. This school of thought, unlike the classical school, promoted the concepts of predeterminism and rehabilitation. It is important to note that both the classical and positive schools govern some of the present-day policies that are aimed at both the punishment and rehabilitation of offenders.

Justifications for punishments, such as retribution and deterrence, both assume that offenders are rational and enjoy the benefit of exercising free will. These themes have continued to have a significant influence in the criminal justice system and the field of corrections even today.

Notes

1. Sutherland, Edwin H., and Cressey, Donald R., *Criminology,* 9th ed. (Philadelphia: J.B. Lippincott and Company, 1974), p. 337.
2. Sutherland, Edwin H., and Cressey, Donald R., *Criminology,* 10th ed. (Philadelphia: J.B. Lippincott and Company, 1978), pp. 355.
3. See Emile Durkheim, *The Division of Labor in Society,* paper ed. (New York: Free Press, 1964), p. 113.
4. Spitzer, Steven, "Punishment and Social Organization: A Study of Durkheim's Theory of Penal Evolution," *Law and Society Review* 9 (Summer, 1975), 634.
5. Siegel, Larry J., (2001) *Criminology: Theory, Patterns, and Typologies* (7th ed.), Wadsworth.
6. Sutherland and Cressey, *Criminology,* 10th ed., p.358.
7. Mannheim, Hermann, ed. *Pioneers in Criminology,* paper ed (Montclair, NJ: Patterson Smith, 1973).
8. Lacroix, Paul, *France in the Middle Ages,* (New York: Frederick Ungar Publishing Co., 1963), p. 394. The examples of punishment are based on this source.
9. Lacroix, Paul, *France in the Eighteenth Century,* p. 291.
10. Durant, Will and Ariel, *The Story of Civilization,* Vol. 7, *The Age of Reason Begins* (New York: Simon and Schuster, 1961), p. 54. The examples of punishments in England are from that source.
11. Durant, Will and Ariel, *Civilization,* Vol. 9, *The Age of Voltaire* (New York: Simon and Schuster, 1965), p. 71. This book is the source of the remaining examples of punishment in England.
12. Beccaria, Cesare, *On Crimes and Punishments,* trans. Henry Paolucci (Indianapolis, IN: Bobbs-Merrill, 1963), pp.ix-xxxiii.
13. Monochese, Eliott, "Cesare Beccaria," in Mannheim, *Pioneers,* p. 49.
14. Schafer, Stephen, *Theories in Criminology* (New York: Random House, 1969), p. 106.
15. Beccaria, On *Crimes and Punishments,* pp. 11-13.
16. Heath, James, *Eighteenth Century Penal Theory* (London: Oxford University Press, 1963), p. 60.
17. Pound, Roscoe, quoted in Frank Tannenbaum, *Crime and the Community* (New York: Ginn and Company, 1938), p. 4.
18. Phillipson, Coleman, *Three Criminal Law Reformers: Beccaria, Bentham, and Romilly* (New York: E.P. Dutton and Co., 1923), p. 234.
19. Geis, Gilbert, "Jeremy Bentham," in Mannheim, *Pioneers,* p. 54.
20. Geis, in *Pioneers,* p. 57.
21. Geis, in *Pioneers,* p. 59.
22. Maestro, M.T., *Voltaire and Beccaria as Reformers of the Criminal Law* (New York: Columbia University Press, 1942), pp. 152-157.
23. Mannheim, *Pioneers,* pp. 386-388, 391.
24. Garofalo, Rafaelle, *Criminology,* trans. Robert W. Millar (Boston: Little, Brown and Company, 1914), p.32.
25. Allen, Francis, "Raffaelle Garofalo," in Mannheim, *Pioneers,* p. 327. For an excellent discussion on Garofalo, see this essay.
26. Sellin, Thorsten, "Enrico Ferri," in Mannheim, *Pioneers,* pp. 370-371.
27. Ferri, Enrico, *Criminal Sociology,* trans. Joseph Killey and John Lisle (Boston: Little, Brown and Company, 1917), p. 209.
28. Ferri, *Criminal Sociology,* pp. 242-277.
29. Ferri, Enrico, *The Positive School of Criminology* (Chicago: Charles H. Kerr and Co., 1913), p. 35.
30. Packer, Herbert L.,*The Limits of the Criminal Sanction* (Stanford, CA: Stanford University Press, 1968).
31. Bureau of Justice Statistics, U.S. Department of Justice (2000), *Prisoners in 2000.*
32. *Furman v. Georgia,* 408 U.S. 238 (1972).
33. 408 U.S. 238, 308.
34. 408 U.S. 238, 395.
35. *Gregg v. Georgia,* 428 U.S. 153, 184-185.
36. 428 U.S. 153, 183428 U.S. 153, 183.
37. Gibbs, Jack P., "The Death Penalty, Retribution and Penal Policy," *The Journal of Criminal Law and Criminology* 69 (Fall, 1978), 294.
38. Gibbs, "The Death Penalty," p. 299.
39. von Hirsch, Andrew, *Doing Justice: The Choice of Punishments* (New York: Hill & Wang, 1976).
40. van den Hagg, Ernest, *Punishing Criminals: Concerning a Very Old and Painful Question* (New York: Basic Books, 1975).
41. van den Haag, *Punishing Criminals,* p. 25.
42. Fogel, David, "*...We Are the Living Proof...*" *The Justice Model for Corrections* (Cincinnati, OH: W.H. Anderson, 1975).
43. Fogel, *Living Proof,* pp. 183-184.
44. Fogel, *Living Proof,* p. 184.
45. Fogel, *Living Proof,* p. 192, emphasis as in the original.
46. Fogel, *Living Proof,* p. 202, emphasis deleted.
47. Fogel, *Living Proof,* p. 206.
48. Lewis, C.S. "The Humanitarian Theory of Punishment," *Res Judicatae* 6 (June, 1953), 224-225.

49. Carlson, Rich J. *The Dilemma of Corrections,* (Lexington, MA: D.C. Heath & Co., 1976), p.135.
50. Carlson, *The Dilemma of Corrections,* p. 126.
51. For more information on the effects of incarceration on deterrence, see http://dwidata.org/sanctions/incarceration.cfm (2000).
52. Chambliss, William, J., *Crime and the Legal Process* (New York: McGraw-Hill, 1969).
53. 115 Can. Crim. Cas. 273 (1956).
54. Quoted in John Kaplan, *Criminal Justice: Introductory Cases and Materials* (Mineola, NY: The Foundation Press, 1973), p. 16.
55. Quoted in Sanford H. Kadish and Monrad G. Paulsen, *Criminal Law and Its Processes* (Boston: Little, Brown and Company, 1969), p. 85.
56. Andenaes, Johannes, "Determinism and Criminal Law," *Journal of Criminal Law, Criminology, and Police Science* 47 (November-December, 1956), 406-413.
57. van den Haag, *Punishing Criminals,* p. 64.
58. van den Hagg, *Punishing Criminals,* p. 64-65.
59. Marcus Felson, *Crime and Everyday Life: Insight and Implications for Society* (Pine Forge Press, 1994).
60. Gibbs, "Crime, Punishment and Deterrence," *Southwest Social Science Quarterly,* 515-530; and Charles R. Tittle, *"Crime Rates and Legal Sanctions,"* Social Problems 16 (Spring, 1969), 409-4515-530; and Charles R. Tittle, *"Crime Rates and Legal Sanctions,"* Social Problems 16 (Spring, 1969), 409-423.
61. See National Center for Policy, *"Does Policy Deter?"* Dallas, Texas, July 5, 2001.
62. Meier, Robert F., "Correlates of Deterrence. Problems of Theory and Method," *Journal of Criminal Justice* 7 (Spring, 1979), 18-19.
63. See *Williams v. New York,* 337 U.S. 241, 248 (1949).
64. Allen, Francis, "Criminal Justice, Legal Values and the Rehabilitative Ideal," *Journal of Criminal Law, Criminology, and Police Science* 50 (September—October, 1959), 226-232.
65. Bazelon, David L., "Street Crime and Correctional Potholes," *Federal Probation* 41 (March 1977), pp. 3-9.
66. Bazelon, *"Street Crime,"* 10.
67. Lewis, *"The Humanitarian Theory of Punishment,"* 225.

Chapter 3

The History of Punishment

Outline

Key Terms

penitentiary
warden
Pennsylvania System
Auburn System
solitary confinement
Elmira Reformatory
progressives
prison overcrowding
indeterminate sanctions
parole
halfway houses
prerelease centers

Chapter 2, "The Social Response to Crime," examined various theoretical justifications of punishment used in reaction to those who violate the laws and mores of society. Although many of the punishments were cruel and unusual in the past, the world was less populated, police protection was nonexistent, and capital punishment and torture were quick methods of incapacitating offenders. "Under the more unstable conditions of the past it would have been difficult to carry out long, continued forms of punishment such as imprisonment."[1] Prison is a recent development, although society has held criminals in custody for a long time. Until recently, confinement was only temporary—while awaiting execution, transportation, or physical discipline—and was not perceived or used as a form of punishment.

This chapter traces the historical development of prisons, focusing attention on the influence of John Howard, a prison reformer. During the emergence of prisons in the United States, two basic types of systems—the Pennsylvania and the Auburn—created the foundation for today's modern prison. The reformation of those incarcerated led to the development of the Elmira Reformatory, which placed emphasis on rehabilitation through education, parole, and indeterminate sentences. Architecture had an important role in all of these systems. Even today, by virtue of the design of prisons and rehabilitation facilities, architecture is related to treatment.

During the development of the prison system throughout the twentieth century in the United States, emphasis was placed on the Progressives and their role in American corrections. Various historical periods, including the transition period and the modern era, will be analyzed, especially the latter's dimensions of prison overcrowding and its effects on the present correctional system.

3-1 Historical Development

The transition from corporal punishment to incarceration as a method of punishment took place in the eighteenth century. This transition was illustrated in 1704, when Pope Clement XI erected the papal prison of San Michele in Rome, and Hippolyte Vilain XIII established a prison in Ghent, Belgium in 1773. Once instituted as a preferred form of punishment, incarceration became the subject of several reforms. In the mid-1700s, John Howard, one of the great prison reformers, visited prisons throughout Europe and notified the world of the sordid conditions under which prisoners were being kept. His work, *State of Prisons,* published in 1777, was extremely influential in the reform of prisons in Europe and the United States. Howard is often credited for the emergence of the **penitentiary**—a facility built with the intent of isolating offenders from society and from each other so that they can reflect, repent, and undergo reformation. The word penitentiary is suggestive of the penance that offenders were to endure. It is important to note that all of these characteristics made the penitentiary different from prisons and jails.

Penitentiary
A state or federal prison that confines offenders convicted of serious crimes and sentenced for terms longer than one year.

In 1776, England was faced with prison overcrowding due to a rising crime rate, the elimination of the need for galley slaves, and decreasing opportunities for transportation of criminals to other countries. In response to the need for new arrangements in the handling of convicts, England legalized the use of hulks, which were abandoned ships converted to hold prisoners. By 1828, 4,000 convicts were confined in prison hulks. "The ships were unsanitary, ill-ventilated and full of vermin." Contagious diseases often killed a great number of prisoners. Punishments were brutal and particularly severe. There was little work for prisoners and idleness was demoralizing. Moral degeneration inevitably set in because of the "promiscuous association of prisoners of all ages and degrees of criminality."[2] This system of penal confinement in England lasted until the mid-nineteenth century.

Among the reasons for the substitution of imprisonment for corporal and capital punishment was the spirit of humanitarianism that arose during the Enlightenment. The influence of the classical criminologists and philosophers was also evident. The emphasis on rationalism served as the ideological basis that provoked and demanded change. This approach was important in the history of prisons because of its influence on social and political philosophy. The philosophers believed that social progress and the "greatest happiness for the greatest number" would occur only through revolutionary social reform. Such social reform could be brought about by applying reason.[3]

It was logical that those ideas would flourish in America because many of the French lived in the United States during the French Revolution. During the same time, many influential Americans lived in France. Since the Constitutional Convention was greatly influenced by French political philosophers, it is reasonable to assume that its members were also aware of the French social philosophy. Those who were most influenced were concentrated in Philadelphia, as it was the birthplace of early penal reform. This is further support of the belief that French philosophy influenced criminal justice reform in the United States.

3-1a Emergence of the Penitentiary System in the United States

Several explanations have been offered regarding the rise of the *penitentiary system* in the United States. David J. Rothman, in his book *The Discovery of the Asylum,*[4] examines the development of the penitentiary and other institutions in the United States. Prior to the Jacksonian period, he notes, Americans handled orphans by placing them in private homes, expected families to care for their insane members, used corporal or capital punishment to punish those who violated the laws of the society, and placed the poor with relatives or friends. Why did Americans develop orphanages, asylums, penitentiaries, and almshouses to care for these classes of deviants during this time?

Rothman maintained that, contrary to the beliefs of some historians, the development of such institutions was avoidable. He looks upon the development of all of these types of institutions as an effort to "promote the stability of the society at a moment when traditional ideas and practices appeared outmoded, constricted, and ineffective." Circumstances were changing rapidly and the people sought a way to maintain stability and retain community cohesion. Students of such social problems, legislators, and philanthropists believed that the nation faced unprecedented dangers. They believed that such institutions could eliminate long-standing problems while restoring social balance.[5]

Rothman began his analysis with the colonial period, taking the position that the social structure must be understood before one can comprehend the changes that took place in the nineteenth century. During the colonial period, it was thought that crime, poverty, mental illness, homeless children, and other social problems were not indicative of a defective social organization and that they could not be eliminated through social action. There seemed to be no reason for the development of institutions to handle such problems. After the Revolution, considerable endorsement was given to the position that the roots of crime and poverty are in the social structure—the faulty organization of the community. The belief in social action to solve such problems was also prevalent. In the case of criminals and delinquents, it was thought that institutionalization would serve the dual purposes of rehabilitating the inmates as well as setting an example for others.[6] It would serve the purposes of both individual and general deterrence.

According to Rothman, the penitentiary was not developed as a place of last resort but rather as a place of temporary confinement in which the criminal changed while society retained its stability. Prisons would also serve the society as demonstrations of proper social organization. The early penologists believed strongly that the penitentiary was a model not only for reforming the criminal but also for society in general; the architecture of the penitentiary would serve as a model for other social institutions.[7]

There is very little doubt that penitentiaries served as a place where offenders would reflect and change their way of being. The name in itself—penitentiary—suggests that offenders would undergo a process of penance as they asked God to forgive them for their wrongdoings. In addition, this institution was meant to serve as a place of moral and physical transformation. Offenders would not only repent to God for their crimes but were also encouraged to make a firm commitment to change the physical activities that allowed them to engage in criminality.

The underlying punitive principle was to keep the inmate busy while relying on techniques to morally change the individual. Inmates were encouraged to constantly think of the crimes they committed while asking God for forgiveness. Prayer was a component of their daily schedule. If one had lived during this time, there would have been little doubt after visiting a penitentiary that they were designed (architecturally) with only one aim—to punish the offender.

3-1b Walnut Street Jail

The Walnut Street Jail was typical of the earliest institutions developed for the purpose of incarceration as punishment in this country. In 1787, the Quakers of Philadelphia formed the Reformist Society for Alleviating the Miseries of Public Prisoners. Under the leadership of individuals such as Dr. Benjamin Rush and Benjamin Franklin, the society aggressively moved to replace corporal and capital punishments with incarceration. Moreover, Rush proposed a new system for the treatment of criminals, which included classification, individualized treatment, and prison labor, to make them self-supporting. In 1790, under Rush's leadership, the society influenced the enactment of a law that established the principle of solitary confinement. The Walnut Street Jail was to be remodeled so that this philosophy could be implemented. Individual cells would be provided for serious offenders. Other prisoners would be separated by gender and by whether they had been sentenced or were only being detained awaiting trial. In this manner, offenders could be isolated from society's bad influences and from one another to allow time for reflection, repentance, and reformation. This law was the beginning of the modern prison system in the United States, for it established the philosophy that was the basis for the Pennsylvania System and later, the Auburn System.

The prisoners at Walnut Street Jail worked eight to ten hours a day and received religious instruction. They worked in their cells and were paid for their work. Guards were not allowed to use their weapons, and corporal punishment was forbidden. Prisoners were allowed to talk only in the nightrooms before retiring. By 1800, problems with the system were obvious. Crowded facilities made work within individual cells impossible, and there was not enough productive work for the large number of prisoners. Vices flourished, and the pardon power was abused. The Walnut Street Jail ultimately failed because of lack of finances, politics, lack of personnel, and crowding, but not before it gained recognition throughout the world. It has been called the "birthplace of the prison system, in its present meaning, not only in the United States but throughout the world."[8]

3-1c Problems Faced by the Early Prisons

Warden
The chief administrator of a correctional facility.

The Walnut Street Jail and other early prisons faced serious problems. Despite tight security and thick walls, escapes occurred. To combat this problem, some **wardens**—chief administrators of correctional institutions—required inmates to wear uniforms. In some prisons, the color of the uniform indicated whether the convict was a first-, second-, or third-time offender. Wardens faced the problem of what to do with inmates who broke rules. In some cases, administrators reacted with a return to corporal punishment, especially whippings, while others used solitary confinement. The prisons faced the problem of the expense of keeping the inmates, especially those with long sentences. Work programs, such as gardening, were devised to alleviate this problem, while allowing the inmates opportunities for exercise. Generally those programs did not work. The inmates were not reliable or efficient and administrators were not skilled in managing the labor situation. The result was that most prisons operated at a loss. "By 1820, the viability of the entire prison system was in doubt, and its most dedicated supporters conceded a near total failure. Institutionalization had not only failed to pay its own way, but also encouraged and educated the criminal to a life of crime."[9]

3-1d Development of the Pennsylvania and Auburn Systems

Pennsylvania System
Prison system based on solitary confinement whereby inmates were isolated at all times.

Auburn, or congregate, system
Prison system that espoused congregate work during the day with an enforced rule of silence; also demanded that the prisoners be housed in isolation at night.

In response to such problems, two distinct types of prison systems were developed—the Pennsylvania System and the Auburn System. The **Pennsylvania System** was based on confinement whereby inmates were isolated at all times. The **Auburn System** was based on the congregate system that placed inmates in workshops during the day, but forbade communication among them. These two systems were the subject of intense debate during the 1800s, and the intensity was not diminished by the fact that most prisons in the United States were modeled after the Auburn System. The two systems were similar, but the arguments over the merits of the systems involved an "extraordinary amount of intellectual and emotional energy." When a state adopted one or the other of the two systems, it entered the debate "with the zeal of a recent convert."[10] Tourists flocked to see the prisons and foreign nations sent delegates to examine the two systems. In 1831, France sent Alexis de Tocqueville and Gustave

Cherry Hill Eastern Penitentiary
Courtesy of The American Correctional Association

Auguste de Beaumont, who wrote, "nothing distracts in Philadelphia, the mind of the convicts from their mediations; and as they are always isolated, the presence of a person who comes to converse with them is the greatest benefit."[11] By the 1830s, the Pennsylvania and Auburn systems were famous around the world.

Development of the Pennsylvania System

With the failure of the Walnut Street Jail, solitary confinement and hard labor did not appear to work. Consideration was given to a return to corporal punishment. In 1817, the Philadelphia Society for the Alleviation of the Miseries of Prisons began a reform movement that eventually led to a law providing for the establishment of solitary cells without labor. The first such prison was opened in Pittsburgh in 1826 and was later known as the Western Penitentiary. Based on the experiences with this prison, however, the law was changed to permit work in solitary confinement before the establishment of the Eastern Penitentiary in Philadelphia. The design of this building eventually became the basic architectural model for the Pennsylvania System. These two systems became so popular that most European countries replicated them and they became the most popular prison systems in the nineteenth century.

Cherry Hill

Eastern Penitentiary, or Cherry Hill—as it was called because it was located in a cherry orchard—opened in 1829. It was the first large-scale attempt to implement the philosophy of solitary confinement at all times with work provided in the cells. The law that authorized the construction of this prison clearly specified that the principle of **solitary confinement** must be incorporated, although the commissioners could make some alterations and improvements in the plan used for the Western Penitentiary. John Haviland, the architect who designed the Eastern Penitentiary, was faced with the problem of creating a design that would permit solitary confinement but would not, at the same time, injure the health or permit the escape of the occupant. His solution was to build seven wings, each connected to a central hub by covered passageways. Each prisoner would have a single inside cell with an outside exercise yard. Prisoners were blindfolded when taken to the prison and were not permitted to see other

Solitary confinement
A type of confinement whereby inmates are isolated at all times; originated in the Walnut Street Jail in Philadelphia, Pennsylvania, in the late 1700s.

The Auburn System
Courtesy of The American Correctional Association

inmates. They were not even assembled for religious worship. The chaplain spoke from the rotunda—a circular hall—while prisoners listened from their individual cells.

Before Cherry Hill was completed, it became the focus of discussion among prison reformers around the world. It served as the architectural model for most of the new prisons in Europe and South America and, later in Asia. The architectural design was not popular in the United States, although today it "dominates the penitentiary system of continental Europe."[12] In Scandinavia, for instance, the "traditional structure is straight out of Pennsylvania, and . . . one of the finest surviving examples of Pennsylvania prison design is the Vestrefaengsel in Copenhagen, where, until not so long ago, chapel seats were still boxed off in vertical coffin-shaped compartments so that privacy of the prisoner would be maintained and his contamination prevented."[13]

Development of the Auburn System

The Auburn System became the architectural model for prisons in the United States. In 1796, New York passed a law that provided for the construction of two prisons—Newgate and Auburn. Newgate, a prison built in New York City, was first occupied in 1797 and soon became overcrowded. To make room for new inmates, the number of prisoners released had to equal the number admitted. The second prison opened at Auburn in the winter of 1817. At first, it followed the same type of system as that of Newgate—workshop groups during the day and several prisoners to a cell at night. Discipline was a problem in this setting, and this method eventually failed, thus allowing the development of a new system—the Auburn System.

The Auburn System, or congregate system, espoused congregate work during the day with an enforced rule of silence, but it also demanded that the prisoners be housed in isolation at night. The architecture created a fortress-like appearance with a series of tiers set in a hollow frame, a much more economical system than that used at Cherry Hill.

The silent system was strictly enforced at Auburn. Inmates were not allowed to talk or exchange glances at any time. They had to stand with their arms folded and their eyes facing the floor so they could not communicate with their hands. They had to walk in lockstep with a downward gaze, and eat face to back. To further isolate the inmates, there was strict regulation of letters and visits with outsiders, and few or no newspapers were provided. Prisoners were brought together for religious services, but they sat in booth-like pews that prevented them from seeing anybody except the speaker. The underlying philosophy of the silent system was the notion that convicts were incorrigible and that industrial efficiency was the main purpose of correctional facilities.

Discipline was also enforced at Auburn. The warden, Captain Elam Lynds, believed that the spirit of a person must be broken before reformation could truly occur. He was largely responsible for the Auburn philosophy of punishment. It is said that he changed the disciplinary rules without legislative authority, instituted the silent system, fed the inmates in their cells, and required lockstep marching. A committee from the legislature visited the prison, approved of the way it was being run, and persuaded the legislature to legalize the new system.

A system of classification that placed dangerous criminals in solitary confinement was instituted in 1821. This led to mental illness, the death of some inmates, and the pleading of others to be let out to work. Although very few in the United States took notes regarding the impact of isolation on an individual's mental state, Germany was the first nation to officially charge individuals with the task of documenting this information. From 1854 to 1909, there were thirty-seven articles printed in German scientific journals regarding the psychotic disturbances promoted by this form of incarceration. However, the scientific community was not the only one taking notes on the impact of solitary confinement. It is reported that prison administrators became concerned that the conditions of solitary confinement were wearing on the population of inmates and their mental state. They were also troubled with the impact mental illness had on the rise of prison violence. It was clear that solitary condition had to either end or be subject to great modification. In 1822, the practice of solitary confinement was abolished.

Comparison of the Pennsylvania and Auburn Systems

There is no question that the Pennsylvania and Auburn systems exhibited radically different methods of punishment. The former emphasized solitary confinement while the latter was based on the congregate system. Both systems stressed the importance of a disciplined routine while isolating the individual from bad influences. It is clear that both the Pennsylvania and Auburn systems reflected the belief that the inmate was not inherently bad, but rather the product of a defective social organization; he or she could be reformed under the proper circumstances. "Just as the criminal's environment had led him into crime, the institutional environment would lead him out of it."[14] The discussions of crime focused on the advantages and disadvantages of these two systems, but no one questioned the premise on which both rested—that incarceration was the best way to handle criminals.

The differences in architecture of the two systems resulted in differences in cost. Even though the design of the Auburn System was less expensive to build, it has been argued that the Pennsylvania System was more economical to administer. Furthermore, the Auburn System was more conducive to productive labor of inmates and less likely to cause mental illness.[15] Finally, it must be noted that the Pennsylvania System sought to produce honest individuals, while the Auburn System aimed at producing obedient citizens. Figure 3-1 compares the two systems.

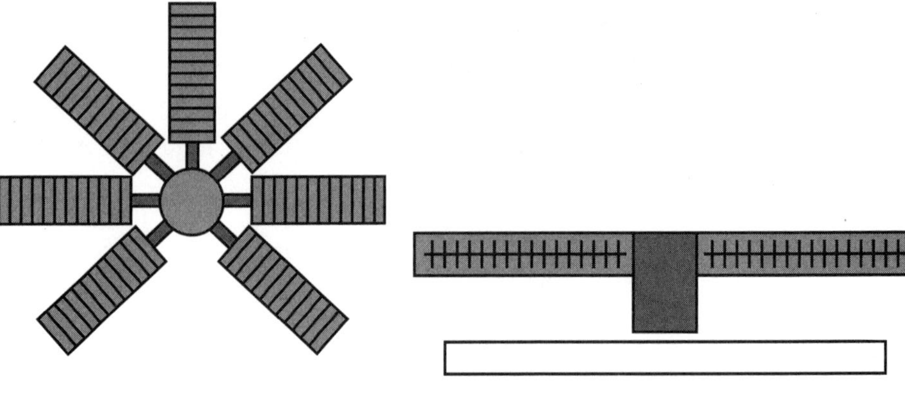

Figure 3-1 Comparison of the Pennsylvania and Auburn Systems

Pennsylvania System
- Twenty-four hour solitary confinement
- Inmates work in cells
- Example: Cherry Hill, open in 1829

Auburn System
- Congregate system but inmates not permitted to speak
- Inmates work in common area
- Example: Auburn, open in 1817

3-1e Prison Architecture

The early proponents of penal and criminal law visualized the close relationship between architecture and behavior. Gabriel de Tarde, one of the most influential prison reformists of the eighteenth century, examined the prison system and decided that prisoners should have individual cells to keep them away from each other. Tarde developed a law of imitation that was based on the notion that individuals committed crimes through their association with other criminals. Tarde thought inmates should have a "stream of kindly disposed visitors whose good influence would be brought to bear" on them.[16] In 1797, Bentham proposed a prison plan called the panopticon, or inspection house. He emphasized the importance of prison architecture. "Morals reformed, health preserved, industry invigorated, instruction diffused, public burdens lightened, economy seated, as it were upon a rock, the Gordian knot of the poor laws not cut, but untied, all by a simple idea in architecture."[17]

The panopticon was the first circular prison plan, and although Bentham got a permit to build such a structure, "fortunately for penology, this monstrosity was never built."[18] The structure was to be constructed of cast iron and glass. Although Bentham's project was never completed, some prisons and jails that resembled his circular plan were built in Europe and America. Pittsburgh's Western State Penitentiary, which opened in 1826, was modeled after Bentham's prison design. It was rebuilt in 1833 because it was "wholly unsuited for anything but a fortress."[19] The plan was also followed in the first four cell houses built at Stateville Prison in Illinois, between 1925 and 1935. The plan was abandoned because of the impracticality of the design. A noted prison architect evaluated the design, saying that it was "the most awful receptacle of gloom ever devised and put together with good stone and brick and mortar."[20]

Those early ideas influenced John Haviland, who designed the Eastern Penitentiary's central rotunda and seven wings in 1820. He gave attention to proper lighting, adequate plumbing, ventilation, and space for exercise and warmth. His plan was the basic architectural design for the Pennsylvania System. It became quite popular in Europe but lost out to the Auburn System in the United States. Nevertheless, his contributions to prison architecture in America cannot be overlooked. "Compared with the penitentiaries of their day, Haviland's prisons were overwhelmingly superior, both technically and stylistically...Haviland's great service to penology would seem to be in establishing high standards of construction, standards which were to have an influence on almost all of the prison construction of the nineteenth century."[21] Furthermore, Haviland's prisons were built in accordance with a treatment philosophy.

The architect of the Auburn prison system, John Cray, also embodied a treatment philosophy in his work. Both Cray and Haviland's designs emphasized strict discipline and non-communication in an institution that was "fearsome and forbidding."[22] Prison architecture was the key to treatment philosophy and the philosophy of those early prisons has dominated the prison system in the United States for over one hundred years. Although many would disagree with the philosophy of non-communication, prison architecture was important because of the effect the structure had on the prisoner.

3-1f Emergence of the Reformatory System

Elmira

On October 12, 1870, penologist Enoch C. Wines led a meeting in Cincinnati, Ohio, that resulted in the organization of the National Prison Association, later called the American Correctional Association. The group drew up thirty-seven principles calling for indeterminate sentences, classification of prisoners, cultivation of the inmate's self-respect, and advancement of the philosophy of reformation. What emerged from this meeting was the **Elmira Reformatory,** which was established in 1876. This institution became the model for housing juvenile offenders. The architecture was similar to that of the Auburn System; however, greater emphasis was placed on educational and trade training. Indeterminate sentences with maximum terms, opportunity for parole, and classification of inmates according to conduct and achievement were the greatest contributions of this new institution.

Elmira Reformatory
The first true reformatory, built in 1876. It advocated the rehabilitation and reformation of offenders.

It was predicted that Elmira would dominate the prison system of the United States. The great contribution of the Elmira Reformatory system was its emphasis on rehabilitation through education and the use of indeterminate sentences and parole. The system eventually declined due to the lack of trained personnel to conduct the education and to classify the inmates adequately.

A great increase in the prison population in the late 1800s resulted in overcrowding. This was due to the perceived threat of the numerous immigrants arriving in America. Most of these immigrants were viewed by some government officials as potential criminals whose only way out of poverty was crime. The fear of immigrants and the rise in crime influenced correctional policy. New prisons were created to house the numerous individuals being incarcerated. During the

The Elmira Reformatory
Library of Congress Prints and Photographs Division
LC-USZ62-83739

late 1800s and early 1900s, the United States was the subject of numerous political and social changes that also influenced correctional practices. New prisons were built, including Attica in New York in 1931 and Stateville in Illinois in 1925. Most of these followed the Auburn architectural plan and were characterized by Sunday services, an on-duty chaplain, increasing costs per inmate, and insufficient educational and vocational training. Vocational training was based on the needs of the institution, not on the interests or needs of the inmates. Insufficient funds were available for adequate prison personnel. As a result, a new era was born in corrections in the United States.

3-2 The Progressives

The period from the 1890s to the 1930s was known as the Progressive Era. Immense industrialization, technological advances, and urban growth characterized this period. With these new developments came an array of social concerns. "The assimilation of immigrants and minorities into the industrial urban centers was particularly difficult to achieve, creating a deep anxiety about social order among many Americans. Some of them responded by advocating exclusionary policies, such as immigration restriction. But others sought answers in a paternalistic vision of the state and in the articulation of a broad reform plan."[23]

Progressives
A group of individuals who espoused social reforms, including individualized treatment of criminals to achieve their rehabilitation. They believed that treating criminals as individuals, each with a different set of needs and problems, would achieve rehabilitation and prepare criminals for mainstream society.

This group of people, known as the **Progressives,** espoused social reforms, including individualized treatment of criminals to achieve their rehabilitation. They believed that treating criminals as individuals, each with a different set of needs and problems, would achieve rehabilitation and prepare them for mainstream society. The Progressives worked toward changing the criminal justice system. They believed that the reasons for crime were biological, psychological, economical, or sociological, and they relied on scientific methods for solutions. "Under this banner, the field of penology became as much territory for social workers, psychologists, and psychiatrists as lawyers."[24]

By the early 1900s, the Progressives had been successful in achieving acceptance of several components of their program: indeterminate sentences, probation, parole, and juvenile courts. These components made a permanent impact on the correctional system in America. The contributions made by the Progressives are unprecedented in the history of corrections.

At the state level, old facilities were stretched to house the increasing number of inmates. "Ten new prisons of the Auburn type style and one modeled after Jeremy Bentham's Panopticon"[25] were built during the period between 1900 and 1935. Due to the large number of inmates entering correctional facilities, little or no attempt was made to classify or segregate the different types of inmates. No effort was made to prevent communication among those incarcerated. The conditions were so strict that only on Sundays were inmates allowed to get out of their cells for an hour.

The role of prisons began to change as they adopted the reformatory philosophy and the reformatories became more like prisons.[26] The only characteristic that distinguished prisons from reformatories in some states was the age of the inmates. Despite this, some reformatories continued to support vocational and educational programs while holding military drills.

From 1900 to 1935, U.S. prisons held programs that were custodial, industrial, and punitive in nature. It was clear that the era of prisons that adhered to classification and moral instruction of offenders had ended. The close of this era is often attributed to the fast-growing number of inmates. In addition, the death of the reformatory program that was in place before the 1900s was made possible by the change in political attitudes about the roles of prisons. Custody, hard labor, and punishment, which were the goals of prisons at the time, began one hundred years earlier. Toward the end of this period, many prisons had eliminated hard labor in favor of custodial and punitive goals. The federal government also participated in the prison changes. In 1929, the U.S. Congress passed the Hawes-Cooper Act. This "diverted prison products of their interstate character on arrival at destination, thus making them subject to state laws."[27] Six years later, the U.S. Congress passed the Ashurst-Sumners Act, which prohibited transportation companies from accepting products made in prison for purposes of transporting them into any state. This act also provided for the labeling of all packages that contained prison-made products. "With the passage of these laws, the Industrial Prison was eliminated. In 1935, for the great majority of prisoners, the penitentiary system had returned once more to its original status: punishment and custody."[28]

3-3 Transition Period (1935-1960)

The penitentiary system returned to its original purpose of custody and punishment during the Great Depression. This period provoked a punitive attitude toward crime.[29] However, many scholars who were developing an interest in reforming the treatment of prisoners did not share this attitude. Their efforts met with resistance and hostility from J. Edgar Hoover, Director of the FBI, as he led the battle against some of these activist professors. The opening of the Alcatraz prison in 1934, under the auspices of the U.S. government, was a way to show the public that the government was taking action to stop the increasing crime rates of those years.

The U.S. Army used Alcatraz, a twelve-acre island in San Francisco Bay, for more than eighty years as barracks. In 1909, it was transformed into a prison with the intent of holding military prisoners. In 1934, Alcatraz became a maximum-security prison with minimum privileges known as "The Rock." It was considered escape-proof.

At Alcatraz an inmate had four rights: clothing, shelter, food, and medical care. Everything else was considered a privilege that had to be earned. Working, recreational activities, visits and letters from family, and library access were privileges that an inmate could gain. After an average of five years in Alcatraz, a prisoner was eligible to be transferred back to another federal prison to serve the remainder of his sentence, provided the inmate was no longer a threat and was considered capable of following rules. Alcatraz remained a prison for twenty-nine years, closing in 1963 because operating costs were too high. It was almost three times more costly to run Alcatraz than other federal prisons due to its physical isolation. In 1972, an act of Congress made Alcatraz a national park.

Between 1915 and 1930, prison administrators began discussing the need for diagnosis and classification. Some of the early efforts include those of Bernard Glueck at Sing Sing, Edgar Doll and W. G. Ellis in New Jersey, and A. W. Stearns in Massachusetts. In 1930, the Bureau of Prisons Act placed federal prisons under the authority of the Federal Bureau of Prisons. In 1934, the act was reorganized under the leadership of Sanford Bates. The Bureau emerged as the leader in corrections nationwide and introduced ideas of diagnosis and classification. The hope of diagnosis was an eventual "cure of the patient." Various forms of treatment emerged to aid this process. The treatment approach was strongly influenced by several disciplines, including social work, psychology, and psychiatry.

Classification has enjoyed a longer history than has diagnosis. It is not a specific treatment, training, or process of labeling. It is a process of analyzing an individual and making a decision about the most effective manner in which to apply the resources of the institution to the inmate. All diagnostic techniques available were employed in analyzing the problems of the individual. Treatment programs were tailored to meet his or her needs. All of these happenings did much for corrections; the Federal Bureau of Prisons provided a pattern that states followed.

Despite all of these changes, prison conditions and treatment of inmates remained an unresolved matter. Conditions were not optimal. Idle time, overcrowding, monotony, and repression led to riots in several prisons, including Alcatraz in 1946. These incidents marked more changes in the field of corrections—a time known as the Modern Era.

3-4 The Modern Era

France was a leader in changing its penal system in 1945. In May of that year, "the Commission for the Reform of French Penitentiaries explicitly endorsed the humane treatment and betterment of prisoners through general and professional instruction. Medical, psychological, and social services were available in every penitentiary, and prison personnel were required to receive specialized, technical training."[30]

In the United States, a great advocating for human rights issues began. The field of corrections, due to its ideological and punitive practices, did not escape criticism. The conditions that led to the political climate during this era in the United States were diverse—the Vietnam War, the Civil Rights movement, and the reinterpretation of criminal law. Prisons suffered from these pressures as riots focusing on poor medical care, poor quality of food, and excessive brutality by the guards occurred in prisons throughout the country. Inmates demanded the same basic rights that were advocated outside prison walls. These riots had an impact on corrections and some of the changes that were implemented were direct results of the unrest.

In 1953, the American Prison Association identified the reasons for the riots as official indifference, lack of financial support, enforced idleness, lack of professional leadership and professional programs, overcrowding of institutions, substandard personnel, political motivation and domination of management, and unwise sentencing and parole practices.[31] As a result, the federal government funded many corrections administrators at both local and state levels to create and carry out new policies. The major thrust of these changes prompted an increase in rehabilitation to treat the psychological disturbances that were considered to be at the root of individuals' criminality. Treatment-oriented corrections were created to ameliorate the existing conditions in prisons.

In 1954, the American Prison Association changed its name to the American Correctional Association. Its members were instructed to "redesignate their prisons as 'correctional institutions' and to label the punishment blocks in them as 'adjustment centers.'"[32] Programs focused on more favorable conditions for inmates and provided libraries, vocational programs, counseling opportunities, and exercise-educational facilities. This period of change, which began during the 1960s, became known as the Modern Era.

The 1970s saw a movement opposing the idea of prisoner rehabilitation because of abuses and therapies that were considered intrusive. No consensus exists today on the best way to initiate prison reform.

3-4a Prison Overcrowding

Although **prison overcrowding** has been in existence for over one hundred years, its popularity as a social phenomenon has recently become one of the United States' most frequently discussed topics. Overcrowding is mostly due to the "War on Drugs" campaign established by the Reagan administration, as it gave rise to longer sentences. In addition, President Clinton's "Get Tough on Crime" tactics continued the Reagan crime policy. The news media also contributed to this effort by convincing the public that society should continue to build more prisons to fight crime effectively. The combination of longer sentences and a powerful media campaign raised public awareness about the increasing problem of prison overcrowding. This is most evident in states such as Florida and Texas, where the public expresses steady support for the increase of correctional budgets aimed at constructing new and more expensive prison facilities.

Between 1990 and mid-year 1999, the number of individuals incarcerated in the U.S. grew an average of 5.7 percent annually. The substantial increase took place in federal facilities. According to the Bureau of Justice Statistics (2001), the federal inmate population grew, from 1998 to 1999, by 9.9 percent. This constitutes the largest increase in twelve months ever reported. However, the growth trend was significantly lower in state prisons and local jails. The population between June 1998 and June 1999 increased by only 3.1 percent while the jail population grew by 2.3 percent.[33] Despite the state and local slow increase, the prison population has increased as a whole. This has resulted in the overcrowding of prisons and the construction of new prisons to accommodate first-time inmates. The building of private prisons and those run by private organizations has also become a trend.

This privatization of prisons has alarmed many. "The delegation by government, to private business, of the power to imprison and, necessarily, the power to use force to maintain order, prevent escape, and the like, raises troublesome legal and ethical questions." Furthermore, many are concerned with the idea of an industry with a vested interest "in maintaining, or even increasing, the number of people incarcerated."[34] This increasing number of inmates limits the ability of correctional officers to do their job and causes escalating tensions among prisoners. The U.S. Supreme Court, as a way to avoid crowding, has established population ceilings. Among the proposed solutions to the problem of overcrowding has been the use of **indeterminate sanctions.** These sanctions, which include boot camps, community service, and home confinement, have been suggested as a way to reduce the total number of inmates within prison walls. Early release, **parole, halfway houses,** and **prerelease centers** have also been suggested as solutions to the problem of overcrowding. These will be discussed in later chapters.

Prison overcrowding
Condition facing prisons today. This condition has been due mostly to the creation of longer and more punitive sentences.

Indeterminate sanctions
Penalties considered to be not as harsh as prison but more stringent than probation. These include, but are not limited to, fines, parole, house monitoring, halfway houses, day treatment centers, boot camps, and intensive supervision probation (ISP).

parole
The continued custody and supervision, at the state and federal levels, of a released offender in the community.

Halfway houses
A prerelease center that helps the offender engage in an adequate transition from prison to community life. Also, a facility that addresses particular problems experienced by some inmates (i.e., alcohol and drug abuse).

Prerelease centers
Centers where individuals would be housed as a last step before being released from correctional supervision. These have been suggested to help alleviate the problem of overcrowding.

Summary

Since the development of the Walnut Street Jail in the late 1700s, the U.S. prison system has undergone many changes. These changes have occurred in tandem with the struggles of society. They have been accompanied by turmoil and constant disagreement about the best way to handle the most current corrections issues. Frequently debated questions include how and which inmates are to be imprisoned; how inmates should be treated when being detained and released; what type of architectural format prisons should follow to ensure safety and an appropriate environment for inmates; how overcrowding can be best handled; and what reforms are needed within the system. These problems continue to exist in the present—whether any progress has been made is still a subject of debate among scholars.

Notes

1. Barnes, Harry Elmer, *The Story of Punishment* (Boston: Stratford, 1930), p.121.
2. Barnes, pp. 117, 122.
3. Barnes, p. 121.
4. Rothman, David J., *The Discovery of the Asylum: Social Order and Disorder in the New Republic* (Boston: Little, Brown, and Company, 1971).
5. Rothman, *Discovery of the Asylum,* pp. xiii-xviii.
6. Rothman, *Discovery of the Asylum,* p. xix.
7. Rothman, *Discovery of the Asylum,* p. xix.
8. Menninger, Karl, *The Crime of Punishment* (New York: Viking, 1968), p. 222.
9. Rothman, *Discovery of the Asylum,* pp. 92-93.
10. Rothman, *Discovery of the Asylum,* pp. 81-82.
11. See Gustave de Auguste Beaumont and Alexis de Tocqueville, *On the Penitentiary System in the United States and its Application in France* (Carbondale, IL): Southern Illinois University Press, [1833] 1964), p.146.
12. Barnes, *Story of Punishment,* p. 144.
13. Conrad, John P., *Crime and Its Correction* (Berkeley, CA: University of California Press, 1965), p. 128
14. Rothman, *Discovery of the Asylum,* p. 83.
15. Barnes, *Story of Punishment,* pp. 142-143.
16. Mannheim, Hermann, ed., *Pioneers in Criminology* (Montclair, NJ: Patterson Smith, 1960), p. 300.
17. Cited in Negley K. Teeters, "State Prisons in the United States: 1870-1970," *Federal Probation* 33 (December, 1969), p. 18.
18. Barnes, Harry Elmer and Teeters, Negley K., *New Horizons in Criminology,* 3rd ed. (Englewood Cliffs, NJ: Prentice-Hall, 1959), p. 484.
19. Barnes, Harry Elmer, quoted in Mannheim, *Pioneers in Criminology,* p. 65.
20. Hopkins, Alfred, quoted in Mannheim, *Pioneers in Criminology,* p. 65.
21. Johnson, Norman B., "John Haviland," in Mannheim, *Pioneers in Criminology,* p.122.
22. Gill, Howard B., "Correctional Philosophy and Architecture," *Journal of Criminal Law, Criminology, and Police Science* 53 (March, 1962), pp. 312-322.
23. Rotman, Edgardo, *The Failure of Reform, The Oxford History of the Prison* (New York: Oxford Press, 1995), pp. 176-177.
24. Rotman, *The Failure of Reform,* p. 187.
25. Killinger, George G., Wood, Jerry M., and Cromwell, Paul, *Penology: The Evolution of Corrections in America* (St. Paul, MN: West Publishing, 1979).
26. Killinger, Wood, and Cromwell, *Penology,* p. 53.
27. Killinger, Wood, and Cromwell, *Penology,* p. 53.
28. "State Prisons in America 1787-1937," in George C. Killinger and Paul F. Cromwell, eds., *Penology* (St. Paul, MN: West Publishing, 1973), p. 53.
29. "State Prisons in America 1787-1937," p. 53.
30. O'Brien, Patricia, *The Prison on the Continent, The Oxford History of the Prison* (New York: Oxford Press, 1995), p. 218.
31. Rotman, *The Failure of Reform,* p. 189.
32. Rotman, *The Failure of Reform,* p. 190.
33. Bureau of Justice Statistics, U.S. Department of Justice (2001), *Corrections Statistics: Summary Findings,* Washington, D.C.
34. Morris, Norval, *The Contemporary Prison, the Oxford History of the Prison* (New York: Oxford Press, 1995), p. 255.

Chapter 4

The Pretrial Process: Bail and Jail

Outline

One of the most critical periods of criminal proceedings is between arraignment and trial. It is a time "when consultation, thorough on-going investigation and preparation . . . [are] vitally important."[1] During this period, the defendant either retains an attorney or is assigned counsel by the court. The defense counsel and the prosecutor negotiate and consider the possibility of plea-bargaining. The defense might request, in order to receive a fair trial, that the location of the proceedings be moved. The judge will then rule on the motion for a change of venue. Witnesses are interviewed and other attempts are made by both sides to secure evidence for the trial. The discovery of additional evidence can change the nature of the case and result in the dropping or reduction of charges. All of these factors make a significant impact on the correctional trends in the United States. As this chapter states, the trial process and the bail system make a significant contribution to the growth of the prison population.

Key Terms

- bail
- Manhattan Bail Project
- jail
- Law Enforcement Assistance Administration (LEAA)
- podular design
- interaction space
- personal space
- direct supervision

This chapter will carefully examine the ways in which accused persons are handled during the pretrial period. The bail system permits some defendants to go free while awaiting trial. The history and purpose of bail is discussed as well as the effects that the denial of bail has on defendants. Criticisms of the bail bondsman system and the money bail system have led to a discussion of reforming the system and the evaluations of bail reform.

Bail and jails are interrelated as changes in the granting of bail directly affect the numbers of inmates detained in jails. Jails are used to detain defendants awaiting trial as well as to incarcerate convicted persons. Pretrial detention is discussed, focusing on United States Supreme Court decisions that considered some of the rights of pretrial detainees. The historical background, organization,

and administration of jails will be studied. The conditions of modern jails is examined, especially those in which the courts ordered a change in jail conditions. Jails serve an important role in corrections. They are detaining facilities where individuals who have recently entered the criminal justice system are either awaiting trial or serving a sentence that is twelve months or less. It is in jails that individuals begin the acculturation process of prisons.

4-1 The Bail System

The American bail system originated from feudal practices in twelfth-century England. It was instituted to assure the presence of defendants at trials. These defendants were often supervised by the reeve (an officer of the court) who was appointed to represent the crown in a specific shire (county). The shire reeve (origin of the word sheriff) preferred to have a third party take care of defendants while they awaited trial and would relinquish them to friends or relatives. These people would serve as sureties (guarantees). When the bail system first began, the surety would be tried if the defendant did not appear for trial after he or she had been placed on **bail.** The party furnishing bail would be reminded that he or she had the powers of a jailer and was expected to produce the accused for trial. This policy of private sureties was also followed in the United States as English settlers brought these traditions to the U.S. colonies. This practice was later replaced by a system of posting bond to guarantee a defendant's presence at trial.

Bail
A system of posting bond to secure a defendant's presence at trial while allowing the accused to be released until the individual faces a trial.

4-1a Purpose of Bail

The purpose of bail is to assure the presence of the defendant at trial. In the United States, this is the only legal reason for bail. The courts have also regulated the monetary boundaries of the bail system. The U.S. Supreme Court ruled "bail set at a figure higher than that reasonably calculated to [secure assurance that the defendant will stand trial] is 'excessive' under the Eighth Amendment."[2] However, many judges use bail for this purpose, especially in connection with people who are considered dangerous or who have been involved in riots and demonstrations. An example of this is illustrated in a story reported by CNN.[3] In 1997, a gunman took dozens of people hostage at a day-care center in Texas. The man, James Monroe Lipscomb, Jr., surrendered to police after thirty hours of negotiation. Lipscomb was having marital problems and entered the Rigsbee Child Development Center to see his wife, who fled after her husband entered. As a result, Lipscomb proceeded to take over the entire day-care facility. After he surrendered, police charged him with various crimes, including one count of aggravated kidnapping. The Texas courts felt that Lipscomb posed a threat to society and set bail at $1 million, which Lipscomb could not reasonably pay. The high bail kept Lipscomb in custody until trial. This case illustrates the practice followed by judges to set bail at high amounts to assure that the defendant will not pose a threat to society before the trial begins. Bail does not, however, serve the claimed purpose of protecting society. Wealthy dangerous offenders who have adequate financial resources might be set free, while persons who are not dangerous to themselves or to society languish in jail.

Bail has a direct relationship to the correctional system. Its presence creates a different type of correctional population in jails—a population of defendants who, although not yet convicted of a particular crime, await trial. Further, it creates a population of individuals who are under correctional custody and have been found guilty by a jury of their peers. These individuals are usually in jail awaiting a sentencing hearing from a judge. Such bail practices have a direct link and impact to the correctional system.

4-1b Bail Bondsman/woman

The professional bondsman/woman (for simplicity, the term "bondsman" will be used throughout this discussion to refer to both males and females) emerged due to the profitable nature of the bail system. In return for a fee, the bondsman posts the bond for the accused. The difference between bail and bond is that the bond (i.e., the guarantee) must be provided in order for an individual to receive bail. A bond is a financial guarantee that the individual, when released from jail on a temporary basis, will appear again in court at the time of the trial. Theoretically, if the accused does not appear, the bondsman is required to forfeit the money to the state. In practice, the courts vacate the forfeitures of bonds in many cases, on the theory that the bondsman has been diligent in his or her attempts to produce the accused for trial. The bondsman often has a lucrative job with little risk. Some bondsmen have not had the necessary money to produce in cases of forfeiture. Because the bond system has been abused, laws have been passed to minimize the exploitation. Some of these require the bondsmen to prove their ability to pay in case of forfeiture and other laws place statutory limits on the fees that can be charged.

The bondsman charges the accused 10 percent for posting bond. He or she may require the accused to sign over a home mortgage or, in some other way, provide collateral security. If the accused does not use a professional bondsman, he or she can post bail by paying the court a specified percentage of the bail or by placing securities with the court. With monetary payment, it is seldom returned even if the accused appears for trial. If bail is high, it can be expensive for the defendant. Minorities are particularly affected by the cost of bail. According to the Bureau of Justice Statistics (1999), in June 1999, 42 percent of the jail population was African American; this was compared to whites (41 percent) and Hispanics (15 percent).[4] Although African Americans and whites only differed by 1 percent, it is important to note that these percentages are compared to the existing composition of minorities and whites in the United States. Thus, given their composition in the United States, African Americans are over-represented in the jail population. This phenomenon could be related to the cost of bail—the higher the cost, the smaller the possibility for an African American suspect to post bail.

In the past, the professional bondsman system has been severely criticized.[5] Some of these criticisms are still pertinent to the bondsman system today. The bondsman might require a larger premium from an offender whom he does not know—a poor business risk—and thereby have considerable control over a defendant. Conversely, bondsmen might consider professional criminals better risks and would not require them to post as much money. As one judge said,

> The effect of such a system is that the professional bondsmen hold the keys to the jail in their pockets. They determine for whom they will act as surety—who in their judgment is a good risk. The bad risks, in the bondsmen's judgment, and the ones who are unable to pay the bondsmen's fees, remain in jail. The court and the commissioner are relegated to the relatively unimportant chore of fixing the amount of bail.[6]

4-1c Alternatives to Bail

The bail system has been the focus of criticism in recent years. These criticisms indicate that a large number of defendants are indigent and cannot afford bail, while others who can afford it are not inclined to appear in court. Due to this reproach, alternative forms of pretrial release (financial and non-financial) have been created. They range from requiring the defendant to post the entire amount of bail to the release of defendants on their promise that they will appear at trial.

Spotlight 4-1

Methods of Pretrial Release

Financial Bond

- **Fully secured bail.** The alleged offender posts the entire amount of bail.
- **Privately secured bail.** A bondsman signs a promissory note to the court for the bail amount and charges a defendant a fee for the service. This fee is usually 10 percent of the bail amount. If the defendant does not appear in court, the bondsman must pay the court the full amount. In most cases, the bondsman requires the defendant to post collateral in addition to the fee required.
- **Deposit bail.** The court allows the accused to deposit a percentage (10 percent in most cases) of the full bail with the court. The complete amount of the bail is required if the defendant fails to appear. The percentage of bail is returned after disposition of the case, but the court frequently retains 1 percent for administrative costs.
- **Unsecured bail.** The accused does not pay any money to the court but is liable for the full amount of bail should he or she fail to appear.

Alternative Release Options

- **Release on recognizance (ROR).** The court releases the accused based on the promise that he or she will appear in court as required.
- **Conditional release.** The court releases the accused subject to specific conditions as set by the courts. These conditions might include attendance at drug treatment therapy, or staying away from the complaining witness.
- **Third-party custody.** The defendant is released into the custody of an agency or individual that promises to assure his or her appearance in court. No monetary transactions are involved in this type of release.
- **Citation release.** Arrested individuals are released pending their first appearance in court on a written order issued by law enforcement personnel.

Source: Bureau of Justice Statistics, *Report to the Nation on Crime and Justice: The Data*, 2nd ed. (Washington, D.C.: U.S. Department of Justice, 1988), p. 76.

This method is often referred to as "release on recognizance" (ROR or OR). Spotlight 4-1 illustrates the various methods of pretrial release.

Some of these methods have been created because of the various reforms made to the bail system and due to the heavy criticisms attributed to the bail system.

4-1d Manhattan Bail Project

Manhattan Bail Project An experiment in the reform of bail that introduced the concept of release on one's own recognizance.

In the 1960s, industrialist Louis Schweitzer became concerned with poor youths who could not make bail and were imprisoned while awaiting trial. As a result, Mr. Schweitzer established the Vera Foundation. This foundation, with the New York University School of Law and the Institute of Judicial Administration, conducted an experiment on bail. This experiment, the **Manhattan Bail Project**, was based on the notion that "more persons can successfully be released . . . if verified information concerning their character and roots in the community is available to the court at the time of bail determination."[7] The publicity received by this experiment led to bail reform initiatives throughout the country.

The project, which began in 1961, allowed New York University law students to interview defendants to gain knowledge that would be relevant to pretrial release. Some of this information included: present or recent residence at the same address for six months or more, present or recent employment for a period of time of six months or more, relatives in the New York City area with whom the defendant is in contact, previous crime conviction(s), and residence in the New York City area for ten years or more.

After the interview took place, the staff would decide whether to recommend release for the defendant. If the staff decided to release, the decision would be sent to the arraignment court and the accused would be randomly assigned to control or experimental groups. For the control group, the recommendation would not be committed to the court. For the experimental group, copies of the recommendation were issued to the judge, prosecutor, and assigned counsel. Ultimately, the decision of whether to grant release was left up to the judge. Of those individuals recommended for release by the staff, the judge released 60 percent. Fourteen percent of those not recommended by the staff were released as well. Due to the existence of the project, four times as many persons were released pending trial. The staff reported that numerous factors (e.g., illness, ignorance of legal processes, family emergencies, and confusion about when and in what court to appear) were responsible for nearly all of those released who did not appear for trial. This was usually corrected by a telephone call to their place of employment, relatives, or homes.

Other cities have adopted bail reform plans that involve release of defendants on their own recognizance (ROR) pending trial. Most of the defendants released on ROR have appeared for trial, and according to the Advisory Commission, this method of release has become a significant alternative to money bail bonds. Despite this, the commission criticizes the plans, noting that in cases involving ROR and other money bail alternatives, the "criteria for these options for the most part have been applied either too conservatively (releasing mostly persons who could have posted bond anyway) or too carelessly (with substantial increases in the default rate)." The commission concluded that despite the fact that the system of using means other than money bail for releasing defendants before trial is a sound one, there have been some administrative problems.[8]

4-1e The Bail Reform Act of 1966

In 1966, the federal government passed the Bail Reform Act. It did not preclude the use of bail as a condition of release in federal courts. It lessened its importance by requiring that before the judge made a decision, he or she must consider alternatives for releasing the accused. The act required a specific procedure for analysis. Judges were to consider alternatives to bail and base decisions on specific types of information. The act established a preference for release without security. It provided that the defendant "shall. . .be ordered released pending trial on his personal recognizance or. . .upon the execution of an unsecured appearance bond in an amount specified by the judicial officer, unless the officer determines, in exercise of his discretion that such a release will not reasonably assure the appearance of the person as required."

The debate over whether to release defendants on bail continued, as evidenced in the following reactions to bail. In his annual state of the judiciary address to the American Bar Association in 1979, Chief Justice Warren E. Burger of the U.S. Supreme Court called for a "fresh examination" of the conditions of bail release for those charged with serious crimes. Burger referred to what he called the "startling increase" in the number of crimes committed by persons on bail while awaiting trial.[9]

The former Director of the Federal Bureau of Prisons, Norman A. Carlson, disagreed, citing crowded jail conditions and inadequate facilities. He felt "our first concern should be to keep as many detainees as possible out of jail."[10] These reactions and the public's growing reluctance to grant bail created the conditions necessary for another bail reform act.

4-1f The Federal Bail Reform Act of 1984

The Bail Reform Act of 1966 established that the judicial officer was to impose the minimal conditions of release needed to assure that the defendant would appear in court. In addition, while an individual could have been held for failure to post bail, detention without bail was allowed only in cases involving capital offenses.

The Bail Reform Act of 1984 changed these provisions. It stated, in reaching decisions on bail and release, that the court should give consideration not only to ensuring the defendant's appearance in court but also to protecting the safety of individuals and the community.

The provisions of the act, as they relate to pretrial detention, make specific reference to particular categories of offenses and offenders. The act authorizes pretrial detention for defendants who are charged with crimes of violence, offenses with possible life sentences or death penalties, major drug offenses, and felonies in which the accused has a specific criminal record. In addition, the act creates a rebuttable presumption that no condition of release will assure the appearance of the defendant and the safety of the community under the following circumstances: The accused committed a drug felony with a ten-year maximum sentence; the defendant used a firearm during the commission of a violent or drug-trafficking offense; or the defendant was convicted of specified serious crimes within the preceding five years while the individual was on pretrial release.[11]

The Federal Bail Reform Act of 1984 does not require that prosecutors request pretrial detention for all defendants in these groups. It also contains provisions for temporary detention (up to ten working days) of illegal aliens or persons under pre- or post-trial release, probation, or parole at the time of the current offense. This provision was included for the purpose of allowing time for other agencies (e.g., law enforcement or immigration officials) to take the appropriate course of action.[12]

4-1g Pretrial Detainees

Pretrial detainees, unlike prisoners, have not been convicted of the crime for which they are being held. They are considered innocent by the law, but were denied bail or did not have the funds to attain bail. They are held under the worst conditions as jails are the least desirable correctional facilities due to the nature of their clientele and poor funding sources. Pretrial detainees are unfortunately exposed to other offenders in a vulnerable and inadequate environment.

The law prescribes that pretrial detainees remain in jail until their trial date. The consequences of this are numerous and have an impact on the outcome of the case. Research suggests that individuals held in jail until the time of trial are at a disadvantage in the preparation of their defense. Pretrial detainees are often in need of an attorney, which most cannot afford. They must rely upon court-appointed lawyers, who, as statistics suggest, are often overwhelmed with cases and cannot spend the necessary time preparing for a good defense. Detainees usually have one or two quick conversations with their attorneys before appearing in court. At the time of their appearance, detainees are often escorted in shackles while wearing jail-issued clothing. This image can make an impact on the judge and jury, as they begin to think that the individual in question looks like a criminal and therefore he or she must be a criminal.

4-1h Pretrial Detainees' Rights

Pretrial detainees are considered innocent until proven guilty. Several courts argued in the 1970s that these individuals should not suffer any more restrictions than those necessary to assure their attendance at trial. The courts also reasoned that the rights of pretrial detainees should exceed those of already sentenced inmates. However, this reasoning did not last long. In 1979, the U.S. Supreme Court overruled the decisions made by the lower courts and limited the rights of all pretrial detainees. A clear example of this is illustrated in the discussion of *Bell v. Wolfish* in Case Study 4-1.

The Court limited its holding to those issues involving double bunking, the publisher-only rule, receipt of packages, visual inspection of body cavities after contact visits, and inspection of rooms while inmates were not present. The Court reviewed these conditions as they related to pretrial detainees, not to convicted persons serving time in jails. The court distinguished this case from those in which inmates are locked in their cells for long periods of time and in which facilities are not as modern and as sanitary as were the facilities at MCC.

The case reaffirmed the Court's position that persons awaiting trial may not be subjected to punishment. The disagreement between the dissenters and the majority, however, was due to the many definitions of punishment. The majority makes it clear that jail officials should have wide discretion in determining what measures are necessary for security within their facilities, and that within reason, such restrictions are not to be considered punishment.

More recently, in *U.S. v. Salerno*, the courts also questioned the constitutionality of the Bail Reform Act of 1984 as it pertains to the preventive detention of dangerous offenders. This case involved the detention of several individuals who were charged with various acts associated with organized crime. At the time of the pretrial detention hearing, the government presented evidence suggesting that Salerno and another individual in this case were prominent figures in the La Cosa Nostra crime family. The government held that the only method used to protect the community from these high-risk offenders was to detain them before trial.[13] The constitutional question posed by this case was whether the Bail Reform Act of 1984 violated the Fifth Amendment's due process clause.

In *Salerno*, the Court held that the Bail Reform Act was constitutional. When the government's interest in protecting the community outweighs individual liberty, pretrial detention can be "a potential solution to a pressing societal problem." In the Court's opinion, the Bail Reform Act applied only to a specific list of serious offenses. This placed heavy burdens on the government to show that the individual arrested posed serious threats to others and did not prevent the accused from enjoying a speedy trial. In its final resolution, the Court also dismissed Salerno's argument that the act had violated the Excessive Bail Clause of the Eighth Amendment.[14]

4-1i Bail and Pretrial Detention: A Conclusion

Pretrial detention clearly places the detainee at a disadvantage in comparison to his or her counterpart who is released pending trial. Beginning with the Manhattan Bail Project in the early 1960s and continuing through the Bail Reform Act of 1984, evidence suggests that the present system of bail is being modified according to the needs of the criminal justice system. It can only be expected that scholars and practitioners will pay close attention to the system of bail and pretrial detention as the inmate population continues to grow.

4-2 Jails

Jail
A locally administered confinement facility used to detain individuals awaiting trial or serving sentences of less than one year.

Jails are one of the most important facilities in the U.S. System of Justice because they affect the most people. However, their definition is inconsistent. Hans W. Mattick, in discussing the problem of defining jails, pointed out that the Latin root of the term jail is *cavea*, which means cavity, cage, or coop. The term "jail" is used to refer to "locally-operated correctional facilities that confine persons before or after adjudication."[15] Inmates in jail usually have a sentence of a year or less, although jails also house persons in a wide variety of other categories,

Case Study 4-1

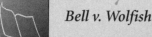

Bell v. Wolfish

Bell v. Wolfish involved inmates at the Metropolitan Correctional Center (MCC), a federally operated facility for short-term custody in New York City. The facility was primarily designed to detain those awaiting trial. It was constructed in 1975 to replace a covered waterfront garage that had served as the federal jail in the city since 1828. The MCC is not a dungeon-type structure with unsanitary facilities that characterizes many of our jails. It is a modern facility that, according to the Court of Appeals, "represented the architectural embodiment of the best and most progressive penological planning." The facility became overcrowded shortly after it opened. Rooms designed for one inmate were used for two and some inmates had to sleep on cots in the common areas.

Less than four months after the MCC opened, several inmates filed a petition that resulted in an appeal to the Supreme Court. Numerous charges were filed, including: inadequate phone service, strip searches, searching of inmates' rooms in their absence, interference with and monitoring of mail, inadequate classification system, inadequate and arbitrary disciplinary and grievance procedures, restrictions on religious freedom, excessive confinement, overcrowded conditions, inadequate facilities for education and recreation and employment opportunities, insufficient staff, and excessive restrictions on the purchase and receipt of books and personal items. The lower court prohibited many of these practices, noting that the pretrial detainees are "presumed to be innocent and held only to ensure their presence at trial." Consequently, a compelling necessity must be shown if they are deprived of any rights beyond those necessary for confinement alone. Most of the rulings of the District Court were affirmed by the Court of Appeals. Not all of the issues were on appeal to the Supreme Court; the four basic issues considered by the latter are discussed briefly.

Double Bunking. The first major issue on appeal to the Supreme Court was the use of double bunking—housing two inmates in a room designed for one. The lower courts held that a compelling necessity must be shown before this practice would be acceptable. The Supreme Court rejected that test and discussed the issue of whether double bunking constituted punishment. The Supreme Court noted that although punishment is permitted in the case of convicted persons (although cruel and unusual punishment is unconstitutional), punishment is not permissible for those not yet convicted. They may be detained for trial, but not punished. The Court held, however, that double bunking does not constitute punishment. Unless it can be shown that by engaging in a particular practice the jail officials intend to punish pretrial detainees, a practice will not be considered punishment if the restriction is reasonably related to a legitimate government purpose. The government has a legitimate purpose not only in assuring the presence of the accused at trial, but also in managing the jail and keeping the facilities secure. "Restraints that are reasonably related to the institution's interest in maintaining jail security do not, without more, constitute unconstitutional punishment, even if they are discomforting and are restrictions that the detainee would not have experienced had he been released while awaiting trial."

The Publisher-Only Rule. Under the publisher-only rule, inmates could receive hardback books only from publishers. The assumption was that publishers could be trusted not to include drugs, weapons, and other contraband items with the shipment. Such books would not have to be inspected. The Bureau of Prisons amended that rule before this hearing to allow inmates to receive books and magazines from bookstores as well as from publishers and book clubs. The bureau had already announced plans to allow receipt of paperbacks, magazines, and other soft-covered materials from any source. The bureau argued that hardback books were the "more dangerous source of risk to institutional security." The Court agreed that prohibiting inmates from receiving hardback books from sources other than publishers, bookstores, and book clubs did not violate First Amendment rights.

Receipt of Packages. The Court also agreed with officials of the institution that receipt of packages from outside the institution (except one package per

including those who have not benefited from receiving bail and must remain in prison until the end of their trial. The number of individuals who are housed in jails across the United States varies from year to year. At mid-year 1999, an estimated 605,943 inmates were held in the nation's jails; this constitutes an increase of 32 percent since the last census in 1993.[16] The consistency in these high numbers suggests that jails are "a major intake center not only for the entire criminal

Case Study 4-1 (continued)

inmate at Christmas) was a security problem and, therefore, the regulation prohibiting such was upheld. It was argued that the probability that such packages would contain contraband was high, thus requiring extensive searches—a time-consuming and expensive process.

Searches. The Court agreed with officials that it was reasonable, because of security needs, to search inmates' rooms when they were absent. Although the Court deems unapproved searches of homes as a violation of their sanctity, the same does not apply to searches of a cell. In fact, correctional officers often disrupt any privacy an inmate may have by conducting cell searches. For security reasons, these are viewed by correctional personnel and the courts as necessary and imminent. The most controversial issue, however, was body searches, which involved visual inspection of body cavities after each contact visit of inmates. Although the Court had difficulty with this practice, it held that such was reasonable to maintain security.

Mr. Justice Powell concurred with part of the majority opinion but dissented on the holding of body cavity searches, which he called a "serious intrusion on one's privacy." Powell advocates some "level of cause, such as a reasonable suspicion, should be required to justify the anal and genital searches described in this case."[17]

Mr. Justice Marshall, in his dissent, argued that the Court's emphasis on the issue of punishment was misplaced. The issue, said Marshall, is what effect the acts have on the pretrial detainees who are presumptively innocent. "By its terms, the Due Process Clause focuses on the nature of deprivations, not on the persons inflicting them. If this concern is to be vindicated, it is the effect of conditions and confinement, not the intent behind them, that must be the focal point of constitutional analysis." He suggested requiring "that a restriction is substantially necessary to jail administration. Where the imposition is of particular gravity, that is, where it implicates interests of fundamental importance or inflicts significant harms, the Government should demonstrate that the restriction serves a compelling necessity of jail administration."[18] With regard to the visual inspection of body cavities, Marshall said:

In my view, the body cavity searches of MCC inmates represent one of the most grave offenses against personal dignity and common decency. After every contact visit with someone from outside the facility, including defense attorneys, an inmate must remove all of his or her clothing, bend over, spread the buttocks, and display the anal cavity for inspection by a correctional officer. Women inmates must assume a suitable posture for vaginal inspection while men must raise their genitals. And, as the Court neglects to note, because of time pressures, this humiliating spectacle is frequently conducted in the presence of other inmates.

The District Court found that the stripping was "unpleasant, embarrassing, and humiliating." A psychiatrist testified that the practice placed inmates in the most degrading position possible, a conclusion amply corroborated by the testimony of the inmates themselves. There was evidence, moreover, that these searches engendered among detainees fears of sexual assault, were the occasion for actual threats of physical abuse by guards, and caused some inmates to forego personal visits.

Not surprisingly, the government asserts a security justification for such inspections. These searches are necessary, it argues, to prevent inmates from smuggling contraband into the facility. In crediting this justification, despite the contrary findings of the two courts below, the Court overlooks the critical facts. As respondents point out, inmates are required to wear one-piece jumpsuits with zippers in the front. To insert an object into the vaginal or anal cavity, an inmate would have to remove the jumpsuit, at least from the upper torso. Since contact visits occur in a glass-enclosed room and are continuously monitored by corrections officers, such a feat would seem extraordinarily difficult. There was medical testimony, moreover, that inserting an object into the rectum is painful and "would require time and opportunity which is not available in the visiting areas," and that visual inspection would probably not detect an object once inserted. Additionally, before entering the visiting room, visitors and their packages are searched thoroughly by a metal detector, fluoroscope, and by hand. Correction officers may require that visitors leave packages or handbags with guards until the visit is over. Only by blinding itself to the facts presented on this record can the Court accept the Government's security rationale.

Without question, these searches are an imposition of sufficient gravity to invoke the compelling necessity standard. It is equally indisputable that they cannot meet that standard. Indeed, the procedure is so unnecessarily degrading that it "shocks the conscience."[19]

justice system, but also a place of first or last resort for a host of disguised health, welfare, and social problem cases."[20] A federal court affirmed "the chilling impact of these numbers dictates the necessity to come to grips with the constitutionality of conditions in the jails in America."[21] The institution of jails has not resisted the change mandated by the different historical eras.

4-2a History of Jails

Law Enforcement Assistance Administration (LEAA)
This administration grew out of the President's Crime Commission between 1965 and 1967. Although it was created to provide resources and coordination to state and local law enforcement agencies, it was short-lived; it was terminated in the late 1970s.

Jails are the oldest U.S. penal institutions, although less is known about them than about any other institution. The existence of jails has been tolerated for centuries with little or no attention. It was not until 1970 that data became available, when the first national jail census was conducted by the **Law Enforcement Assistance Administration (LEAA)**.

Jails can be traced back to the twelfth century when they debuted "in the form of murky dungeons, abysmal pits, unscaleable precipices, strong poles or trees, and suspended cages in which hapless prisoners were kept."[22] At the time, the purpose of jails was to detain individuals awaiting trial, transportation, the death penalty, or corporal punishment. These facilities were not escape-proof. Guards received additional fees for shackling prisoners. Inmates were not classified according to their special needs, physical conditions were awful, food was inadequate, and there were no treatment rehabilitation programs. The prison reformer John Howard asserted in 1773, after touring European institutions, that more prisoners died of jail fever than were executed.[23] This was an alarming statement as executions were very common at the time.

In the 1600s, the Pennsylvania Quakers argued for more humane treatment of those who violated the law. Criminals were often exposed to the harsh effects of corporal punishment. Due to the humanitarian contributions of the Quakers, the Walnut Street Jail was founded in 1790 in Philadelphia. Other jails were built soon after, marking a more sympathetic handling of criminal offenders. Despite these attempts, jails still represented the worst conditions possible for those unfortunate enough to be incarcerated. Joseph Fishman, the only federal prison inspector, investigator, and consultant in the United States, best depicted these horrible conditions in 1923. In his book, *Crucible of Crime*, Fishman described the jails in the United States at the time. He based these descriptions and evaluations of jails on his visits to 1,500 of these facilities. He stated that some convicts would ask for a year in prison instead of six months in jail due to the horrible conditions at the time.[24] Prisons were better facilities as they hired staff that provided adequate support to inmates.

Fishman's conclusion is summarized by his definition of jail as follows:

> An unbelievably filthy institution in which are confined men and women, serving sentences for misdemeanors and crimes, and men and women not under sentence who are simply awaiting trial. With few exceptions, having no segregation of the unconvicted from the convicted, the well from the diseased, the youngest and most impressionable from the most degraded and hardened. Usually swarming with bedbugs, roaches, lice, and other vermin; has an odor of disinfectant and filth which is appalling: supports in complete idleness thousands of able-bodied men and women, and generally affords ample time and opportunity to assure inmates a complete course in every kind of viciousness and crime. A melting pot in which the worst elements of the raw material in the criminal world are brought forth blended and turned out in absolute perfection."[25]

Today, jails have changed their physical appearance dramatically, although they still suffer from inadequate funding and resources. In large cities like Miami, jails often blend with suburban neighborhoods in their design, which makes them appear as if they are large corporate offices.

Despite this, residents of these suburban neighborhoods often plead for legislators to move these facilities in an attempt to save the integrity of the community.

A Current Jail in Washington County, Missouri (built in 1997)

These pictures illustrate a jail in Washington County, Missouri. Notice the fact that it blends in with the neighborhood. That is, from plain view, it does not resemble the previous jail designs with small windows and prison bars that made them "stand out."

Photographs by Esther M. Ziock Carroll.

4-2b Jail Populations

Jail populations are characterized by a high rate of turnover and a more heterogeneous population than other types of incarceration facilities. Jails are occupied by persons awaiting trial, witnesses being held for trial, and convicted persons serving short sentences. This includes men, women, and juveniles. Most of the convicted inmates are serving sentences for the commission of misdemeanors rather than felonies. Misdemeanors are the less serious types of offenses, such as disorderly conduct, prostitution, and public drunkenness. Sentences for such violations are less than one year. The more serious offenders have been convicted for felonies such as murder, armed robbery, and rape. Felons receive sentences for longer than a year and are confined in prisons or similar institutions, not in jails. Today's emphasis on crime control has prompted inmates to receive longer sentences, thus overcrowding both jail and prison facilities.

The popularity of imprisonment as punishment is evident in the growth of jail inmates. The Bureau of Justice Statistics (BJS) conducted the first national jail census in 1970. Since then, the BJS has conducted a jail census in 1972, 1978, 1983, 1988, 1993, and 1999. A jail census taken in 1999 indicated that the rate of incarceration has increased, from one in every 532 U.S. residents to one in every 450.[26] In addition, the BJS indicated that the jail population increased 32 percent in "the six years between censuses, from 459,804 at mid-year 1993 to 605,943 at mid-year 1999."[27] The growth of the jail population is further illustrated in Figure 4-1.

4-2c Administration of Jails

Typical U.S. jails are small and were built between 1880 and 1920. Most of these facilities have had little or no renovation. They are located in small towns that are often the county seat of a predominately rural county. These facilities contribute to the majority of jails but house a minority of the jail population. These institutions are seldom used and are rarely crowded. This is not the case in urban settings, where jails are overcrowded and are subject to numerous lawsuits.

The typical jail is locally financed and administered, which inevitably involves jail administration in local politics. Throughout history, U.S. jails have been under the direction and supervision of the sheriff who is usually an elected official. These administrators have shown little interest in jail inspections or improvements. However, that trend has changed since the 1980s when the American Correctional Association sponsored the Commission on Accreditation for Corrections. This commission not only developed standards for jails, but also cer-

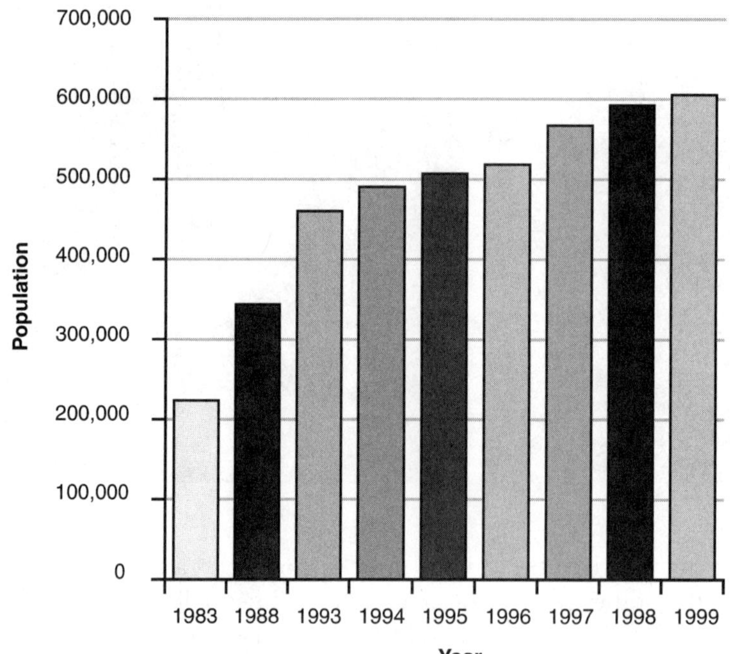

Figure 4-1
Jail Population (1983, 1988, 1993-1999)
Source: Bureau of Justice Statistics (1999). U.S. Department of Justice Census of Jails, 1999. Washington, D.C.

tified those that met such standards. This has led to a movement in which states have assumed partial control of their jails, thus establishing minimum standards. Despite this, today's jails suffer from limited budgets that are often under a fee system—the costs of food, housing, and services are averaged and a specific amount is allocated to the sheriff's department. This practice results in poor jails that offer inmates inadequate food, lack of inmate support, and poor services.

4-2d Staffing of Jails

Today's jails face serious staffing problems. Staff members receive low pay and usually have little or no training for working with the incarcerated. Most jails have small budgets as they are considered the lowest priority of local governments. These local governments often have less money to spend than state or federal governments. Jails are sometimes administered by law enforcement officials who adhere to a law-abiding administrative approach while ignoring any rehabilitative goal. Jails were largely understaffed until recently. The Bureau of Justice Statistics has reported that jails employed, at mid-year 1999, an estimated 207,600 individuals. This constitutes a growth of 42,100 between 1993 and 1999—an increase of 25 percent. During this same period, the number of inmates in jails also grew an estimated 32 percent. Overall, the jail staff grew more rapidly between 1983 and 1988 than the inmate population. As a result, the overall employee/inmate ratio diminished from 3.5 inmates per jail staff member in 1983 to 3.4 inmates per staff member in 1988. During the 1990s, this trend rapidly changed as the number of inmates rose faster than jail staff. The ratio increased to 2.9 inmates per staff in 1999.[28]

Jails have few professional staff members (including medical personnel) due to budgetary constraints. It is ironic that most of the jail population is in need of medical, psychiatric, and social care. Inmates are often drug addicts and they may suffer from venereal diseases or be HIV positive. This presents an even greater problem for jail administrators who are constantly avoiding legal challenges introduced by inmates. Under the Civil Rights Act of 1871 (codified as 42 U.S. Code 1983), employees in jails may be held legally liable for their actions. This provision includes wardens, who are also liable for the actions of their employees. Many critics of this legislation have argued that inmates have an open door to sue the jails and their administrators. Statistics have supported these critics—

inmates often sue on every conceivable aspect of incarceration, including the poor quality of food.

The present wave of inmate lawsuits was initiated by previous judicial action that emphasized the need for change in jail facilities. The state of Texas has reported that it handles approximately 5,000 inmate-initiated lawsuits per year. This is despite several steps taken to discourage inmates from filing frivolous lawsuits. A Congressional act requires inmates to pay $150 each time he/she files a federal lawsuit. This fee can be waived, however, if the inmate claims to be poor, although the full amount is due if the individual files a frivolous lawsuit three times.[29]

An additional problem facing jails today is the conflict that exists between professional and non-professional jail staff. Robert G. Culbertson pointed out that the primarily custodian-oriented jail personnel are suspicious of the court decisions regarding the rights of inmates as well as the state department attempts to place correctional personnel in jails. This problem, combined with inadequate numbers of personnel, creates predicaments, one of which is role overload. "The role occupant finds it impossible for him to complete all the tasks requested by various people. He is placed in a position whereby he must deny some of the requests, creating conflict, or be taxed beyond the limits of his abilities." To avoid the problems of role overload, one will seek ways in which to reduce the conflict. One of those ways might be to ignore the requests that originate from treatment personnel. "The consequence again, is the escalation of conflict between rehabilitation and custody personnel."[30]

4-2e The New Generation Jail

An unprecedented wave of jail constructions took place until recently. This trend has begun to slow down and the national figures suggest that between 1993 and 1999 the number of jails increased from 3,304 to 3,365. This depicts an increase of only 61 jails in 6 years; a clear sign that a deceleration in jail construction has commenced.[31]

Most of the new jails under construction follow a different philosophy of design and management than that of the old jails. They are designed to improve the staff's ability to manage the inmate population. The new generation jails, as they are often called, are built upon three architectural concepts: **podular design**, **interaction space**, and **personal space**.

Podular units are self-contained living areas that house approximately twelve to twenty-four inmates. These units are composed of single-occupancy rooms for inmates and a common multi-purpose dayroom for recreational interaction. Living areas with comfortable furniture, porcelain lavatories, tile and carpet floor coverings, and windows also characterize podular units. The pods are equipped with radios, telephones, outdoor exercise areas, and televisions. All daily activities occur within the pod.[32]

The design of the new generation jail provides an environment in which inmates are expected to exhibit civilized behavior, and proponents believe the inmate interaction within the podular units to be normative. Each living area is designed to enhance the observation and communication between inmates and staff members. This management philosophy is referred to as **direct supervision** and it operates under the premise of prisonization theory. This is one of the most crucial components of the new generation jail philosophy. It refers to a method of correctional supervision in which one or several jail officers are stationed inside the living area and are in direct contact with those housed in the pod.

Jail practitioners in the United States are slowly accepting this philosophy due to the reported success of the effectiveness of the operation and design of these jails in reducing negative inmate behavior. Today, sociologists are conduct-

Podular design
This design proposes living areas designed to enhance the observation of and communication (i.e., interaction) between inmates and staff members.

Interaction space
This concept offers architectural designs aimed at controlling inmate interaction in the prison environment.

Personal space
The design of the new generation jail is based on the philosophy that podular units create an environment that is normative; civilized behavior of inmates housed is expected. It is believed that personal space should be encouraged to attain the previously mentioned goals.

Direct supervision
Prisonization theory based on the notion that podular units create an environment that is normative; civilized behavior of inmates housed in is expected. Each living area is designed to enhance the observation of and communication between inmates and staff members.

ing longitudinal studies to follow what happens when a traditional jail makes the transition to a podular, direct supervision facility.[33]

4-2f Trends and Profiles of Jail Inmates

The number of jail inmates has grown to unprecedented proportions in recent years. Since 1993, the rate of jail incarceration increased from one in every 532 U.S. residents to one in every 450. This is also true for juveniles. On June 30, 1999, an estimated 9,458 persons under age eighteen were housed in adult jails in the United States.[34]

The gender of jail inmates is slowly changing. In 1993, men made up 90.4 percent of the jail population. In 1999 the figures suggested that males made up 89 percent of the overall jail population. Although the change is not significant, a clear decline in the male jail population has begun to take place. In 1993, females made up 9.6 percent of the jail population. The 1999 figures claim female inmates make up 11 percent of the overall jail population.[35]

Statistics also show that more than half (54 percent) of adult jail inmates were not convicted. When compared to the 1993 figures, a higher percentage of inmates in 1999 were awaiting trial and not serving a sentence. Between 1993 and 1999, "the number of white non-Hispanics increased from 39.3 percent to 41.3 percent; blacks non-Hispanics decreased from 44.2 percent to 41.5 percent; Hispanics increased from 15.1 percent to 15.5 percent; and American Indians, Alaska Natives, Asians, and Pacific Islanders increased from 1.3 percent to 1.7 percent."[36] Slowly, jail population demographics are changing. It is clear that the correctional staff must strive to meet the challenges this change is likely to bring.

4-2g Jail Services

Both historic and recent literature indicates that jails generally warehouse inmates while providing few services. Many inmates who participate in the few programs offered in jails do so for reasons other than self-help. It is rare that inmates regard their participation in these jail services as positive.

Some jail facilities offer services to treat the medical needs of inmates. They offer substance abuse although programs are usually at full capacity as drug users are arrested more frequently than in the past. These programs are scarce and often suffer from budgetary constraints. Advocates of these programs urge the funding of more jail services as many jail inmates have poor reading skills and few job skills. Inmates have a hard time finding jobs after they are released from jails, leaving them with few options, one of which is a life of crime. Jail services supporters often quote studies in which inmates who improve their educational level during confinement are less likely to break the law again. These supporters ignore the fact that these studies are flawed as they do not include the possibility that motivated inmates—who would have done better after release even without the programs—are the ones who improve their basic academic skills. A study of federal inmates that attempted to adjust for this selection bias found that inmates who participated in educational programs were less likely to commit offenses again.[37] A study of inmates in Wisconsin concluded that education programs in prison were cost-effective because they reduced recidivism or increased the amount of time before released inmates returned to prison.[38] Although most prisons include the programs researched in these studies, few jails offer them, as necessary funding to build suitable classroom space is unavailable and jail inmates are incarcerated for a brief period.

One of the few jail divisions in the United States that overcame these predicaments is the Corrections Division in Orange County, Florida. This division provides intensive educational and vocational services to its inmate popula-

Spotlight 4-2

Services Provided by Florida's Orange County Jail

- Structured educational and vocational programs (from adult basic education to carpentry) designed to accommodate the inmate's short stay
- Job readiness and placement services
- Incentives to participate in programming—and to avoid misconduct
- Management of most inmates through direct supervision to contain costs, promote inmate responsibility, and allow for open areas that are often used as classrooms

Source: U.S. Department of Justice, Office of Justice Programs, The Orange County, Florida Jail Educational and Vocational Programs; December, 1997.

tion (which currently averages 4,200). This jail is the seventeenth largest in the United States.[39] When these services were implemented, dramatic changes occurred in its daily operations. Today, the entire jail revolves around its educational and vocational programs. Spotlight 4-2 illustrates the major services offered by the Orange County Jail.

Each of the services mentioned forms a part of a comprehensive corrections strategy aimed at saving the county money while keeping inmates occupied and out of trouble. The hope is that this strategy will reduce recidivism. All services provided by jail facilities are supposed to be administered to all inmates without regard to their ethnicity, socioeconomic status, religious affiliation, or any other prejudice that may exist. Unfortunately, this is not always true. On March 12, 1998, the *Chicago Tribune*[40] reported that favoritism was shown to actor Robert Downey, Jr. in a California jail. The newspaper reported that Downey was given a film furlough, allowing him to travel via a shuttle to a Hollywood studio while he completed a movie. He was also allowed to leave jail to visit his plastic surgeon after an altercation with another inmate left him with a facial wound.

One of the biggest hurdles of the implementation of programs such as those offered at the Orange County Jail is the overcrowding of inmates in the correctional system. These jails are running at their full capacity. This problem is exacerbated by the overcrowding of prisons that continues to worsen. Prisons will occasionally transfer inmates to jails to serve the remainder of their sentences. Jail administrators are then faced with another challenge—that of a new and experienced inmate. The trend of prison and jail overcrowding will continue on its current path of growth, even if this has slowed down in recent years. States such as Missouri have had to hire private prisons in other states to handle some of their correctional clientele. This pattern will continue to hinder programs offered in jails as monetary allocation continues to decline. Organizations such as the American Jail Association are attempting to educate the public as well as correctional personnel on the challenges associated with an increasing jail population.

Summary

This chapter examined the handling of the accused after arrest and before trial as this is one of the most crucial periods in the entire criminal justice process. A person detained in jail may be adversely affected by the experience. However, if the person is released, society may be endangered. This time is also the period during which the accused, with his or her attorney, is preparing for trial.

The purpose of the bail system is to secure the presence of the accused at trial. Judges often use bail as preventive detention without statutory authority. Various attempts to reform the bail system have been outlined as well as the constitutional rights of pretrial detainees. The history of jails includes their utilization as a form of social control. Various characteristics of today's jail system were examined in this chapter, including the population increase in jails, the administration and staffing of jails, the new generation of jails, the trends and profiles of jails, and the services provided.

Notes

1. *Powell v. Alabama*, 287 U.S. 45, 57 (1932).
2. *Stack v. Boyle*, 342 U.S. 1, 5 (1951).
3. CNN, December 19, 1997.
4. Bureau of Justice Statistics (1999), *U.S. Department of Justice Census of Jails, 1999*, Washington, D.C.
5. See Forrest Dill, "Discretion, Exchange and Social Control: Bail Bondsmen in Criminal Courts," *Law and Society Review* 9 (Summer, 1975), 639-674.
6. *Pammell v. U.S.*, 320 F. 2d 698, 699 (1963), (Judge Skelley Wright, concurring).
7. Ares, Charles E., Rankin, Anne, and Sturz, Herbert, "The Manhattan Bail Project," *New York University Law Review* 38 (January 1963), 68. See this article, which is the basis for the comments in this section, for a more detailed discussion of this project.
8. National Advisory Commission on Criminal Justice Standards and Goals, *Corrections* (Washington, D.C.: U.S. Government Printing Office, 1973), p. 103.
9. "Butler Seeks Study of Bail Releases in Major Crime," *The New York Times* (February 12, 1979), p. A14, col. 3.
10. *The New York Times* (May 5, 1977), p. A19, col. 1
11. Bureau of Justice Statistics. *Pretrial Release and Detention: the Bail Reform Act of 1984* (Washington, D.C.: U.S. Department of Justice, February, 1988), p. 2. The Bail Reform Act is codified in U.S. Code, Chapter 18, Sections 3141 et. Seq. (1994).
12. Bureau of Justice Statistics, *Pretrial Release and Detention: The Bail Reform Act of 1984.*
13. *U.S. v. Salerno*, 481 U.S. 739 (1987), remanded, 829 f. 2d. 345 (2d circ. 1987) cases and citations omitted.
14. *U.S. v. Salerno*, no. 86-87.1
15. U.S. Department of Justice, Bureau of Justice Statistics, 1988, *Jail Statistics.*
16. Bureau of Justice Statistics (1999), U.S. Department of Justice *Census of Jails, 1999*, Washington, D.C.
17. *Bell v. Wolfish*, 441 U.S. 520 (1979).
18. *Bell v. Wolfish.*
19. *Bell v. Wolfish.*
20. Mattick, Hans, "The Contemporary Jails in the United States: An Unknown and Neglected Area of Justice," in Daniel Glaser, ed., *Handbook of Criminology* (Skokie, IL: Rand McNally, 1974), p. 781.
21. *Rhuem v. Malcol*, 371 F. Supp. 594 (1974). On appeal, the "findings of facts and conclusions of law that various conditions of the Tombs are unconstitutional" was affirmed, but the case was remanded for "further consideration...of the relief to be granted." 587 F. 2d 333, 342 (1974).
22. Flynn, Edith Elizabeth, "Jails and Criminal Justice," in Lloyd E. Ohlin, ed., *Prisoners in America* (Englewood Cliffs, NJ: Prentice-Hall, 1973), chap. 2, p. 49.
23. Hall, Jerome, *Theft, Law, and Society* (Boston: Little Brown and Company, 1935), p. 108. See also John Howard, *State of Prisons*, 2nd ed. (Warrington, England: Patterson Smith, 1792).
24. Fishman, Joseph F., *Crucible of Crime: The Shocking Story of the American Jail* (New York: Cosmopolis Press, 1923), p. 823
25. Fishman, *Crucible of Crime*, pp. 13-14.
26. Bureau of Justice Statistics (1999),U.S. Department of Justice *Census of Jails, 1999*,Washington, D.C.
27. Bureau of Justice Statistics (1999),U.S. Department of Justice *Census of Jails, 1999*,Washington, D.C.
28. Bureau of Justice Statistics (1999),U.S. Department of Justice *Census of Jails, 1999*,Washington, D.C.
29. Herrick, Thaddeus, "Inmates no longer get their 'free day in court'," *Houston Chronicle*, July 18, 1999.
30. Culbertson, Robert G., "Personnel Conflicts in Jail Management," *American Journal of Corrections* 39 (March-April, 1977), 29.
31. Bureau of Justice Statistics (1999), U.S. Department of Justice *Census of Jails, 1999*,Washington, D.C.
32. Bayens, Gerald J., Williams, Jimmy J., and Smykla, John Ortiz, "Jail Type Makes a Difference: Evaluating the Transition from a Traditional to a Podular, Direct Supervision Jail Across Ten Years," *American Jail Magazine.*

33. For more information, see Bayens, Williams, and Smykla, *Jail Type.*
34. Bureau of Justice Statistics (1999), U.S. Department of Justice *Census of Jails, 1999,* Washington, D.C.
35. Bureau of Justice Statistics (1999), U.S. Department of Justice Census of Jails, 1999, Washington, D.C.
36. http://www.orangecountyfl.net/Reference/archive/chairman_2001/jail_visit.htm
37. Harer, M.D., "Recidivism Among Federal Prison Releases in 1987: A Preliminary Report," Unpublished paper (Washington, DC: U.S. Department of Justice, Federal Bureau of Prisons, Office of Research Evaluation, March, 1994).
38. Piehl, A.M., "Learning While Doing Time," Unpublished paper (Cambridge, MA: Harvard University, John F. Kennedy School of Government, April, 1994).
39. http://www.orangecountyfl.net/Reference/archive/chairman_2001/jail_visit.htm
40. *The Chicago Tribune* (March 12, 1998), p. 2.

Chapter 5

Sentencing

Sentencing is one of the most important stages in the criminal justice system. For the offender, it is the culmination of events in his or her life and the determination of how the coming months or years will be spent, or in the case of capital punishment, whether the defendant will be allowed to live. For society, it is a time for a decision that necessitates action in a particular case and recognition of the philosophy of punishment and rehabilitation. For the correctional system, sentencing has a direct impact—it sets the amount of time an individual may spend in a correctional facility.

Sentencing includes all decisions the court makes regarding the official handling of a person who pleads guilty or is convicted of a crime. This may include probation, with or without specified restrictions on the behavior of the defendant, imposition of a fine, capital punishment, commitment under a special statute such as a sexual psychopath law, work assignments, restitution to the victim, corporal punishment, or incarceration. Although the courts have the most significant impact on sentencing practices, all three branches of government (legislative, executive, and judicial) have influence on the sentencing laws and practices in the United States. This chapter discusses the concepts, philosophy, procedures, strategies, and trends associated with sentencing.

Key Terms

sentencing disparity
mandatory sentences
prison confinement
jail confinement
probation

Outline

5-1 The Sentencing Decision

The decision of sentencing someone to prison, probation, or another form of punishment rests within the discretionary authority of judges unless the legislature of a particular jurisdiction has removed all judicial discretion. Juries also have sentencing power; however, in some circumstances, the judge is not required to follow the sentencing recommendation given by the jury.

Recently, the United States Supreme Court examined the issue of jury input in two states—Alabama and Florida. The Court declared that the Alabama system did not deny the defendant's Eighth Amendment rights.[1] Alabama's system is based on the principle that the trial judge is to consider the sentence issued by the jury, but the weight the judge places on the recommendation is not specified. After examining the system used in the state of Florida, the U.S. Supreme Court declared (in *Proffitt v. Florida*) that the existing capital punishment procedures were constitutional (see Case Study 5-1).[2]

The U.S. Supreme Court has upheld the Arizona plan, which established that after an individual is found guilty of first-degree murder, a different sentencing hearing would be held before the court could determine whether to impose life imprisonment or the death penalty. This statute refers to specific factors that must be considered for and against leniency when making that particular decision.[3]

When the jury exercises sentencing power, the judge issues instructions to the jury regarding the law and its application to sentencing. Several factors are taken into consideration when the sentencing decision is made. Although some of these factors may be designated by statute, some states have formalized and restricted their usage.

5-2 Impact of Sentencing on Corrections

The purposes of punishment are closely connected to sentencing. The adoption of a punishment philosophy of retribution or rehabilitation, deterrence or reintegration, incapacitation or reparation will affect the nature of sentencing and ultimately corrections. If capital punishment is used frequently, the number of long-term inmates will be reduced. If probation, (a form of sentencing in which the offender is placed under supervision in the community), is used extensively, persons who would otherwise be incarcerated for a short time will be freed. Any sudden, significant change in the use of probation could gravely affect correctional institutions and the programs they offer. A quick drop in the use of probation could increase the inmate population. A sudden increase in the use of probation could result in employee layoffs in correctional institutions and reduction in the number of programs and medical care of those institutions. In addition, a change in the use of one type of sentence over another could alter the stay for those in prison, thus either reducing or increasing the number of inmates incarcerated.

The impact of sentencing on corrections reaches beyond the number of people who will enter or remain in the correctional system. The goals of sentencing, which are controlled by the judicial branch, may be incompatible with those set by professionals in the correctional field. For instance, if sentencing is based on a philosophy of justice or social defense, the implementation of that philosophy will, in some cases, be in conflict with a correctional goal of changing or rehabilitating the offender. The recent movement of handling punishment and sentencing in terms of just deserts or retribution is not necessarily the philosophy taken by professionals in the field of corrections. They are still involved with the approach of attempting to change, assist, or resocialize the offender. Whether such goals have been accomplished continues to be a hot topic of debate. This

Case Study 5-1

Proffitt v. Florida

The Issue:

"Following his Florida conviction for first-degree murder and the imposition of the death penalty, Proffitt challenged the constitutionality of both his death sentence, alleging it was a 'cruel and unusual' punishment, and Florida's capital-sentencing procedure, alleging is was arbitrary and capricious insofar as it permitted judges rather than juries to act as sole sentencing authorities." Thus, the questions are: "Is the death penalty a 'cruel and unusual' punishment? Is Florida's capital-sentencing procedure unconstitutional?"

The Opinion:

"No and no. The Court held that the death penalty was not a 'cruel and unusual' punishment per se, and that Florida's capital-sentencing procedure was not unconstitutionally arbitrary and/or capricious. Although empowering trial judges with sole sentencing authority, the statutory procedure tightly prescribed their relevant decision-making process. The procedure requires sentencing judges to focus on both the crime's circumstances and the defendant's character by weighing eight statutory aggravating factors against seven statutory mitigating factors. Furthermore, sentencing judges are required to submit a written explanation of their death-sentence finding for the purpose of automatic review by Florida's Supreme Court. Such strict requirements sufficiently safeguard against the presence of any constitutional deficiencies arising from an arbitrary and/or capricious imposition of the death penalty."

Source: Courtesy of The OYEZ Project, Northwestern University (www.oyez.org)

conflict of interest and goals between those in the judicial branch who advocate a punitive sentence and those correctional professionals who support rehabilitation illustrates one of the internal contradictions of the criminal justice system. The struggle between these two components over the retribution approach can be expected to continue unless those in corrections abandon the philosophy of rehabilitation. Conversely, if one takes the position that the new approaches to sentencing have not abandoned the philosophy of rehabilitation, but that they represent only a shift from rehabilitation as a justification for punishment, the conflict may not be so great. This approach might even enhance the goals of corrections if the result is to view corrections in terms of voluntary programs for offenders. Only those offenders who wish to be treated enter the treatment programs while they are confined, resulting in greater success rates.

5-3 Sentence Disparity

In the past, it was the responsibility of judges to determine criminal sentences. They considered all of the facts of a case including the circumstances of the offense and the life history of the offender. They would then choose a sentence they regarded as fair. The only legal requirement for judges to meet was that the sentence was within a statutory range. The ranges, however, were extremely broad. Statues typically authorized sentences such as "not more than five years," or in some instances "any term of years or life."[4] Judges could impose any sentence as long as it was within the range specified by the statutes. Many felt this gave judges too much discretionary power.

Once the sentence was imposed and the person was in prison, it was up to the parole board to determine the actual release date. The parole board would then consider an individual's behavior in prison and the efforts made toward his or her rehabilitation. Parole boards released people when they felt they were ready. This most often occurred after just half of the individual's sentence had been completed. If the released person did not behave as expected, parole could be revoked and that person would return to prison.

In the 1970s, discretionary sentencing became strongly opposed as a result of its inconsistency.[5] A large number of judges sentenced similar offenders differently, while a great deal of power was acquired by parole boards. The sentence disparity became so extreme that offenders were often serving anomalous sentences in prison despite their similar offenses and backgrounds. There was a strong accumulation of evidence suggesting that the system led to arbitrary decision-making and sometimes discrimination against poor individuals and members of minority groups.

Sentencing disparity
The variations that take place when defendants convicted of the same crime receive sentences of different types or lengths.

Sentencing disparity is based on the concept that offenders with similar backgrounds and similar offenses may receive different sentences with no reasonable justification. In his book, *The Rich Get Richer and the Poor Get Prison*, Jeffery Reiman argued that it is a "simple fact that the criminal justice system reserves its harshest penalties for its lower-class clients and puts on kid gloves when confronted with a better class of crook."[6] In addition to Reiman's arguments, various studies have been conducted to measure whether sentence disparity exists. All of the studies concluded that it does exist, and occurs quite frequently.

Stewart D'Alessio and Lisa Stolzenberg studied a random sample of 2,760 offenders who had been committed to the care of the Florida Department of Corrections in 1985. They did not find any sentence disparity for poor offenders found guilty of property crimes but found that poor offenders received longer sentences for violent crimes and narcotics possession.[7] Others have made similar findings. Theodore Chiricos and William Bales discovered that unemployed defendants with similar records who were found guilty of similar offenses were more likely to be incarcerated while awaiting trial and for longer periods than were employed defendants. Furthermore, these authors reported that these unemployed defendants were more than twice as likely as their employed counterparts to be incarcerated upon a guilty finding.[8]

Mandatory sentence
A sentence determined by statutes that requires that a specific penalty is imposed for certain convicted offenders.

Other studies have explored the question of whether criminal justice officials' discretionary choices in the application of **mandatory sentencing** laws are made in a racially neutral manner. Results of these studies are particularly relevant. A study conducted by B.S. Meierhoefer, which involved cases of federal offenders, examined whether sentencing severity varied by the amount and type of drugs involved in the current crime, the use of weapons, the defendant's offense record, role in the offense, history of drug use, age, gender, and race.[9] Meierhoefer found sentencing differences associated with the offender's race, even after taking into consideration differences associated with other traits. However, it is important to note this difference was small.

The U.S. Sentencing Commission expanded this study and found that there were significant differences in the proportion of whites (54 percent), Hispanics (57 percent), and African Americans (68 percent) who received mandatory minimum sentences for the most serious offense they had committed.[10] A reanalysis of the data used by the U.S. Sentencing Commission in 1991 provided a different conclusion.[11] Their study showed that when legally relevant case-processing factors were considered, a defendant's race and ethnicity were not related to the sentence imposed.

In 1995, this same commission reached a different conclusion than the one made earlier. The U.S. Sentencing Commission reassessed the sentencing disparity between crack and powder cocaine offenses. These sentences were created in 1986, by the United States Congress when it enacted mandatory minimum sentences for cocaine and crack trafficking—the sale of five grams of crack or 500 grams of powder cocaine is punishable by a mandatory minimum sentence of five years in federal prison. Additionally, the sale of fifty grams of crack or 5,000 grams (5 kilos) of powder cocaine is subject to a mandatory minimum of ten years in federal prison. By 1988, Congress enacted a five-year mandatory minimum prison term for possession of more than five grams of crack. The same law mandated a maximum of one year in prison for first-time offenders who were convicted of possession of any other drug, including powder cocaine.[12] It was on these laws that the U.S. Sentencing Commission based its findings in 1995. In its report, the commission details the disparate impact that crack sentences have had on African Americans and makes recommendations for changes in the current sentencing strategy. The report found that over 88 percent of those sentenced for crack offenses were African Americans, while only 4.1 percent of those sentenced for that same offense were white. This is despite the fact most of those who use crack are white (52 percent) while 38 percent of users are African Americans.[13] The commission's recommendations involved (1) establishing methods within the guidelines' structure to deal with the crimes of possession and distribution of both crack and powder cocaine; (2) revisiting the 100-to-1 ratio (100 grams of crack or powder cocaine equals one year in prison); and (3) reassessing the penalty structure for simple possession. The recommendations were turned down by several officials, including President Clinton. In a statement, Clinton said that "we have to send a constant message to our children that drugs are illegal, drugs are dangerous, drugs may cost you your life—and the penalties for dealing drugs are severe." He also added that he was "not going to let anyone who peddles drugs get the idea that the cost of doing business is going down."[14]

In April 1997, the U.S. Sentencing Commission made recommendations suggesting reformation on the disparity between powder cocaine and crack cocaine mandatory sentences.[15] These recommendations, unlike those made in 1995, did not encounter much resistance from officials. This is because the recommendations made by the commission in 1997 were based on an effort to compromise with Congress and former President Clinton. They were not in agreement with the commission's earlier advice that the 100-to-1 ratio to trigger mandatory penalties be eliminated. The commission acknowledged that the sale of crack should be more harshly punished than the sale of powder cocaine on a quantity basis. For the five-year mandatory sentence, the commission recommended that the 500-gram powder cocaine trigger be reduced to between 125–375 grams, and that the 5-gram cocaine trigger be raised to between 25–75 grams. Among those who supported this latest recommendation is Judge Richard P. Conaboy, chairman of the commission, who stated, "The ranges suggested provide Congress the flexibility to make an informed judgment about the appropriate penalties for these two forms of cocaine. . . . We feel strongly, though, that the current policy must be changed to ensure that severe penalties are targeted at the most serious traffickers. Adopting a ratio within the ranges we recommend will more accurately accomplish this purpose."[16]

Despite the lack of resistance by some officials, it is important to note that the recommendations made by the U.S. Sentencing Commission in 1997 also found criticism among some individuals, including Eric W. Sterling, President of the Criminal Justice Policy Foundation. Sterling has been involved in analyzing drug sentencing in the United States since the early 1980s. He said "there are at least six reasons why this proposal stinks. First, sentences should not be raised or lowered simply to include or exclude more offenders of a given race. Second, the quantity triggers were established irrationally. The low quantities have no relation to the high level of culpability that Congress wanted to punish in 1986 when it wrote this law. This tinkering does not bring rationality. Three, lowering powder cocaine quantity triggers means more low-level cocaine mules, couriers, and lookouts will be subject to kingpin level sentences. Four, more blacks—who remain at the low rungs of the cocaine trafficking ladder—will get long mandatory sentences for powder cases. Five, federal prosecutors will decline cases they now accept and accept cases they now decline, and the percentage and number of black low-level crack defendants will remain largely unchanged. Six, this proposal is offered in the spirit of we have to do something. It will delay real reform."[17] Despite these criticisms, the good news for the commission was that Republicans in Congress, including former Senate Judiciary Committee Chairman Orrin Hatch (R-UT), agreed with the suggestion that there should be an increase in punishment for powder cocaine among low-level dealers. Passing legislation addressed this form of sentencing disparity. NOTE: The most recent USSC report can be found at the United States Sentencing Commission's Web site (http://www.ussc.gov/).

Sentence disparity has been in existence for many years and will continue to take place. The difference between the past and present sentence disparity practices is that, in earlier days, it was regarded as part of the judge's "wise" discretion, whereas now it is subject to public outrage. Most conflict criminologists regard sentence disparities as evidence that the criminal justice system is often the source of exploitation and unfair treatment toward the underclass—the most likely group to use the cheapest form of cocaine, which is crack.[18]

5-4 Sentencing Guidelines

In 1984, the U.S. Congress addressed sentence disparity concerns by forming the United States Sentencing Commission with the aim of expounding the Federal Sentencing Guidelines. The new system curtailed parole and confined sentences imposed by judges into narrow ranges. A few years later, the U.S. Congress enacted the guidelines into law, and in 1989, the U.S. Supreme Court held that this effort was constitutional.[19]

Judges who use sentencing guidelines utilize worksheets to calculate a sentence. This process has often been associated with the calculation of income taxes using the federal 1040 form. The worksheet used by judges when calculating a sentence is complex and intricate but in theory is to guide all judges to the same conclusions. A sample of the worksheet used in the state of Minnesota can be seen in Table 5-1. The numbers in italics in the grid represent the range within which judges may impose a sentence. The criminal history of the offender is calculated by adding a point for each prior felony conviction, half a point for each prior conviction including a gross misdemeanor, and one-quarter point for each prior conviction involving a misdemeanor.

In Florida, a similar worksheet is printed and distributed quarterly to clerks of the circuit courts, state attorneys, and probation and parole services field staff. Using an Innovations Incentive Grant of $35,000, Florida contracted an agency to develop a computer system to automate score sheet preparation and to allow for storage and retrieval of offender information. The resulting software, Sentencing Analysis Guidelines Entry System (SAGES), is currently operational in the Florida Department of Correction's mainframe computer. SAGES is not only available to the Department of Corrections but also to probation/parole field staff and half of the state attorneys offices in Florida.[20]

The guidelines assign an offense level to each specific crime—low offense levels for minor crimes and high offense levels for major criminal acts. This offense assignment takes place while the guidelines direct the calculation of the criminal history of each defendant. For example, a person with a clean background starts with zero criminal history points, with a possibility of having points added for the first and each subsequent offense. The goal of the judge is to

TABLE 5-1 Minnesota Sentencing Guidelines Grid (Presumptive Sentence Length in Months, Effective August 1, 2002)

Italicized numbers within the grid denote the range within which a judge may sentence without the sentence being deemed a departure. Offenders with nonimprisonment felony sentences are subject to jail time according to law.

Severity Level of Conviction Offense (Common offenses listed in italics)		Criminal History Score: 0	1	2	3	4	5	6 or more
Murder, 2nd Degree (intentional murder; drive-by-shootings)	XI	306 *299-313*	326 *319-333*	346 *339-353*	366 *359-373*	386 *379-393*	406 *399-413*	426 *419-433*
Murder, 3rd Degree Murder, 2nd Degree (unintentional murder)	X	150 *144-156*	165 *159-171*	180 *174-186*	195 *189-201*	210 *204-216*	225 *219-231*	240 *234-246*
Criminal Sexual Conduct, 1st Degree[2] *Assault, 1st Degree*	IX	86 *81-91*	98 *93-103*	110 *105-115*	122 *117-127*	134 *129-139*	146 *141-151*	158 *153-163*
Aggravated Robbery, 1st Degree	VIII	48 *44-52*	58 *54-62*	68 *64-72*	78 *74-82*	88 *84-92*	98 *94-102*	108 *104-112*
Felony DWI	VII	36	42	48	54 *51-57*	60 *57-63*	66 *63-69*	72 *69-75*
Criminal Sexual Conduct, 2nd Degree (a) & (b)	VI	21	27	33	39 *37-41*	45 *43-47*	51 *49-53*	57 *55-59*
Residential Burglary Simple Robbery	V	18	23	28	33 *31-35*	38 *36-40*	43 *41-45*	48 *46-50*
Nonresidential Burglary	IV	12[1]	15	18	21	24 *23-25*	27 *26-28*	30 *29-31*
Theft Crimes (Over $2,500)	III	12[1]	13	15	17	19 *18-20*	21 *20-22*	23 *22-24*
Theft Crimes ($2,500 or less) Check Forgery ($200-$2,500)	II	12[1]	12[1]	13	15	17	19	21 *20-22*
Sale of Simulated Controlled Substance	I	12[1]	12[1]	12[1]	13	15	17	19 *18-20*

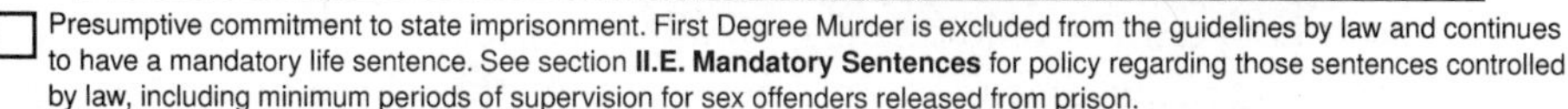

☐ Presumptive commitment to state imprisonment. First Degree Murder is excluded from the guidelines by law and continues to have a mandatory life sentence. See section **II.E. Mandatory Sentences** for policy regarding those sentences controlled by law, including minimum periods of supervision for sex offenders released from prison.

■ Presumptive stayed sentence; at the discretion of the judge, up to a year in jail and/or other non-jail sanctions can be imposed as conditions of probation. However, certain offenses in this section of the grid always carry a presumptive commitment to state prison. These offenses include Third Degree Controlled Substance Crimes when the offender has a prior felony drug conviction, Burglary of an Occupied Dwelling when the offender has prior felony burglary conviction, second and subsequent Criminal Sexual Conduct offenses and offenses carrying a mandatory minimum prison term due to the use of a dangerous weapon (e.g., Second Degree Assault). See sections **II.C. Presumptive Sentence** and **II.E.Mandatory Sentences.**

1 One year and one day

2 Pursuant to M.S.§ 609.342, subd. 2, the presumptive sentence for Criminal Sexual Conduct in the First Degree is a minimum of 144 months (**see II.C. Presumptive Sentence** and **II.G. Convictions for Attempts, Conspiracies, and Other Sentence Modifiers**).

Source: Minnesota Sentencing Guidelines Commission

"look up on a grid the spot where the offense level intersects the criminal history."[21] The grid automatically assigns light sentences to individuals who have low criminal histories and commit less serious crimes, while it assigns stiff sentences to those who have long criminal histories and commit severe crimes. The judge then imposes a sentence that is in accordance with the sentencing guidelines grid unless there is a strong reason to depart from this norm.

The guidelines have been welcomed as they attempt to reduce the high number of cases with sentencing disparity. Due to the popularity of these sentence guidelines, they are currently used in the federal system and in approximately one-third of the states. However, this popularity has met some resistance. In an analysis of the federal sentencing guidelines, researchers found that African Americans received longer sentences than whites, not because of differential treatment by judges but because they made up the large majority of those convicted of trafficking crack cocaine.[22] In addition, critics argue that the attempt of sentencing guidelines is a failure because the discretionary power has shifted to prosecutors and others in the criminal justice system. Despite these criticisms, it is important to mention that various jurisdictions use distinct guidelines and have different experiences with them. The overall experience has been that guidelines are representative of an improvement but they must be well-structured and subject to careful scrutiny to be successful.

5-5 Strategies in Sentencing

There are three major sentencing strategies in the United States—indeterminate, determinate, and mandatory. The philosophies of punishment discussed in previous chapters are often represented in the various sentencing strategies. These are often used in combination by some states. Spotlight 5-1 illustrates the major characteristics of each of the three sentencing designs.

5-6 Mandatory Sentences

5-6a Three Strikes Law

Of all of the strategies mentioned earlier, mandatory sentences have gained the most popularity in recent years. Due to the growing conservative public attitude toward crime, many state officials have recently considered proposals to enhance sentencing for adults and juveniles who have been convicted of violent crimes. These sentences usually involve longer prison terms for violent offenders who possess a record of serious crimes. A prominent example of this is the creation of the new form of mandatory sentencing called the Three Strikes Law (and in some jurisdictions, Two Strikes Law). By 1994, this law was enacted in all fifty states. The Three Strikes Law states that a repeat violent offender will be incarcerated up to life after he or she has been convicted three times for the same violent offense. California was a pioneer in the implementation of this type of mandatory sentence. California Governor Pete Wilson argued that by implementing the Three Strikes Law, crime would be substantially reduced.

It is not surprising that the implementation of the Three Strikes Law has resulted in longer prison terms for recidivists than did earlier mandatory minimum sentencing laws. The state of California's Three Strikes Law requires that offenders who are convicted of a violent crime, and who have had two prior convictions, serve a minimum of twenty-five years.[23] This same law also doubles the prison terms for those offenders who are convicted of a second violent felony.[24] However, it is important to recognize that the Three Strikes Law varies in breadth. Some stipulate that both of an offender's prior convictions and the current offense should be violent felonies while others require that the offender's prior felonies be violent. Some Three Strikes Laws count only past adult violent felony convictions while others allow consideration of juvenile adjudications for violent crimes. It is hard to determine whether these laws are effective in reducing crime. Although there has been a decline in crime in recent years, many attribute this phenomenon to the economic stability of the country instead of the Three Strikes Laws. Supporters of these laws argue that they have made their contribution in reducing the overall crime trend in the United States. It is diffi-

Spotlight 5-1

Sentencing Strategies

Indeterminate sentence. This involves ranges made by the legislature that allow correctional personnel to exercise discretion in determining sentences. This type of sentence usually involves a maximum and a minimum term for each offense, and is based on the rehabilitative ideal. The corrections professional has total discretion to release an offender once the individual has been successfully rehabilitated. Most penal codes with indeterminate sentences dictate a minimum and maximum amount of time to be served in prison (e.g., one to five years, three to ten years, twenty years to life).

Mandatory sentence. This states that a sentence must be imposed upon conviction. Mandatory sentences, which often involve incarceration, are usually specified by legislatures or by Congress. These sentences are designed to deny the judge of his or her discretionary powers regarding incarceration. If the sentence dictates a specific prison term, the judge does not have the ability to impose a different term or an alternative to prison. Mandatory prison sentences are mostly given to violent and habitual offenders, drug offenders, and those who used a weapon in the commission of a crime. An example of this type of sentence is a Massachusetts gun law that mandates a one-year jail term to anyone convicted of possessing an unregistered firearm.[25]

Determinate sentence. As society encourages a punitive approach toward offenders, more support is being given to determinate sentences. These sentences mandate fixed periods of incarceration minus any good time credits that offenders earn. The release of an inmate is not based on his or her participation in a rehabilitation program offered in prison and is not subject to the discretion of a parole board. Today, as different states adopt intermediate sentencing laws, some states have incorporated determinate sentences into penal codes that mandate a specific prison term for a particular crime, while others still allow judges to decide a particular prison sentence from an array of choices.

cult to know who is correct and it is impossible to measure the impact of these laws on crime.

Despite the increasing popularity of these laws, a case *(Lockyer, CA Attorney General v. Andrade, Leandro / Ewing, Gary v. California)* is currently being considered by the U.S. Supreme Court. This case presents the following questions:

1. Does the California Three Strikes Law (twenty-five year sentence) violate the Eighth Amendment to the U.S. Constitution against cruel and unusual punishment?
2. Does a twenty-five year-to-life sentence violate federal Constitutional provisions against cruel and unusual punishment since the punishment is disproportionate with the crime (e.g., stealing golf clubs)?
3. Did the California courts apply, in an unreasonable manner, federal law within the meaning of Antiterrorism and Effective Death Penalty Act's habeas corpus provision, 28 U.S.C. when considering the state of California's Three Strikes sentencing law?[26]

5-6b Truth in Sentencing

Another type of mandatory sentencing enhancement is truth in sentencing. Provisions for this type of mandatory sentence are found in the Violent Crime Control and Law Enforcement Act of 1994. Truth in sentencing requires that all

Spotlight 5-2

Tonry's Research Findings on the Impact of Mandatory Sentencing Laws

- Criminal justice officials and practitioners (e.g., police, lawyers, and judges) exercise their discretion to avoid the application of the laws they consider unduly harsh.
- Arrest rates for specific crimes decline soon after the implementation of mandatory sentencing laws.
- Dismissal and diversion rates increase at the early stages of case processing after the implementation of sentencing laws.
- For defendants whose cases are not dismissed, plea-bargain rates decline while trial rates increase.
- Sentencing delays increase for convicted defendants.
- The implementation of mandatory sentencing laws has little impact on the probability that offenders will be imprisoned. This is the case when the effects of declining arrests, indictments, and convictions are taken into consideration.
- In general, sentences become longer and more severe.

imprisoned offenders serve at least 85 percent of their sentences and aims at achieving two goals—deterrence and incapacitation. By passing mandatory sentencing laws, legislators are attempting to convey that some crimes are considered especially grave and that people who commit such crimes deserve punitive sanctions. The creation of these laws has been attributed to the public outcry for more severe sanctions because of high-profile crimes. Such laws will continue to increase in popularity as the fear of crime continues to grow among Americans.

5-7 Impact of Mandatory Sentencing Laws

Due to the growing popularity of mandatory sentences in recent years, scholars have devoted their attention to the evaluation of these sentences. Most of the evaluations have focused on two types of crimes—those committed with handguns and those related to drugs. It is important to note that drug offenses are most commonly subjected to mandatory minimum penalties in state and federal courts. A Massachusetts law, regarding crimes committed with handguns, imposed mandatory jail terms for those convicted of possession of unlicensed firearms and concluded that the law was not an effective deterrent of gun crime.[27]

Similarly, studies in Michigan[28] found no evidence that mandatory sentences reduced the number of crimes committed with firearms. Other evaluations of mandatory gun-use sentencing in six major cities (Detroit, Tampa, Miami, Jacksonville, Pittsburgh, and Philadelphia) concluded that these mandatory sentences deterred homicide but they did not have the same effect on any other violent crime.[29] Another study of New York's 1973 Rockefeller drug laws did not support the long-held claim that these laws were efficient in deterring drug-related crimes in New York City.[30] Although these studies questioned the efficiency of mandatory sentencing laws, a few of them measured the incapacitation effects of these laws.

Studies have also been done to assert the impact of mandatory sentencing laws on the criminal justice system. A study conducted by Michael Tonry (1987), summarizes the findings of all of these studies.[31] In general, he reported that officials make earlier and more selective arrests, charges, and diversion decisions while bargaining less. Spotlight 5-2 summarizes some of Tonry's findings.

Spotlight 5-3

Tonry's Research Review on the Impact of Mandatory Sentencing Laws

- Mandatory sentences do not achieve certainty and predictability since officials circumvent them if they believe that the results are unduly punitive.
- Mandatory sentencing laws are redundant when proscribing probation for serious cases since such cases are generally disposed of by sentencing the offender to prison.
- Mandatory sentences are arbitrary for minor cases.
- Mandatory sentences usually result in undeserved severe punishment for a marginal offender.

Spotlight 5-3 presents the research review that Tonry conducted on the most important studies of mandatory sentencing laws.

5-8 Sentencing Trends

The most recent sentencing trends were published in 1999. Between 1992 and 1996, the number of felony convictions increased 14 percent in state courts and 11 percent in federal courts. In 1996, state and federal courts together imposed a prison sentence on 39 percent of all persons convicted of a felony. Federal courts sentenced 64 percent of felons to prison, and state courts, 38 percent. Together, state and federal courts sentenced to prison 57 percent of the 170,400 felons convicted of a violent crime in 1996.[32]

5-8a Comparison of State and Federal Sentences for Felonies

Three types of sentences comprise most of the judgments imposed in federal and state courts for felony convictions. These include **prison confinement** (usually for a year or more), **jail confinement** (usually less than a year), and **probation,** which accounted for most of the sentences that state and federal courts imposed as punishment for a felony conviction. However, state and federal sentences are not entirely comparable, since there are differences between the type of offense processed in state and federal courts.[33]

In 1996, violent crimes comprised 17 percent of felony convictions in state courts but only 6 percent of those in federal courts. Violent crimes made up 25 percent of state prison sentences but only 8 percent of federal prison sentences. Drug-related offenses comprised 35 percent of all felony convictions in state courts while they made up 41 percent of those in federal courts. Drug crimes made up 32 percent of state prison sentences but 54 percent of federal prison sentences. When comparing these statistics, it is important to note that individual offense categories differ in state and federal courts. For example, federal offenses labeled "robbery" are almost entirely bank robberies (over 95 percent) while state robbery offenses seldom involves those of banks.[34] These statistics can be confusing. However, they all show that states' criminal justice systems oversee much more activity than does the federal government. They present the tremendous amount of sentences rendered in a given year— these impact the correctional system by overwhelming it with individuals assigned to serve extended prison sentences.

Prison confinement
One of the three types of sentences that comprises most of the sentences imposed in federal and state courts for felony convictions. Prison confinement usually entails a sentence of one year or more in prison.

Jail confinement
One of the three types of sentences that comprises most of the sentences imposed in federal and state courts for felony convictions. This type of confinement usually involves less that one year in a jail facility.

Probation
A type of sentence in which the offender is subjected to conditioned supervision in the community.

5-8b Average Sentence Length

A great deal of debate has occurred regarding the necessary amount of prison time each defendant should receive. The direction that state and federal courts have taken regarding the length of sentences is important. Felons sent to state and federal prisons have an average imposed sentence length of approximately five years.[35] Although these averages differ slightly from those in 1990, 1992, and 1994, the changes since 1990 have not been directed toward either consistently longer or shorter sentences. Unlike the lengths of jail sentences, which vary little from the six month overall national average, prison sentence lengths vary widely from one offense to the other. The average prison sentence for murder is approximately twenty-one years; for sexual assault, ten years; for robbery, eight and a half years; for motor vehicle theft, three and a half years; and for drug possession, three and a half years. The only category that exceeds the average prison sentence of five years is that of violent offenses.[36] For the complete listing of lengths of felony sentences imposed by state and federal courts, see Table 5-2. State courts impose longer sentences for serious violent offenses than the federal courts. This coincides with the fact that states oversee most of the criminal justice activity.

5-8c Sentence Length versus Time Served

It is important to examine the relationship between the sentences imposed by the courts and the time actually served by inmates. The amount of prison time an offender is prescribed at sentencing is longer than the actual amount of time the offender will serve. According to the Bureau of Justice Statistics,[37] there are two primary reasons that explain the difference between the sentences imposed and the actual time served by inmates:

- Most states, but not the federal system, have a parole board that decides the time when a prisoner is released. In those particular states, the sentence imposed is the same as the amount of time the offender serves before being released. This is only if the offender is never paroled. Since almost all offenders are eventually paroled, relatively few serve their entire sentence before release.
- In the state and federal system, inmates can earn early release through time credits for good behavior or special achievements. Automatic good-time credits are awarded in many states.

Due to the public outcry demanding that inmates serve longer periods of their sentence, any federal prisoner who is sentenced for a crime committed after November 1987 is subject to the law setting the 85 percent minimum. This federal law is based on the notion that all federal inmates have to serve at least 85 percent of their specified sentence. The only exception to this involves those inmates sentenced to life in prison—these prisoners have to serve their sentences in full. Inmates are subject to laws that vary from state to state. However, statistics suggest that in 1996, at the state level, rapists served 51 percent of their sentence while drug traffickers served 42 percent of their sentence. If one is to assume that state inmates sentenced in 1996 served the same percentage of their sentence as those released in 1996, state felons sentenced in 1996 served about two and one-half years (45 percent of a sixty-two month sentence).[38]

The average federal prison sentence (six and a half years) and the average state sentence (five years and two months) do not differ substantially. Newly sentenced federal inmates are expected to serve, on the average, three years and three months longer than the newly sentenced state offenders (five and a half years versus two and a third years). One of the reasons for this difference is that federal drug traffickers receive longer sentences than those received by state inmates (seven and a half years versus four and a half years). In addition, federal drug traffickers make up a significantly larger proportion of the prison population (52 percent of all sentenced to prison versus 22 percent); they also serve a larger percentage of their sentence (85 percent) than state offenders who usually serve 40 percent of their sentence.[39]

TABLE 5-2 Length of Felony Sentences Imposed by State and Federal Courts, by Violent Offenses, 1996

Most Serious Violent Offense	Mean Maximum Sentence Length for Felons Sentenced to Incarceration			
	Total Incarceration (in months)	Prison Incarceration (in months)	Jail Incarceration (in months)	Straight Probation (in months)
Murder/ manslaughter[a]				
State and federal	244	253	8	71
State	249	257	8	72
Federal	110	128	8	44
Sexual Assault[b]				
State and federal	98	119	8	66
State	98	120	8	66
Federal	73	79	8	45
Robbery				
State and federal	88	101	10	52
State	87	101	10	52
Federal	107	110	8	43
Aggravated Assault				
State and federal	43	69	6	41
State	43	69	6	41
Federal	34	46	7	40
Other Violent Crimes[c]				
State and federal	35	61	6	44
State	34	59	6	44
Federal	24	141	8	40

Note: For individuals who received a combination of sentences, the sentence designation was originated from the most severe penalty imposed—prison being the most severe, followed by jail, then probation. All of the mean sentence lengths excluded sentences to death or life in prison.

[a] Includes non-negligent manslaughter

[b] Includes rape.

[c] Includes offenses such as negligent manslaughter and kidnapping

Source: U.S. Department of Justice, Department of Justice Statistics (July, 1999), *Felony Sentences in the United States,* 1996.

Governor Ryan's Decision to Commute Death Sentences in Illinois

Outgoing Illinois Governor George Ryan commuted the death penalty sentences of all inmates on Illinois' death row before leaving office at the beginning of 2003. This was a surprise to some who had predicted Ryan would not conduct this action as it was deemed irresponsible and outrageous. Immediately after Ryan's announcement, victims' advocacy groups throughout the United States began to condemn Ryan's actions. They claimed he had made the decision to commute the sentences for political reasons on his last day as governor as his tenure had been surrounded by political controversy. Regardless of his reasons, Ryan's actions will forever change the death penalty practices in Illinois. According to experts, it may inspire other states to follow, as Ryan's decisions have led to a revival on the death penalty debate.

Summary

The sentencing process presents a perplexing problem in the system of criminal justice. Some people believe in the philosophy of individualized treatment although they are faced with insufficient knowledge of treatment to implement it successfully. Conversely, some believe in "justice" and the realities of current sentencing disparities. There is no easy answer to the question of how to combine justice and individualization. Some discretion must exist or the system regresses to the mechanical and harsh philosophy of Beccaria, who argued successfully in the eighteenth century that the punishment should fit the crime. It was a philosophy that made sentencing easy. The legislature determined the sentence for each offense and the court's only function was to determine whether the accused had committed the offense. That system was soon abolished in many countries because it was felt that such justice was unnecessarily cruel. It did not take into account mitigating circumstances, which were emphasized by the neoclassical school. In the United States, a philosophy of individualized treatment developed in the twentieth century that was supported by legislatures and recognized by the courts. This philosophy reached its most extreme form in the indeterminate sentence. Recently, this philosophy has come under attack. At the time of this writing, the American Criminal Justice System is experiencing a "get-tough" policy with regard to sentencing. Some states have already returned legislatively to a mandatory sentencing process, and others have started procedures to abolish parole.

This chapter examined several dimensions of the sentencing dilemma. A brief look at the impact that sentencing has had on the system of justice and the various sentencing strategies developed was discussed. Attention was given to mandatory sentences and the complexities surrounding these types of sentences. There are also characteristics associated with sentencing disparity. In the process of this discussion, several studies from recent years were examined to determine whether there is sentencing disparity and, if so, the severity of the problem. The history and function of sentencing guidelines was outlined while paying particular attention to the role these have played in reducing the sentencing disparity. The recent trends associated with the sentencing procedures of federal and state courts were considered as well.

It is reasonable to conclude that the control, not the abolition, of discretion is one of the main issues associated with sentencing. The legal profession should recognize and accept the challenge of successful control of judicial and prosecutorial discretion, especially as discretion relates to sentencing decisions. The legal profession alone, however, cannot solve some of the problems of the criminal justice system. Society must take responsibility for providing the necessary resources that will enable us to provide adequate legal services for all. The social structure should be realistically appraised as the criminal justice system does not exist in isolation from the rest of society. Research must be fostered and supported. The tendency to abandon philosophies, such as treatment, before they have been given a real trial, should be reexamined.

Notes

1. See *Harris v. Alabama,* 115 S3 CT. 1031 (1995), Rehg, denied, 115 S. CT. 1725 (1995).
2. *Proffitt v. Florida,* 428 U.S. 242 (1976).
3. See *Walton v. Alabama,* 497 U.S. 639 (1990), Rehg, denied, 497 U.S. 639 (1996).
4. Coalition for Sentencing Reform, *History of the Guidelines.* (February, 1997).
5. *History of the Guidelines.*
6. Reiman, Jeffery, *The Rich Get Richer and the Poor Get Prison,* 6th ed. (Needham Heights, MA: Allyn & Bacon, 2001).
7. D'Alessio, Stewart J., and Stolzenberg, Lisa, "Socioeconomic Status and the Sentencing of the Traditional Offender," *Journal of Criminal Justice* 21 (1993), 71-74.
8. Chiricos, Theodore, and Bales, William, "Unemployment and Punishment: An Empirical Assessment," *Criminology* 29, No. 4 (1991), 701-24.
9. Meierhoefer, B.S. (1992), *General Effect of Mandatory Minimum Prison Terms,* (Washington, D.C.: Federal Judicial Center, 1992); Meierhoefer, B.S., "Role of Offense and Offender Characteristics in Federal Sentencing," *Southern California Law Review 66,* 1 (November, 1992); 367-404; Meierhoefer, B.S. *General Effect of Mandatory Minimum Prison Terms: A Longitudinal Study of Federal Sentences Imposed* (Washington, D.C.: Federal Judicial Center, 1992).
10. U.S. Sentencing Commission, *Federal Sentencing Guidelines: A Report on the Operation of the Guidelines Systems and Short-Term Impacts on Disparity in Sentencing, Use of Incarceration, and Prosecutorial Direction and Plea Bargaining* (Washington, D.C.: U.S. Sentencing Commission, 1991).
11. Langan, P., *Federal Prosecutor Application of Mandatory Sentencing Laws: Racially Disparate? Widely Evaded?* (Washington, D.C.: U.S. Department of Justice, Bureau of Justice Statistics, 1992).
12. News Brief (March 1995), "U.S. Sentencing Commission Releases Long Awaited Report on Crack/Powder Sentences."
13. News Brief "U.S. Sentencing Commission."
14. News Brief (December 1995), "Clinton Signs Bill to Disapprove of Equalizing Crack Powder Cocaine Sentences."
15. U.S. Sentencing Commission, *Cocaine and Federal Sentencing* (April, 1997); Mary Pat Flaherty and Joan Biskupic, "Hill Urged to Reduce Gap Between Sentences for Crack and Powder Cocaine," *Washington Post* (April 30, 1997), p. A12.
16. News Brief (May-June 1997), "Sentencing Commission Proposes Reduction in Disparity in Powder and Crack Cocaine Sentences."
17. News Brief, "Sentencing Commission."
18. Sen. Richard Quinney, *The Social Reality of Crime* (Boston: Little Brown, 1970), and M. Lynch and W.B. Groves (1989), *A Primer in Radical Criminology* (New York: Harrow and Heston).
19. *Mistretta v. U.S.,* 488 U.S., 361 (1989).
20. Sentencing Guidelines, "1994-1995 Annual Report," *The Guidebook to Corrections in Florida,* 1995.
21. Coalition for Sentencing Reform, *History of the Guidelines.*
22. McDonald, D.C., and K.E. Carlson, "Sentencing in the Courts: Does Race Matter?" *The Transition to Sentencing Guidelines, 1986-90* (Washington, D.C.: U.S. Department of Justice: Bureau of Justice Statistics, 1993).
23. U.S. Department of Justice, Office of Justice Programs, National Institute of Justice, *Mandatory Sentencing* (January 1997).
24. In mid-1996, the California Supreme Court ruled that the state's Three Strikes Law constituted an undue intrusion on judges' sentencing discretion. State legislative leaders immediately announced plans to introduce legislation that would reinstate the law.
25. Tonry, Michael, "Mandatory Penalties," *Crime and Justice: A Review of Research,* vol. 16, Michael Tonry ed. (1990).
26. See *Lockyer, CA Attorney General v. Andrade, Leandro / Ewing, Gary v. California* 01-1127/01-6978. Appealed From: 9th Circuit Court of Appeals (270 F.3d 743) / California Court of Appeal (April 25, 2001, unpublished).
27. Tonry, *Crime and Justice,* p. 243.
28. Loftin, C., Heumann, M., and McDowall, D., "Mandatory Sentencing and Firearms Violence: Evaluating and Alternative to Gun Control," *Law and Society Review,* 17 (1983): 287-318.
29. McDowall, D., Loftin, C., and Wiersema, B., "A Comparative Study of the Preventative Effects of Mandatory Sentencing Laws for Gun Crimes," *Journal of Criminal Law and Criminology* 83, 2 (Summer, 1992): 378-394.
30. Joint Committee on New York Drug Law Evaluation, the Nation's Toughest Drug law; Evaluating the New York Experience, a Project of the Association of the Bar of the City of New York; the City of New York and the Drug Sentencing Council, Inc. (Washington, D.C.: U.S. Government Printing Office, (1978).
31. Tonry, Michael, *Sentencing Reform Impacts* (Washington, D.C.: U.S. Department of Justice, National Institute of Justice, 1987).
32. U.S. Department of Justice, Bureau of Justice Statistics, "Felony Sentences in the United States, 1996" By Jodi M. Brown and Patrick A. Langan. Washington, D.C.
33. Ibid.
34. Ibid.
35. Ibid.
36. Ibid.
37. Ibid. Dept. of Justice, *Felony Sentences.*
38. Ibid.
39. Ibid.

Chapter 6

Probation

Outline

Due to the increasingly overcrowded prisons, more and more attention is being devoted to alternatives and modifications of confinement sentences. It has been long recognized that crime and delinquency are failures of the community as well as of individual offenders. The task of corrections is one of reintegrating the offender into the community, restoring family ties, educating or employing the offender, and securing a place for the inmate in the normal functioning of society. According to recent statistics, the most frequently used method of such reintegration is probation. In fact, 3,773, 600 adults were on probation in the United States at the end of 1999.[1] More than half of these probationers (51 percent) had been convicted for committing a felony, 48percent for a misdemeanor, and 1 percent for other infractions. When considering the rate of supervision, national data showed that, by the end of 1999, 77 percent of probationers were being actively supervised while 10 percent were inactive cases and 9 percent had been abandoned.[2]

Key Terms

split sentence
shock incarceration
intermittent incarceration
modification of sentence
probation officer
PSI (Pre-sentence Investigation Report)

Probation is a sentence granted by a judge, in which the offender is not confined to an institution but must fulfill some condition(s) imposed by the court. The offender must remain in the community and must be under the supervision of a probation officer, who is usually a court-appointed official. The original sentence imposed on the offender remains and can be invoked at any time should the provisions of probation be violated. Probation differs from parole in that the latter requires the offender to serve a portion of his or her sentence in an institution before being released to the community. An individual being sentenced to probation is, in most cases, released to the community at once.[3] Ideally, the decision to allow a convicted person to live in the community under supervision is made after careful study of the person's background, behavior, and potential for success. The decision is based on the philosophy that the rehabilitation of some individuals might be hindered by imprisonment and will be aided by supervised freedom.

This chapter begins with a brief historical overview of probation and recent data on the use of probation as an alternative to prison. The purposes of probation and its organizational system are discussed, including supervision and the conditions of probation. Considerable attention is placed on the decision to grant probation—as well as to revoke it—while discussing variants of traditional forms of probation. Finally, the discussion turns to an evaluation of probation including an analysis of its future.

6-1 Historical Overview

Scholars disagree on the origins of probation, but its use is often traced to English common law. The earliest incorporation of a system that resembled probation was the concept of "benefit of clergy." The church maintained that it was the only organization to have jurisdiction over members of the clergy. Thus, if clergy members committed crimes, they would not be subjected to the criminal courts and would be handled by the church courts. Henry II objected to this system and insisted that clerics suspected of crimes be tried in secular courts. The resulting compromise provided that clergy accused of crimes would be tried in secular courts but with benefit of clergy. This meant that their bishops could claim dispensation for them. The charge would be read, but the state would not present evidence against the accused cleric. Instead, the accused would be allowed to give his view of the accusation and bring witnesses. With the only evidence coming from witnesses selected by the accused, most cases resulted in acquittals. Later, benefit of clergy was extended to all church personnel as protection against capital punishment, and eventually to all people who could read. The ability to read signified a person's association with the church. To test the clerical character, the individual accused of a crime was given a Psalm, usually the fifty-first, to read. If he demonstrated an ability to read, he was released from secular court and turned over to the ecclesiastical courts. The device was used to mitigate the harsh sentences of the criminal law. However, because of its severe abuse, it fell into disfavor. Parliament later declared that certain acts would be felonies without benefit of clergy and finally abandoned the use of the device.[4] In addition to benefit of clergy, the English also released people on their own recognizance and used a device called "judicial reprieve," which was a forerunner to the suspended sentence.[5]

In the United States, probation can be traced to John Augustus, a prominent Boston shoemaker. In 1841, Augustus, who is now considered the father of probation, became the first probation officer when he encountered a man who was going to be sentenced in the Boston courts. Augustus bailed the man out of jail and succeeded in getting his sentence reduced. From that day forward, he would often petition the Boston courts to suspend an individual's sentence and grant the accused conditional liberty under his supervision.[6] The people Augustus bailed out and supervised varied in background. He first started with drunkards, then with women and children, and later with offenders of all types. He would find them shelter, food, clothing, and a place to work.[7] In fact, records indicate that between 1841 and 1859, judges released almost 2,000 offenders into Augustus's custody instead of incarcerating them.[8]

Due to the high degree of success enjoyed by Augustus, the state of Massachusetts legislated an official, localized trial of his practices. As a result, in 1880, the Massachusetts legislature approved the nation's first statewide hiring of probation officers.[9] The Massachusetts law required that officers "carefully inquire into the character and offense of every person arrested for crime . . . with a view to ascertaining whether the accused may reasonably be expected to reform without punishment."[10] The popularity of the Massachusetts law gave rise to the enactment of similar laws in other states. By 1925, every state had some type of probation for juveniles, and by 1939, at least thirty-nine states had laws for adult probation. By 1967, every state had adult probation laws.[11] Unlike the individual states, the federal government lagged behind in its implementation of probation laws, and it was not until 1925 that the Federal Probation Act was passed.

6-2 The Impact of Probation on the System of Justice

In late 1976, the Criminal Justice Directory Survey of Probation and Parole agencies was conduced by the Bureau of the Census for the Law Enforcement Assistance Administration. It was the first systematic effort to collect data on probation and parole on a large scale. The survey revealed that on September 1, 1976, almost 1.5 million men, women, and children were on probation and parole in state and local systems. The study also revealed the existence of 3,868 state and local probation and parole agencies in the United States, employing 55,807 persons, of whom 60 percent were involved in counseling clients. An additional 20,263 volunteers were involved in probation and parole programs.[12]

In the 1970s, probation was imposed in as high as 70 percent of the sentences in some states and 54 percent in the federal system.[13] In 1967, the President's Commission on Law Enforcement and Administration of Justice concluded that the "best data available indicate that probation offers one of the most significant prospects for effective programs in corrections." However, the commission also noted that in most jurisdictions, probation fell short of meeting the two basic requirements for success: a system that facilitates the accurate selection of persons to receive probation, and adequate community resources for probationers.[14]

In 1995, a national survey was conducted on all adults on probation under the supervision of state and local agencies. This survey used a nationally representative sample and was administered in two parts. The study consisted of a review of the administrative records of 5,867 adult probationers, providing detailed information on current offenses and sentences, criminal histories, levels of supervision and contacts, participation in treatment programs, and disciplinary hearing outcomes. Administrative records were obtained from 167 state, county, and municipal probation agencies nationwide. Systematic samples of probationers were drawn from rosters prepared by each of the participating probation agencies. The response rate was 87.4 percent.[15] Since then, additional studies on the population distribution and characteristics of probation have been produced. Spotlight 6-1 presents some of the main highlights of a 1999 report on probationers.

6-2a Purpose of Probation

The purpose of the federal probation system was described by the Federal Judicial Center as follows:

> The central goal of the probation system is to enhance the safety of the community by reducing the incidence of criminal acts by persons previously convicted. The goal is achieved through the counseling, guidance, assistance, surveillance, and restraint of offenders to enable their reintegration into society as law abiding and productive members.[16]

In 1970, the American Bar Association approved a set of standards in support of more extensive use of probation. The standards are presented in Spotlight 6-2.

Spotlight 6-1

Highlights of the Characteristics of Adults on Probation in 1999

- In 1999, most probationers were supervised at the state level; 3,637,201 state and 3,670,591 federal probationers
- Texas had the largest probation population (443,688); the state with the lowest (2,726) probation population was North Dakota.
- Most probationers were white (63%), male (78%), who received probation due to a felony (51%) and did not receive incarceration (79%) as a component of their sentence.
- An estimated 3,773,600 adults were on probation by the end of 1999.
- Women represented 22% of all probationers in 1999.
- Almost 2/3 of all probationers were white; Blacks made up more than 1/3 of probationers at year-end 1999.

Source: Bureau of Justice Statistics. *U.S. Department of Justice, U.S. Correctional Population Reaches 6.3 Million Men and Women Represents 3.1 % of the Adult U.S. Population,* Sunday, July 23, 2000.

6-2b Organization and Conditions of Probation

As mentioned earlier, probation originated in a Boston courtroom. The first probation agencies were part of the judicial branch of government. As the idea of probation moved from east to west, variations in its organizational structure began to take place. Today, probation is not only part of the executive branch of government, but has statewide unification. This began at a time when the pros and cons of each organizational system were considered. The Advisory Commission examining this issue made the statement that probation services should be located within the executive branch of government. "Such placement would facilitate a more rational allocation of probation staff services, increase interaction and administrative coordination with corrections and allied human services, increase access to the budget process and establishment of priorities, and remove the courts from an inappropriate role."[17] The commission noted that when the probationers are located within the judiciary, they are often required to perform functions that are not only unrelated to probation supervision, but that might be detrimental to that function.

Split sentence
A type of sentence whereby a judge renders a sentence involving incarceration for a specific period of time followed closely by a probationary period for a fixed period of time.

Shock incarceration
The process of incarcerating an individual for a brief period of time and then releasing him or her on probation.

Intermittent incarceration
Type of incarceration that allows the offender who was sentenced to probation to spend weekends or nights in a local jail. The offender is part of the community while still being supervised in a controlled correctional facility.

Modification of sentence
The adjustment of an offender's sentence based on a number of factors, including the individual's good behavior in prison.

Today, probation has changed not only in its organizational structure but also in the way it is administered. Probation is seldom issued as a single punishment aimed at replacing incarceration. Judges, who are under constant pressure by the public to act tough on criminals, are sentencing offenders to probation along with some other type of sanction. The modern forms of sentencing in which probation is issued along with other punitive measures are as follows:

- **Split sentence:** An individual is sentenced to a specific period of incarceration. This is usually followed by a period of probation.
- **Shock incarceration:** An offender who has been sentenced to prison is released and resentenced to probation. The prison time is supposed to "shock" the individual offender.
- **Intermittent incarceration:** An offender who was sentenced to probation spends weekends or nights in a local jail. The idea is that the offender is part of the community while still being supervised in a controlled correctional facility.
- **Modification of sentence:** An individual's original sentence is reconsidered within a limited time frame. The sentence is modified to include probation.

Spotlight 6-2

Desirability of Probation

1. It maximizes the liberty of the individual while at the same time vindicating the authority of the law and effectively protecting the public from further violations of the law.
2. It affirmatively promotes the rehabilitation of the offender by continuing normal community contacts.
3. It avoids the negative and frequently stultifying effects of confinement that often severely and unnecessarily complicate the reintegration of the offender into the community.
4. It greatly reduces the financial costs to the public treasury of an effective correctional system.
5. It minimizes the impact of the conviction upon innocent dependents of the offender.[18]

These types of probation sentences include specific restrictions or conditions that vary from jurisdiction to jurisdiction. However, some of these conditions are common to all regions. For example, probationers are required to report to an officer periodically, at specified times and places. The officer may also visit the client. Probationers may change residence only with the permission of the supervising officer. They must work, attend school, or engage in an approved activity. If those plans change, it must be reported to the supervising officer or court. Probationers are often required to submit periodic reports of their activities and progress. They are restricted in the use of alcoholic beverages and appearance in bars or other questionable places. In some jurisdictions, they are not allowed to drink any alcoholic beverages or liquors. Probationers are not permitted to own, possess, use, sell, or have under their control deadly weapons or firearms.

Probationers' associations are also restricted. They are generally not allowed to associate with former inmates, although the supervising officer can approve it. Some jurisdictions forbid probationers from associating with people with bad reputations, a vague requirement that is hard to interpret.

Probationers are not allowed to leave the state or country without the permission of an official. Such permission is granted infrequently and only for extraordinary reasons. They are required to refrain from violating laws and must cooperate with their supervising officers. Occasionally, curfews or restrictions on where they live are imposed. Finally, the civil rights of probationers are affected. Probationers are sometimes not allowed to engage in businesses or sign contracts without the permission of their probation officer.[19]

Other conditions of those being sentenced to probation in the 1990s have been examined. Recent statistics show that in 1995, nearly 100 percent of current drug users (defined as those who claimed drug use in the month before the offense) reported having some kind of special condition included in their probation sentence. The most common punitive condition imposed on offenders was monetary (82 percent), including fees, fines, and court costs. A majority of drug users also reported restrictions as stipulated in their probation sentence against the use of alcohol and drugs (56 percent). Half of the current drug users received a sentence that required them to attend some kind of substance-abuse treatment, and 42 percent reported receiving drug treatment on their current sentence.[20] It is estimated that this trend will continue as long as individuals convicted for drug-related offenses are being sentenced at disproportionate rates to either prison or probation.

Probation has changed since the time of Augustus to keep up with the needs of the correctional system. Today, as the correctional population is growing beyond expected proportions, there is a greater need to issue probation. However, the growing fear of crime among the citizenry has created public pressure to sentence individuals to probation along with some other sanction.

It is also important to examine the activities conducted by those who enforce the conditions of probation. Some have argued that the role of the probation officer should be studied in an attempt to understand the complexities surrounding modern-day probation sentences.

6-2c The Probation Officer

Probation officers, since the years of John Augustus, were responsible for the rehabilitation of the offender. However, the role of the probation officer has recently changed. The challenges of bigger caseloads and limited powers make the duties of a probation officer very hard to perform. Every state prescribes a unique mission for its probation officers. Probation officers are asked to perform two functions—investigation and supervision of offenders. The investigative function involves the preparation of the **Pre-Sentence Investigation Report (PSI)**, which is often used in the sentencing of the individual offender. In addition, the supervisory role involves the close control of the offender's actions.

6-2d The Pre-sentence Investigation Report

Probation officer
An official employed by a probation agency who is mostly responsible for preparing presentence investigation reports, supervising offenders on probation, and helping to incorporate offenders back into society as lawful citizens.

PSI (Pre-sentence Investigation Report)
A report that is filed by probation or parole officers. It provides background information about the offender for the purpose of influencing the sentence imposed by the judge or parole board.

The functions of a probation officer begin before the individual under consideration is actually placed on probation. The probation officer usually prepares the PSI, which is based on the social work concept of looking at the individual's life history. The PSI can be of invaluable assistance to the sentencing judge, who decides what methods of treatment should be used with the offender. If the accused is committed, the PSI may be helpful to classification personnel at the correctional facility, as well as to the parole board. The report also aids the probation officer if the accused is placed under their care. Such information can be helpful to researchers who may seek data on those sentenced to probation.

The content of the PSI has changed since its original form. During the early years of the PSI, the belief was that the more information it contained, the more comprehensive it was. The thought was that to effectively rehabilitate an offender, the courts and probation personnel needed to know as much as possible about the offender. Over time, PSI reports have changed in length. The belief today is that short PSI reports are just as effective as the long reports. Due to the growing amount of cases, judges used to simply skim through long PSI reports looking for specific information that would assist them in their sentences. Most of those involved in the process of creating and interpreting these reports unanimously agree that shorter is better.

The new PSI is short and standardized. Questions pertaining to the offender's background and habits are frequently asked then verified by other sources. When a probation officer asks an offender if he or she has a drug problem and the answer is no, the probation officer will confirm this information by asking family members or friends the same question. If the offender was telling the truth, the probation officer will write in the PSI report that there is no apparent drug problem.

In addition, the PSI report usually includes information regarding the impact that the crime committed had on the victim. This addition is the direct result of the victim's rights movement of the 1970s. The probation officer interviews the victims and asks a series of questions about their perception of how much and what type of damage the criminal caused. When this new line of questioning was introduced, there was a concern among many that victims would often exaggerate the harm caused by the offender in an attempt to seek retalia-

Spotlight 6-3

Pre-sentence Investigation Report

Basic Information Regarding the Following:
Date
Name
Address
County
Court number
Offense
Class
Custody status
Maximum penalty
Detainers or pending chargers
District attorney
Presiding judge
Counsel
Plea
Verdict
Birth date
Height
Eye color
Age
Weight
Hair color
Race
Sex
Marital status
Education
Citizenship
Employment status
Concerned agencies
Place of birth
Distinguishing marks
Number of dependents

A More Detailed History of the Following:
Offense summary
Plea bargain/negotiations and stipulations
Official version
Defendant's version
Accomplices/codefendants
Prior record
Arrests not resulting in conviction
Driving record
Prior parole, probation, and institutional performance
Family history
Marital history
Education
Health

tion. However, studies suggest that this is not true. Spotlight 6-3 shows the information requested in a typical PSI report.

After preparing the PSI, the probation officer might also be expected to make a pre-sentence recommendation to the judge, which may or may not be followed. In the past, some studies have shown that in making such recommendations, probation officers do not consider all the data in the PSI, but rely heavily on the offense committed and on the prior record of the offender in question.[21]

6-2e Supervision of Probationers

One of the primary functions of the probation officer is to supervise probationers. However, the type and degree of supervision varies. In some probation departments, it is the probation officer's job to counsel probationers, particularly when they are juveniles. In other departments, the probation officer is expected only to supervise the activities of his or her probationers, and that supervision might be extremely limited. The choice of these models depends on variables such as the availability of resources, the caseload of probation officers, their professional training, and the needs of the probationers. The officer's basic function is to assist the probationer in making important transitions—from free citizen to one under supervision.

Many probation officers prefer to have a close interpersonal relationship with the client whom they are assisting.[22] The role of most probation officers—advocacy of due process and enforcement of the law—is successfully achieved by relying heavily on close interaction with the offender. The criminological literature contains numerous articles discussing ways in which probation officers can improve their supervisory relationships with their clients and serve as treatment agents.[23]

Treatment of probationers can be multidimensional. The greatest need of the probationer is to learn the social skills involved in successful interpersonal bonds. Criminality may be seen as a failure to relate to other people successfully. The offender does not have command of the tact, insight, and judgment needed to relate to others. Most offenders have long histories of personal failures and the probation officer is responsible for helping them build their self-confidence and acquire the social skills and habits necessary for successful relationships.

Claude Mangrum discussed the importance of what he calls "the humanity of probation officers." He argued that people live in an environment that creates inhumanity, manifested in poverty, violence, and crime. People no longer take time to relate to other human beings as people; they feel little commitment to each other and to the community.[24] Probationers may feel this most; they have often been the victims of social injustice, rejection, and stigma. It is important that probation officers not discourage them by questioning their essential dignity and worth as human beings.

Probation officers must be genuine in their relationships with clients. They must be sensitive to their clients' needs and relate to them as people, not simply as cases. This does not mean that probation officers cannot be firm. "There is nothing necessarily incompatible between warmth and acceptance and firm enforcement of the laws of the land. We must take whatever corrective measures are necessary; but these must not permit us to demean the dignity of the individual."[25] Probation officers must be effective in their communication with offenders, talking with them, not to them. Above all, the client must be treated with dignity and made to feel that he or she is important, at least to the probation officer.

When probation officers go beyond supervision of their clients and begin a treatment process, however, some problems can occur. Shelle G. Dietrich has discussed three potential problems in an article on probation.[26] First, when probation officers try to serve as therapists, because they lack qualifications, difficulties can occur. Many officers are not specifically trained as treatment personnel. According to Dietrich, "this lack of specialized training is rarely addressed and seems to be frequently forgotten."[27] A second problem arises when probation officers are given short-term, simplistic advice that might have potentially harmful consequences. Dietrich quoted as an example some of the comments of Mangrum. For example, probation officers are told to treat their clients with dignity, to be honest with them, to be concerned and genuine. Dietrich characterized such suggestions as "descriptive generalities," leaving the reader with "the feeling that the advice has evaporated into amorphous, vague directives which are frequently contradictory and difficult to apply to specific situations." When specifics are given, the advice is often "questionable and reflects cognitive, simplistic conceptions of human relationships."[28] In some cases, the advice, if taken, has a harmful effect on the client. Dietrich concludes, the "assumption of responsibility for being 'helpful' in untrained areas should be soberly reconsidered."[29]

Finally, Dietrich argued, even if the probation officer is trained and skilled in treatment techniques and is licensed in such work, the very nature of the position precludes some kinds of treatment. Because of the legal nature of probation work, the probation officer can never promise the confidentiality that an effective treatment relationship requires. In reality, the probation officer has a conflict of interest. The officer represents the interests of the state in violations of the probation agreement or the law, as well as the interests of the client in treatment and supervision.

Dietrich proposed that the probation officer be seen not as an agent of change, but as a case manager. While having knowledge of community agencies and resources, the function of the probation officer could be to "make such possibilities available to the probationer." It would not be the function of the probation officer to engage in therapeutic treatment, but to refer the probationer to qualified treatment personnel in the community, as well as to introduce the client to vocational, educational, and other resources.[30] This position received some support from the Advisory Commission, which clearly rejected the traditional concept of one person—a probation officer—as the sole treatment agent of a probationer. The commission characterized the probation officer as a community resource manager. In that capacity, the officer would "utilize a range of resources rather than be the sole provider of services—his role until now and one impossible to fulfill." It must be noted that Dietrich and his comments have come under heavy criticism by some who argue that probation officers serve as therapists and perform as such in a successful manner.

One of the problems associated with the supervision of offenders in today's correctional system is that due to overcrowding, more and more judges are sentencing some violent offenders to probation. It is necessary for most probation officers, who are often overworked with large caseloads, to take some steps to ensure their personal safety. Some have recommended that probation officers attain the mental preparedness needed to ensure their safety through rigid training. This training should include crisis rehearsals as well as crisis identification.[31]

Recently there has been a trend of large numbers of probationers—especially those of violent backgrounds—violating their probation conditions. This is the case mostly among offenders who have been sentenced to intensive supervision. Statistics from the National Institute of Justice show that approximately 65 percent of intensive supervision probationers and parolees violate their sentences, compared to 38 percent for traditional programs. It is worth noting that many of the violations are for special conditions of supervision that apply only to intensive supervision probation.[32]

Due to the problems currently facing probation officers, technology is being used as a method to conduct their supervisory role effectively. In Westchester County, New York, cameras have been used to supervise probationers more closely. Rocco Pozzi, probation commissioner, proudly announced that his probation agency developed an aggressive enforcement program that would keep a closer watch on 1,800 probationers who had been charged with driving while intoxicated or while ability was impaired. The agency had set up a sting operation that began by inviting 172 probationers to meet with probation officers to review their cases over a three-day period. At the location where the probationers were meeting with their probation officers, surveillance units were in position. When the probationers left, officers followed them to see whether they used public transit or taxis or drove away in their own vehicles. If they drove, police videotaped them and made note of their license plates. The testimony made by each officer and the videotape evidence was used to secure arrest warrants. The subsequent arrests were announced publicly and attracted extensive local media attention. The message was that Westchester County took probation seriously.[33]

6-2f Recruitment of Probation Officers

In the 1970s, the Advisory Commission pointed out that probation officer salaries must be high enough to attract qualified applicants. The committee suggested that the baccalaureate degree should be considered the basic educational requirement, but greater efforts should be made to create opportunities for those who have not completed the degree. The commission stated that such persons, with proper training, could carry out some of the activities of probation officers. In addition, it was recommended that special attention be given to the recruitment and training of persons who are from the socioeconomic and minority groups from which most probationers come, as well as to the recruitment of women. Probation offices throughout the United States have since made an effort to increase the salaries of probation officers while attempting to attract women to the probation job market. States such as Illinois have passed legislative acts that depict salaries and rights for probation officers working in that state. Despite these efforts, critics argue that probationers, to this day, earn less than adequate salaries that promote high turnover rates and low morale among probation officers.

National studies have been conducted in an effort to resolve staffing problems. In the past, states and local governments have attempted to solve the problem by raising the salaries of probation officers, making an effort to recruit minorities while reducing workloads, and providing greater opportunities for education and training. These attempts have been curtailed by the overwhelming amount of cases processed in the criminal justice system and the attempts to abolish affirmative action programs (which are expected to reduce the number of minority members hired as probation officers).

The commission concluded that a more effective approach would be for states to develop staffing programs that include effective job classification. The commission recommended that "each state immediately should develop a comprehensive manpower development and training program to recruit, screen, utilize, train, educate, and evaluate a full range of probation personnel, including volunteers, women, and ex-offenders." Included in that program should be "effective utilization of a range of manpower on a full or part-time basis by using a systems approach to identify service objectives and by specifying job tasks and range of personnel necessary to meet the objectives. Jobs should be re-examined periodically to insure that organizational objectives are being met."[34]

The commission further recommended that after personnel are employed in probation services, continuing education and training should be made available. Personnel should be able to choose one of two tracks: "direct service to probationers or administration. Each track should have sufficient salary and status to provide continuing job satisfaction."[35]

In today's competitive job market, most criminal justice practitioners and probation officers are seeking academic degrees from universities and colleges throughout the United States. Most have attributed this trend to the emergence of on-line courses that allow individuals that hold a full time job while seeking an academic degree during evenings. Despite the educational trend of probation officers, most newly hired probation officers are young high school graduates who seek a career in corrections.

6-2g Services Provided to the Probationer

If the purpose of probation is to assist the probationer in his or her adjustment problems, serious consideration must be given to the individual needs of that person. The Advisory Commission pointed out that too often probationers are considered a homogeneous group in assuming that they all need treatment. In reality, their needs are quite varied. Attention should be given to those needs and to the possibility of letting the individual participate in a treatment program designed for him or her. In addition, probation officers need to know what it means to be a probationer and what problems the individual faces as a consequence of his or her status under the law.

TABLE **6-1** **Treatment History of Alcohol- or Drug-Involved Probationers, 1995**

Participated in an Alcohol or Drug Treatment Program	% of Alcohol- or Drug-Involved Probationers
Ever	64.2
While incarcerated	10.2
Before current sentence	39.8
During current sentence	53.6
Currently in program	30.1
Number of probationers	1,390,572

Note: Probationers may have received treatment at multiple times in the past. It is clear from the statistics cited previously that today's probation services are geared toward offenders who abuse drugs frequently. This is a direct response to the overwhelming number of drug users who have entered the correctional system in the past few years. There are those who argue that as long as severe punishments attached to drug-related laws exist, the correctional system will continue to be overwhelmed with its admission of drug offenders. This will also have a negative effect on probation in the near future.

Source: *Substance Abuse Treatment of Adults on Probation,* 1995, Bureau of Justice Statistics, U.S. Department of Justice (March, 1998).

The commission recommended classification of probationers and identification of their needs. To implement effective delivery of the services, the commission recommended the probation administrators:

- Develop a goal-oriented system.
- Identify service needs of probationers systematically and periodically, and specify measurable objectives based on priorities and needs assessment.
- Differentiate between those services that the probation system should provide and those that should be provided by other resources.
- Organize the system to deliver services, including purchase of services for probationers, and organize the staff around workloads.
- Move probation staff from courthouses to residential areas and develop service centers for probationers.
- Redefine the role of probation officers from caseworkers to community resource managers.
- Provide the services to misdemeanants.

The Advisory Commission concluded that probation services should be goal-oriented. The goal should be the reintegration of the probationer into society so that he or she can manage without outside assistance. Probationers can help determine what their own needs are, then priorities can be established and problems identified. Objectives must be specified before one can judge whether those objectives have been accomplished.

A great number of probation programs are drug-related. Data from the Bureau of Justice Statistics on the subject suggest that in 1995, nearly 70 percent of probationers reported they used drugs in the past. This frequency of drug use presents a problem to probation officers in their attempt to rehabilitate offenders. Drug treatment programs are frequently offered to probationers who are regarded as having a drug-related problem. Statistics suggest that in 1995, nearly one-third of alcohol- or drug-involved probationers were enrolled in an alcohol or drug treatment program. As shown in Table 6-1, half of alcohol- or drug-involved probationers said they had received treatment on their current sentence and about one-third had been treated at some time in their lives.[36]

6-2h The Decision to Grant Probation

The granting of probation, which may be done only by the court, is a form of sentencing. It is considered, however, to be a disposition in lieu of sentencing. In some cases, the court will sentence a defendant to a term of incarceration but suspend the sentence for a specified period of time during which the offender will be on probation. If the offender does not violate the terms of probation, the sentence will never be imposed. If violations occur, the offender will be incarcerated. Because of the close relationship between probation and sentencing, which the Supreme Court considers a crucial stage in the criminal justice process, the defendant is entitled to due process at the probation hearing. The fundamental idea of due process under the U.S. Constitution is that a person should not be deprived of life, liberty, or property without reasonable and lawful procedures. This means that the judge may not be unreasonable, arbitrary, or capricious in the decision whether to grant probation. The defendant is entitled to an attorney at this stage, as well as if or when the probation is revoked and the suspended sentence is imposed.[37]

Recently, several questions have been raised about disparity in probation sentences. A study was conducted in 1995 that measured the differences that exist among rural and urban adult probation admissions. Interviews were conducted with 3,698 adult offenders on probation in Illinois. The questions were based on the probationer's supervision and treatment experiences. It was found that offenders in non-metropolitan counties were much less likely to be on probation for drug offenses and more likely to be on probation for other offenses. However, there were some similarities. It was determined that the average length of probation was the same in both metropolitan and non-metropolitan counties—twenty months. This was the case for various categories of offenses, including violent offenses, property offenses, drug offenses, and DUI (driving under the influence).[38] As this study states, differences do exist in the administration of probation from jurisdiction to jurisdiction.

6-2i Court Limitations

The American Bar Association has suggested the following restriction on the conditions of probation— every probationer should be required to lead a law-abiding life but no other conditions should be required by statute. Additional conditions of probation should be made by the sentencing court on an individual basis, according to the needs in each case. It is appropriate to develop standards for such conditions "as long as such conditions are not routinely imposed." The conditions imposed in each case should be for the purpose of assisting the probationer to lead a law-abiding life. "They should be reasonably related to his rehabilitation and not unduly restrictive of his liberty or incompatible with his freedom of religion. They should not be so vague or ambiguous as to give no real guidance." The ABA proposal lists areas in which conditions might be appropriately made:

- Cooperating with a program of supervision
- Meeting family responsibilities
- Maintaining steady employment or engaging or refraining from engaging in a specific employment or occupation
- Pursuing prescribed educational or vocational training
- Undergoing available medical or psychiatric treatment
- Maintaining residence in a prescribed area or in a special facility established for or available to persons on probation
- Refraining from consorting with certain types of people or frequenting certain types of places
- Making restitution of the fruits of the crime or reparation for loss or damage caused thereby.[39]

In the past, the courts did not interfere with the administration of prisons or probation systems. Consequently, the courts did not disturb conditions for probation, once established, unless such conditions were illegal, immoral, or impossible for the individual to fulfill. Courts have since abandoned this hands-off concept. *People v. Blankenship* is an example in which the court upheld the requirement that a defendant undergo a vasectomy as a prerequisite to probation. The case was decided in 1936 and probably would not be decided the same way today.

The male defendant was twenty-three years old and pleaded guilty to the rape of a thirteen-year-old girl. Both had syphilis, although there was no evidence that he transmitted the disease to her. The court recognized that syphilis can be cured but "it was not so much concerned with curing the disease with which appellant was afflicted as it was with preventing appellant from transmitting the disease to his possible posterity."[40]

In *People v. Dominguez,* the defendant was a twenty-year-old mother of two illegitimate children, convicted of armed robbery. The trial court imposed as a condition of probation that she not become pregnant out of wedlock again. She did, and the court revoked the probation. On appeal, the case was reversed. The court noted that while the trial court has wide discretion in setting the terms of probation, that discretion in determining probation "must be impartial, guided by 'fixed legal principles, to be exercised in conformity with the spirit of the law.'" The court said that when the condition of probation has no relationship to the crime for which the probationer was convicted or to future criminality, and which is not in itself criminal, it is invalid. "Contraceptive failure is not a indicium of criminality."[41]

In *Irman v. State,* an appeals court ruled that requiring a young man to cut his hair for two years, as a condition of probation, was unconstitutional. The court recognized that a probationer occupies a special status and the court may require conditions that it could not impose on free persons. Such conditions, as refraining from associating with immoral persons, abstaining from alcohol or drugs, and even holding an approved job, all fall within the category of "no temptation" conditions. These conditions are intended to assist a person in avoiding temptations that might be related to law-breaking behavior. These conditions are designed to help the individual become a law-abiding citizen. In another case, *In re Bushan* (1970), the court ruled that requiring as a condition of probation that a person undergo psychiatric care at his own expense with a psychiatrist approved by the court was unreasonable.[42]

The probationer's right to marry was questioned in a 1968 case. A defendant pleaded guilty to selling marijuana and was placed on probation. Before that sentence was decided, she married. She did not tell her attorney, because he had advised her that at the sentencing hearing she should not mention the name of the fellow she was dating because he had been arrested on a drug charge. She was given a short jail sentence and was placed on probation with stipulations, one of which was that she live with her parents. Later, to get the probation order changed, she claimed that the conditions of probation denied her the right of cohabitation with her husband. The court said it would decide such cases on a case-by-case basis and that it was not suggesting that probation would normally separate husband and wife. Due to the circumstances in this case, the probation order was not only upheld but also made more stringent. The court noted that probation is not a right but an act of "grace and clemency" and that the "judge is vested with a wide discretion, which will not be disturbed in the absence of abuse."[43]

Finally, in the case of a woman convicted of child abuse, the lower court ordered as a condition of probation that she have no children during the five-year probationary period. The appellate court struck that order, ruling that it was an unconstitutional violation of the right to privacy and an abuse of judicial discretion.[44]

6-2j Revocation of Probation

Historically, probation could be easily and quickly revoked, and without due process. The U.S. Supreme Court recently handed down cases that indicate a requirement of some elements of due process at the revocation of probation. This approach is based on the belief that probation is an important phase of the rehabilitation process, and that if offenders are to be rehabilitated, they must see the system as fair. If the system is arbitrary, offenders will lose respect for it and are more likely to repeat crimes. It is therefore in the interest of society, as well as the probationer or parolee, that they be treated fairly.[45]

In a later case, *Gagnon v. Scarpelli,* the Supreme Court extended rights involving revocation of parole to revocation of probation, indicating that in general, parole and probation revocation are the same for purposes of due process. The Court stated "probation revocation, like parole revocation, is not a stage of a criminal prosecution, but does result in a loss of liberty."[46] The Court therefore held that a probationer, like a parolee, "is entitled to two hearings": a preliminary hearing at the time of arrest and detention for the purpose of determining whether there is probable cause to believe that the terms of probation were violated; and a second, more comprehensive hearing when the final revocation decision is made.

In *U.S. v. Johnson,* the Supreme Court reversed and remanded a lower court's decision to deny relief to a case regarding the meaning of "time served" to a probationer. The case pertains to a respondent who had been serving a prison sentence in federal prison for multiple drug and firearms felonies when two of his convictions were noted as invalid. As a result, the respondent was determined to have served two and a half years too much prison time and was subsequently released. However, a three-year term of supervised release was yet to be served on the outstanding convictions. Upon hearing the case, the District Court denied relief in this case noting that the supervised release started upon the respondents' actual release from prison, and not before that time. However, the Sixth Court reversed the case agreeing with the respondent's argument that his supervised release term started not on the day he left prison but on the day his prison term expired. As noted earlier, the Supreme Court reversed and remanded the Sixth Court's decision.[47]

6-2k Measuring the Success of Probation

The success of probationers is usually measured by their degree of recidivism (habitual criminality) compared to the rate of recidivism of persons who have been incarcerated. Recidivism can be measured by violations of law or merely by violations of one or more of the conditions of probation. Technically, a probation failure could result if a probationer marries without the consent of the supervising officer. Such a measure of success is crude and does not necessarily measure rehabilitation. It measures only whether a person is caught violating another law or probation rule. The measure cannot reach those who do not possess the proper skills and mature judgment that are considered essential to rehabilitation.

Comparison of success from jurisdiction to jurisdiction is also difficult. The types of persons placed on probation differ, as do the definitions of probation violation utilized in the collection of data. Jurisdictions that place a small percentage of persons on probation may have fewer violations than those that place a larger percentage, because the former do not grant probation to anyone who might be a risk. Probation's success is subject to a critical public that constantly demands quick, inexpensive solutions to crime.

6-2l Empirical Evidence

In the late 1980s, a study of adult felons on probation examined the enforcement of sanctions that were part of the probation sentence. The analysis was conducted from results of a follow-up survey of convicted adult felons placed on state probation in 1986. The survey tracked 12,370 probationers for three years, from 1986 to 1989. Results indicated that a sizable number of offenders were discharged from probation before having fully complied with the conditions of their sentences. Among those released without compliance, 24 percent were ordered to participate in alcohol treatment, 20 percent in mental-health counseling, 32 percent in a drug-treatment program, 25 percent ordered to reside in a residential facility, 33 percent referred to drug testing, 33 percent ordered to house arrest, 35 percent ordered to day reporting, 21 percent ordered to perform community service, 69 percent ordered to pay supervision fees, and 40 percent ordered to make restitution.[48]

These results suggest that sanctions imposed with probation are not rigorously enforced. A reason for this may be that inadequate resources are in place to enforce and monitor drug tests, house arrests, community service, payment of fines, and treatment participation. This lack of resources might be a result of the growth of incarceration rates in the past years, with prisons and jails benefiting the most from state and local budgets (an average of two cents for every dollar spent in most states). At the same time, spending on probation and parole has been limited (an average of two-tenths of one cent of every dollar spent in most states).[49]

It is equally important that the recidivism rates of those who attend treatment programs are lower when compared to the rates of those who do not attend. New York is hosting a program targeted at probationers who have been convicted two or more times of driving while intoxicated and are not presently receiving any treatment service. This program merges probation with the treatment of these offenders at facilities such as the Hudson Mohawk Recovery Center and Seton Addiction Services for one or two years. In 1996, a ten-year study of the program was concluded. This study compared outcomes for participants in a control group and probationers not offered formal treatment.[50] The results of this study suggest the following:

- Program graduates were arrested 40 percent fewer times for DUI offenses and two-thirds fewer times for non-DUI offenses.
- On average, a person in the treatment program went nineteen months longer before being rearrested for any crime.
- Program participants were only one-fifth as likely to violate probation as were members of the control group.[51]

It can be argued that the program has been effective in lowering the recidivism rates of probationers who have been convicted of DUI offenses. In making concrete assumptions or generalizations about the effectiveness of this program, however, one must be careful when considering its implementation in another jurisdiction.

Unlike the New York program, recent studies have indicated that probation in the 1990s is a failure and that the only option is to reinvent it. Joan R. Petersilia, former director of RAND's criminal justice research program, calculated that the U.S. currently spends about $200 per probationer for supervision.

She notes, "It is no wonder that recidivism rates are so high."[52] An additional study argues that it should be no surprise that probationers have a high recidivism rate when we consider the problems facing probation officers.[53] These include being underpaid, overworked, and having scores of cases to manage. This same study suggests that probation must be reinvented by investing more money, allocating more agents, and maintaining a closer supervision of offenders. Some also argue that probation should be teamed with police agencies as part of a larger crime-prevention initiative.[54] The collective effort of all the social control agencies in the criminal justice system would be put to work. It is not clear whether the suggestions made by this study will work once implemented—however, the number of probation studies are sure grow as correctional administrators and the general public explore alternatives to incarceration.

6-2m The Future

The future of probation is unclear. Some jurisdictions have begun implementing different modernized versions of probation that they claim to be highly successful. In 1995, probation departments in Oklahoma, Utah, Oregon, and Texas began to test telephone-reporting programs to monitor low-risk offenders. Probationers are asked to call a 900 number once a month to answer a number of computerized questions.[55] This approach aims at reducing paper reporting—both mail-in and office reporting. This program has been praised by most of the agencies presently using it. Patty Davis of the Oklahoma Department of Corrections stated that this was one way "to work smarter and free up officers for more meaningful contact with offenders who really need intervention activity."[56] Davis added that the program is "used with more than low-risk cases, that is, if you have to report and pay fees, then the offender is eligible."[57] Everyone involved in this new approach to monitor the activities of probationers cautioned that this was not the solution—just one approach toward the improvement of probation.

In other jurisdictions, probation and police executives are establishing partnerships that highlight information-sharing and joint supervision projects to improve the efficiency of community safety services. Most of these community justice programs involve high-risk offender monitoring and the creation of police, citizen, corrections, and human service provider networks. Some of these jurisdictions include Redmond, Washington's high-risk offender monitoring program, Boston's Night Lite and Tracker programs, and Knoxville, Tennessee's network of citizens, police, corrections, and human service providers working together to reduce crime.[58] The outcome of these programs is unknown, although the preliminary results are positive and several probation agencies have recently expressed interest in adopting similar programs in their particular jurisdiction.

In another article, Charles J. Kehoe holds that technological advances will directly affect probation, especially among juveniles.[59] Kehoe predicts that, in the near future, centralized probation offices will be extinct. Communication technology will enable probation officers to do their jobs without ever having to report to an office. By logging into a home computer and modem, officers will be able to check a daily schedule, send and receive documents, and communicate with co-workers and supervisors.[60]

Kehoe adds that in the future, most court hearings will be held on closed circuit television, which will minimize the risk of violence and escape attempts when transporting offenders to and from court. The state of Florida is already implementing this approach. The satellite usage will also be implemented to educate all probation personnel more effectively. Probation officers will enjoy the benefit of video conferences that will allow unlimited access to training and other programs by probation staff all over the country and the world. Kehoe also warns about the dangers associated with the use of this new technology. One of these dangers is the sacrifice that will be made to our privacy. The following question is asked: How far are we willing to go to reduce crime and at what cost?[61]

The terrorist attacks of September 11, 2001, changed the people of the United States, but significantly impacted the manner in which the criminal justice system handles suspects and offenders. Some cite the public cry to engage in conservative practices of fighting crime and terrorism as responsible for the change of practices in probation. Many argue that probation will not be the most frequently used form of punishment in the future. This is due to the fear that certain probationers will commit crimes while serving their probation sentence.

Summary

This chapter reviewed the history and practice of probation, one of the most controversial and frequently used programs in the criminal justice system. This form of sentencing was considered, and the problems, both legal and sociological, were discussed. Previous and current empirical evidence of the success or failure of probation was examined, although effectiveness has not been measured.

Despite the cries of leniency and the trend toward harsher reactions to those who have been convicted of crimes, probation continues to be the most frequently used form of sentencing. More attention should be given to the goals of probation in given cases and to the conditions imposed on particular probationers. Are the conditions really related to the goals of probation? Probation is intended to be a flexible form of reaction to the convicted person—a method by which the court can devise an individualized sentence. This is especially important in cases in which incarceration appears unnecessary for the safety of society and in which it would perhaps be detrimental for the offender. As the correctional population grows to unprecedented proportions, one would be tempted to guess that probation will hold an even more important role in our system of criminal justice. Some predict that the September 11 terrorist attacks are likely to alter the popularity of probation, as people will request tougher sentences that include incarceration.

Notes

1. United States Department of Justice, *U.S. Correctional Population Reaches 6.3 Million Men and Women Represents 3.1 % of the Adult U.S. Population,* Sunday, July 23, 2000. Washington, D.C.
2. United States Department of Justice, *U.S. Correctional Population,* 2000.
3. The Columbia Encyclopedia, Edition 6, "Probation," p. 30172 (New York: Columbia University Press, 2000).
4. For a more detailed discussion of benefit of clergy, see David Dressler, *Practice and Theory of Probation and Parole,* 2nd ed. (New York: Columbia University Press, 1969), pp. 16–18.
5. "The Origins of Probation: From Common Law Roots," in George G. Killinger and Paul F. Cromwell, Jr., *Corrections in the Community: Alternatives to Imprisonment* (St. Paul, MN: West, 1974), pp. 159–160.
6. Montgomery, Reid, Jr., and Dillingham, Steven N., *Probation and Parole in Practice* (1983).
7. Montgomery and Dillingham, *Probation and Parole,* p.13.
8. Champion, Dean, "Felony Plea Bargaining and Probation: A Growing Judicial and Prosecutional Dilemma," *Journal of Criminal Justice* (1988), vol. 16, no. 4, p. 291.
9. See Act of Mar. 22, 1880, cah. 129, 1880 Mass. Acts 87.
10. Act of Mar. 22, 1880, cah. 129, 1880 Mass. Acts 87.
11. Montgomery and Dillingham, *Probation and Parole,* Supra note 25, at 24.
12. U.S. Bureau of the Census, National Criminal Justice Information and Statistics Service, *State and Local Probation and Parole Systems* (Washington, D.C.: U.S. Government Printing Office, 1978), pp. vii, 1.
13. Carlson, Norman A., "The Future of Prisons," *Trial* 12 (March, 1976), 32.
14. The President's Commission on Law Enforcement and Administration of Justice, *Task Force Report: Corrections* (Washington, D.C.: U.S. Government Printing Office, 1967), p. 27.

15. Bonczar, Thomas P., *Characteristics of Adults on Probation*, 1995, Bureau of Justice Statistics, U.S. Department of Justice (Washington, D.C.: U.S. Government Printing Office, December, 1997).
16. The Federal Judicial Center, *An Introduction to the Federal Probation System* (Washington, DC: U.S. Government Printing Office, 1976), p. 1.
17. National Advisory Commission on Criminal Justice Standards and Goals, *Corrections* (Washington, D.C.: U.S. Government Printing Office, 1973), p. 159.
18. American Bar Association Project on Standards for Criminal Justice, *Standards Relating to Probation* (Approved Draft, 1970), p.27.
19. For a listing of conditions of parole, by states and designations, see *The Sourcebook of Criminal Justice Statistics* (Washington, D.C.: U.S. Government Printing Office, 1996).
20. Bureau of Justice Statistics, U.S. Department of Justice, *Substance Abuse and Treatment of Adults on Probation*, 1995 (March, 1998).
21. See James Robinson, Leslie T. Wilkins, Robert M. Carter, and Albert Wahl, *San Francisco Project*, Research Report No. 14 (Berkeley: University of California School of Criminology, 1969).
22. See, for example, the earlier work of Daniel Glaser, *The Effectiveness of a Prison and Parole System* (New York: The Bobbs-Merrill Co., 1964).
23. The literature is discussed in Shelle G. Dietrich, "The Probation Officer as Therapist; Examination of Three Major Problem Areas," *Federal Probation* 43 (June, 1979), 14–19.
24. Mangrum, Claude T., "The Humanity of Probation Officers," *Federal Probation* 36 (June, 1972) 47–50.
25. Mangrum, "Humanity," p. 48
26. Dietrich, "Probation Officer as Therapist," p. 15.
27. Dietrich, "Probation Officer as Therapist," p. 15.
28. Dietrich, "Probation Officer as Therapist," p. 15.
29. Dietrich, "Probation Officer as Therapist," p. 18.
30. Dietrich, "Probation Officer as Therapist," p. 19.
31. Brown, Paul W., "Probation Officers Need to Rely on More Than Luck to Ensure Safety," *Corrections Today* (April, 1994), vol. 56, no. 2, 180(2).
32. Morrison, Richard D., "The Risk of Intensive Supervision," *In Complete Control: Correctional Security* (July, 1994), vol. 56, no. 4, 118(3).
33. Evans, Donald G., "Probation Undercover: Westchester County's DUI," *Drinking While Impaired* (August, 1996) vol. 58, no. 5, 172(2).
34. National Advisory Commission on Criminal Justice Standards and Goals, *Corrections*, p. 337. For a critique of the use of volunteers as probation officers, see David A. Dowell, "Volunteers in Probation: A Research Note on Evaluation," *Journal of Criminal Justice* (Winter, 1978), 6:9 357–361.
35. Advisory Commission, *Corrections*, p. 338.
36. Bureau of Justice Statistics, U.S. Department of Justice, *Substance Abuse and Treatment of Adults on Probation*, 1995.
37. *Mempha v. Rhay*, 389 U.S. 128 (1967).
38. Ellsworth, Thomas, and Weisheit, Ralph A., "The Supervision and Treatment of Offenders on Probation: Understanding Rural and Urban Differences," *The Prison Journal*, (June, 1997), vol. 77, no. 2, 209 (20).
39. American Bar Association, *Standards Relating to Probation*, p. 45.
40. *People v. Blankenship*, 61 P.2d 352, 353 (1936).
41. *People v. Dominguez*, 64 Cal. Rptr. 290, 293 (1967).
42. *In re Bushman*, 463 p. 2d 727 (1970).
43. *In re Peeler*, 72 Cal. Rptr. 254, 258 (1968).
44. *Ohio v. Livingston*, 372 N.E.2d 1335 (1978).
45. Plamer, John W., *Constitutional Rights of Prisoners* (Cincinnati, OH: Anderson, 1973), p. 114.
46. *Gagnon v. Scarpelli*, 411 U.S. 778, 782 (1973).
47. *United States v. Johnson*, (98-1696)154 F.3d 569 (2000).
48. Langan, Patrick A., "Between Prison and Probation: Intermediate Sanctions," *Science*, (May 6, 1994), vol. 264, no. 5160, 791(3).
49. Langan, "Between Prison and Probation," p. 792.
50. "New York Program That Merges Treatment, Probation Gets Results," (Rensselaer County Probation Alcohol Treatment), *Alcoholism and Drug Abuse Week* (February 5, 1996), vol. 8, no. 6, 6(1).
51. "New York Program That Merges Treatment, Probation," p. 6.
52. Dilulio, Jr., John J., "Reinventing Parole and Probation," *Brookings Review* (Spring, 1997), vol. 15, no. 2, 40(3).
53. Dilulio, "Reinventing Parole," p. 40.
54. Dilulio, "Reinventing Parole," p. 41.
55. Evans, Donald G., "Four States Experiment with Telephone Technology" (Telephone-Reporting Technology to Monitor Offenders), *Probation and Parole Forum* (December, 1995), vol. 57, no. 7, 170.
56. Evans, "Four States Experiment," p. 170.
57. Evans, "Four States Experiment," p. 170.
58. Evans, Donald G., "Probation and Police Collaboration: Promoting Public Safety," *Corrections Today*, (June, 1997), vol. 59, no. 3, 126(2).
59. Kehoe, Charles J., "Dramatic Changes in Store for Juvenile Probation Agencies" (Juveniles: A Generation at Risk), *Corrections Today* (December, 1994), vol. 56, no. 7, 96(3).
60. Kehoe, "Dramatic Changes in Store," p. 98.
61. Kehoe, "Dramatic Changes in Store," p. 97.

Chapter 7

Community Corrections and Intermediate Sanctions

Outline

Key Terms

intermediate sanctions
boot camps
community-based corrections
deinstitutionalization

A philosophy of revenge, followed by the dominant theme of restraint, characterized early penal institutions. In the United States, a humanitarian effort strongly influenced early correctional philosophy, with an emphasis on reformation of the individual. The Quakers thought this could be accomplished by giving the offender time to think and reflect, through religious training, and by isolating the offender from the harmful influence of questionable people. The emphasis was on the total institution, resulting in the removal of the individual from home and society. In that atmosphere, it was thought, the person could be rehabilitated.

The philosophy of rehabilitation has been challenged, resulting in a variety of trends in corrections. A return to retribution in sentencing has been one of the results. Another has been the emphasis on community-based treatment. One of the key words in corrections today is reintegration. Institutionalization has not been effective and has created more serious problems for offenders. Some argue that the emphasis should be on keeping as many offenders as possible in the community. "It is believed that reintegration of the offender with the law-abiding community . . . cannot be accomplished by isolating the offender in an artificial, custodial, setting."[1] This mentality has led to the creation of penalties considered to be less harsh than prison but more stringent than probation. These are known as **intermediate sanctions**. They include fines, parole, house monitoring, halfway houses, day treatment centers, **boot camps**, and intensive supervision probation (ISP).

This chapter explores the trend toward community-based corrections. A historical view of community corrections and the position taken by previous national commissions is discussed as well as various models, legislation, and recent trends in community-based corrections.

Later, the compliance of those sentenced to community-based corrections programs is explored, in addition to the findings of recent studies evaluating the effectiveness of intermediate sanctions imposed by the judicial system. Finally, we examine the need for research, and explore major perceptions and recommendations regarding intermediate sanctions.

7-1 Overview of Community-Based Corrections

7-1a History

Intermediate sanctions
Penalties considered to be not as harsh as prison but more stringent than probation. These include fines, parole, house monitoring, halfway houses, day treatment centers, boot camps, and intensive supervision probation (ISP).

Boot camps
A correctional program modeled after military boot camps and aimed at reforming first-time juvenile offenders.

Community-based corrections
An approach to punishment that emphasizes reintegration of the offender into the community through the use of local facilities.

The concept of **community-based corrections** has existed for centuries but the organized approach to this form of handling offenders is very recent. In the United States, this approach can be traced from the first halfway house in 1887 in New York City to a highly complex array of current programs. The major impetus for the movement was the Federal Prisoner's Rehabilitation Act of 1965 and the President's Crime Commission Report of 1967. The Prisoner's Rehabilition Act provided for furloughs, work release, and community treatment facilities for federal inmates. The President's Crime Commission Report stated that the new direction in corrections recognized that crime and delinquency are failures of the community and the individual offenders. The commission saw the task of corrections as one of reintegrating the offender into the community, restoring family ties, obtaining education or employment, and securing a place in the normal functioning of society. The commission said to achieve this requires changes in the community and the offender. The commission described the traditional method of institutionalizing offenders as a "fundamental deficiency in approach" and concluded that reintegration is "likely to be furthered much more readily by working with offenders in the community than by incarceration."

In 1973, the National Advisory Commission on Criminal Justice Standards and Goals called for an increased emphasis on probation, the most frequent form of sentencing. The commission concluded, "The most hopeful move toward effective corrections is to continue and strengthen the trend away from confining people in institutions and toward supervising them in the community."[2]

Why this movement? The National Advisory Commission stated the reasons:

> First, state institutions consume more than three-fourths of all expenditures for corrections while dealing with less than one-third of all offenders. Second, as a whole they do not deal with those offenders effectively. There is no evidence that prisons reduce the amount of crime. On the contrary, there is evidence that they contribute to criminal activity after the inmate is released.
>
> Prisons tend to dehumanize people...Prison regimentation makes prisoner's weaknesses worse and erodes their capacity for responsibility and self-government. Add to these facts the physical and mental conditions resulting from overcrowding and the various ways in which institutions ignore the rights of offenders, and the riots of the past decade are hardly surprising. Safety for society may be achieved for a limited time if offenders are kept out of circulation, but no real public protection is provided if confinement serves mainly to prepare men for more, and more skilled, criminality.[3]

The importance of integrating or reintegrating the offender into the community was emphasized by Paul C. Friday and Jerald Hage. After a brief look at the approaches used by sociologists to explain delinquent behavior, Friday and Hage employed those approaches to develop an integrated perspective. "The objective is to indicate what factors influence youth reliance on groups supporting delinquent values by considering the patterns of role relationships." They based their approach on the social integration theory of Durkheim.[4] Friday and Hage point out that for adolescents in our society, the development of an integrated role pattern is greatly hindered by the social structure of society, which often isolates them from basic social institutions. "When adolescents have meaningful kin, educational, work, and community relationships, they are more likely to become socialized to the dominant norms of society. Integration is facilitated by interaction across all role patterns." When these do not exist, a young person is more likely to move into deviant behavior, with the youth group being "the only meaningful role relationship."[5]

Reintegration of the offender into the community is not a one-way process. Lloyd E. Ohlin, Alden D. Miller, and Robert B. Coates, in their evaluation of **deinstitutionalization** in Massachusetts, emphasized the need for the community to take an active role in the process of treating the offender—a strategy they call advocacy—which goes beyond reintegration. They maintained that it might not be sufficient to try to reintegrate the offender into the community—the latter may need to change more than does the offender. For example, if resources for reintegration are not available, they must be developed. The advocacy approach involved getting the community to provide the resources for offenders.[6]

Deinstitutionalization
The process of institutional incarceration with community-based correctional facilities and programs.

7-1b Definition of Community-Based Programs

Ohlin, Miller, and Coates emphasized that the words "'community-based' focus attention on the nature of the links between programs and the community." When determining which programs are the least community-based and which are the most, one looks to the extent and quality of the relationships between those involved in the program—both clients and staff—and the community. For example, the old chain gangs (which are being reintroduced in some states), worked in the community but are not what we mean by community-based corrections.[7] "Generally, as the frequency, quality, and duration of community relationships increase, the program becomes more community-based."[8]

Community-based treatment should be distinguished from diversion, a term that often refers to community-based corrections. Technically, diversion means to turn the offender aside from the criminal (or juvenile) justice system. It should not be used to refer to "a different routing *within* the correctional component of this system." The appropriate term to use for the process of the "development and use of community-based correctional programs as alternatives to institutions" is the term deinstitutionalization.[9] Diversion is an important process that has implications for improvement of the system of corrections. This is true today, with the incarceration rate at an all-time high. While correctional facilities are attempting to "catch up" in their constructions, diversion of inmates may be the only option that correctional administrations have.

The concern over the definition of community corrections continues to haunt correctional administrators. In January 1995, during the Winter Conference in Dallas, the president of the American Correctional Association charged a Community Corrections Committee to prepare a statement describing the purpose and mission of community corrections. The committee, in response to the president's charge, decided that it would be necessary to develop a definition of community corrections before creating a mission statement and supporting principles.[10] However, the committee quickly realized that the task of defining community corrections was not an easy one. It was full of obstacles. In the past, most practitioners who attempted to define it have concentrated on the factors that do not make a program part of the community corrections family.

The committee continued to work on the challenge of defining community corrections at a meeting at the headquarters of the American Correctional Association (ACA) in Maryland on May 10, 1996. In arriving at the proposed definition, the committee made note of the fact that some elements of a definition needed to be taken for granted. These included the following:

- Community corrections is part of the justice system, which involves both adults and juveniles, and also includes a broader context containing elements of social justice.
- Community corrections agencies are involved in administering sanctions and providing services. Services are provided to victims, defendants, and offenders.
- Community corrections agencies acknowledge that they exist to enhance public safety.
- Community corrections is effective and efficient when it works in partnership with local communities and other agencies interested in safer communities and justice.[11]

Finally, the committee agreed that community corrections can be defined as the "part of the justice system providing sanctions and services to enhance public safety and maintain offenders/defendants within the community. These goals are accomplished by selecting appropriate participants, holding offenders accountable, repairing the harm done to victims and the community, supervising and treating offenders/defendants, involving citizens, and maintaining positive ties between the community and the offender."[12] Supporters of this definition argue that the most important component is the fact that it acknowledges that community corrections is a part of the broader justice system. Many praise this definition as it specifies the mechanisms that can be implemented to achieve the specified goals while acknowledging that the work of community sanctions is accomplished by keeping offenders within the community. The latter will continue to challenge corrections administrators as the citizenry demands more severe sanctions, most of which include long prison sentences.

7-2 Intermediate Sanctions

The demand for more intermediate sanctions comes from judges, correctional administrators, and the public. As explained earlier, most intermediate sanctions aim at punishing the offender while keeping him or her in the community. The advantages of this approach are numerous. For example, the offender may be able to keep his or her job and then continue to support any dependants. This will prevent the dependant family from drawing welfare or other types of social benefits. The community will benefit from these sanctions by not being forced to pay for the incarceration of the inmate. The increase in the number of people the department of corrections is supervising continues to justify intermediate sanctions. This is particularly true in jurisdictions where overcrowded prison conditions are forcing correctional administrators to take extraordinary measures (e.g., contracting out with a private prison facility, transferring inmates to other states). Overall, the benefits of intermediate sanctions are numerous and they vary according to the type of sanction being imposed. Spotlight 7-1 shows each of the major forms of intermediate sanctions in place today.

7-2a Four Major CCA Models

In the early 1970s, Minnesota, Iowa, and Colorado adopted Community Corrections Acts (CCAs) that were to serve as models for community corrections programming and financing in the following years. The implementation of these acts was largely a result of concerned professionals and community groups, with the aim of bringing funding to local and county agencies for the planning, development, and delivery of correctional services and sanctions at the local level.[13]

Spotlight 7-1

Forms of Intermediate Sanctions

1. **Fines**: The courts issue these very frequently. Statistics suggest that U.S. courts collect over $1 billion in fines every year. Fines are usually issued along with another type of sanction. For example, a judge may impose one year of probation and a fine of $300.
2. **Community Service**: This specific condition requires that the accused give a determined number of hours of free labor in public service. This includes cleaning a park, repairing an old house, or painting over a graffiti-covered wall. The idea is that the offender will be able to repair some or all of the damage that has been committed against the community. Some argue that this condition is beneficial psychologically to offenders who begin to take pride in their community and are less likely to commit another crime.
3. **Restitution**: This condition requires the offender to pay a specific sum of money to the victim, the victim's family, or a crime victim support fund. The assumption is that the offender will repair the wrongdoing via a financial contribution.
4. **Intensive Supervision Probation (ISP)**: These programs target offenders who are subject to incarceration and require a more intensive supervision of probationers. This attention is allowed as each ISP officer has a small caseload.
5. **Home Confinement**: Offenders under this program are sentenced to incarceration in their homes. The terms of home confinement vary from state to state. In some cases, home confinement programs allow offenders to leave their home for specific periods of the day. Others are more restrictive and do not allow the offender to leave the home at any time. The benefits of home confinement are numerous. It reduces or eliminates the cost associated with incarceration, can allow the offender to maintain a job, and does not break up the family composition.
6. **Shock Incarceration**: Offenders are sentenced to a jail or prison term for a specific amount of time. After the offender serves thirty to ninety days in jail or prison, a judge reduces the sentence and then releases the offender to the community under a probationary status. The idea is that the offender will be shocked after the prison experience to such an extent that he or she will be unlikely to engage in criminal activity in the future.
7. **Boot camps**: Offenders usually serve a short sentence and are then sent to a rigorous, military-like regimen. This program is aimed at developing discipline and respect for the law—it targets first time juvenile offenders. Boot camps usually last up to four months and contain routines full of physical training (PT), marches, drills, and hard labor. The success of these programs has been debated. Some argue that they offer a way to discipline those who are thought of as being impressionable, while others believe that these programs legitimize violence and make offenders more physically and emotionally fit to enhance their criminal careers.
8. **Halfway Houses**: Termed "halfway" as an indicator of their mission to incorporate an offender back into the community. Halfway houses are a middle point between prison and the community. These homes are usually located in residential settings, based on the rationale that the individual must heal and correct the errors in the same community that served as a backdrop to criminality.

Three decades later, more than half of the American states have implemented laws that are patterned after these early acts. It is imperative to examine the evolution, commonalities, differences, and various traits of these acts are examined in an attempt to identify their influence on the creation of what is now known as intermediate sanctions.

In 1973, Minnesota was the first state to adopt a CCA. State officials were interested in reducing fragmentation in service delivery, controlling costs, and redefining the population of offenders. At the time, local officials were willing to assume increased correctional responsibilities for less serious offenders as long as they were also given state subsidies.[14] Soon after, Iowa and Colorado followed the example set forth by Minnesota. All of the CCAs in these states reflected the characteristics, values, and attitudes of midwestern people. All of these acts placed a strong emphasis on "doing the right thing" while developing rational policies and humane practices. An additional model, which incorporated characteristics of the Minnesota and Colorado CCAs but also included unique elements, can be characterized as a southern model that began with the Virginia Community Diversion Incentive Act and later assumed a form that would be followed by the Tennessee CCA.

All four of these models shared a number of characteristics that have been replicated by other states. The original four Community Corrections Acts:

- Were legislatively authorized: Statues provided the framework and authority for the other defining features of CCAs.
- Were authorized statewide: CCAs mandated or authorized all localities, individually or in combination, to take advantage of the funds and authority granted.
- Provided for citizen participation: CCAs provided for citizen involvement and specified roles that citizens played.
- Defined an intergovernmental structure: CCAs delineated the roles to be performed and the power and authority to be exercised by involving state and local agencies or units of government.
- Required local planning: CCAs provided that local planning would precede and serve as the basis for the development, implementation, and modification of local correctional sanctions and services.
- Provided for state funding: CCAs provided for state subsidies to support local correctional programs and services.
- Called for decentralized program design and delivery: CCAs provided for local control of the processes employed to assess local needs, to establish local priorities, and to plan local programs.
- Endorsed locally determined sanctions and services: CCAs provided resources and authority for sanctions and services to be developed and delivered at the local level.[15]

Some argue that the original implementation of CCAs contributed to the creation of intermediate sanctions. Others have claimed that CCAs must be regarded as the equivalent of intermediate sanctions. Which one of these two positions is correct? The definition of intermediate sanctions is "dispositional options that lie between traditional probation and total confinement in state prisons on a spectrum of intrusiveness, level of punishment, and control."[16] Most of the literature suggests that the development of CCAs that took place in the 1970s influenced the creation of the first intermediate sanctions in the mid-1980s. It is argued that CCAs gave acceptance to the notion that sanctions needed to be implemented at the intermediate level. Whether CCAs are equivalent to intermediate sanctions depends upon the state implementing the CCA. For example, the early models were inclusive of all or most local correctional programs and services, including probation and parole. In the states that utilized these early models, CCAs included intermediate sanctions, but were not limited to midrange options. In other states such as Kansas and Indiana, the CCAs that were adopted did not provide for the integration of probation and parole services. Consequently, some CCAs have focused largely on intermediate sanctions but others have included probation, parole, and other services. Some of the other areas in which CCAs are different include the extent of decentralization of correctional services, the nature of citizen participation, the relative emphasis on deinstitutionalization, and the level of focus on rehabilitation of offenders through community-based approaches.[17]

The contribution of CCAs toward the development of intermediate sanctions is unprecedented. Many have argued that without CCAs, no state would have ever implemented what is now known as intermediate sanctions. It is imperative to understand the benefits and lessons taught by the creation and implementation of the original four CCA models in order to better understand the function of community corrections. The commonalities, differences, and some of the contributions of these four original CCA models represent those in other states that have since enacted legislation for the purpose of modifying or creating community corrections programs. The following is a discussion of one of the original CCA models (Minnesota) and the implementation of the first CCA in the state of Michigan.

Minnesota

Kenneth F. Schoen, Commissioner of the Minnesota Department of Corrections, gave his opinion of Minnesota's statutory response to the move toward community-based corrections:

> Incarceration is extremely expensive and it does not affect crime rates. The Minnesota Community Corrections Act changes the role of corrections. Instead of serving to cage society's rejects, corrections becomes a joint effort by the community and the offender to reintegrate that offender into society. If we want a more realistic approach to corrections, this act represents an option well worth considering.[18]

For each offender committed to a Minnesota state facility, a "charge-back" from the state subsidy was given to the community, which served as a powerful incentive against state commitment. If a county wished to participate in the Community Corrections Act, it had to select a local advisory board for corrections, composed of local citizens and persons from the local criminal justice system. The board had to devise a plan for community corrections and then submit the plan to the county commissioners. If approved, the plan then had to be submitted to the State Commissioner of Corrections. If the latter thought the plan was workable, the subsidy from the state began. The amount that each county received in state subsidy was determined by a formula based on the correctional needs, population, and financial resources of the county, minus projected costs for the number of people the county committed to state institutions, as well as any other state subsidies received by the county.[19]

Did the plan achieve its goals? The first goal, reduction of state commitments, occurred. The second goal, increased cost-effectiveness, was more difficult to measure. Schoen said that in the long run, the second goal was probably reached, but in the short run, the state had to operate parallel systems of corrections. The third goal was to decrease the demand for state institutions, which would eventually be phased out. That did not happen.When the plan was implemented in 1973, the demand for increased incarceration began.

Critics of the Minnesota plan have pointed out that there has been no indication that serving time in jail is more therapeutic for inmates than serving time in prison, and the inclusion of jails in the program is therefore questionable. The formula used for determining the subsidy has also been the source of criticism as the greater needs of high-crime urban areas were not taken into consideration.

Criminologist David Ward stated:

> [I]t has yet to be proven to me that local communities can do a better job at providing services or that program interest is high at the community level. I think these people have good intentions, but it has been my experience with community groups that they're not sophisticated enough to stick with programs, and in the end they wind up being taken over by professionals. I'm skeptical that communities can be made to become more responsive and effective.[20]

Michigan

In Michigan, probation first became viable in the early twentieth century. It was not until the early 1900s that the state assumed responsibility for offenders other than those who were committed to state prisons. In 1937, the Model Corrections Act created the Michigan Department of Corrections (MDOC).[21] It provided state-funded probation services for the first time. However, no other community alternatives were offered until the 1960s when the MDOC implemented a work pass/release program for state prison inmates. In 1975, Governor William Milliken officially acknowledged the problem of prison overcrowding and requested that the other agencies of government assist in solving the problem. The director of corrections at the time, Perry Johnson, implemented the Probation Incentive Program, through which the state reimbursed counties that diverted offenders to local intermediate sanctions programs. This was later aided by funds available through the Law Enforcement Assistance Administration.

After the request made by director Johnson, the Michigan legislature funded two community corrections programs and a residential probation program in Detroit in 1977. That same year the Michigan State Senate introduced the first formal legislation aimed specifically at subsidizing local community-based programs. In 1981, after a series of prison riots, community corrections legislation was reintroduced in the state of Michigan. This legislation proposed subsidies to counties as well as legislation allowing two-year jail sentences. Finally, in 1989, the Michigan Community Corrections Act (Public Act 511) became law. Not only did the CCA create an autonomous agency, but it also required that advisory boards be established for the purpose of developing and implementing community corrections plans. The CCA had specific language regarding the aims of diverting sentences: "The plan shall include . . . provisions that detail how the city, county, or counties plan to substantially reduce, within one year, the use of prison sentences for felons for which the state felony sentencing guidelines upper limit for the recommended minimum sentence is twelve months or less."[22]

According to reports, Michigan's CCA is regarded as an enormous success. Since it was enacted, most of Michigan's eighty-three counties have voluntarily formed local advisory boards, which are made up of local corrections officials, judges, prosecutors, law enforcement agents, and local government representatives. Michigan's CCA has also expanded the use of intermediate sanctions in local jurisdictions. As a proportion of all sentences, it is reported that prison dispositions decreased from 37.2 percent in 1989 to 29.3 percent in 1993. Data obtained from the Michigan Department of Corrections (2002) suggested that this this trend has continued.[23] In addition, the implementation of Michigan's CCA, community service work, electronic monitoring, day reporting, employment, drug testing, and treatment programs have been expanded in most communities in the state. These programs are helpful to corrections officials in the monitoring of offenders in the community, they enhance public safety, and increase the accountability of Michigan's criminal justice system. It must be noted that the reported success has been overshadowed by the continued growth of the state's inmate population. This growth, as is the case in many other states, can be attributed to the passage of more than one hundred state statutes that have increased penalties and the use of prison sentences. In Michigan, these laws include prison sentences for third-offense drunk driving and for those found guilty of possession of fifty grams or less of a controlled substance.[24]

7-2b The Classification Process

Inmates facing the possibility of being sentenced to an intermediate sanction are subject to the classification process. This process is different in every jurisdiction. However, many jurisdictions have recently begun to classify their inmates inside jail facilities. This is particularly important for correctional administrators who claim to have the advantage of placing low-risk offenders in intermediate sanction programs by classifying inmates early in the process. The intermediate sanction sentence is influenced by both the classification process and judicial discretion.

Correctional administrators are not the only group that classifies inmates. Those who make policy also need to frequently select target populations as they test new programs, especially in the area of community corrections. For the past few years, policymakers have begun to use data on jail populations as they consider implementing new, innovative programs in this area. The data includes admission date, pre/post-sentence, primary offense severity, classification level and date classified, release reason and release date. Breaking down this data can often lead policymakers to not only target a particular group, but also to gain insight of the two main factors driving jail populations: admissions and length of stay.[25]

A data-driven policy approach to selecting target populations for intermediate sanctions and community corrections must begin with an understanding of the individual passing through the jail facility. Two of the most frequently selected inmate populations targeted for diversion from jail are those placed on pre-trial status and minimum-security inmates.[26] Inmates who have not yet faced trial (especially if they are nonviolent and have no prior assault record, no escape history, no warrants, and no institutional problems) are prime candidates for placement on some type of intermediate sanction.

As Americans become conscious of the prejudices that exist in the criminal justice system, more and more classification procedures will be adopted by jail and prison administrators in their attempt to make the process as objective as possible. This will be the subject of criticism as it is argued that the basis used to send an individual to prison, or some form of intermediate sanction, is biased and unfair to the disadvantaged.

7-2c The Effectiveness and Enforcement of Intermediate Sanctions

Effectiveness

The history of CCAs, the classification methods used when considering recipients of intermediate sanctions, and the effectiveness of those programs is important. To determine whether these goals have been reached, several studies are reviewed. A survey that was conducted on convicted adult felons placed on state probation in 1986 tracked 12,370 probationers for a period of three years, from 1986 to 1989.[27] The purpose was to explore the effectiveness and compliance of some forms of intermediate sanctions. Statistically weighted, the sample of 12,370 represented 79,000 probationers. The sanctions that were considered included:

- Alcohol treatment
- Counseling
- Drug treatment

- Residential placement
- Drug testing
- House arrest
- Day reporting
- Intensive supervision
- Split sentence
- Community service
- Supervision fees
- Victim restitution[28]

The preliminary results indicated that sizable numbers were discharged from probation before having fully complied with their specific condition. These included 24 percent of those ordered to participate in alcohol treatment, 20 percent ordered for mental health counseling, 32 percent ordered for drug treatment, 25 percent ordered to be placed in residential facilities, 33 percent ordered for drug testing, 31 percent ordered for house arrest, 35 percent ordered for day reporting, 21 percent ordered to perform community service, 69 percent ordered to pay supervision fees, and 40 percent ordered to make restitution. When considered together, 49 percent of those sanctioned were found to have been in noncompliance at the time of their probation discharge. Further analysis indicated that of those who did not comply, only 21 percent had been punished with jail confinement for their noncompliance.[29]

The author of this study, Patrick Langan, argued that there may be several reasons why intermediate sanctions were not working or were not being enforced. He suggested that lack of adequate resources for enforcing and monitoring drug tests, house arrests, community service, payment of fines, and treatment participation could be to blame. Although budgetary restrictions were not the only reason for the high incidence of noncompliance of intermediate sanctions, they may be partially responsible. The budgetary situation is so grave that according to the author, prison, jail, parole, and probation populations all tripled in size from 1977 to 1990. Yet, only spending for prisons and jails have increased. Specifically, "In 1990, prison and jail spending accounted for two cents of every state and local dollar spent, twice the amount spent in 1977. Spending for probation and parole accounted for two-tenths of one cent of every dollar spent in 1990, unchanged from what it was in 1977."[30] Recent data suggests that this trend continues. According to the Bureau of Justice Statistics (2002), in 1999 the nation spent $146.5 million on the federal, state, and local justice systems.[31] Based on this information, the cost per inmate in 1999 was as follows:

- Corrections, spending alone: $26, 134 per inmate
- Corrections, judicial and legal costs: $43,297 per inmate
- Corrections, judicial, legal, and police costs: $78,154 per inmate[32]

Critics who object to the increasing cost of incarceration and support the notion that more funds should be appropriated for intermediate sanctions argue that these effectively reduce recidivism rates while decreasing the prison population. Approximately two dozen major reviews of the existing literature that explored what works have been conducted in the last fifteen years.[33] Although the items mentioned in each study vary from program to program, some common characteristics are shared by most of the sucessful intermediate sanction programs. This was determined by low recidivism rates. These characteristics are listed in Spotlight 7-2.

Unlike successful programs, unsuccessful services offered usually target low-risk offenders and noncriminological needs such as anxiety, depression, and self-

Spotlight 7-2

Characteristics of Successful Intermediate Sanction Programs

1. Services are intensive and last three to nine months. These services are based on pscyhological, cognitive, and social learning theories and are used for higher risk offenders.
2. Services target criminological needs. These include antisocial attitudes and values.
3. The style and mode of treatment is matched to the learning style and personality of the offender.
4. The behavior exhibited directly influences the reinforcement of the program. Contingencies are enforced in a firm, but fair, manner. Positive reinforcement (e.g., tangible rewards, activities, social reinforcers) is used much more frequently than punishment (e.g., fines and restitution). The reported ratio is four to one.
5. Most therapists relate to offfenders in sensitive and constructive ways and are trained and supervised appropriately.
6. The structure of programs and their activities disrupt the criminal network by placing offenders in situations in which pro-social activities predominate.

Source: Paul Gendreau (February, 1995), "Examining What Works in Community Corrections," *Corrections Today*, vol. 57, no. 1. p. 28(3). Reprinted with permission of the American Correctional Association, Lanham, MD.

esteem. They have also relied on Freudian psychodynamic and Rogerian nondirective therapies. They have frequently used medical model approaches such as drug treatments and "punishing smarter" approaches such as Intensive Supervision Probation (ISP) and boot camps.[34]

The success rate of modern intermediate sanctions (e.g., boot camps) is also being questioned. The main goal of boot camps is to develop discipline and respect for authority through a military-like regimen. They have been the subject of criticism due to increasing incidents involving the abuse of power. An example of this is found in the boot camps in Wisconsin and Oklahoma, which were the subject of an investigation by their respective state legislatures.[35] The most cited criticism comes from criminologist Doris MacKenzie of the University of Maryland, who completed a study of boot camps. She found that boot-camp graduates had the same rate of recidivism as did felons released from traditional prisons (approximately 30 to 40 percent).[36] Her conclusion was that boot camps do not work. This is because the offender, upon successful completion of the boot camp program, is released to the same crime-ridden neighborhood from which he or she came. These criticisms, although growing, are still meeting resistance from the true believers in the effectiveness of boot camps. Supporters of these camps argue that MacKenzie's figures are not accurate because every boot camp is run differently. Some operate strictly on a military format, while others offer more integrated programs. Supporters also add that most recidivists who successfully graduated from boot camps were being sent back to prison for technical parole violations. It is unclear which position is accurate; however, the effectiveness of this form of intermediate sanctions will continue to be questioned as more of these programs are established.

Enforcement

As a result of the large number of individuals who do not comply with the conditions set forth by intermediate sanctions, there are negative ramifications. It is estimated that each of the offenders who does not comply with these conditions will require at least one court hearing. At the national level, this means that up to 1.5 million offenders require at least one more additional court hearing and modification of their sentence.[37] This noncompliance adds significantly to the current budgetary and personnel burden experienced by the criminal justice system. In the past several years, some parole and probation agencies have begun to examine the processes with the goal of increasing compliance and reducing the amount of violations. Most of these agencies have started to focus on policies and practices within probation and parole services to improve offender accountability and agency response. A researcher of criminal justice policies, Peggy Burke, pointed out:

> We realized that it was not simply a revocation decision that was the issue—but rather how the system responded to violations. We began seeing revocation as only one piece of a process that began with release and the setting of conditions, involved the supervision process in its entirety, and focused particularly on how the system responded to violation behavior, even short of the issuance of a formal violation report or a revocation.... There is something that lies between benign neglect, or "letting it slide" on the one hand, and revocation and reincarceration on the other for parole violators. Their behavior presents a range of severity or danger to the community. Surely probation and parole agencies' responses to these behaviors might well be structured along some continuum of intermediate sanctions, in much the same way that an initial sentencing decision might be made. And this might well yield supervision of offenders, more responsible use of resources, and perhaps even better outcomes with offenders.[38]

Many agencies are realizing that not all noncompliant behavior deserves the same attention. The type of noncompliant behavior is assessed and then ranked according to its level of seriousness. This ranking usually determines how the probation agency will respond. In most cases, the more serious behavior is forwarded to the court, while the less serious is handled by the probation agency. The state of South Carolina is one of the jurisdictions that has developed guidelines for the purpose of ranking violators. Its program is an aggressive attempt to formalize responses to noncompliant behavior. In South Carolina, violation behavior is categorized on the basis of the offense and risk imposed. The following categories are included:

- **Category A** This category involves the most serious violations, with the agent issuing a warrant or citation. These violations include convictions for a new offense, a second violation of home detention, the failure to report within thirty days, the possession of a weapon, the failure to pay financial penalties within six months, and termination from community service due to unsatisfactory performance.
- **Category B** The violations that occur in this category indicate the offender is unwilling to cooperate or is demonstrating signs of community instability, such as unacceptable employment or residence patterns. The agent has the choice to place the offender in an intermediate sanction program or to simply refer the entire case to a hearing officer.
- **Category C** Minor violations take place within this category and are usually resolved at the supervisory level.[39]

In South Carolina, the violation process begins once an offender violates any of the conditions of release prescribed by the courts. At that time, the agent has a series of options, including reprimands, counseling, treatment referrals, day-care placement, restructured supervision plans, increased drug testing, and increased supervision contacts. If the agent is not fully satisfied with the response, he or she still has other options. These include placing the offender in a halfway house for up to seventy-five days, increasing the number of public service hours, and imposing other unlimited conditions.[40] If the offender continues to violate his or her conditions of release, a warrant is usually issued. Once this occurs, the offender is mandated to appear before an administrative hearing officer who usually determines whether incarceration is necessary given the severity of the offense and the potential risk the offender poses to the community. The hearing officer can determine whether a partial or full revocation from probation is appropriate. The enforcement process in South Carolina is an illustration of many systems that are currently in place through the United States. In some cities, such as Seattle, an individual who does not appear before a hearing officer is considered a fugitive. The individual is apprehended by the Fugitive Apprehension Team, which has recently been created to protect the community.[41]

7-2d Sex Offenders: Community Corrections Bound?

Although unthinkable to many, statistics suggest that sexual offenders are often released to the community while they are monitored or registered as offenders. According to a study by The Bureau of Justice Statistics (1997), in 1994, almost 60 percent of the 234,000 convicted sex offenders that were under the care, custody, or control of corrections were on probation or parole. This same report estimated that approximately 99,300 offenders convicted of rape or sexual assault were housed in local jails or state/federal prison facilities. Further, approximately 134,300 convicted offenders were under some form of correctional supervision in the community. This included parole or probation.[42]

When compared to national correctional trends, the Bureau of Justice Statistics (1997) suggests that sexual offenders constitute approximately 4.7 percent of the almost five million offenders who were under the supervision of the correctional system in 1994. In that same year, sex offenders comprised:

- 1 percent of the federal prison population
- 9.7 percent of the state prison population
- 3.4 percent of jail inmates
- 3.6 percent of offenders on probation
- 4 percent of all offenders on parole[43]

The Bureau of Justice Statistics study showed that sex offenders are more likely than other violent offenders to be rearrested for a new offense when discharged from prison or probation.[44] It is not surprising that with the growing concern over crime, citizens are less willing to tolerate a sexual predator living in their community—even if the sex offender is fulfilling all aspects of their court sentence. Evidence of this can be traced to the passage of Megan's Law, which mandates public notification of the whereabouts of sex offenders. Although this law prohibits neighbors of sex offenders from seeking retribution against the offender, it enhances the possibility of labeling.[45]

In March 1998, the Bureau of Justice Statistics established the National Sex Offender Registry Assistance Program (NSOR-AP). This program assists states in their efforts to participate in the FBI's permanent National Sex Offender Registry (NSOR). This federal registry contains a database of all registered sex offenders in the United States.[46] It is believed tracking sex offenders is helpful in the overall effort of law enforcement personnel to solve sex-related crimes. Further, the NSOR is currently surveying states in an attempt to evaluate their offender registries while identifying areas of priority. Despite the law enforcement claims that keeping a current federal registry of sex offenders will be helpful to authorities when a sex crime is commited, many individuals and advocacy groups (e.g., ACLU) have expressed concerns regarding this effort. Some of the criticisms are based on alleged violations of civil and constitutional rights. The debate over the registry of sex offenders has also focused on the potential for rehabilitating these offenders once they reenter the community. If offenders are tracked and must be part of a registry, they may be less likely to change their criminal activities.

7-2e The Need for Further Research

In addition to the mandate of registering sex offenders, there are other sanctions that accompany those being released conditionally. They are called intermediate sanctions. Although some research is available on intermediate sanctions, there is still a need for more detailed information regarding these alternative programs. The need for further data is fueled by the overcrowding currently facing most correctional institutions. More detailed research in the area could assist policymakers in determining appropriate sanctions for offenders. According to Lawrence Bennett, "Research has provided a good deal of information that can benefit administrators in planning intermediate sanction and community correction programs. However, it is obvious that more research needs to be done to help practitioners determine not only what programs work but also which aspects of each program play critical roles in observed outcomes."[47] Perhaps the source of concern is the September 11 terrorist attacks which have prompted people to be unconcerned with the reintegration of inmates and society. If this were to occur, research on intermediate sanctions would be immediately affected, leaving many questions still unanswered.

7-2f Perceptions of Intermediate Sanctions

Supporters of intermediate sanctions have become increasingly concerned about the public perception of sanctions as a form of punishment. This is particularly relevant in our current society in which political figures base their stance on a particular issue on public opinion polls. Some argue that intermediate sanctions have the same punitive effect as prison sentences. However, very little research in this area suggests a verdict one way or another. In Minnesota, a groundbreaking study was conducted to explore the perceptions of intermediate sanctions as a form of punishment.[48] The study was designed to measure how offenders and staff in Minnesota rank the severity of several criminal sanctions and which specific sanctions they judge as being equivalent in punitiveness.

The study offered various results. First, the study discovered that some intermediate sanctions equate, in terms of punitiveness, with prison. For example, inmates viewed one year in prison as equivalent in severity to three years of intensive probation supervision or one year in jail, while at the same time, they viewed six months in jail as equivalent to one year of intensive supervision. Inmates and staff ranked most sanctions in the same way but the staff ratings were higher for three and six months in jail and lower for one and five years of probation. These two groups differed on the difficulty of complying with individual probation conditions. The staff judged most probation conditions as being harder for offenders to comply with than did inmates. The findings of this study also suggested that it is no longer necessary to equate criminal punishment with prison alone.[49] The results determined that at some level of intensity and length, intensive probation and prison are equally severe, and that probation may actually be the least desirable form of punishment.[50] These findings are important as a warning sign to political figures who pride themselves in their belief that the longer they incarcerate offenders, the more effective they are in reducing the fear of crime among the citizenry.

7-2g Recommendations

During the 125th Congress of Corrections which was held on August 9, 1995, in Cincinnati, the American Correctional Association's executive committee approved nine legislative position statements. Of these, one pertained to community corrections and intermediate sanctions.[51] During this meeting, it was asserted that support needed to be given to community corrections while increasing the use of intermediate sanctions. The American Correctional Association (ACA) made a statement supporting a balanced approach to crime reduction that included a range of criminal justice services, including confinement in prison or jail, community corrections, intermediate sanctions, and other nonincarcerative options for nonviolent offenders. One of the most important recognitions the ACA made pertains to the combination of incarceration with other effective programs aimed at prevention, policing, punishment, treatment, restitution, reparation, and education. The ACA statement concluded by making a strong statement calling for adequate funding to federal, state, and local governments for construction and operation of correctional facilities and programs for a complete range of effective interventions.[52]

Others argue that correctional intervention at the community level needs to have a more restorative perspective. They feel that restorative justice:

- Holds the offender directly accountable to the individual victim and the community affected by the criminal act
- Requires the offender to take responsibility to "make things whole again," to the degree that it is possible
- Provides victims purposeful access to the court and correctional processes, which allows them to shape offender obligations
- Encourages the community to become involved in supporting victims, holding offenders accountable, and providing opportunities for offenders to reintegrate into the community[53]

To achieve and institute the restorative perspective, the Community Corrections Acts should be amended. Despite the fact that CCAs provide states with a subsidy and an authority to plan and implement correctional programs, they have not achieved a satisfactory level for victims. Victims are often forced to reenact or relive the traumatic criminal episode that they experienced, at the request of the criminal justice system. In order for the system to be successful, it must include the protection of fundamental rights.[54] It is not clear if these recommendations will work. However, community corrections and intermediate sanctions will continue to change as they become one of the preferred methods of punishment in the United States.

Summary

In 1972, the National Advisory Commission Progress Report stated that "the thrust towards community-based corrections supports the most significant philosophical trend corrections has experienced in years."[55] In this chapter, a brief discussion of the historic concept of community-based corrections was examined. Although the concept has been around for centuries, the organization and systematization of community-based corrections in this country is a relatively recent phenomenon, gaining its greatest impetus from the 1967 President's Crime Commission Report. The emphasis then became reintegration of the offender, which replaced the emphasis on rehabilitation, resulting in suspended philosophies of revenge, restraint, and reformation. A growing awareness that traditional, costly institutionalization of offenders was not achieving the goal of rehabilitation, along with the increasing evidence of the harmful effects of imprisonment, fueled the movement.

After examining the meaning of community corrections, the major forms of intermediate sanctions being implemented today, including fines, community service, restitution, intensive supervision probation (ISP), home confinement, shock incarceration, and boot camps were discussed. In addition, the various community corrections systems that were implemented in four states served as models for other states in their attempt to establish community correctional programs. The legislative movement and its influence on the creation and implementation of community corrections acts (CCAs) throughout the country, as well as a brief explanation of the classification process which determines whether offenders are fit to participate in intermediate sanction programs, was outlined. Finally, various issues pertaining to the effectiveness, enforcement, and perception of intermediate sanctions were examined and it has been found that further research in this area is needed as well as a series of recommendations to improve the quality of intermediate sanctions in the future.

The movement toward community-based treatment may represent a desperate attempt to do something without knowledge of its impact. Disillusionment over attempts at rehabilitation through institutionalized treatment has led to the current trend toward harsher sentencing for serious offenders, decriminalization of juvenile status offenders, and the increased use of community-based treatment. The largest problem is that when citizens adopt a new approach, that approach is burdened with the responsibility of reducing the crime rate. It may be that the burden of reducing recidivism is too great for any treatment method or approach and other measures of success or failure should be explored.

Notes

1. Klapmuts, Nora, "Community Alternatives to Prison," Chapter 15 in *Community Health and the Criminal Justice System,* John Monahan, ed. (New York: Penguin Press, Inc., 1976), p. 206.
2. National Advisory Commission on Criminal Justice Standards and Goals, *A National Strategy To Reduce Crime* (Washington, D.C.: U.S. Government Printing Office, 1973), p. 121.
3. *A National Strategy To Reduce Crime,* p.121.
4. Durkheim, Emile, *Suicide* (New York: Free Press, 1951).
5. Friday, Paul C., and Hage, Jerald, "Youth Crime in Postindustrial Societies: An Integrated Perspective," *Criminology* 14 (November, 1976), 347–367; quotations are on pp. 348–349, 365, 366.
6. Ohlin, Lloyd E., Miller, Alden D., and Coates, Robert B., *Juvenile Correctional Reform in Massachusetts, A Preliminary Report of the Center for Criminal Justice of the Harvard Law School,* National Institute for Justice and Delinquency Prevention, LEAA (Washington, D.C., 1997).
7. Ohlin, Miller, and Coates, *Juvenile Correction Reform,* p. 23.
8. Rutherford, Andrew, and Bengur, Osman, *Community Based Alternatives to Juvenile Incarceration,* National Evaluation Program; Phase I, Summary Report, National Institute of Law Enforcement and Criminal Justice, LEAA (Washington, DC: U.S. Government Printing Office, 1976), p. 11.
9. Vinter, Robert D., Downs, George, and Halls, John, "Juvenile Corrections in the States: Residential Programs and Deinstitutionalization: A Preliminary Report" (Ann Arbor: University of Michigan Press, 1975).
10. Evans, Donald G., "Defining Community Corrections," *Corrections Today,* October 1996) vol. 58, no. 6, 124 (2).
11. Evans, "Defining Community Corrections," 124 (2).
12. Evans, "Defining Community Corrections," 124 (2).
13. Harris, Kay, "Key Differences Among Community Corrections Acts in the United States: An Overview," *The Prison Journal* 76:2 (1996), 192–238.
14. Harris, "Key Differences,"192(47).
15. Harris, "Key Differences," 192(47).
16. Harris, "Key Differences," 192(47).
17. Harris, "Key Differences," 192(47).
18. Schoen, Kenneth F., "The Community Corrections Act," *Crime and Delinquency* 24 (October, 1978), 464.
19. Minn. Stat. Ann. and 401.01 et seq. (West).
20. Quoted in "Minnesota's Community Corrections Act Takes Hold," *Corrections Magazine* 4 (March, 1978), 54.
21. Clark, Patrick M., "The Evolution of Michigan's Community Corrections Act" (Michigan Community Corrections Act), *Corrections Today* (February 1995), vol. 57, no. 1, 38(3).
22. Clark, "Evolution," 38(3).
23. Michigan Department of Corrections. Office of Community Corrections (2002), Annual Report. http://www.michigan.gov/documents/occannual_4987_7.pdf

24. Clark, "Evolution," 38(3).
25. Wells, David, and Brennan, Tim, "Jail Classification: Improving Link to Intermediate Sanctions," *Corrections Today* (February, 1995), vol. 57, no. 1, 58(4).
26. Wells and Brennan, "Jail Classification," 58(4).
27. Langan, Patrick A., "Between Prison and Probation: Intermediate Sanctions," *Science* (May 6, 1994), vol. 264, no. 5160, 791(3).
28. Langan, "Between Prison and Probation," 791(3).
29. Langan, "Between Prison and Probation," 791(3).
30. Gifford, Sidra Lea, U.S. Department of Justice, Bureau of Justice Statistics, Justice Expenditure and Employment in the United States, 1999 (Washington, D.C.: U.S. Department of Justice, February 2002), p. 4, Table 6; Beck, Allen J., PhD, and Jennifer C. Karberg, U.S. Department of Justice, Bureau of Justice Statistics, *Prison and Jail Inmates at Midyear 2000* (Washington, D.C.: U.S. Department of Justice, March 2001), p. 2, Table 1.31.
31. Ibid.
32. Gendreau, Paul, and Paparozzi, Mario A., "Examining What Works in Community Corrections," *Corrections Today* (February, 1995), vol. 57, no. 1, 28(3).
33. Gendreau and Paparozzi, "Examining What Works," 28(3).
34. Sileo, Chi Chi, "Abuse, Absolution Found at Boot Camp" (Failure of Alternative Prisons that Provide Discipline and Training in Behavior Modification), *Insight on the News* (June 27, 1994), vol. 10, no. 26, 6(5).
35. Sileo, "Abuse, Absolution," 6(5).
36. Taxman, Faye S., "Intermediate Sanctions: Dealing with Technical Violators," *Corrections Today* (February 1995), vol. 57, no. 1, 46(7).
37. Taxman, "Intermediate Sanctions," 46(7).
38. Taxman, "Intermediate Sanctions," 46(7).
39. Taxman, "Intermediate Sanctions," 46(7).
40. Olsson, Kurt S., "CCO Leaves No Stone Unturned in Tracking Down Fugitives" (Seattle Fugitive Apprehension Team Corrections Officer Sean Zelka), *Corrections Today* (June, 1996), vol. 58, no. 3, 88(1).
41. Bureau of Justice Statistics, U.S. Department of Justice(1997), *Sex Offenses and Offenders*, Washington, D.C.
42. Bureau of Justice Statistics, *Sex Offenses and Offenders*, 1997.
43. McMurry, Kelley, "Fewer Sex Offenders on Community Release Programs Than Other Criminals," *Trial* 33 (April, 1997), no. 4, 88–89.
44. Bureau of Justice Statistics, *Sex Offenses and Offenders*, 1997
45. Bureau of Justice Statistics, U.S. Department of Justice (2002), *Summary of State Sex Offenders Registries*, 2001, Washington, D.C.
46. Bennett, Lawrence A., "Current Findings on Intermediate Sanctions and Community Corrections," *Corrections Today* (February, 1995), vol. 57, no. 1, p.86(4).
47. Petersilia, Joan, and Piper Deschenes, Elizabeth, "Perceptions of Punishment: Inmates and Staff Work the Severity of Prison versus Intermediate Sanctions," *Prison Journal* (September, 1994), vol. 74, no. 3, 306(23).
48. Petersilia and Piper Deschenes, "Perceptions of Punishment," 306(23).
49. Petersilia and Piper Deschenes, "Perceptions of Punishment," 306(23).
50. Smith Ingley, Gwyn, "Position Statements Released" (Legislative Priorities on Corrections) (Legislative Issues), *Corrections Today* (April, 1996), vol. 58, no. 2, 206(3).
51. Smith Ingley, "Position Statements," 206(3).
52. Carey, Mark, "Restorative Justice in Community Corrections," *Corrections Today* (August, 1996), vol. 58, no. 5, 152(4).
53. Carey, "Restorative Justice," 152(4).
54. U.S. Department of Justice, *Progress Report of the National Advisory Commission on Criminal Justice Standards and Goals* (Washington, D.C.: U.S. Government Printing Office, 1972), p. 32.
55. U.S. Department of Justice, *Progress Report of the National Advisory Commission on Criminal Justice Standards and Goals* (Washington, D.C.: U.S. Government Printing Office, 1972), p. 32.

Chapter 8

Modern Prisons: Classification and Correctional Programs

Outline

Early advocates of imprisonment in this country believed that incarceration was not only an appropriate form of punishment but that it would also have a reforming effect on offenders. The Pennsylvania System was based on the assumption that if offenders had time to think, reflect, and to read and study the Bible, they would repent and be reformed. In the Auburn System, whipping was assumed to have a reforming effect. Wardens believed that the inmate's spirit had to be broken before reformation could take place. Later, reformers argued that hard work would have a corrective effect on inmates. Others emphasized vocational training as a prerequisite for changing the offender.

Since the latter part of the twentieth century, reformation of offenders was considered through a medical model. This model is based on the principles of diagnosis and treatment utilized, with the hope of an eventual cure of the patient. In the process of applying this model, various forms of treatment programs were developed to aid in rehabilitation. More recently, the philosophies of reform and rehabilitation have been questioned. In the current climate, many members of society believe that treatment has not worked and we should return to a philosophy of retribution or just deserts. People feel that prison should be a place of punishment and not a source of rehabilitation. They feel that inmates should not enjoy any free services for which citizens in the community have to pay. According to the principle of least eligibility, inmates should be the least eligible of all citizens to receive any social benefits beyond those required by the law. If this principle were taken to the

Key Terms

principle of least eligibility
Federal Bureau of Prisons
supermax prisons
maximum-security prisons
medium-security prisons
minimum-security prisons
classification clinic
integrated classification system
diagnostic/reception center
reception program
individual psychotherapy
group psychotherapy
reality therapy
transactional analysis
social therapies
behavior modification
lease system
contract system
piece-price system
public (state) account system
state-use system

Principle of least eligibility The idea that inmates should be the least eligible of all citizens to receive any social benefits beyond those required by the law.

extreme, it would prohibit inmates from receiving a free college education while in prison. In reality, this principle has created many problems for correctional administrators. They face constant criticisms from the public for the free services provided to inmates. People feel that it is not fair for law-abiding citizens who have obeyed the rules pay for services that law-breakers receive free.

The principle of least eligibility has also influenced the performance and existence of prison programs. Inmates should have the opportunity to be rehabilitated but no one wants to incur the monetary cost associated with the funding of such programs. The result is that most prison programs suffer from inadequate funding, poor staffing, and poor success rates. Inmates who claim that it is their constitutional right to have a sex change operation or receive plastic surgery have provoked some of the public criticisms of prison programs. In their claims, inmates have argued that a denial of their request constitutes a violation of their constitutional rights. Such claims anger people who feel that these luxuries should not be funded by taxpayers.

In this chapter, programs designed to aid in the reformation and rehabilitation of inmates and the techniques that have been used are discussed. The organization of corrections and the examination of the classification process of correctional institutions and inmates is outlined. This is very important in determining which inmates are placed in treatment programs. Finally, treatment, educational, and vocational programs are explored, focusing on the various effects of incarceration.

8-1 Organization of Corrections

There are various systems of corrections in the United States. One system is administered at the federal level while the others are managed in each of the fifty states. Since all these systems differ in their operations, management, and programs, the statement can be made that there are fifty-one correctional systems in the United States.

8-1a The Federal Bureau of Prisons

Federal Bureau of Prisons Institution created in 1929 by the House Special Committee on Federal Penal and Reformatory Institutions.

The **Federal Bureau of Prisons** was created in 1929 by the House Special Committee on Federal Penal and Reformatory Institutions. After much deliberation, this committee offered various recommendations, including the establishment of a centralized administration of federal prisons at the bureau level, increased expenditure for federal probation officers, the establishment of a full-time parole board, and the provision of facilities by the District of Columbia for its inmates. President Hoover signed this legislation into law on May 14, 1930, creating what is now known as the Federal Bureau of Prisons within the U.S. Department of Justice.

Today, the Federal Bureau of Prisons oversees 102 correctional institutions throughout the United States. As of January 2002, the total number of inmates it supervises is 156,879 (130,692 in Bureau of Prison facilities and 12,660 in privately managed facilities). These privately managed facilities are run by the private sector under contract with the federal government. The federal inmate population is compromised of white (56 percent) males (93 percent). It is important to note that African Americans are the second largest group (40.9 precent) in federal prisons.[1]

Statistics also show that at the federal level, the average age of an inmate serving time is thirty-seven, while the most common sentence imposed is five to ten years (28.6 percent). Most inmates at a federal correctional facility are serving time for a drug-related offense (55.1 percent). Although this number has decreased since the late 1990s, it is still close to the all-time high recorded in 1994, when 61.4 percent of sentenced inmates were serving time at a federal facility for a drug-related offense.[2]

Spotlight 8-1

Highlights of States' Correctional Systems in 1995

- In 1995, states operated 1,375 facilities.
- More state facilities of all security levels were in operation in 1995 than were present five years earlier.
- Facilities operating under state authority in 1990 grew 14 percent from 1,207 to 1,375.
- State prison authorities operated more than four-fifths of the nation's correctional facilities.
- More than nine of every ten inmates were held in facilities operated by state authorities.
- The South accounted for nearly 50 percent of state correctional facilities and more than 40 percent of state prisoners at midyear 1995.
- State facilities housed nearly 150,000–200,000 inmates in the Northeast, Midwest, and West regions; the South housed more than 400,000 prisoners.
- The South had the largest number of prisoners per 100,000 state residents (437) and the Northeast had the lowest number (293).
- In the prison population, 49 percent of inmates were African American non-Hispanic; 35 percent were white non-Hispanic; 14 percent were Hispanic; 1 percent was Native American; and 1 percent were Asian or Pacific Islander.
- In both 1990 and 1995, equal proportions of state prisoners were kept in each of the maximum (under 40 percent of all inmates), medium (almost 50 percent), or minimum (10 percent) security facilities (these levels of security are discussed later in this chapter).
- The number of inmate deaths rose from 2.4 per 1,000 state inmates in 1990 to 3.4 in 1995.
- At midyear 1995, 378 correctional facilities (27 percent) were under court order or consent decree for specific conditions (to limit population) or for the totality of conditions.

Source: Bureau of Justice Statistics.

8-1b The State Prison Systems

As stated previously, each of the fifty states operates its correctional system in a specific way. It is hard to describe all the state prison systems because most of them are unique. California, Texas, Florida, and New York are known for their correctional systems and represent some generalities that are common to most of the states' correctional systems. These are highlighted in Spotlight 8-1. It is important to recognize that although this information is captured every five years, the Bureau of Justice Statistics does not publish the information until two years after the last census. At the time the second edition of this textbook was produced, the 2000 prison census data was not available.

8-2 Classification

As early as the 1800s, inmates were classified. At the Elmira Reformatory, Zebulon Brockway began the process of classifying inmates according to their security level and program needs. This trend continued through the years. A century ago, the American Prison Association articulated the concept of individualized treatment in its Declaration of Principles. Ironically, that concept became popular long before anyone realized that for treatment programs to succeed, there must be an understanding of the particular offender. It was not until the 1920s that a few prison administrators began talking about the need for diagnosis, which resulted in the establishment of some diagnostic centers for prisons. This was also the result of the rehabilitation ideal, which was based on the notion that inmates could be rehabilitated through appropriate treatment.

Classification was regarded as the diagnostic method necessary to assess the treatment needs of offenders. One of the most influential figures in the continuing use of classification was psychiatrist Karl Menninger. In the 1950s, Menninger advocated the use of the classification method for the effective treatment of offenders. His rehabilitative principles were based on the notion that prison life could be compared to an individual's childhood. Menninger asserted that both of these rely on a state of dependency in which the necessities of food, shelter, clothing, and supervision have to be met by a supervising authority.[3] He concluded there is a good possibility that offenders subconsciously seek a more secure environment (e.g., prison) when they commit a crime.

Despite Menniger's attempts, which some regard as idealistic in nature, classification has really meant segregation—by race, age, and sex. No serious attempts have been made in the classification process to assess the problems of a particular offender within the context of a treatment program. Because of the emphasis given to confinement in the 1980s, classification is understood by many today to mean segregation. Despite this, most criminologists regard classification as a process with a deeper meaning than simply separating inmates by risk level.

Classification can be defined as "a method by which diagnosis, treatment planning, and the execution of the treatment programs are coordinated in the individual case."[4] Classification begins after the individual has been sentenced to serve time in prison. The inmate is transferred out of a local jail to a diagnostic center. This correctional facility specializes in the diagnosis of inmates entering the correctional system. In this facility, an inmate's custody assessment and treatment needs are produced.

Classification is supposed to be a process that assesses the individual's custody requirements and determines the most effective way to apply institutional resources to the individual's case. However, it is often a process in which inmates are labeled as predators. This label stays with them throughout their tenure in prison and sometimes even after they fulfill their sentence. For classification to be effective, all available diagnostic techniques should be used when analyzing the individual's problems and a treatment program should be tailored to each individual's needs. The plan should then be executed and revised when necessary. Finally, the program should be coordinated with the activities of the individual on parole or unconditional release. In reality, however, this is not always the case.

It is worth noting that classification does not only take place among inmates—correctional facilities are also classified according to their security level. Before examining the inmate classification process, it is important to look at the various levels of security attributed to U.S. correctional facilities.

8-2a Prison Classification

Once the inmates have been exposed to the classification process, a determination of the inmate's security level is made. Assessors, who are usually correctional officers, take into account factors such as the seriousness of the offense, the possibility of escape, and the potential for violent behavior when determining the appropriate security level. Most states do not enjoy the benefit of having a specific institution for each level of security. Consequently, facilities are often divided into sections for different categories. Because there are no universal standards for designing a prison, an institution that holds high-risk offenders in one state may be regarded as a low-security facility in another. Despite this, general statements can be made about the different security levels attributed to correctional facilities in the United States.

Supermax Prisons

U.S. prisons are classified according to their level of security. Any correctional site can be categorized as a maximum, medium, or minimum security facility. Most states have built prisons that are considered to have higher security mechanisms than those of a maximum facility—these are often referred to as maxi-max or **supermax prisons**. The concept began in 1983 at a federal prison in Marion, Illinois, after inmates killed two correctional officers and a prison-wide twenty-three-hour lockdown was implemented. This allowed inmates to leave their cells for only one hour a day for solitary exercise. As the concept grew, the number of maxi-max prisons increased. All of these facilities have been built with the aim of housing the most violent and aggressive individuals in the correctional system. Some of the most notorious maxi-max institutions include California's Pelican Bay institution and the supermax prison built in Florence, Colorado. Despite their rapid growth, experts argue that the solitary confinement of maxi-max prisons is harmful to inmates, who suffer from symptoms ranging from "memory loss to severe anxiety to hallucinations to delusions and, under the severest cases of sensory deprivation, people go crazy."[5] Another factor contributing to the recent attention these facilities are receiving is the fact that more and more inmates (some of them involved in high profile cases) are being sent to maxi-max facilities. For example, on January 9, 1998, the man behind the first World Trade Center bombing, Ramzi Yousef, received one of the harshest sentences in history. Judge Kevin T. Duffy sentenced Yousef to 240 years plus life in solitary confinement. Judge Duffy recommended that Yousef be allowed to see his lawyers but he was not allowed to make telephone calls, even to his family. Although some welcomed the sentence, other argued that it violated Yousef's constitutional protection against cruel and unusual punishment. After the September 11, 2001 terrorist attacks against the United States, the American public has become supportive of a punitive approach towards inmates. Some argue that it will be many years until most Americans will consider the due process aspect of punishment, particularly when it involves individuals accused of committing acts of terrorism.

Supermax prisons Often referred to as "maxi-max." These institutions are built to house the most violent and aggressive individuals in the correctional system.

Maximum-Security Prisons

According to the most recently published prison/jail census (1995), **maximum-security prisons** comprised 25 percent of state and federal facilities in the United States. Larger states usually have one or more maximum-security prisons. In 1995, over half of these institutions housed over 1,000 inmates.[6] High walls that contain guard towers usually surround these facilities, leaving the impression that their aim is to punish the most serious offenders the system can hold. They are often located in rural areas away from society.[7] Inside the maximum-security prison, inmates live in small cells that contain their own sanitary facility. When one walks through the corridors of these facilities, there is no question that their purpose is custody and discipline. Some of these facilities are very old. It is estimated that in 1995, 10 percent of inmates housed in maximum-security prisons lived in facilities that were over 100 years old.[8]

Maximum-security prisons Correctional institutions that hold inmates requiring the highest degree of custody and control.

In maximum-security prisons, head counts are conducted frequently despite that inmates are allowed out of their cells only if a guard accompanies them. This has had a severe effect on inmates who have been incarcerated in these types of facilities for an extended time. Critics hold that such treatment constitutes cruel and unusual punishment.

Medium-Security Prisons

Medium-security prisons Correctional institutions in which inmates are allowed to engage in recreational activities.

Although the architecture of these prisons usually resembles that of maximum-security institutions, in reality their method of operation is somewhat different. The **medium-security prison** concept was born in an attempt to seek alternatives to the maximum-security institution. Most of the construction in corrections in the past half-century has been for medium-security institutions. The recent architecture of the medium-security facilities is based on the campus design, which includes residence areas with single rooms and dormitories for inmates. In most of these medium-security prisons, inmates have more freedom than those confined in maximum-security institutions. Inmates in medium-security facilities have privileges and contact with the outside world via visitors, television, radios, and mail. These facilities aim at rehabilitating offenders through the implementation of various programs. In 1995, medium-security facilities comprised 38 percent of the total number of state and federal facilities. In 1995, medium-security facilities were of every size: 31 percent were small, 29 percent were medium, and 40 percent were large capacity.[9] In 1995, at the state level, approximately 43 percent of inmates were classified as medium-security, in contrast with 32 percent at the federal level.[10]

Minimum-Security Prisons

Minimum-security prisons Correctional institutions in which inmates are allowed extensive freedoms under limited correctional supervision.

The architecture of **minimum-security prisons** is substantially different from that of maximum- and medium-security prisons. Because these prisons do not house the most serious offenders in the correctional system, they do not need guard towers or high walls. Most of the inmates who reside in these institutions live in private rooms or in dormitories, allowing them to have a substantial level of personal freedom. Some of the minimum-security prisons of today allow inmates to wear their own clothing and they are privileged to have their own television sets. In 1995, inmates in minimum-security facilities were the least likely (85 percent) to be in male-only institutions. In that same year, approximately 2 percent of the inmates in minimum-security prisons resided in buildings that were at least 100 years old. In 1995, most inmates at the federal level (57 percent) resided in minimum-security prisons—this constitutes an increase of inmates (35 percent) since 1990.[11] Despite this growth, most of these prisons still offer rehabilitative programs to inmates. It is common to find inmates working outside these campus-like facilities wearing regular work clothes. Although this may give the impression to the public that the inmates are not receiving sufficient punishment for their wrongdoing, it should be remembered that they are still deprived of their freedom. The correctional staff controls every aspect of their lives.

8-2b Types of Inmate Classification Systems

Classification clinic Location where an individual was classified according to security and rehabilitative programs. This concept failed because it was independent from the institution that incarcerated the offender.

After examining the different security classifications of correctional institutions, it is important to discuss the various types of inmate classification systems that have been used in the past and those that are in use today. The first type, the **classification clinic,** was a failure because it was autonomous within the institution that incarcerated the individual under study. Elaborate diagnosis could take place and then be ignored by the administrative officials of the institution, for they were in no way bound by the recommendations of the clinic. This represented a clash of opinions between those seeking treatment and correctional personnel whose priority was custody.

The **integrated classification system,** one of the most popular methods in the past, involved both the professional and the administrative personnel of the institution. A classification committee was formed and chaired by the warden or superintendent of the institution. The decisions of the committee were binding on the administration and any changes in the inmate's treatment program had to be approved by the committee. An important advantage of this system was that it permitted professional and administrative personnel to work together and to gain insight into the problems that each group faced.[12]

Integrated classification system Inmate classification system in which a classification committee, usually chaired by the warden or superintendent of the institution, was formed. The decisions of this committee were binding on the administration, and any changes in the treatment program of the inmate had to be approved by the committee.

A third type, which is the most widely used system today, is the **diagnostic**, or **reception center**. The convicted individual is sentenced to a particular institution and then classified, while others are sentenced to the reception center. In the center, inmates are usually diagnosed for three to six weeks. The inmate is studied carefully and examined by psychologists, psychiatrists, physicians, social workers, and other personnel. A treatment program is then planned, including a decision concerning which of the institutions in the jurisdiction would be most appropriate for rehabilitation. This system reflects the alleged goal of the existing classification system—to classify inmates based on their security and rehabilitative needs.

Diagnostic/reception center Correctional units in which professional staff determines which treatment program and correctional facility are appropriate for the individual offender.

Some states have a reception center at each institution while others have a reception center that receives all inmates before they are diagnosed and sent to a specific prison to serve their prescribed sentence. A number of criminologists have regarded the reception center as a place where the individual inmate begins to accept the reality of being incarcerated. After contemplating the possibility of loss of freedom in a court of law, the convicted offender now begins to accept the reality of confinement for the next few months or years. In reception centers, inmates are often stripped of their street clothing and are given a uniform, a code of conduct book, and a full medical examination. In some cases, this occurs as soon as the inmate arrives from the local jail.

In some jurisdictions, inmates are classified based only on their past criminal history, age, severity of the criminal act, and institutional conduct (if any). The priority in these cases is to assign the individual to a proper security level (minimum, medium, or maximum). This has been the recent trend, as the general population continues to challenge the existence and function of rehabilitative programs and is constantly demanding a more punitive approach toward the handling of inmates.

In jurisdictions where rehabilitation is a realistic goal, inmates often receive a series of psychological and medical examinations to determine their program needs as well as their custodial level. Those inmates who are in most need of assistance usually receive it. It is important to mention that before considering the program needs of the inmate, the institution's needs are usually met. The enrollment in some programs is sometimes very high and, as a result, the availability of programs is limited. This is becoming more of a trend as rehabilitative programs suffer from budgetary cuts and public scrutiny.

Most reception facilities have committees that make the classification decision. These committees are made up of the deputy warden and the heads of each department, including those who oversee custody, industry, education, and treatment. An inmate appears before the committee, which makes a recommendation regarding the inmate's program as well as his or her custody status. At the time of consideration, the committee is presented with enough information to make a decision regarding the inmate. This information includes pre-sentence reports, police records, and the results of the various examinations conducted in the reception center. In some jurisdictions, the committee consists of a few staff members who are appointed to make these decisions. This occurs because top-level prison administrators are unavailable due to their hectic schedules and long hours.

8-2c An Ideal Classification System

Reception program First element of a classification program; new inmates should be segregated for purposes of medical tests and for orientation.

Most of the current classification systems are far from ideal. To assess the weaknesses and strengths of the existing systems, it is important to examine the traits associated with an ideal inmate classification system. The first element should be a **reception program.** New inmates should be segregated for purposes of medical tests and orientation. Traditionally, inmates were initiated into the correctional system by other inmates. Under modern reception programs, orientation is theoretically conducted by professional staff. The inmate should be taken on a tour of the institution where he or she will be confined. The rules and regulations of the institution should be carefully explained. Personnel should be trained to work with the individual on personal problems, such as the loss of family and friends, as well as with the hostilities the individual may have developed toward the police or other elements of the legal process.

Activities are an important element in the orientation process. Most people committed to a correctional facility have already spent time in jail, a time usually characterized by idleness. "Further idleness during the admission period tends to increase the tensions and ill feelings it is so necessary to break down."[13]

It is important to build a case summary of the diagnostic studies. This summary should contain a legal history of the case, criminal record (if any), a social history, physical conditions, vocational abilities and interests, educational and religious background, recreational interests, reports of psychologists and psychiatrists, and the individual's initial reaction to the treatment programs. The behavior of the individual at the reception center should also be noted in the case summary. This initial adjustment phase should be only the beginning of a complete record on the inmate. The final case history should include not only the case summary but also all correspondence about the inmate, a photograph, fingerprints, reports of probation officers, progress reports, and legal documents. Staff members should be trained to use these documents effectively and the documents should be kept confidential from other inmates. Unfortunately, current prison overcrowding coupled with a growing punitive attitude among the citizenry prevents us from having an ideal classification system.

Classification Committee

The classification committee is the key element in the classification process. It is important to have well-trained staff members on the board. If the recommendations of the committee are to be binding throughout the institution, the warden or superintendent should chair the committee. Other committee members should be staff persons who will help evaluate and work with the inmate. The composition of the committee varies from inmate to inmate, and includes the appropriate work supervisor and counselor, a staff member from the prison school if the inmate has expressed an interest in education, and the psychiatrist, psychologist, and physician who tested and examined the inmate.

The inmate should be allowed to participate in the initial classification meeting and he or she should be made to feel comfortable and at ease during the interview. The committee may have to decide on (1) whether to transfer the inmate to another institution, (2) how much custody will be required, (3) work assignments, (4) academic program, (5) religious classes and counseling based on the chaplain's recommendation, and (6) recreational programs. In special cases, the committee may recommend psychiatric counseling, or participation in Alcoholics Anonymous (AA), Check Forgers Anonymous, or other such organizations.[14]

8-2d Contributions of the Inmate Classification System

In addition to facilitating the treatment of inmates, classification in its ideal state makes other positive contributions to corrections. While breaking down many of the problems created by overspecialization, classification aims at facilitating discipline, increasing productive industrial output, and improving the morale of inmates. If utilized properly, it results in success that the inmate can see.

> Classification has demonstrated that [inmates] appreciate real effort to help them and the opportunities for self-improvement provided. Classification results in the development of materials that will aid the parole board in making a decision. It provides data for criminological research. Finally, it provides the information needed for long-range planning for building correctional facilities.[15]

8-2e Correctional Programs

The classification process as it pertains to institutions and inmates has been examined and various correctional programs offered to inmates in today's prison system will be discussed. They sometimes aim at achieving goals that have been regarded by some correctional administrators and staff personnel as being unrealistic in nature. It is equally important to remember that most, if not all, of these correctional programs suffer from budgetary constraints and public criticisms for being too soft on inmates. Some of these public sentiments are often based on well-publicized cases in which a particular prison program failed in its attempt to treat, train, or educate an inmate who committed a serious offense after being released from prison.

Treatment Programs

Don Gibbons, in his treatise on the treatment of delinquents and criminals, emphasized the need to distinguish between treatment and humanitarianism. The rise of the spirit of humanitarianism has often been confused with the belief that people, specifically inmates, should be treated humanely. The result has been that efforts implemented to make prisons more humane have been interpreted by some as an attempt to treat or rehabilitate the incarcerated. Many argue that there is no convincing evidence which suggests that attempts to make prisons more humane places have resulted in rehabilitation.

What is the difference? According to Gibbons, "Humanitarian reform designates those changes that have been introduced into corrections in recent decades which serve to lessen the harshness or severity of punishment."[16] The humanitarian movement in prisons is based on the early philosophy that deprivation of liberty is the punishment. It would be excessive punishment and inhumane to force the person deprived of his or her liberty to live in filth or among rats, in damp, cold, dark cells, to eat poorly prepared food constituting an unbalanced diet, and to suffer corporal punishment. In the past, changes in privileges have been made for inmates, such as increases in the number of visits they may have with their families and friends. Gibbons points out that such visits can decrease tension in prisons and can have positive effects on the inmates. They can also have negative effects. He argues that the visits are not related to treatment and should not be considered therapeutic. Increased visits, classification, and educational and vocational training might be referred to as adjuncts to treatment. Religious activities, recreational participation, and prerelease planning are other adjuncts. These programs are not aimed at particular therapy problems of inmates and therefore do not constitute treatment per se.[17]

Types of Treatment

The term "treatment" is often used to define, very broadly, what takes place in prisons or in alternatives to incarceration. Although there is no consensus on the definition of treatment, most experts regard it as the implementation of remedies in order to obtain a particular cure. Treatment includes all programs or approaches that are aimed at the reformation or rehabilitation of the individual, making it impossible to examine any of the issues in detail. This following discussion is a brief overview of the kinds of treatment that have been used in prison facilities in the United States.

Some inmates do not have adequate access, if any, to treatment. This is because some inmates are regarded as too dangerous to be given an opportunity to participate in a treatment program in the company of other inmates. Another reason for the lack of inmate accessibility to treatment programs is the overcrowding prison conditions that make these programs scarce and extremely competitive.

Not all offenders should be treated alike. Offenders are not a homogeneous group—different variables influence each offender to turn to crime. No one treatment technique is effective with all inmates.[18]

In his work, Don Gibbons constructed a typology of treatment forms that contained two categories representing the basic orientations toward causation of crime—psychological and social therapies.[19]Psychological therapies include individual depth psychotherapy, group psychotherapy, and client-centered therapy. Included among social therapies are group therapy and milieu management.

Psychological Therapies: Individual Depth Psychotherapy

It has been asserted that the treatment of criminals implies changing their personalities, beliefs, or motivations so that they have internal controls to prevent criminal behavior. Some believe that a psychiatrist's most effective therapeutic tool is psychotherapy. The aim of psychotherapy is to instigate a process of growth in patients so that they can manage their own affairs. When therapists work individually with patients, they try to help individuals understand the early life experiences that are thought to be important in causing personal problems. Through these psychoanalytic techniques of in-depth therapy, therapists bring out these experiences and assist their patients in dealing with them. Gibbons has referred to the basic elements of psychotherapy proposed by Richard Jenkins:

1. A sense of emotional security that the patient develops from interaction with the therapist.
2. Respect for the integrity and self-determination of the individual or respect for the patient's identity.
3. The release of pent-up emotional tension.
4. Reduction or stimulation of the patient's sense of responsibility for his actions.
5. Attenuation or stimulation of the guilt-anxiety of the person.
6. Reduction of feelings of inferiority or inadequacy of patients.[20]

Individual psychotherapy A form of psychotherapy aimed at addressing the specific needs of an individual. The success of this type of therapy in a controlled environment such as prison is highly questionable.

Despite the aims of this therapy, in a controlled environment such as prison, **individual psychotherapy** seldom works. One of the most obvious impairments is that the therapist is not working for the patient, as is common in clinics outside the correctional system, but rather for the government with the aim to develop a crime-free mentality in the offender. This problem, among others, has challenged the existence of programs addressing the emotional state of inmates. In most prisons, counselors and other correctional staff members attempt to directly address some of the most common problems of inmates (e.g., adjustment into the correctional facility, concerns with existing dependants outside the facility) instead of practicing in-depth psychotherapy techniques.

Group psychotherapy A type of psychotherapy aimed at an individual within a group setting.

Group Psychotherapy and Human Potential Therapies

Gibbons distinguishes between **group psychotherapy**, which is aimed at an individual within a group setting, and group therapy, which is aimed at changing an entire group. S. R. Slavson argued that group therapy is valuable because the group members give support to one another and that reduces their individual fears and defenses. But Jenkins contended that some problems may be so painful that an individual may not want to discuss them in a group.[21]

Since Gibbons formulated his treatment typology, human potential therapies have become widely used in society and, in the past few decades, have been introduced into prison. Since their introduction, these types of therapies have retained their popularity because they address inmates' emotions and thoughts in a group setting while allowing individuals to develop a support mechanism with their peers. There are several kinds of human potential therapies and all are a form of group psychotherapy. They are at times led by persons who are not trained as well as clinical psychologists or psychiatrists.

Reality Therapy

Unlike depth psychotherapy, **reality therapy** does not involve delving into the past. It operates on the principle that the past is significant in an individual's behavior only to the extent that he or she permits. The focus is on the present. Reality therapy has been developed by those who question the value of conventional psychiatric treatment.

Reality therapy Therapy that operates on the principle that the past is significant in an individual's behavior only to the extent that he or she so permits; the focus is therefore on the present.

The use of reality therapy in the treatment of offenders was started in the early 1960s by Dr. William Glaser, who is known as the "Father of Reality Therapy." The premise of this therapy is that the basic problem of inmates is irresponsibility. The therapist tries to teach offenders to become responsible and to achieve their own needs without harming others.

Reality therapy is based on the assumption that all people have two basic psychological needs: the need to give and receive love and the need to feel that they are important to others as well to themselves. It is further believed that behavior has some meaning to the individual, but that people who are not meeting their own needs "refuse to acknowledge the reality of the world in which they live. This becomes more apparent with each successive failure to gain relatedness and respect. Reality therapy mobilizes its effort toward helping people accept reality and aims to help them meet their needs within its confines."[22] People meet their needs through involvement with others, so the therapist must become involved with patients and not reject them because of their deviant behavior. As therapists become involved with patients, they help these patients adapt to reality by being both a model and a mirror of reality. They take a more active role in the relationship with patients than the traditional approach. Reality therapy, in contrast to traditional therapy, encourages patients to face the moral aspect of their behavior. They must decide whether behavior is right or wrong. No attempt is made to study the unconscious—reality therapy forces the individual to examine the conscious self and behavior.

Rachin notes that patients who have not responded well to conventional treatment methods often do not respond to reality therapy, although it is less costly than traditional methods since it does not require as much time. He concludes, "The principles of reality therapy are common sense interwoven with a firm belief in the dignity of man and his ability to improve his lot. Its value is twofold: it is a means by which people can help one another, and it is a treatment technique, applicable regardless of symptomatology."[23] After having explored the methodology used in reality therapy, it is easy to understand why it is a popular method in corrections. Not only does this type of therapy adhere to the concept that society's rules are real and cannot be escaped, but it is feasible that this type of therapy can also be implemented over a short period of time in any type of correctional setting. The latter makes reality therapy very attractive to correctional administrators concerned with the rehabilitation of inmates.

Transactional Analysis

Transactional analysis Theory based on the belief that each person has three persons within—a parent, an adult, and a child. Games, psychodrama, and script analysis help the individual to understand how these three persons control his or her behavior. The goal is to understand and develop spontaneity and a capacity for intimacy.

Transactional analysis, or TA, was created by Dr. Eric Berne, author of *Games People Play*.[24] Some correctional institutions use transactional analysis in treatment programs. William Nagel briefly referred to TA, stating that it is based on the belief that each person has three personas within: a parent, an adult, and a child. By the use of games, psychodrama, and script analysis, individuals are helped to understand how these three persons control his or her behavior. The goal is to understand and "develop spontaneity and a capacity for intimacy."[25] Some institutions have space problems that prevent them from offering TA programs. They must have room for the small groups to meet and offices for the back-up counseling sessions. According to Nagel, transactional analysis has been used as a treatment method at the federal penitentiary at Marion, Illinois, and at the O.H. Close School near Stockton, California. This type of therapy has been considered to be appropriate for most correctional facilities since it is simple, short term, and straightforward.

Social Therapies

Social therapies Social therapies promote the idea that the client is not to be rehabilitated in isolation from the environment. The two major social therapies are group therapy and milieu management. Also known as environmental therapies.

Gibbons regards **social therapies** as environmental therapies, and divides them into three categories—environmental change, group therapy, and milieu management. Environmental change takes place outside correctional facilities and is not discussed here. Group therapy and milieu management can be utilized within correctional institutions.

Group Therapy

Group therapy is designed to change the behavior of an entire group through a process of socialization. It is believed to be highly effective in prison settings that aim at improving inmate socialization skills. In showing that the principle of differential association could be utilized in treatment, Donald R. Cressey stated that if criminals or delinquents are to be changed, they must become assimilated into groups that emphasize law-abiding behavior and alienated from those that emphasize law-violating behavior. The "more relevant the common purpose of the group to the reformation of criminals, the greater will be its influence on the criminal members' attitudes and values" and the "more cohesive the group, the greater the members' readiness to influence others and the more relevant the problem of conformity to group norms." In addition, all of the members of the group must be able to achieve status within the group for activities that are conducive to reform. The more effective reformation groups will be those in which criminals join with noncriminals for the purpose of changing other criminals. Finally, when the entire group is the focus of change, the process of reformation can be enhanced by convincing the group that change is needed. The group will then exert the pressure for change on its members.[26]

Group therapy has been distinguished from group counseling by some who argue that the former is more intensive. Gibbons believes that the distinction is unfortunate. He has argued that if the purpose is to "create real groups with new attitudinal and normative patterns," it is group therapy.[27]

Milieu Management

Milieu management has the same goals as does group therapy, but is more extensive, including the entire environment of the group in the treatment program. It is usually conducted within institutions. One example is the Synanon method for treating drug addicts. Synanon houses have been established with an environment structured toward treatment and rehabilitation of the addict. Great success has been claimed for such programs. The patients in many of these programs, however, participate voluntarily, which clearly distinguishes these situations from those of the correctional facility. One of the crucial criticisms of the milieu approach is that the participants might learn to live within the structured milieu; however, they are not able to live within society without the protection of the group. That criticism could be made of any program that does not attempt to integrate the person into society.

In addition to the categories of treatment discussed by Gibbons, behavior modification, which has been used extensively by corrections, is examined.

Behavior Modification

Traditional psychotherapy is based on the theory that deviant behavior is symptomatic of a deep, underlying personality problem that must be uncovered and treated. In contrast, **behavior modification** is based on learning theory and is concerned with observable behavior. According to the argument, it is not the unconscious that is important, but rather the behavior that can be observed and manipulated. It is assumed that neurotic symptoms and some types of deviant behavior are acquired through an unfortunate quirk of learning and are in some way rewarding to the patient. The significant aspect of this approach is the belief that deviant behaviors are learned in the same way that all other behavior is learned. The undesirable behavior can be eliminated, modified, or replaced by taking away the reward value. Alternatively, the behavior can be replaced by rewarding conduct that is more appropriate.

Behavior modification Method based on learning theory; applied to change behavior by rewarding appropriate behaviors and removing reinforcements for negative actions.

Following the theories of B. F. Skinner and his associates, behavior modification is behavior controlled by its consequences. "Behavior modification, then, is the systematic application of proven principles of conditioning and learning in the remediation of human problems."[28] When dealing with conduct that is undesirable, behavioral therapy attempts to produce a change in the person's long-established patterns of response to himself or herself and to others.[29]

The following is an illustration of how behavior modification works. Blaine, a fourteen year boy whose IQ was in the low 80s, had adjustment problems both at school and at home. He was antagonistic toward his peers and incorrigible at school. At home, he disrespected the house and set fires. School officials tried various punishments with little success. His father tried spankings and lectures with little result, but experienced some success with denying television privileges. Under the behavior modification program devised for Blaine, a daily chart was kept. For each day he did not play with matches, he received a star on his chart, praise from his father, and an opportunity to watch television in the evening. If he got a star each day for a week, he received twenty-five cents. If he played with matches one day, he lost the star, the television privileges for that day, and the quarter for the week. In the six months that the chart was used for Blaine, he missed only one opportunity for reinforcement. Furthermore, he and his brothers began doing their chores at home regularly—for this action they received praise and reinforcement. Blaine's behavior at school improved greatly. "Follow-up showed no changes—the school was full of praise for his behavior and playing with matches" did not recur.[30] This type of treatment is also available in most correctional facilities. Statistics suggest that in 1995, psychological, life skills, and psychiatric counseling were available in 69 percent of correctional facilities, while in the same year, 67 percent of these institutions offered community adjustment counseling.[31]

Physiological Behavior Control

Considerable attention has been given recently to mind-controlling behavior techniques, such as the use of drugs, psychosurgery, chemotherapy, and electrode implantation. Such popular attempts to control behavior are included under the umbrella of behavior modification. It has been argued that even though these procedures are used to control behavior, "they should not be confused with behavior-modification procedures for they are not applications of the principles of conditioning and learning. Techniques such as these involve instead physiological alterations that fall within the domain of the physician, the surgeon, the psychiatrist—certainly not the behavior modifier."[32] Nor does the controversy end with the definition of the treatment program. There is disagreement on the issue of what constitutes consent to these treatment methods and whether the methods have actually been administered without consent.

Today, most correctional facilities enjoy the benefit of drug rehabilitation programs. This is not surprising as most offenders housed in today's prisons have been convicted for drug-related offenses. The Clark Foundation report, *Americans Behind Bars,* concluded that "much of the growth in prison population has resulted from a doubling of the number of arrests for drug law violations and a tripling of the rate of incarceration for arrested drug offenders."[33] Some of the psychological therapies explained earlier are being used as part of the inmate's drug treatment program. Some studies on the effectiveness of long-term residential treatment programs have indicated that without aftercare and follow-up support, offenders are more likely to relapse into drug use and crime. These studies, which evaluated the Federal Bureau of Prisons' drug treatment programs in public health service hospitals in Lexington, Kentucky, and Fort Worth, Texas, revealed a 96 percent relapse rate among treatment participants. It has been recommended that the implementation of additional months of drug and job treatment programs would reduce the recurrence of drug use among those released.[34] Other studies have suggested that intensive case management delivered for six months to drug-involved arrestees released after booking has significantly reduced drug use and lowered criminal recidivism.[35] Other types of programs are offered in today's institutions to support those who suffer from various problems, including the HIV virus and mental disorders.

Education Programs

Despite today's punitive attitude, the public still supports educational programs offered in correctional facilities. It is believed that educated individuals will turn away from a life of crime. This belief has been substantiated by various research studies suggesting that education may be a key to preventing criminal behavior.

According to statistics released in 1995, 80 percent of the correctional facilities in the United States provide secondary educational programs, while 75 percent of them provide basic adult education. In that same year, vocational training was offered in 54 percent of the correctional institutions while college-level course work was available in 33 percent of these same institutions. In addition, about 23 percent of inmates were enrolled in some type of education in 1995, including 22 percent of state inmates and 29 percent of federal inmates.[36]

Historical Overview

Prison education programs are recent in development. "The first school system for all prisoners was established in Maryland in the 1830s followed by a New York law of 1847 appointing instructors in its prisons."[37] High rates of illiteracy among early prisoners gave impetus to prison education programs. The ministers who went to prison for religious training and to attempt to convert the inmates were the first teachers. The ministers had to teach the inmates how to read before they could study the Bible. The Quakers, who initiated many early prison reforms, were the first laypeople to advocate education of criminals. They ran into opposition, however, from individuals who thought that educated criminals would be more dangerous than uneducated inmates upon their release.

Prison education in the United States began formally with the development of the reformatory system, which started at Elmira in 1876 under the leadership of Zebulen Brockway. His desire was to establish an educational system that would teach inmates self-discipline as well as academic subjects. College professors headed the division of academic and moral education. Professors, public school principals, and lawyers taught specific courses.[38] It is ironic that in 1876, prison courses were taught by highly qualified professionals, while in the facilities of recent decades, courses are often taught by people who do not have college degrees. Brockway's other contribution was the industrial program at the Detroit House of Corrections in 1861, the "first grading system based on the degree of reformation (reformation attitude), [and] one of the first trade schools and manual arts programs for those prisoners incapable of benefiting from the more academic courses."[39]

Current Programs

The U.S. Department of Education was authorized in 1991 to create a new office to provide national leadership for correctional educational issues. This was named the "Office of Correctional Education" (OCE). Specifically, the OCE provides technical assistance to all states, schools, and correctional institutions. Under the federal grant program, the U.S. Department of Education awards grants to state correctional institutions in order to facilitate the educational process of all inmates.[40]

Educational programs not only serve the interest of the inmate but also that of the correctional administrator. These programs provide incentives to inmates in surroundings that are otherwise devoid of constructive activities. In addition, these programs provide exposure to positive civilian role models while engaging inmates for many hours in quiet, productive activity. Some have claimed that education programs make up a key component of what has been referred to as dynamic security within correctional facilities.

The review of studies regarding education programs offered in prisons suggests that participation in prison educational programs is related significantly to lower recidivism rates. Some studies have also suggested that pre-college programs have a significant relationship with post-release employment. Offenders who participated in pre-college education programs were more likely to continue their education after release. Some of the findings have suggested that participation in college programs in prison is associated with lower recidivism rates, higher rates of post-release employment, and higher rates of participation in education programs after release.[41] Overall, positive benefits for those who attend education programs in prisons have been detected. Although some studies suggest the contrary, most experts argue that the benefits of these programs outweigh any negative effects.

Vocational Training

Vocational training programs attempt to teach offenders job skills with the hope that they can employ them once released. This is one of the oldest approaches toward the rehabilitation of offenders. At times, these programs are designed to keep the prison running and to provide some type of income. At the federal level, industries operated by the Federal Bureau of Prisons (UNICOR), produced goods including furniture and electronic equipment. In some states, such as Florida, inmates produce the desks, tables, and stationery found in colleges. Vocational training suffers from the principle of least eligibility in that it is offered only for less desirable jobs. If programs were to offer training for better jobs, the public would resent it, arguing that inmates do not deserve quality training.

Inmates often learn trades that are not marketable outside the prison facility. This leads the released offender to resort to their illegitimate ways to survive. Historically, the vocational training programs offered in prisons have been impacted by the economic needs of society.

Prison Labor and Industry

Correctional administrators have argued for years that "the most difficult prison to administer is the one in which prisoners languish in idleness. Absence of work leads to moral and physical degradation and corrupts institutional order."[42] This view leads to the attitude that "no single phase of life within prison walls is more important to the public or to the inmate than efficient industrial operations and the intelligent utilization of the labor of prisoners."[43] This attitude toward prison labor reflects a belief that work is an important element in the program of rehabilitation. It also reflects the popular belief that prisoners should work and help support themselves. Yet, prison labor in the past has resulted in restrictive legislation.

Historical Overview

Work was an important element of the early U.S. prisons. Even in the solitary confinement cells of the Pennsylvania System, prisoners were expected to work at crafts. That system became outmoded with the Industrial Revolution.

The early prison labor systems, beginning at Auburn, New York in 1823, were profitable, although in the process they exploited prisoners, who were often treated like slaves.[44] In prison, hard labor was often considered a major component of the daily routine, discipline, reformation, and profit in institutions across the country. The first prison-labor programs in the United States operated within a free and open market but were later curtailed by legislation. Several forms of prison labor were characteristic: the lease system, the contract system, the piece-price system, and the public (or state) account system.

Lease system System whereby the prison labor force was placed in the hands of a lessee for a previously agreed-upon fee.

Contract system System under which the state maintained inmates but sold their labor to a contractor, who, in turn, supervised them while providing the necessary work equipment.

Piece-price system System in which a contractor pays a fixed price for each finished piece of work done by inmates.

Public (state) account system A system that brought the entire prison labor system under the control of the state.

Under the **lease system,** the entire prison labor force was placed in the hands of a lessee for an agreed-upon fee. "The system developed in the South where prisoners where sent to lumber camps, in effect as slave laborers, and the state received a fixed rate per man per month."[45] The state worked the prisoners and earned revenue from their labor, but had no responsibility for their custody. In the 1920s, public indignation terminated this system. The **contract system** developed as a result, wherein the state maintained the prisoners but sold their labor to a contractor who provided the necessary machinery and supervision. This system exploited the inmates and provided revenue for the state and the contractor. It was abolished by federal legislation.

Under the **piece-price system,** the contractor paid a fixed price for each finished work done by inmates. The state was in charge of maintaining the prisoner and supervising his or her work. Federal legislation also eliminated this system.

The **public** (or **state**) **account system** placed the entire labor system under the control of the state. The state maintained the inmates, supervised their work, and marketed their products.

Private industries complained that they could not compete with the cheap prison labor which affected legislation, and ultimately, these labor systems. Although some states passed laws regulating prison industry, the biggest setback occurred in 1929 with the passage of the Hawes-Cooper Act (which became effective five years later). This act prohibited prison goods from being shipped into states that had laws prohibiting their sale. The power to regulate the sale of such goods was held by the states. In 1925, the passage of the Ashurst-Sumners Act made it a federal offense to transport prison goods into states that prohibited their sale and also required the labeling of prison-made goods shipped in interstate commerce. The United States Supreme Court upheld the constitutionality of these laws.

By 1940, all fifty states passed laws prohibiting the sale of prison-made products within their borders, which forced the prison labor system to change. The **state-use system** was then developed, which permitted the sale of prison-made goods only to state institutions. Consequently, prison goods consisted of soap, clothing, office furniture, license plates, road signs, and other products used by state agencies and institutions.

State-use system A system whereby inmates were allowed to sell their goods to state-run institutions.

The Congressional Impact on the Prison Industry

In 1979, Congress authorized the Prison Industry Enhancement (PIE) program through the Justice System Improvement Act. This program brings the private sector into the prison industry by exempting certified correctional agencies from any type of legislative restriction imposed on the transportation and sale of prison-made goods in interstate commerce. Inmates must be paid minimum wage and other criteria must be met. In addition, the PIE program authorizes deductions of up to 80 percent of gross wages for taxes, room and board, family support, and victim compensation. This program was revised in 1984 under the Justice Assistance Act and amended again in the Crime Control Act of 1990.[46] While this program does not repeal the Ashurst-Sumners Act, it does deny its application to specific certified prison industries. The program's popularity has grown in recent years, however, prompting Congress to gradually expand the number of allowable certifications from seven to fifty.

The PIE program offers various advantages to states that implement it in addition to the benefits it provides inmates. The PIE program offers a strong financial incentive to the state by generating goods and services that produce income, and offenders can make a contribution to society while defraying their own cost of incarceration. Statistics show that between December 1979 and September 1994, $2,914,236 had been contributed to victim's programs; $8,251,225 had been collected for room and board; $2,875,088 had been paid for family support; and $5,189,950 had been collected in taxes.[47] Despite this, PIE remains a small program, employing only 1,663 inmates nationwide.[48]

Some states, such as California, have implemented programs that allow inmates to help in the fight for a better environment. The California Prison Industry Authority established a waste recycling plant inside the premises of Folsom State Prison to enable parole violators to engage in community service while generating revenues for the state. Some of these revenues were aimed at offsetting prison costs and alleviating the city's waste problem. Inmates were asked to sort out garbage that was moving through a conveyor. Evaluations of this program indicate that it was a success.[49] Other states have implemented similar programs in an attempt to defray incarceration costs while allowing inmates to spend their time in a productive activity.

Summary

This chapter considered the important issue of treatment of offenders in correctional institutions. A discussion of the federal and state correctional systems began the chapter. Then, the classification process of institutions and inmates was discussed. The various characteristics associated with maximum-, medium-, and minimum-security prisons were examined while considering the psychological impact of the inmate classification process. The various programs offered in most correctional settings in the United States were outlined and the establishment and operation of the various treatment, educational, and vocational programs offered by different correctional systems in the United States were detailed.

During the discussion of treatment programs, the typology offered by Don C. Gibbons, psychological and social therapies, was emphasized. The various dimensions of behavior modification were considered and educational programs were discussed. The historical development of these programs was reviewed. The most recent studies in this area have shown a strong positive correlation between attendance at correctional educational programs and low recidivism.

Finally, the vocational programs offered in the correctional system were examined as well as the historical background which describes their evolution and continuing popularity. These programs are popular among the citizenry and correctional administrators because they claim to reduce some of the costs associated with imprisonment while reducing incidents of violence and recidivism rates among inmates. At a time when a conservative public holds terrorism at the forefront of most discussions, it is striking that these programs are continuing to survive and achieve high levels of success.

Notes

1. Federal Bureau of Prisons, *Quick Facts* (January, 2002), Washington, D.C.
2. Federal Bureau of Prisons, *Quick Facts.*
3. Menninger, Karl, *The Crime of Punishment* (New York: Viking Press, 1968), p. 176.
4. Loveland, Frank, "Classification in the Prison System," in Paul W. Tappan, ed., *Contemporary Correction* (New York: McGraw-Hill, 1951), p. 91.
5. CNN, January 9, 1998, *Trend Toward Solitary Confinement Worries Experts,* statement made by Dr. Henry Weinstein.
6. Census of State and Federal Correctional Facilities, 1995 (August, 1995), U.S. Department of Justice Statistics.
7. Prison Research Education Action Project, "Prisons Cannot Protect Society," in Bonnie Szumski, *America's Prisons: Opposing Viewpoints,* 4th ed. (St. Paul, MN: Greenhaven Press, 1985), p. 46. See also *America's Prisons: Opposing Viewpoints,* Roman Espejo (St. Paul, MN: Greenhaven Press, 2002).
8. Census of State and Federal Correctional Facilities, 1995 (August, 1995), U.S. Department of Justice, Bureau of Justice Statistics.
9. Census of State and Federal Correctional Facilities, 1995.
10. Census of State and Federal Correctional Facilities, 1995.
11. Census of State and Federal Correctional Facilities, 1995.
12. Loveland, "Classification in the Prison System," p. 91. For a discussion of teamwork in the classification of inmates, see John Hepburn and Celesta A. Albonetti, "Team Classification in State Correctional Institutions: Its Association with Inmate and Staff Attitudes," *Criminal Justice and Behavior* 5 (March, 1978), 63-73.
13. Loveland, Frank, "Classification in the Prison System," p. 95.
14. American Correctional Association, *Manual of Correctional Standards* (Washington, D.C., 1996), pp. 285-287.
15. Loveland, "Classification in the Prison System," pp. 100-103.
16. Gibbons, Don C., *Changing the Law Breaker: The Treatment of Delinquents and Criminals.* (Englewood Cliffs, NJ: Prentice-Hall, 1965), pp. 130-131.
17. Gibbons, *Changing the Law Breaker,* pp. 133-135.
18. Gibbons, *Changing the Law Breaker,* p. 142.
19. Gibbons, Don C., *Society, Crime, and Criminal Careers* (Englewood Cliffs, NJ: Prentice-Hall, Inc., 1968), p. 493.
20. Quoted in Gibbons, *Changing the Law Breaker,* p. 145.
21. Slavson, S. R., "Group Psychotherapy," *Scientific American* 183 (December, 1950), 42.
22. Quoted in Richard L. Rachin, "Reality Therapy: Helping People Help Themselves," *Crime and Delinquency* 20 (January, 1974), 49.
23. Rachin, "Reality Therapy," p. 53.
24. Berne, Eric, *Games People Play* (New York: Grove Press, 1962).
25. Nagel, William, *The New Red Barn: A Critical Look at the Modern American Prison* (New York: Walker, 1973), p. 134. See also John Blackmore, " 'Human Potential' Therapies, Behind Bars," *Corrections Magazine* 4 (December, 1978), pp. 29-38.
26. Cressey, Donald R., "Changing Criminals: The Application of the Theory of Differential Association," *American Journal of Socioloy* 61:9 (September, 1955), 116-120. See also Vold, George B., Bernard, Thomas J., and Snipes, Jeffrey B., *Theoretical Criminology,* 5th ed. (New York: Oxford University Press, 2002).

27. Gibbons, *Changing the Law Breaker,* p. 163.
28. Milan, Michael A., and McKee, John M., "Behavior Modification; Principles and Applications in Corrections," in Daniel Glaser, ed., *Handbook of Criminology* (Skokie, IL: Rand McNally, 1974), p. 746.
29. For a review of the literature on behavior modification, see V. Scott Johnson, "Behavior Modification in the Correctional Setting," *Criminal Justice and Behavior* 4 (December, 1977), 397-428.
30. Thorne, Gaylord L., et al., "Behavior Modification Techniques: New Tools for Probation Officers," *Federal Probation* 31 (June, 1967), 21.
31. Census of State and Federal Correctional Facilities, 1995.
32. Quoted in Milan and McKee, "Behavior Modification," p. 746.
33. Edna McConnell Clark Foundation, *Americans Behind Bars* (New York: Edna McConnell Clark Foundation, 1994), p. 8. For more discussion on drug offenders, see Samuel Walker, *Sense and Nonsense About Crime and Drugs,* 5th ed. (Belmont, CA: Wadsworth Publishing Company, 2001).
34. Corrections–Based Continuum of Effective Drug Abuse Treatment (June, 1996), National Institute of Justice.
35. Case Management With Drug-Involved Arrestees (November, 1995), National Institute of Justice.
36. Census of State and Federal Correctional Facilities, 1995.
37. Tappan, Paul, *Crime, Justice, and Correction* (New York: McGraw-Hill, 1960), p. 390.
38. Johnson, Elmer Hubert, *Crime, Correction, and Society* (Homewood, IL: Dorsey, 1978), pp. 371-372.
39. Morris, Delyte W., "The University's Role in Prison Education," in Harvey S. Perlman and Thomas B. Allington, eds., *The Tasks of Penology* (Lincoln, NE: The University of Nebraska Press, 1969), p. 199.
40. U.S. Department of Education Web Site. http://www.ed.gov/offices/OVAE/AdultEd/OCE/mission.html
41. Adams, Kenneth, et al., "A Large-Scale Multidimensional Test of the Effects of Prison Education Programs on Offenders' Behavior" (December, 1994), *Prison Journal,* vol. 74, n. 4, p. 433 (17).
42. Johnson, *Crime, Corrections, and Society,* p. 559.
43. U.S. Bureau of Prisons, Handbook of Correctional Institutional Design and Construction, quoted in Tappan, *Crime, Justice and Corrections,* p. 681.
44. See Thorsten Sellin, *Slavery and the Penal System* (New York: Elsevier, 1976).
45. Handbook of Correctional Institutional Design and Construction, in Tappan, *Crime, Justice and Corrections,* p. 682.
46. Misrahi, James J., "Factories with Fences: An Analysis of the Prison" Industry Enhancement Certification Program in Historical Perspective" (Winter, 1996), *American Criminal Law Review,* 33, n. 2, 411-436.
47. Misrahi, "Factories with Fences," p. 413.
48. Misrahi, "Factories with Fences," p. 414.
49. Harrison, Larry, and Lovell, Douglas G., "Inmate Work Program Helps Solve City's Waste Problem" (April, 1996), *Corrections Today,* vol. 58, n. 2, p. 132 (3).

Chapter 9

Prison Administration in the 21st Century

Outline

The administration of prisons is one of the most important topics in any corrections course. Since the creation of the correctional system in the United States, legislators and other government officials have recognized the importance of leadership and control in the administration of prison facilities. In 1967, the President's Crime Commission stated that in many jurisdictions the administration of prisons is the greatest barrier in establishing programs for reintegrating the inmate into society. Once such programs are established, prison administrators will be more influential than the professional treatment personnel in determining whether the programs are successful.

This chapter discusses different areas related to correctional officers, wardens, and restorative justice. The challenges currently affecting the correctional officer are examined as well as the complex task of being a prison warden. In the final section of this chapter, the nature of the restorative justice principle as it relates to the correctional system in the United States is reviewed.

Key Terms

correctional officer
inmate conditioning
corruption through friendship
corruption through reciprocity
corruption through default
trustee
professional staff
James B. Jacobs
Joseph E. Ragen
bureaucratic management style
technocratic management style
idiosyncratic management style
participative management style

9-1 Correctional Officers

Correctional officer
Individual in charge of the custody of inmates in a correctional facility.

The job of a **correctional officer** is unique when compared to other positions within the criminal justice system. Many correctional officers feel that they are not appreciated or respected by a public that is seldom aware of their existence.[1] In the words of a correctional officer:

> "We are some of the best-trained and most caring professionals in the law enforcement community. We put our well-being on the line every day to protect society from some of its worst individuals. Nearly every inmate we come into contact with is a felon—murderers, rapists, robbers, child molesters and drug dealers. Every inmate has the potential to cause great bodily harm at any time. Still we go inside those walls and fences every day and do a job that few others would attempt."[2]

There is little doubt then, of the reason why correctional officers often leave their jobs for other, more suitable forms of employment. Even in slow economic times, it is not hard to find employment ads seeking qualified applicants for the position of correctional officer. As one drives into Huntsville, Texas—a place known in the correctional community for its number of executions—it is not difficult to find a sign with the following sentence: "Become a Correctional Officer: Follow a Rewarding Career."

The problem, though, is not necessarily in recruiting. The correctional system will always find individuals seeking a career as a correctional officer. The problem lies in the quality of the applicants. More and more stories today examine the number of correctional officers that follow unethical and illegal practices in their professional capacity as a guardian of the law. Some states hire civilians and place them immediately, sometimes in correctional settings, without the proper training. This has been prompted by the need to fill in the empty slots in correctional facilities. Some states are being forced to hire personnel and give them a correctional assignment before they are sent to the appropriate site for training. In some states, a short crash course on defensive tactics is issued so that the newly hired officer knows how to control various situations. Experts on security issues argue that although this small training session is better than no training at all, it should not substitute for correctional academy training, which often comes months after a person has been working as a correctional officer.

Correctional officers constitute the majority of the personnel working in most institutions. According to the U.S. Department of Labor, in 2000, correctional officers held approximately 457,000 jobs. Further, "almost six of every ten jobs were in state correctional institutions such as prisons, prison camps, and youth correctional facilities."[3]

Despite their numbers, these officers have infrequently been the subjects of intensive and systematic analysis. The two studies of prison communities conducted by Donald Clemmer and Gresham N. Sykes mention the role of correctional officers in the prison community but were not focused on the career of the officer or even on a systematic sociological analysis of the officer's role.[4] Both found the correctional officers to be primarily custody oriented, however, with Clemmer indicating that the idea of reformation was "utterly foreign to the average guard."[5] With regard to the emphasis on security, Sykes pointed out that only a small percentage of prisoners attempt escape. But, said Sykes, since the prison officials do not know which inmates may try to escape, they continue to maintain security against all.[6]

Another function of prison officials, one of concern to the public who fear prison riots, is the maintenance of internal order. The prison staff in Syke's study rated this function second only to custody. Inmates are expected to follow strict rules of the institution as well as to conform to rules imposed by the culture of the outside world.[7]

9-1a Maintenance of Control

How do correctional officers control inmates? One way is has been with physical force. Another way—and some would argue, a more effective one—is through the correctional officer's use of the inmate community. That is, the control is actually based on an informal system of **inmate conditioning**. Inmates are often permitted to hold a degree of power over other inmates and in some cases are allowed infractions of the rules without penalty. In return for this treatment, inmates keep order within the correctional institution. Despite these methods of control, most correctional officers will tell you that if it were not for some of the privileges they are allowed to offer and/or take away from inmates, most correctional facilities would currently experience riots.

Inmate conditioning A form of controlling inmates. Inmates are often permitted to hold a degree of power over other inmates, and in some cases are allowed infractions of the rules without penalty. In return for this treatment, inmates keep order within the correctional institution.

Inmates are often treated as if they were children, as the correctional officers reward them for good behavior and punish them for bad behavior. Because use of force is a delicate matter in correctional facilities, most correctional officers would agree that the preferred method of maximizing control is to condition inmates and refer to the use of perks. In some correctional institutions, if inmates behave well throughout the day (usually measured by lack of violent episodes in a given day), they are rewarded by watching a movie on a VCR during that evening's recreation time. A movie, which easily removes two hours of a long sentence, is a welcomed event.

Another form of control is the privilege of using the exercise room, which includes weights. Inmates who do not behave well are punished by being banned from the weight room and they have to express their frustrations in other ways that are not related to physical activity. This, coupled with the fact that most correctional officers will place an unruly offender in an isolation cell, gives momentum to the aim of deterring inmates from misbehaving.

9-1b Corruption Among Correctional Officers

Most correctional officers are decent, hard working people, but there are a few, as in other professions, that are corrupt and follow unethical practices in the course of their work.[8] According to a fairly recent study, the following are the most often encountered unethical activities in correctional settings:

- Abuse of inmates
- Inappropriate relationship with inmates
- Introduction to contraband
- Fiscal improprieties
- On-duty misconduct
- Off-duty misconduct
- Investigative violations[9]

All of these are grounded in the interactions of correctional officers and inmates. According to a study conducted by Lloyd McCorkle, the interrelationship of correctional officers and inmates may lead to corruption in one of three ways. These are:

- **Corruption through friendship**
- **Corruption through reciprocity**
- **Corruption through default**[10]

Corruption through friendship The corruption of correctional personnel that results from the absence of traditional devices that separate the ruler from the ruled. The officer cannot withdraw physically, act through intermediaries, or fall back on dignity.

Corruption Through Friendship

The correctional officer is without the traditional devices that separate the ruler from the ruled. The officer cannot withdraw physically, act through intermediaries, or fall back on dignity. Inmates have, in the past, referred to the correctional officer as a hack or screw. They pressure the officer with "a sort of moral blackmail," threatening ridicule and hostility if he/she will not be a "good Joe." As the middle person between the bureaucratic top and the prison floor, "the guard is caught in a conflict of loyalties." Correctional officers may resent the higher authorities that give them orders but show little appreciation for what they do. Ironically, officers resemble the inmate who resents correctional officers for similar reasons. Although inmates are condemned by society, the low-paid officer may actually be gratified to associate with notorious criminals. The correctional officer "often believes that these men are not seriously to be viewed as criminals, as desperate prisoners to be rigidly suppressed."[11]

Corruption Through Reciprocity

Corruption through reciprocity Correctional personnel ignore minor infractions. This takes place because of the pressure experienced by officers who realize that their merit rating depends on the cooperation they receive from those they control.

"To a large extent the guard is dependent on inmates for the satisfactory performance of his duties and, like many figures of authority, the guard is evaluated in terms of the men he controls." The correctional officer's pay, promotion, and merit ratings depend on the cooperation they receive from those they control, although they have few rewards to offer those under their authority. One of the rewards is to ignore minor infractions. Officers must also realize that they may face danger from the inmates. For example, during a prison riot they could be taken as hostage. "A fund of good will becomes a valuable form of insurance," so officers must have friends among the inmates.[12]

Corruption Through Default

Corruption through default The form of corruption takes place because of the indifference, laziness, or naiveté on the officer's part. As a result, the officer's job is gradually taken over by others.

Trustee An entrusted inmate who, due to his loyalty to correctional officers, receives extra benefits.

"Finally, much of the guard's authority tends to be destroyed by the innocuous encroachment of inmates on the guard's duties."[13] Indifference, laziness, or naiveté on the officer's part may mean that his/her job is gradually taken over by others. A second result of the earlier type of interrelationship between correctional officers and inmates is the use of some inmates as **trustees**. These inmates gain such power in the prison that they take on a role very similar to that of a correctional officer. In the past, they were often armed but not trained in the use of firearms. When shooting was used a form of disciplining, they often injured inmates. Trustees also engage in "loan sharking, extortion, and other illegal conduct in dealing with inmates subject to their authority and control." Although today most correctional facilities do not arm their trustees, they still hold special responsibilities while benefiting from additional perks which are often denied to other inmates. The idea is that these inmates will provide information to correctional administrators regarding upcoming plans for a riot or an escape.

9-1c Rehabilitation versus Security: A Correctional Officer's Dilemma

At a time when the United States is fighting terrorism, there is much suspicion that the already conservative American public is expecting a more serious governmental approach to secure the nation. This perspective may also have an impact on the correctional system as personnel are being retrained in order to identify and detect terrorist movements inside the prison system.

This growing conservative agenda, coupled with the recent movement to reform and rehabilitate, is creating conflict among most correctional officers. This conflict is clouding their judgment as they contemplate the rehabilitation potential of an inmate versus the punishment they deserve (and the public expects the inmates to receive). This has resulted in what some have called the state of anomie. The anomie is created by the conflict between the philosophies of treatment and custody and by the undermining of the officer's ability to maintain security while utilizing the rehabilitative approach. Before the adoption of the rehabilitative approach in the 1960s, correctional officers were regarded as and performed the duties of a guard. The rules of inmate behavior were specific. Correctional officers maintained security and regulated the inmates' lives. Under the reforms, guards became correctional officers, and although they were still in charge of security, their jobs took on added functions. They were to aid in rehabilitation but were never told how this was to be accomplished. No longer were there specific rules for inmate behavior. Correctional officers were faced with having to make decisions on such issues as what happens if an inmate makes unnecessary loud noise. Is that a threat to the security of the institution that demands action by the officers? Or, should it be ignored on the assumption that inmates have a need (and a right) to express themselves?

The adaptation to the new rehabilitation objectives was made more difficult as a new type of personnel entered the correctional system. The correctional system experienced yet one more change—the entrance of thousands of rehabilitation workers and other **professional staff**. This angered and frustrated correctional officers who did not share the same vision about the ultimate goal of rehabilitating inmates.

Professional staff Typically individuals who hold a college degree and work in a correctional setting conducting some form of service (e.g., counselors).

Since the entrance of professional staff (e.g., doctors, nurses, counselors) to the correctional field, additional factors have contributed to the suspicion existing between correctional officers and professional staff members. There is an apparent difference in the nature of their corresponding assignments and in educational levels. Professional staff members tend to have more education than correctional officers; some have had exposure to college, and some have attained a college and/or advanced degree. In contrast, correctional officers are mostly high school graduates who have not taken college courses. This educational dilemma seems to increase the suspicion of correctional officers towards their college educated counterparts. It is not unusual to hear comments that suggest (when referring to correctional staff) that they are "clueless" about the work that must be done in prisons. These comments help correctional officers understand the liberal approach of their counterparts.

It is difficult for these two groups to get along and work towards the same goal. This is one of the most significant problems for the correctional system. While it benefits from the work of talented personnel at all levels, it is also negatively affected by the contrast and conflict of different ideologies. Experts argue that the only manner in which these and other similar problems can be addressed is through a change of culture in the correctional system—formalizing educational standards while enhancing the existing training of all correctional professionals.

9-2 The Warden

Although the role of correctional officers and the professional staff is important for the success of any correctional facility, the warden sets the tone that impacts the manner in which a particular facility will operate. The importance of this position cannot be overemphasized. The philosophy of the warden is crucial in determining which orientation the programs of the institutions will take. If the warden believes the main function of prison is custody, the allocation of funds will likely be reflected in security to the detriment of rehabilitation programs. Although a warden's belief in the philosophy of rehabilitation will not ensure success within the institution, it probably is a prerequisite to any success that might occur.

In its 1967 report, the President's Crime Commission expressed great concern over the possibility that the position of warden might attract persons primarily interested in power and authority. The traditional position of warden held unlimited power over both staff and inmates. It was usually a political appointment and brought with it fringe benefits such as the use of a car, living expenses, extensive domestic service provided by inmates, and even household furnishings. The commission, however, noted some positive changes. At the time of the report, twenty-three states had established a merit system for filling the position of prison warden. In other states, governors had begun to appoint professionally trained persons to these important roles.[14]

James B. Jacobs Performed a classic correctional study on the role of wardens in correctional institutions. Further, he analyzed the involvement of the administration of the penitentiary in Stateville, Illinois.

Joseph E. Ragen Served as the warden at Stateville, Illinois for thirty years. A former sheriff of a small Illinois town, Ragen had only a ninth-grade education and became the Stateville warden in 1936 after serving as warden of another institution in Illinois, where he had the reputation of being a strict disciplinarian.

A study performed by **James B. Jacobs**, on the role of wardens in correctional institutions, analyzed the involvement of the administration of the penitentiary in Stateville, Illinois, as it relates to sociological organizational theory. This study is considered one of a kind. Jacobs used a Weberian analysis, tracing events from the traditional to charismatic, to rational-legal forms of authority, and finally to increasing bureaucratization.[15]

Joseph E. Ragen was the warden at Stateville for thirty years. A former sheriff of a small Illinois town, Ragen had only a ninth-grade education when he became the Stateville warden in 1936. After serving as warden of another institution in Illinois, he developed the reputation of being a strict disciplinarian. At Stateville, Ragen exercised control over minute details of prison life and administration and would not tolerate changes by anyone from the inside or outside, without his prior approval. Referred to as the "old boss," Ragen established a prison that was so orderly and efficient that it became known throughout the world.[16]

Ragen demanded absolute loyalty from those who worked for him. Their reactions and feelings were characterized as ranging from love and respect to fear and deep resentment, from intensive loyalty to a feeling that Ragen was arbitrary and authoritarian. Correctional officers and inmates had strong negative feelings about the intense supervision.

He imposed severe rules on the inmates and on the correctional officers, whose behavior he tried to control off-duty as well as on-duty. For the inmates, the silent system was enforced in marching and in dinning halls. When the emphasis on prison reform and concern for inmates began spreading across the country in the mid-1950s, Ragen simply redefined his system of total control by calling it rehabilitation. He rearranged some of the programs. For example, he put more men in the vocational school, but at the same time oriented the school to the personal needs of his favored staff. All of the inmates worked but only about 20 percent of them worked in the industries of which Ragen spoke so proudly. The rest sewed hems on red flags, buttons on jockey shorts, or engaged in similar vocations.[17]

Contacts with the outside world were carefully monitored. Those who defied the warden and those who tried to complain to outside the facility were beaten. "Inmates who challenged the system could be 'salted away' in segregation for as long as a decade."[18]

In 1961, Ragen left Stateville to become the Director of Public Safety in Illinois. In that position, he was in charge of managing the entire Illinois prison system. He appointed many of his people from Stateville to high positions in the system. His loyal assistant warden, Frank Pate, became warden in Stateville. Ragen left behind a 132-page rulebook that codified his system and until 1965, that book ruled the institution. Ragen himself spent considerable time there, and in essence, still controlled the prison.[19]

In 1965, Ragen became ill and suffered from an alleged mental breakdown. He had to resign and was replaced by long time rival Ross Randolph, who relaxed the prison rules considerably. The prison began to feel the effects of the 1962 revision of the Illinois criminal code, which shortened sentences. Many of the prisoners who had been at Stateville for a long time and held supervisory positions in the industries left the prison, and were replaced by civilians.

With the shortening of sentences in Illinois, the rising proportions of minorities, and the fast turnover of inmates at Stateville, the traditional inmate social system disintegrated. Black nationalism and other movements were on the upswing and inmates were less willing to accept the authoritarian system they had experienced during the reign of Ragen and Pate. The institution became more bureaucratic. This occurred for three reasons. First, the creation of the Illinois Department of Corrections left virtually no local autonomy to prisons. The second was:

> "[the] emergence of a highly educated elite occupying the top administrative positions. This elite does not share the homogeneity of the guard force, nor does it view Stateville as an institution with an independent moral value over and above its instrumental function in the criminal justice system. It has brought to the prison the values and attitudes of the American University and embodies within it an ethos of public service."[20]

The final reason was that the civilians who were appointed as treatment personnel were specialized, resulting in more narrowly defined job descriptions for all the staff. These new appointments frequently criticized the old patriarchal regime. Staff training, research and long-range planning, implementation of the grievance mechanism, and the maintenance of written records were other changes.[21]

The last stage of the institution, which Jacobs calls the stage of restoration, was characterized by a strengthening of security, improved services, and improved morale of correctional officers. Jacobs concluded that if the warden could maintain security and the increase in services that were extended to inmates during the period of bureaucratization, the facility would become a model of prison administration. However, there are limits, such as resources. Secondly, at some point, the administration can no longer be responsive to the problems and needs of the inmates. Third, the warden has already encountered conflict with prison reformers, private interest groups, the media, and some correctional officers. Finally, politics is a source of problems.

Today, the office of the warden is subject to political realities not present during Ragen's time. That is, wardens are considered a combination of politician and correctional professional. They are often evaluated for their performance and measured by virtue of the absence of riots or other disturbances. The successful warden is one who does not receive much media attention as a result of discipline-related issues. Further, the successful warden is one who reassures society that just punishment is being carried out while at the same time understanding the reality that the harsher the treatment in prison, the less likely an individual will be to succeed once released to society. A warden from a correctional institution located in the Midwest stated that the most difficult job he had to do was to "appease the public who often demanded punishment while acknowledging that one day, most of the inmates housed in his facility would leave the institution and return to society to live next door to those that had, at one point or another, demanded restitution."

It is not surprising to acknowledge the fact that some wardens in today's correctional system often leave their posts in order to retire or to find alternative jobs.[22] Many consider it the ideal post to hold after a long career, but just before retirement; however, this is not the attitude to have when one accepts the invitation to become a warden. Despite this, there are some that are considered to be successful in their attempt to make an impact in the lives of inmates.[23] Stories that relate successful techniques are being passed on from one generation of wardens to the next. The facilitator of communication between old and new wardens is the U.S. National Institute of Corrections (NIC). Just recently, NIC has announced additional grants being offered to state wardens in an attempt to seek the replication of existing management models regarded as successful.[24] Retired warden Jim Willett stated the following in his article "What I Have Learned":

- I presided over eighty-nine executions; eighty-eight men and one woman—and every one was different.
- I would signal that it was time to start the chemicals by taking off my glasses.
- The best part of leaving the job is not having to watch anybody die.
- People think we enjoy this.
- I made it through eight years as a warden and never had one run off.
- If I could do one thing differently, I would have lived a better Christian life.
- We in this nation have gotten to where we can't laugh at ourselves anymore.
- People who are sure about the death penalty one way or the other must have greater insight than me.
- The greatest movie line ever? Coming from a warden, it ought to be "what we have here is a failure to communicate."
- I can't be certain I didn't help execute an innocent person. There may have been people who said "I did it" to protect somebody else.
- I gave my inmates as much respect as they allowed me to give them.
- I had a guy on the gurney look me straight in the eye and say "God bless you." And I said, "God bless you, too."[25]

9-2a Management Styles

Although each warden has a particular management style, most adhere to professional standards. Most correctional professionals understand that success will depend not only on organization analysis, management by objectives, and planning, but also on style of management. There are four styles of management: bureaucratic, technocratic, idiosyncratic, and participative.

Bureaucratic management style Form of management which specifies that a manager has little, if any, personal contact with those who work below him or her; it is felt that personal contact will lessen the bureaucrat's authority.

Technocratic management style Style of management which suggests that a manager may react personally with others in the organization but sees himself or herself as the outstanding expert in the organization, the chief technocrat, who directs change as necessary.

Bureaucratic Management Style

In the **bureaucratic management style**, the manager has little, if any, personal contact with those who work below him or her—it is felt that personal contact will lessen the bureaucrat's authority. The emphasis is on rules and loyalty to the manager as well as to the objectives of the organization. This form of management is effective in some situations but is not a good style for identifying problems and the need for change.

Technocratic Management Style

In the **technocratic management style**, the technocrat may react personally with others in the organization but sees himself or herself as the outstanding expert in the organization who directs change as necessary. Within corrections, psychologists and social workers are often examples of technocrats.

Idiosyncratic Management Style

The **idiosyncratic management style** is the "big brother" approach. The administrator tries to manage by stimulating and encouraging others to carry out their roles. This type of manager may also manipulate individuals, reserve considerable decision making for himself or herself, and "frequently bypasses subordinates in his efforts to influence the behavior of individuals several echelons below in the hierarchy." This leader may become preoccupied with minute details or may have trouble delegating decision-making power, even in areas that are of no concern to him or her. When the leader does make decisions, they are often based on personalities and not on the significance of the decision to the organization. In the applications of this style, which are manipulative in nature, the organizational consequences will be that the organization will not hold its more interpersonally skillful subordinates any longer or that it will deteriorate in a pathology of intrigue. [26]

Idiosyncratic management style This management style is referred to as being part of the "big brother" approach where the administrator tries to manage by stimulating and encouraging others to carry out their roles. This type of manager may also manipulate individuals personally.

Participative Management Style

The manager who practices the **participative management style** maintains an informal and friendly relationship with subordinates and may even sacrifice work requirements of the organization in order to keep harmony with the staff. The opinions of subordinates are solicited and are considered in decision-making. The goal of this manager is to build an effective team of workers and the approach is group-oriented.

Correctional administrators, including wardens, use all of these management styles. Wardens and other correctional administrators are asked to embrace new and innovative concepts that are likely to influence the nature of the correctional system. Recently, prison administrators have embraced the concept of restorative justice.

Participative management style This management style sustains that a manger should maintain an informal and friendly relationship with subordinates and may even sacrifice work requirements of the organization at times in order to keep harmony with the staff.

9-3 Restorative Justice

The aim of restorative justice is to restore justice in cases where justice has not occurred. It is defined as "a systematic response to wrongdoing thate emphasizes healing the wounds of victims, offenders, and communities caused or revealed by crime."[27] The underlying theme is that the offender is forced to restore the wrongdoing done to the victim. Some retail stores have adopted this approach and implemented it in cases involving shoplifting incidents. Stores have asked convicted shoplifters, as components of their punitive conditions, to reimburse the store (who in these cases are the victims) for money spent on court fees and/or expert testimony. In cases where the shoplifter damaged goods belonging to the store, he or she is often asked to pay for them or replace them with new items.

The primary practices and programs that currently reflect restorative justice will aim to:

- Identify and repair the harm done
- Involve all pertinent groups
- Convert the traditional relationship of communities and their governments[28]

In the correctional field, restorative justice takes place in reintegration programs for inmates. Upon being eligible for release, some inmates qualify for programs that aim at slowly reintegrating them back to their lives before they were incarcerated. These programs consider the inmate and the family members who must become accustomed to the idea that their loved one is now outside of prison. In addition, these programs allow the inmate to regain control of his or her life by seeking employment and following a legitimate lifestyle that won't commit him or her back to prison.[29]

Although it is not clear if these programs are successful, most criminal justice practitioners and correctional personnel claim that it is a positive step. As long as the concept of restoring justice is in place, the criminal justice system will keep the focus on the victims.

Summary

Some of the most important issues related to prison management were examined in this chapter. Particular emphasis was placed on the nature and role of correctional officers while demonstrating the complexities associated with this particular job. Some of these included the discussion of the rehabilitative versus security approaches. In addition, the responsibilities of the prison warden while examining the historical dimensions related to this position were discussed.

The final section in this chapter was devoted to the concept of restorative justice with particular emphasis on how this concept has affected the correctional system. Programs related to the reintegration of inmates back into the community follow the restorative justice approach that restores justice back into the community and victims. It is likely that this approach will continue to challenge correctional administrators to creatively think and focus on crime victims and their rights.

Notes

1. For further discussion of correctional officers, see Andrew D. Alpert's "Probation Officers and Correctional Treatment Specialists," *Occupational Outlook Quarterly,* Fall 2001.
2. Davis, Ray Curtis, "Correctional Officers Deserve Respect," *Corrections Today,* December 1999, P. 29.
3. U.S. Department of Labor, Bureau of Labor Statistics, "Occupational Outlook Handbook," 2001, Washington, D.C.
4. Donald Clemmer, *The Prison Community* (New York: Holt, Rinehart and Winston, 1958); and Gresham Sykes, *Society of Captives* (Princeton, NJ: Princeton University Press, 1958).
5. Clemmer, *The Prison Community,* p. 84. Note that the term "prison guard" was later replaced by "correctional officer." This was done in an attempt to professionalize the work of correctional personnel.
6. Sykes, *Society of Captives.*
7. Sykes, p. 23.
8. For a more in-depth discussion on correctional officer misconduct, read Nina Siegal's "Stopping Abuse in Prison," *The Progressive,* April 1999 v.63, i.4, p. 31(1).
9. Henry, Mark A., "Unethical Staff Behavior: A Guide to Identifying and Investigating Staff Misconduct," *Corrections Today,* June, 1998.
10. Lloyd W. McCorkle, "Social Structure in a Prison," In Norman Johnson et al., eds., *The Sociology of Punishment and Correction,* 2nd ed., (New York: Wiley, 1970), p. 421.
11. McCorkle, "Social Structure."
12. McCorkle, p. 421.
13. McCorkle, p. 421.
14. The President's Commission on Law Enforcement and Administration of Justice, *Task Force Report: Corrections* (Washington, D.C.: U.S. Governmental Printing Office, 1967), p. 59.
15. James B. Jacobs, *Statesville: The Penitentiary in Mass Society* (Chicago: University of Chicago Press, 1977), pp. 10-11.
16. Jacobs, p. 29.
17. Jacobs, p. 47.
18. Jacobs, p. 50.
19. Jacobs, pp. 51-52.
20. Jacobs, p. 73.
21. Jacobs, p. 78.
22. For additional information on the challenges facing wardens in the twenty-first century, read Gary I. Dennis's "WY2K: The Challenge of Being a Warden in the New Millennium," *Corrections Today,* December 1999, pp. 80-82, 131.
23. For further discussion of the impact of wardens on the lives of inmates, read Elizabeth A. Klug's "Warden Helps Inmates, Staff Improve Their Lives," *Corrections Today,* April, 2002, p. 14.
24. Susan M. Hunter, "NIC Provides Training for Wardens," *Corrections Today,* August 2001, pp.147-148.
25. Patrick Beach, "What I've Learned: Jim Willett (Interview)," *Esquire,* March 2002, v.137, i.3, p.140(2).
26. George G. Killinger, Paul F. Cromwell, and Bonnie Cromwell, *Issues in Corrections and Administration: Selected Readings,* (St. Paul, MN: West Publishing Company, 1976).
27. Restorative Justice Online (2002), http://www.restorativejustice.org/rj3/intro_default.htm
28. Restorative Justice Online (2002).
29. For more information on these programs, go to http://www.restorativejustice.org/rj3/Introduction-Definition/Tutorial/Prisoner_Assistance.htm and read about the Alternatives to Violence project (AVP) and the Detroit Transition of Prisoners (TOP).

Chapter

Chapter 10

Parole and Release from Prison

Outline

On a daily basis, inmates from correctional institutions throughout the United States are being released back into society after serving long prison sentences. To many, the thought of waking up in their own beds while enjoying their many freedoms is a dream come true. However, most former inmates ask the question, "Now what?" upon being released from prison. They do not know what they will do and how they will cope with a life that is radically different from the life they have known while incarcerated.

Key Terms

contract theory
continuing custody theory
due process theory

Some inmates find that a minimum wage job does not pay the amount of money they need and they resort to a life of crime that offers immediate gratification. Others may end up committing suicide as they struggle to cope with a lifestyle they have forgotten. If they cannot find jobs and face continued discrimination and harassment, their chances of returning to the institution on another charge are greatly increased.

This chapter explores the problems that inmates face upon release from prison and considers the programs that have been designed to prepare inmates for their discharge. Furlough and work release programs are discussed, which have been designed to provide the inmate with a gradual reentry into society. Pre-release programs within the institutions are discussed— these programs do not actually place offenders in the community but attempt to provide them with an opportunity to discuss some of the problems they will encounter upon release. Some of the problems inmates most frequently encounter upon release are: financial problems, lack of employment, and social concerns.

The last section of this chapter is devoted to a discussion on parole—the most frequent form of release from prison. The text examines parole historically, considers the purposes of parole, and discusses various ways in which parole is organized. Consider-

able attention is given to the process of parole decision-making and the conditions that may be imposed on the parolee. Parole supervision, both in terms of the services offered to the client as well as the qualifications and functions of parole officers, is discussed. Several court cases that have placed limitations on the authority of the state to remove an individual from parole are described. Finally, attempts to evaluate the success or failure of parole and consider the future of this method of release are explored.

10-1 Preparation for Release

The regular use of work release and furlough programs in the United States is a recent phenomenon. It stemmed from the provision for these programs in the federal system by the Prisoner Rehabilitation Act of 1965. However, at the state level, the first work release law was the Huber Law, which was passed in Wisconsin in 1913. The next statute was not passed until 1957 in North Carolina. The first furlough program was introduced by legislation in Mississippi in 1918. A few states passed laws providing for work release or furloughs before 1965, but most of the programs in existence today were established by state laws after the 1965 federal law was passed. Work release programs have grown to such proportions today that they represent another form of release for inmates. According to the Bureau of Justice Statistics (2001), jail personnel in the United States supervised 7,780 inmates who worked in programs outside correctional institutions in 1999.[1] Although state prison statistics do not separate work release figures from other forms of community-based initiatives, in 1998, authorities reported to have supervised more than 72,000 individuals committed to electronic monitoring, home detention, or work release.[2] These figures suggest that work release programs are currently a major component of the correctional systems in the United States.

It is necessary to distinguish work release programs from furlough programs. A furlough allows an inmate to leave the institution for a specified purpose other than work or study. For example, the offender may be given a furlough to visit a sick relative, to attend a family member's funeral, or to look for a job. The leave is only temporary and is granted for a short period of time.

In work release programs, the inmate is released from incarceration to work or attend school. Inmates may participate in work-study, take courses at an educational institution, or work at a job in the community. The primary aim of such programs is to allow "selected prisoners to hold normal, productive, paying jobs and return to the prison for all nonworking hours."[3] Work release is also referred to by other names such as day parole, outmate program, day work, daylight parole, free labor, intermittent jailing, and work furlough.

State legislation varies in regards to who decides whether an inmate should be put on work release and how the money earned by the inmate is to be used. Most legislation permits states to contract with other political subdivisions for housing of inmates because they cannot always find work near the institution. Some states provide halfway houses—a non-confining residential facility designed for readjusting offenders to the community after incarceration—while others use county jails.

Among the conditions for outside employment are that inmates cannot work in areas where there is a surplus of labor; they must be paid the same wage that others receive for the same job; if a union is involved, it must be consulted; and the inmate cannot work during a labor dispute.

10-1a Evaluation

The first and most important advantage of these programs is that they place the offender in contact with his or her family and the community. In the past, several studies have shown that "those inmates with strong family ties, and who have maintained those ties during incarceration, are more successful on release than those offenders without such ties."[4] Work release programs enable offenders to engage in positive contact with the community, while assuming that work placement is satisfactory. It also permits men and women to support, to some extent, themselves and their families. This can eliminate the self-concept of failure that can be the result of the loss of the supportive role important in American society. Under the work release programs, the offender can obtain more satisfying jobs than the prison could provide. Work release and furlough programs provide a transition for the incarcerated inmate—from a closely supervised way of life in prison to a more independent life within society. These programs also give the community a transition period during which it accepts the offender back into society. Finally, the programs have permitted some states to close one or more correctional facilities, thus decreasing the cost to the taxpayer. Despite these benefits, some argue that these programs are a failure. They cite low levels of supervision with a general disinterest in the success of the inmate as primary reasons for their failures.

The popularity of the benefits associated with the work release programs has been obscured in recent months by the public's demand that inmates serve most, if not all, of their prison sentences. This public attitude has been gaining popularity since the terrorist attacks of September 11, 2001. The effort to fight terrorism has convinced the public that punishment should be in place without considering the idea of rehabilitation.

Some have questioned the arguments made supporting work release programs. Most critics cite the problems with methodology in the samples used in order to determine that these programs are successful. Gordon P. Waldo and Theodore G. Chiricos, in their review of the studies of work release, maintain that most of those who favor such programs "have ignored both theoretical premise and empirical evidence in asserting" the advantages of work release.[5] Based on their study in which they used random assignments of subjects to both the control and experimental groups, Waldo and Chiricos concluded:

> At this initial point in our analysis, it would appear that participation in work release has no bearing on the rates of recidivism for all subjects in the present inquiry. In short, there is no evidence that participation in work release makes any difference in recidivism, regardless of the operational definition of recidivism or the control variables utilized.[6]

10-1b Pre-release Programs

Use of furloughs and work release programs is limited by staff, resources, and the possibility that some offenders will commit crimes while participating in the programs. Consequently, not all offenders may participate. All offenders must, however, be released when they have served their court-imposed sentences. Pre-release programs have been developed to assist offenders in making the adjustments back to life in the community.

It has long been recognized that most offenders who eventually commit more crimes do so within a very short time after release. This suggests that immediate adjustment problems might be quite severe for offenders. It was not until the 1940s that prison officials began to develop programs within their institutions aimed at assisting inmates with these adjustment problems.[7]

Most of the work release programs currently available are designed for inmates who have from ten to eighteen months remaining to complete their sentence, and it is possible for inmates to be released from prison up to one year before they complete their sentence. This can be done as long as they qualify for a work release program. The eligibility requirements are different from state to state but most require that the applicant:

- Be placed in a community treatment center
- Be of minimum to low security
- Must have no more than eighteen months remaining to complete the sentence
- Have a clear institutional conduct record
- Cannot have any violence, organized crime, high drug, or public safety factors that are involved in the inmate's case
- Must be fully employable with no medical constraints that would have an impact on a given work assignment
- Must be willing to participate in a work release program[8]

Most programs involve living in a halfway house while working at a prearranged site. Participants are eligible for furloughs—they can qualify to be released away from the halfway house for the weekend. This privilege is extended as long as the inmate continues to perform at a level that is deemed as satisfactory.[9]

A study at the United States Penitentiary in Lewisburg, Pennsylvania, suggested that pre-release programs needed to adopt part of the philosophy of Alcoholics Anonymous. Inmates need to recognize that they must want help, that they do not want to be recommitted, and that they accept the fact that release to the community will present problems. This pre-release program involved three types of programs: mandatory considerations (legal problems, rules of supervision); planning and resources (employment information, job responsibilities, financial planning, community resources); and emotional factors (race relations, attitude problems). Attendance was required at some, but not all, meetings. Special sessions were held on clothing, alcoholism, and other topics.

Inmates who participated in the program at Lewisburg were asked to complete a questionnaire ninety days before leaving the institution and again six months after their release. In the pre-release questionnaire, the main interests expressed by inmates were finding a job, having money to meet their needs, and staying out of trouble. In the group meetings of the pre-release program, they had additional concerns including being accepted by others and relationships with police. The post-release questionnaire revealed that the predominant problems were in the areas of employment, finances, and becoming adjusted to a free society. Two-thirds of the inmates thought the pre-release program had helped but said that group sessions should have been longer because the individuals profited most by discussing problems with others who were also soon to be released. Respondents said that the most valuable things they received in prison were job training, academic improvement, and better understanding of interpersonal relationships.[10] Today, the effectiveness of pre-release programs remains unclear. A consensus does exist, however, in the belief that the absence of these programs would result in even more extreme overcrowded conditions for the prison system.

10-1c Halfway Houses: Traditional Pre-release Centers

Halfway houses are often used as transitions from prison to the community and they have a long history. The earliest documentation of a proposal for a halfway house in the United States was in 1817 in the Commonwealth of Massachusetts, but the first one actually established was the Temporary Asylum for Discharged Female Prisoners in 1864 in Boston. Not many followed until 1950, when the disenchantment with rehabilitating persons within prisons began to gain momentum. In the 1950s, a movement to develop halfway houses began. It grew during the 1960s with the formation of the Halfway House Association.[11]

Traditionally, there have been two types of halfway houses: places for released persons to receive assistance in adjusting to the community (a general purpose residence) and places for specific problems of adjustment, such as drug treatment centers. The Shaw Residence in Washington, D.C., which was regarded as one of

Spotlight 10-1

LASER Treatment: A Program That Changes Criminal Behavior

The Dauphin County Prison in Pennsylvania implemented the Life, Attitude, Skills, Educational Retraining (LASER) project in January 1994.[12] This program aims at changing the criminal behavior of the individual by altering lifestyle patterns. Although it is cited here as an example of a pre-release program, this program aids not only those who are incarcerated, but also at those on parole or on release. The program usually lasts thirteen weeks and teaches participants skills that will improve their quality of life, while decreasing in-house disciplinary infractions and reducing recidivism. A recent evaluation of the program revealed that recidivism rates for LASER participants were 62 percent for a control group as opposed to 78 percent for the Dauphin County prison population.[13] It was also found that LASER graduates committed fewer in-house disciplinary infractions while showing increased self-esteem and a higher educational level. It is claimed that the LASER program "whole person" approach teaches inmates the skills required to give them what they need most—freedom. Although the findings of this particular evaluation are encouraging, a certain degree of caution must be exercised before this program can claim success and be replicated in other jurisdictions.

the general-purpose types, assisted people released from the Federal Bureau of Prisons. It operated like a family home. Residents were given financial counseling assistance and help adjusting to an independent life. They were encouraged to spend weekends away from the residence. Halfway houses such as the Shaw residence can be found throughout the United States. Most operate closely with the community in an attempt to address the reintegration-related needs of the offender.

10-1d Halfway Programs: Pre-release Guidance Centers

In the early 1960s, the Federal Bureau of Prisons opened six pre-release centers where prisoners could serve the last few months of their sentences while adjusting to the community. Some were located in YMCA facilities. In these centers, offenders ate in the cafeteria and used the recreational facilities. They traveled to the pre-release center by public transportation and without escort. Offenders were confined to the center for a few days of orientation but then were mobile. They were permitted to move out of the facility before the end of their term, returning only for conferences. These pre-release centers were staffed by people associated with the correctional institution who visited the offenders for counseling sessions and by some permanent staff. The centers were tied in with some probation offices. The advantage of having this counseling available was that the professional staff handled problems as they took place. Even though some of the offenders got into trouble (for example, getting drunk), their actions did not invalidate the program. They would probably have these problems when released from prison and in the program they had access to counseling when the problem occurred.[14]

Recently, halfway houses have lost some of their attractiveness. States are now facing a great deal of criticism about their inability to rehabilitate offenders. Consequently, the popularity and funding of halfway houses have suffered. This problem has reached such proportions that some jurisdictions have transformed halfway houses into museums or other public facilities. This has occurred because citizens see a halfway house in their community as a presence that will devalue their property. Despite this, halfway houses continue to provide offenders an opportunity for an adequate transition to life after prison. In addition to halfway houses, some pre-release programs, such as the one described in Spotlight 10-1, continue to make a difference as they ease the transition from prison life to the outside world.

10-2 Problems Encountered upon Release

Inmates who have been incarcerated face many problems upon release. One of the most obvious problems is the labeling that often follows the inmate. This is most evident in states that make a point of releasing photographs of ex-offenders and placing them in local newspapers and on bulletin boards. Some states place photos of former inmates on the Internet. The information often includes the reasons why the individual served a prison sentence. This practice is found among individuals accused of sexual offenses. The reasoning is to inform the community that a sexual predator is living among them. While trying to protect the community, this practice makes it very difficult for the recently released offender to attain a job or lead a crime-free lifestyle—the label of being a criminal can hamper job marketability. The most frequently encountered problems by inmates upon release are financial, employment, and personal (including family problems).

10-2a Financial Needs of Inmates upon Release

Inmates do not receive much financial assistance from correctional institutions. Many scholars, such as Jeffery Reiman (2001), have argued that the criminal justice system is unfair to those who are poor. Poor individuals facing criminal charges are more likely to receive a harsher sentence when compared to those that have substantial incomes that affords them a good defense team. This also makes a significant impact on inmates who, when released from prison, find themselves in a critical state of poverty.[15]

This phenomenon is not recent. In the early 1960s, the results of the National Survey of Financial Assistance to Released Prisoners were published. The survey revealed that the most frequent kind of assistance that American prisons gave to released prisoners was civilian clothing. This is even truer today, as most institutions require that prisoners send their personal clothing home. At the time of release, it is necessary for the institution to replace prison clothing with something less conspicuous. Some institutions save the personal clothing of inmates and give it back to them upon release. Others permit relatives to ship clothing to inmates. The survey, which included all state prison systems in the United States except Arkansas, revealed that all states except Hawaii issue free clothing to a released inmate who would otherwise have none.

The next most frequent type of assistance is money for transportation from the prison to the individual's destination. These grants are minimal, however, and are only given for transportation to an approved location. Some states give cash only to those who have been discharged and not to parolees. Some states base the amount of money given to the inmate on length of term or financial need. Others give the same sum to all although the amount is small.[16] Out of those funds, they must pay for additional clothing, room and board, and, in many cases, debts incurred before incarceration. They may also have to support a family and may not have a job upon release. Inmates are thrown into the outside world with few financial resources and little moral support.

A change of clothing, a ticket home, and a few dollars will not get one very far in today's inflationary world. Add to that a person who is rejected by society and by his or her family, and the ex-offender, in the words of Norman C. Colter, is a "handicapped human being, one who needs all the things the rest of us need and a little bit more." Colter advocates giving the inmate a large subsidy upon release. He concludes:

> The choice is simple. We can continue the current practice of releasing a man with so little money that we virtually guarantee he will return to prison and thus add about $50,000 to our tax burden to pay for his arrest, trial, and several years of wasteful and destructive support. Or we can give him about $1,200 over a six-month

period, an investment in the likelihood that this assistance will do much more to make him law-abiding than a $20,000 cell would.[17]

10-2b Employment

A second problem faced by offenders upon release is employment. Although offenders who have served all of their time must be released, those who have been granted parole will generally not be released without a job. The institution may or may not provide assistance in seeking employment for offenders. Again, their inability to attain a job is exacerbated by their lack of skills, their criminal label, and non-support from correctional agencies. This is a negative cycle, as the offender cannot be released until he or she obtains employment, while at the same time, he or she lacks the skills or the background to attain a job successfully. Unfortunately, this problem is most evident among drug offenders who, having been used to the high monetary rewards of selling drugs, refuse to be paid minimum wage in jobs they regard as undesirable. They often argue that they could make as much money in a single drug transaction as they would be paid during an entire month at a regular job.

Legal Reactions

Many states have statutes that prohibit granting licenses to ex-offenders to become members of certain professions, such as law and medicine. The American Bar Association's Commission on Correctional Facilities and Services and its Criminal Law Section sponsored the National Clearinghouse on Offender Employment Restrictions, funded by contract with the United States Department of Labor's Manpower Administration. Through its newsletter and other publications, the clearinghouse has made available to interested persons "information on the laws, regulations, and administrative practices and procedures which prevent the ex-offender from obtaining employment," as well as information on manpower programs.[18]

It is understandable why some claim that it is very difficult for former inmates to find a job, as most employers consider hiring an ex-con a liability. When applying for a job, one is asked about prior arrest and/or convictions. In some states and for some jobs, it is illegal to hire individuals who have a criminal past.

10-2c Social Problems of Ex-Offenders

Daniel Glaser, in his study of the U.S. federal correctional system, devoted an entire chapter to "The Ex-Prisoner's Social World." Glaser found that the blood ties of inmates improve during incarceration but that relationships with friends and spouses weaken. Over 90 percent of ex-offenders return to the communities in which they resided before the time of incarceration. Although their offenses may be known, they can usually expect to receive the greatest assistance from their families and/or close friends. This situation may be disadvantageous, however, in the case of ex-offenders who have experienced or are experiencing discord with relatives in the town to which they return. Of particular interest was the finding that the "most unfavorable post-release residential arrangement, in terms of post-release failure rates, is that in which the ex-prisoner lives alone."[19]

Ideally, counseling for families should take place while the spouse/parent is in prison and should continue after the inmate has been released. The problems of inmates' children should also be considered, especially if the caretaker in a single parent household is incarcerated. The strongest sign that children are affected by the confinement of a parent is poor school performance. Children who have at least one parent incarcerated are more likely than their counterparts to score low on exams while offering a greater likelihood of dropping out of school.

Although each of the two parents is regarded as important in a given household, a mother has a central role in the lives of her children. Consequently, the separation of a mother and child, when she is incarcerated, is particularly traumatic to the children. The most difficult of these situations is found in single parent households where the mother is the sole provider.

10-3 Parole

In the United States, most offenders reenter society via some form of parole program after serving time in a correctional facility. The Attorney General's Survey of Release Procedures has defined parole as "the release of an offender from a penal or correctional institution after he has served a portion of his sentence, under the continued custody of the state and under conditions that permit his reincarceration in the event of misbehavior."[20]

Parole resembles probation in that both permit a convicted person to live in the community under supervision. Theoretically, the decision to parole someone is made after careful study of the person's background, behavior, and potential for success. Both parole and probation are based on the philosophy that the rehabilitation of some individuals might be hindered by imprisonment (or further imprisonment) and will be aided by supervised freedom. The processes differ in that parole is granted after a portion of the prison term is served, while probation is granted in lieu of incarceration. Probation is a sentence while parole is not. In addition, a judge grants probation, while the decision to parole is usually made by a board appointed specifically for that purpose.

Parole should also be distinguished from other forms of release that occur when a person has served his or her full term, or when there is a statutory provision that a person may be released for good behavior after serving a specified portion of his or her term. Good behavior sometimes entitles inmates to a reduction in the length of their sentence. Their release is not, however, dependent upon the administrative decision of a parole board. Parole should also be distinguished from mandatory release, in which release is granted to an offender who has served all of his or her term. Such persons are released without supervision, in contrast to the continued supervision that the state (or the federal government in the case of a federal offender) exercises over a parolee. The government is entitled to continue that supervision until the parole period expires.

The origin of parole has been traced to the English system of transporting criminals to the American colonies. Criminals were pardoned by the English government after being sold to the highest bidder in America. The buyer then became the master of the individual, whose new status was that of indentured servant. The system is similar to parole in that the individual, to receive the change in status, agreed to certain conditions similar to the ones currently imposed by parole boards (e.g., restriction of movement).[21]

Others have claimed that the concept of conditioned liberty was first introduced in France around 1830. It was an intermediary step of freedom—supervision between prison confinement and complete freedom in the community. This system is the beginning of the concept known today as parole. In the United States, parole for juveniles goes back to the last half of the nineteenth century to the House of Refuge for children. In 1876, New York's Elmira Reformatory gave the first official recognition to a parole system.[22] The parole idea in the United States was closely linked to the introduction of indeterminate sentences. Parole began to be widely used upon state adoption of indeterminate sentences. It is reported that by 1900, twenty states had parole systems and by 1925, forty-eight states had parole systems.[23] By 1910, each federal correctional facility had

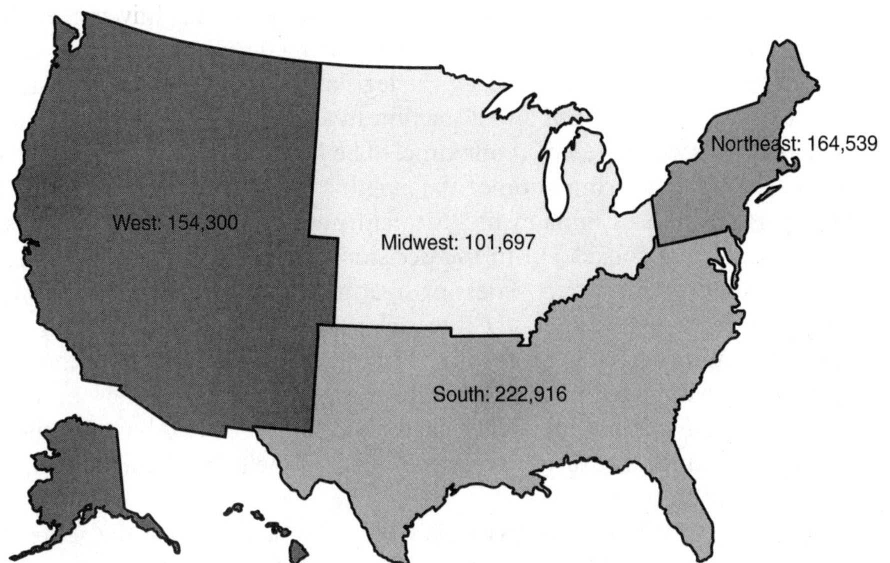

Figure 10-1
Parole Population in the United States by Region
Source: Bureau of Justice Statistics, Glaze, L., *Annual Parole Survey,* 2000.

its own parole board. These were replaced in 1930 when Congress created the U.S. Board of Parole. Today, all states have a mechanism in place to release offenders back to the community while under supervision.

10-3a Data on Parole

By January 1, 2000, there were 714,457 individuals on parole in the United States. This figure represents 71,005 at the federal level and 643,452 at the state level. Most individuals granted parole by 2000 were in the south (222,916) while the lowest number of parolees was in the midwest (101,697). The state with the highest number of parolees in 2000 was California (114,046); this state was closely followed by Texas, which had 109,310 parolees in January 2000. The state with the lowest number of parolees was Maine (28).[24] Figure 10-1 shows the parole populations in 2000 for the four regions of the United States: northeast, south, midwest, and west.

Statistics suggest that 88 percent of parolees are males while only 12 percent are females. Most are white (55 percent), followed by African Americans (44 percent). Approximately 21 percent of parolees in 2000 were of Hispanic origin. Among all parolees, 97 percent had been sentenced to more than one year in prison and 83 percent of them were determined to have an active supervision status. When comparing the statistics of 2000 with those of 1990, a trend is obvious. In the past ten years, females (+4 percent), whites (+3 percent), and Hispanics (+3 percent) have increased their presence among parolees. However, others have diminished their presence among parolees. These include males (-4 percent), African-Americans (-3 percent), and individuals entering discretionary parole (-22 percent).[25]

10-3b Parole and Sentencing

Parole is not a form of sentencing. The latter is determined by the court and the former by an administrative agency—the parole board. The two practices are, however, closely related. Although the occurrence of parole has increased since 1980, its popularity has been slowly declining. This phenomenon is the direct result of the immense overcrowding that the correctional system is presently experiencing. Despite the fact that very few individuals want to release offenders from prisons via parole (due to the belief that once out of prison they will again engage in criminal activity), correctional administrators must release those they consider to be less harmful so that others (preferably violent offenders) can occupy their space. Sentencing has had an effect on this recent trend.

America has experienced a sentencing movement that has ranged from allowing judges considerable discretion in sentencing decisions, to flat sentencing (in which sentences are established by the legislature), to the indeterminate sentence (often with a minimum and a maximum established by law), and back to flat sentencing. It was believed, at one time, to be important for judges and parole boards to share the determination of the length of incarceration. Also important was the participation of inmates in treatment programs. His or her progress in those programs was considered in the decision whether to release. No judge at sentencing could predict effectiveness of treatment and the release decision was left to a later decision-making body. It was also thought that this approach would give the community greater protection. Persons who were dangerous, and had not yet been rehabilitated would not be released. Norval Morris has argued, "It was a fine idea having only the defect that it did not work."[26] Abuses of the system resulted in sentencing disparity, with individuals held in prison for long periods with little or no treatment.

In the past, well-known individuals have taken a stance on the sentencing issue as it relates to parole. Massachusetts Senator Edward M. Kennedy took the position that sentencing disparity has been compounded by parole. In addition to the abuse of discretion that may occur at the time of deciding parole, Kennedy argued that the very existence of a parole system might encourage judges in their lengthy sentences. Judges might impose harsh sentences to make the community think that they are being tough with offenders—for example, in the case of drug possession offenses—with the expectation that the parole board will release the individuals early. Unfortunately, judges are not required to state reasons for their sentences and it is possible that parole boards inadvertently act contrary to the expectations of the judge. Even when the parole board members know what the judge presumes, they are not required to follow those expectations.[27] Kennedy concluded that with flat or determinate sentencing, parole release would not be needed. "Under this system of judicially-fixed sentences, parole release would be abolished and whether or not a prisoner has been 'rehabilitated' or has completed a certain prison curriculum would no longer have any bearing on his prison release date."[28]

10-3c Organization of Parole

The organization of parole is complex. One reason for this is the variety of sentencing structures under which parole systems must operate. Despite suggestions by the American Bar Association, the President's Crime Commission, the American Law Institute (which proposed a Model Penal Code), and the National Council on Crime and Delinquency (which proposed the Model Sentencing Act), jurisdictions differ in their sentencing structures. The type of sentence is closely related to the parole system. For example, in jurisdictions where sentences are long with little time off for good behavior, parole can involve a long period of supervision. In jurisdictions where sentences are short, parole can be relatively unimportant as a form of release and supervision will be for shorter periods. Historically, the authority to release prisoners rested with a state's governor. Today, governors no longer have this power but they still influence the process by possessing the authority to appoint most of the parole board members.

The Advisory Commission recommended eight objectives for a sentencing system consistent with parole goals. Those objectives involved the legislature and sentencing judges determining maximum sentences, but they could not restrict parole-granting authorities. Consequently, no minimum sentences existed. In addition, there were no offenses for which parole was denied by legislation. The commission recommended relatively short sentences with a five-year maximum for most offenses. The purpose of the commission's recommendations appeared to be twofold: to keep offenders from spending long terms in correctional facilities and to give a large degree of discretion concerning their release to parole boards. Abuse of that discretion by parole boards would be limited by the short maximum terms and by the requirement that parole boards give written reasons for refusal to grant parole.

The commission discussed the variety of functions parole boards must perform, in addition to making decisions on parole—from granting pardons in some states to holding clemency hearings and appointing the parole supervision staff. Despite the wide variety of parole programs, the states are equally divided between two models—the independent and the consolidated.

Independent Authority Model

Some parole boards for adult correctional facilities follow the independent authority model, establishing the parole board as an agency independent of the institution from which individuals are paroled. This model is supposed to establish a more objective process; however, the independent authority model has been severely criticized. The parole board is often composed of people who know little or nothing about corrections. The board is removed from the institution and often does not understand what is taking place there. Decisions may be made for inappropriate reasons, such as the desires of the local police chief. Consequently, parole boards often release those who should not be paroled and reject those who should be paroled.

Consolidated Model

The newer model is based on the belief that it is best to consolidate the parole activities within the department of corrections or any other multifunctional department of human services. Under the consolidated model, the parole board is able to retain its independent decision-making authority while being organizationally close to the department of corrections and sensitive to the department's needs. Some argue that this model is better as its parole board has more information about the offender (e.g., behavior while in prison, offense committed), which is needed to grant parole properly.

10-3d Parole Board Members: Selection and Qualifications

In most states, the governor appoints members of the parole board. The department of corrections appoints the board in whole or in part (in some jurisdictions). In some states, members of the board serve part-time; in others, board membership is a full-time position. It has been argued that full-time parole members are well-educated and well-paid individuals who have the proper training to successfully conduct parole hearings. Others argue that part-time parole members, although perhaps paid less than their full-time counterparts, represent the community more effectively.

What qualifications should parole board members possess? Some argue that parole boards should be made up of people who are trained in law, the behavioral sciences, and corrections. It has been recommended that they be sensitive to public concerns and willing to challenge the system when necessary. Boards have too often been rubber stamps of the correctional authorities, eliminating the possibility of a check on their abuse of discretion. The backgrounds of parole members vary throughout the United States. In the state of Mississippi, recent parole board members consisted of a businessman, a contractor, a clerk, and a farmer, whereas the parole board in Washington was made up of individuals with adequate training in the law, ministry, sociology, and government.

10-3e The Parole Granting Decision

Historically, American parole boards had almost total discretionary power. The theory behind this power was that parole was to be regarded as a privilege and not a right. "The prisoner has no statutory right, even if 'qualified,' to be granted conditional liberty or allowed to remain on parole."[29] Since parole is not to be considered a right, no reasons are offered for denial. Elements of due process are not required at the time the decision is made. As stated by a federal court in 1971,

> The Board of Parole is given absolute discretion in matters of parole. The courts are without power to grant a parole or to determine judicially eligibility for parole. . . . Furthermore, it is not the function of the courts to review the discretion of the Board in the denial of the application for parole or to review the credibility of reports and information received by the Board in making its determinations.[30]

The U.S. Supreme Court refused to review the case. That opinion was cited with approval by the same court in another case in 1973.[31]

The reasoning of the federal court in ruling that due process is not required at the determination of parole is that the granting of parole is not an adversary proceeding. The granting of parole is a complicated decision and the parole board must be able to use evidence that would not be admissible in a trial.

This lack of due process at the parole decision stage resulted in bitter complaints from inmates. One described his observations of fellow inmates who went before the parole board:

> They would get their hopes up and do all of the "right things," like going to church and AA meetings and behaving properly. The parole board would encourage them during the hearing. Then they would wait for a long time, sometimes six weeks, before they heard. If their applications for parole were denied, their feelings of despair would later turn to hatred at being rejected with no reasons given for the decisions. This inmate decided not to go for a parole hearing. He did not "wish to go through the very ugly and unpleasant cycles that my fellow inmates have. . . . You, my keepers, have my body, but my mind is somewhat my own. I feel free in the strength of my convictions."[32]

John Irwin discussed some of the ways in which the parole system can be disrupted. This resulted in a different set of standards applied at the time of a parole hearing than those that existed at the time the inmate was incarcerated. When this happens, says Irwin, a sense of injustice develops in inmates which further increases their loss of commitment to conventional society.[33] Justice Hugo Black best summarized the view of many inmates toward the parole board:

> In the course of my reading—by no means confined to law—I have reviewed many of the world's religions. The tenets of many faiths hold the deity to be a trinity. Seemingly, the parole boards by whatever names designated in the various states, have in too many instances sought to enlarge this to include themselves as members.[34]

10-3f The Parole Hearing

The most important stage in the administration of parole is the parole hearing. Until a few years ago, the legal requirements at this stage were unclear and the nature of the hearing differed from state to state. Most states allowed the inmate to be present although some only reviewed the inmate's files. The parole board might hear cases with all members present or might break into panels, with each panel hearing and deciding different cases. The hearings were usually private, attended only by the inmate, members of the board, and a representative of the institution in which the inmate was incarcerated. Reports from family members, institutional staff members, psychologists, or other treatment personnel might be included. The board might want information on the inmate's plans upon release. Reasons for denial may or may not be given.

The federal courts were divided over the requirements of due process at the parole hearing, but in 1979, the U.S. Supreme Court decided a case on appeal from the U.S. Court of Appeals for the Eighth Circuit. In *Greenholtz v. Inmates of Nebraska Penal and Correctional Complex*,[35] the Court held that due process requirements were met by the Nebraska statute that allowed an inmate, at the time of the first parole release decision in his or her case, an opportunity to be heard and the right to receive a statement of the reasons for a parole denial. The Court stated the Nebraska statute did create an expectation of parole that must be protected by due process. Whether that expectation exists in other state statutes would have to be determined by examining those cases. The Court did not agree, however, that the United States Constitution requires that a parole hearing involve all of the same elements of due process required at the stage of trial. The Court also stated that due process at that stage did not require the parole board to specify the particular evidence that influenced its parole denial.

Today, the previously held discretion by the parole board has been limited by the implementation of guidelines. These guidelines are designed to reduce disparities among the time served by individuals who have committed the same or similar crimes. The guidelines are so precise that they give parole board members the specific time the offender will serve, given the nature of the offense and the individual's criminal history. Release is usually granted to individuals who serve the specified time and who have abided by the rules of the institution, to those whose release will not diminish the seriousness of the offense, and to those whose release will not place public safety at risk.

In most states, inmates who are subject to these guidelines are eligible for a release hearing within 120 days after they have been incarcerated. However, the previously held release date may be modified at regularly scheduled parole review hearings. These are usually held every eighteen months.

10-3g The Parole Officer and Parole Services

It is important that conditions of parole be reasonable; perhaps more important is the way in which those conditions are enforced. Revocation of parole can occur when parolees violate its conditions. The parole officer has considerable power in the determination of parole revocation.

Qualifications of Parole Officers

Parole officers should be highly qualified. In many respects, they should have the same qualifications as those of probation officers. The Advisory Commission, in Standard 12.8, "Manpower for Parole," took the position that by 1975, all states had to "develop a comprehensive manpower and training program which would make it possible to recruit persons with a wide variety of skills, including significant numbers of minority group members and volunteers, and use them effectively in parole programs." The commission specified a bachelor's degree as a minimum requirement for a beginning parole officer, but stated that persons without such a degree should be trained to work with parole officers "on a team basis, carrying out the tasks appropriate to their individual skills." A strong emphasis was placed on the need to utilize volunteers and ex-offenders, combined with "new and innovative training programs in organizational development . . . to integrate successfully the variety of skills involved in a modern parole agency and to deal with the tensions and conflicts which will inevitably arise from mixing such a variety of personnel in team supervision efforts."[36]

Case Study 10-1

Morrissey v. Brewer

If parole boards were required to grant hearings, adversarial in nature, with the full rights accorded in criminal proceedings, their function as an administrative body acting in the role of *parens patriae* would be aborted. The probable result of the imposition of such stringent requirements would actually decrease the number of paroles granted due to the heavy burden placed upon the administrative processes of supervision and investigation.

Today, the parole officer position requires individuals with many skills. Among these, the individual seeking a career as a parole officer must have competence in working with people and in developing relationships with law enforcement agencies. This person must be able to work under pressure and be able to manage large caseloads.[37]

10-3h Revocation of Parole

Contract theory Theory that holds that the parolee agrees to assume the conditions of release when parole is offered. If those conditions are violated, the contract has been broken, and parole may be revoked.

Not long ago, parole could be revoked easily and without due process. Such revocation was justified on the basis of the privilege versus right theory as well as two other theories: contract theory and continuing custody theory.

The **contract theory** states that the parolee agrees to the conditions of release when parole is offered. If those conditions are violated, the contract has been broken, and parole may be revoked. The problem with this theory is that the parolee has little or no bargaining power. He or she has no other alternative by which to obtain early release.[38]

Under the **continuing custody theory**, the parolee remains in the custody of the granting authority, subject to the same rules and regulations governing daily conduct as before he or she was released from prison. The person's daily life is still regulated by authorities who establish rules regarding both the personal and the work life of the releasee. The problem with this theory is that parole is supposed to be rehabilitative and is viewed as a different system from incarceration, so it is irrational to attempt to apply the same rules to parolees and inmates.[39]

10-3i Due Process Theory

Continuing custody theory Theory that holds that the parolee remains in the custody of the granting authority. The subject is under the same rules and regulations that governed the daily conduct of the offender before release from prison.

Due process theory Theory based on the concept that parole is an important phase in the process of rehabilitation.

In the case of parole revocation, the U.S. Supreme Court has applied a different theory. This is the **due process theory**, which embodies the concept that parole is an important phase in the process of rehabilitation. If inmates are to be rehabilitated, they must see the parole system as being fair. Some argue that fairness demands that an individual be granted due process at the time his or her parole is revoked. The Eighth Circuit did not agree, however. In an early 1970s Iowa case, quoted in Case Study 10-1, the court expressed its fear that allowing due process at parole revocation would endanger the system of parole.[40]

The U.S. Supreme Court rejected these and other arguments.[41] In summary, the Court said:

1. Parole is an integrative part of the correctional system and its primary purpose is to aid in rehabilitation.
2. The parole system implies that an individual may remain on parole until the rules are violated.
3. Revocation of parole "is not part of a criminal prosecution and thus the full panoply of rights due a defendant in such a proceeding does not apply to parole revocation."
4. Whether parole is a right or privilege is not the crucial question. The issue is the extent to which an individual would be "condemned to suffer

grievous loss." The liberty enjoyed by a parolee is important; if terminated, some elements of due process must be involved.
5. The state's interest in protecting society does not preclude or hinder an informal hearing at parole revocation.
6. Society has an interest in not revoking parole unless parole rules have been violated.
7. The requirements of due process fluctuate with particular types of cases.

The elements of due process required at parole revocation were:

1. Written notice of the alleged violations of parole.
2. Disclosure to the parolee of the evidence of violation.
3. Opportunity to be heard in person and to present evidence as well as witnesses.
4. Right to confront and cross-examine adverse witnesses unless good cause can be shown for not allowing this confrontation.
5. Right to judgment by a detached and neutral hearing body.
6. Written statement of reasons for revoking parole as well as of the evidence used in arriving at that decision.

More recently, the Court has heard cases involving revocation of probation as it continues to address issues concerning the due process of correctional clients. These cases—*Bearden v. Georgia*[42] and *Black v. Romano*[43]—have shown that due process must be present in the restriction mechanisms of probation revocation. In *Bearden*, the Court held that it was improper to revoke the probation of an indigent who had made an effort to pay the required fine. In *Romano*, the Court held that due process did not mandate that other alternatives be considered before committing the offender to prison on the original sentence.

10-3j Parole: Its Present State and Its Future

Today, parole has many faces. These faces vary and are mostly dependent upon the tolerance and opinions of citizens of a particular jurisdiction. In California, a waste recycling plant has been constructed inside the premises of Folsom State Prison. This has been done to enable parole violators to render community service and generate revenues, reducing prison costs while alleviating the city's waste problem. So far, the preliminary reports are favorable and suggest that this program is a success in accomplishing most of its goals.[44]

Other programs in California are being implemented for the purpose of determining a more successful way of handling offenders released on parole. California's Parole and Community Services Division is using state-of-the-art technology to monitor its growing parolee population. Powerful electronic monitors such as ankle transmitters and voice verification systems are only a few of the innovative technological conditions imposed on parolees. Other jurisdictions are considering the use of global satellite positioning, video imaging, and electronic kiosks to enhance supervision.[45]

Although these and other programs continue to be implemented, the future of parole is unclear. There are those who claim that parole has to change or it will perish. These critics believe that society should not destroy parole but merely attempt to modify its present-day version. It is alleged that one of the modifications needed is to place responsibility back on the offender. The responsibility to look for a job and find an adequate place to live should be with the offenders so they feel they will be at a loss if these goals are not met. To achieve this, it has been proposed that the offender be issued a voucher that could allow him or her to seek a job, education, and drug treatment from a state-selected provider for a specific period.[46] This way, the parolee chooses to seek help, while allowing parole officers to conduct other pressing activities.

There are still those who claim that parole will continue to fail as long as it is in existence. These individuals cite Virginia as an example. This particular state witnessed a 28 percent increase in criminal violence between 1990 and 1995 and this trend has continued since the early 1990s. Three out of four violent crimes—murder, armed robbery, rape, and assault—are being committed by repeat offenders. As a result, effective January 1, 1995, severe penalties for rape, murder, and armed robbery were imposed.[47] These punishments were implemented at the same time that parole was abolished. The belief is that by enacting these laws, most violent offenders will be in prison, while the state will save revenues and lives. Virginia's plan has been presented by many as an illustration of the future of parole in America. No one knows what lies ahead for parole. However, as citizens become concerned with the crime issue, there is a strong likelihood that more politicians will begin to consider plans abolishing parole.

Summary

Parole has come under attack in the United States. In the early 1970s, the American Friends Service Committee, after its report on the criminal justice system in this country, called for the abolition of parole.[48] The movement to eliminate parole did not, however, gain momentum until the mid-1970s, when some states passed flat sentencing laws. Senator Edward M. Kennedy, one of the writers and sponsors of the bill to revise the United States Criminal Code, Attorney General Griffin Bell, and United States Bureau of Prisons Director Norman Carlson, all spoke at hearings on the proposed revision in the summer of 1977 and argued for the abolition of parole.[49] Norval Morris, Dean of the University of Chicago School of Law, in his widely read book, *The Future of Imprisonment*, called for considerable reduction in the power of the parole board, although he did not call for its dissolution.[50]

The various dimensions of parole as well as other forms of release from prison were described in this chapter. Furloughs and work release programs, both designed to permit a gradual reentry of the offender back into society, were discussed. The attempts to prepare the offender for release through the establishment of pre-release programs were detailed. Some of these programs are carried out within the institutions while some involve moving the offenders into halfway houses, another form of gradual return to society. The problems that offenders face upon returning to society—financial, employment, and social—were analyzed.

The focus of this chapter was the most frequently used method of release from incarceration. After distinguishing parole from probation, as well as from other forms of release from prison, its history was discussed. The organization of parole outlined the two traditional models of parole systems: the independent and consolidation models. A discussion of the process of selection by the parole board, along with a discussion of qualifications for members of the board, led to an outline of the parole decision.

For years, federal courts took a hands-off policy toward parole board decisions. The reasons for that position and the problems it created were analyzed. The parole hearing was discussed in light of a Supreme Court case involving the due process issue at this stage. Some of the empirical studies of parole decisions—how and why they are made—were examined. Parole officers, their qualifications, functions, and the services that they provide, were also discussed.

The important decision of parole revocation was with the due process requirements articulated by the United States Supreme Court. The final portion of the chapter was devoted to the prediction of parole success. This was followed by a discussion on the present and future conditions of parole in the United States.

Notes

1. Bureau of Justice Statistics (2001), Census of Jails, 1999, U.S. Department of Justice. Washington, D.C.
2. CNN, March 14, 1999, "U.S. Imprisonment Doubles Over 12 Years."
3. Case, John D., "Doing Time in the Community," *Federal Probation* 31 (March, 1967), 9.
4. Markley, Carson V., "Furlough Programs and Conjugal Visiting in Adult Correctional Institutions," *Federal Probation* 37 (March, 1973), 19.
5. Waldo, Gordon P., and Chiricos, Theodore G., "Work Release and Recidivism: An Empirical Evaluation of a Social Policy," reprinted in Marcia Guttentag and Shalom Saar, eds., *Evaluation Studies Review Annual* 2 (Beverly Hills, CA: Sage Publishers, 1977), p. 626, references omitted.
6. Waldo and Chiricos, in Cuttentag and Saar, eds., p. 637. See also Waldo and Chiricos, *Work as a Rehabilitation Tool: An Evaluation of Two State Programs,* U. S. Department of Justice, LEAA, Final Report, (Washington, D.C.: U.S. Government Printing Office, 1974).
7. Baker, J. E., "Preparing Prisoners for Their Return to the Community," *Federal Probation* 30 (June, 1966), 43.
8. National Legal Professional Associates (2001), *Community Corrections Urban Release Programs,* (Cincinnati, Ohio).
9. National Legal Professional Associates, 2001.
10. Baker, "Preparing Prisoners," pp. 43-50.
11. Seiter, Richard P., et al., Halfway Houses, National Evaluation Program, Phase I, Summary Report, National Institute of Law Enforcement and Criminal Justice, *LEAA* (Washington, DC: U.S. Government Printing Office, 1977).
12. Orosz, Connie L., "LASER Treatment Changes Criminal Behavior," (Life, Attitude, Skills, Educational Retraining) (Programs That Work), *Corrections Today* (August, 1996), vol. 58, n.5, 74(4).
13. Orosz, "LASER Treatment," 74(4).
14. The President's Commission on Law Enforcement and Administration of Justice, *Task Force Report: Corrections,* (Washington, D.C.: U.S. Government Printing Office, 1967), pp. 40-41.
15. Jeffery Reiman (2001), *The Rich Get Richer and the Poor Get Prison,* (Boston: Allyn and Bacon).
16. Glaser, Daniel, *The Effectiveness of a Prison and Parole System* (Indianapolis, IN: Bobbs-Merrill, 1964), pp. 317-318.
17. Colter Norman C., "Subsidizing the Released Inmate," *Crime and Delinquency* 21 (July, 1975), 285. For a listing of state financial provisions for releasees, see Kenneth J. Kenihan, "The Financial Condition of Released Prisoners," *Crime and Delinquency* 21 (July, 1975), 266-281.
18. Robinson, James W., "Occupational Licensing, the Ex-Offender, and Society," *The Justice System Journal* 3 (June, 1974), 69.
19. Glaser, *The Effectiveness of a Prison and Parole System,* p. 400.
20. Attorney General's Survey of Release Procedures, *Parole,* vol. 4 (Washington, D.C.: U.S. Government Printing Office, 1939), p. 4, quoted in Vincent O'Leary, "Parole Administration," Chapter 25 in Daniel Glaser, ed., *Handbook of Criminology* (Chicago: Rand McNally College Publishing Co., 1974), pp. 909-949; quotation is on p. 909.
21. "The Origins of Parole," in George G. Killinger and Paul F. Cromwell, Jr., eds., *Corrections in the Community: Alternatives to Imprisonment* (St. Paul, MN: West Publishing Co., 1974), p. 400.
22. The President's Commission, *Corrections,* p. 60. See also O Leary, "Parole Administration," pp. 909-912.
23. Friedman, Lawrence M., *Crime and Punishment in American History* (New York: Basic Books, 1993), p. 304.
24. Bureau of Justice Statistics (2001), U.S. Department of Justice, "Adults on Parole, 2000," Washington, D.C.
25. Bureau of Justice Statistics (2001).
26. Morris, Norval, *The Future of Imprisonment* (Chicago: University of Chicago Press, 1974), p. 47.
27. According to a decision of the United States Supreme Court, "The decision as to when a lawfully sentenced defendant shall actually be released has been committed by Congress, with certain limitations, to the discretion of the Parole Commission. Whether wisely or not, Congress has decided that the Commission is in the best position to determine when release is appropriate, and in doing so, to moderate the disparities in the sentencing practices of individual judges. . . . [T]he [sentencing] judge has no enforceable expectations with respect to the actual release of a sentenced defendant short of his statutory term. The judge may well have expectations as to when release is likely. But the actual decision is not his to make, either at the time of sentencing or later if his expectations are not met." *U.S. v. Addonizio,* 99 S.Ct. 2235, 2242 (1979).
28. Kennedy, Edward M., "Toward a New System of Criminal Sentencing: Law with Order," *The American Criminal Law Review* 16 (Spring, 1979), 361.
29. *Morrissey v. Brewer,* 433 F.2d 942 (8th Cir. 1971), rev'd, 408 U.S. 471 (1972).
30. *Tarlton v. Clark,* 441 F 2d 384, 385 (5th Cir. 1971), *cert. denied,* 403 U.S. 934 (1971).
31. *Scarpa v. U.S. Board of Parole,* 447 F.2d 278 (5th Cir. 1973), vacated, 414 U.S. 809 (1973).
32. Miller, Robert Clarence, "Parole," *Fortune News* (October, 1972), 10.
33. Irwin, John, *The Felon* (Englewood Cliffs, NJ: Prentice-Hall, Inc., 1970), p. 173.
34. Quoted in Jessica Mitford, *Kind and Usual Punishment: The Prison Business* (New York: Alfred A. Knopf, 1973), p. 216.
35. *Greenholtz v. Inmates of Nebraska Penal and Correctional Complex,* 99 S.Ct. 2100 (1979).

36. The Advisory Commission, *Corrections,* pp. 435-436.
37. Smith, Albert G., "Organizational Skills for Managing Your Probation and Parole Workload," *Corrections Today,* vol. 54, no. 5 (July, 1992), pp. 136-142.
38. Palmer, John W., *Constitutional Rights of Prisoners* (Cincinnati, OH: Anderson, 1973), p. 114.
39. Palmer, *Constitutional Rights,* p. 114.
40. *Morrissey v. Brewer,* 443 F.2d 942 (1971), rev 'd 408 U.S. 471.
41. *Morrissey v. Brewer,* 408 U.S. 471.
42. *Bearden v. Georgia,* 461 U.S. 660 (1983).
43. *Black v. Romano,* 471 U.S. 606 (1985).
44. Harrison, Larry, and Lovell, Douglas G., "Inmate Work Program Helps Solve City's Waste Problem," *Corrections Today* (April, 1996), vol. 58, no. 2, 132(3).
45. Morris, Marisela, "Technological Advances in Parole Supervision," *Corrections Today* (July, 1996), vol. 58, no. 4, 88(3).
46. Dilulio, Jr., John J., "Reinventing Parole and Probation," *Brookings Review* (Spring, 1997), vol. 15, no. 2, 40(3).
47. Allen, George, "The Courage of Our Conviction: The Abolition of Parole Will Save Lives and Money," *Policy Review* (Spring, 1995) no. 72, 4(4).
48. American Friends Service Committee, *Struggle for Justice: A Report on Crime and Punishment in America* (New York: Hill & Wang, 1971).
49. Wilson, Rob, "Parole Release: Devil or Savior?" *Corrections Magazine* 3 (September, 1977), 52.
50. Morris, Norval, *The Future of Imprisonment,* pp. 28-50.

Chapter 11

The Male Inmate

Outline

Key Terms

- deprivation model
- importation model
- segregation
- HIV
- conjugal visits
- furlough

The way prisoners are treated upon entering prison serves as an illustration of society's rejection of those who break the law. They are stripped of most of their personal belongings, assigned a number, examined, inspected, weighed, and documented. These acts represent efforts to deprive them of their identities. The actions are often conducted in a humiliating way that further advances the prisoners' degrading status. They face correctional officers who are there to make sure that inmates conform to the rules of the institution. The guards have ultimate control over inmates, furnishing "constant reminders of the social degradation to which . . . [they have] been subjected."[1] Gresham M. Sykes referred to the psychological and social problems that result from the worst punishment—deprivation of liberty—as the "pains of imprisonment." In his study of male inmates in the 1960s, Sykes discussed the moral rejection given by the community, which represents a permanent threat to the self-concept of the inmate; the deprivation of goods and services in a society that places a substantial emphasis on material possessions; the deprivation of heterosexual relationships and the resulting threat to the inmate's masculinity or femininity; and the deprivation of security in which the individual is constantly facing threats to his or her safety, health, and life.[2]

The prison staff regulates the life of the inmate and the latter has no opportunity to function in adult roles. This chapter discusses how male prisoners react to these regulations and deprivations. The sociological studies of the prison community, the inmate subculture, and approaches to an understanding of the ways in which inmates adapt to prison life will be explored. The chapter begins with a look at Donald Clemmer's study of the prison community, which was published in 1940, and his concept of prisonization. The types of social roles that have been analyzed within the prison community are examined. The prison community, in its role

as an agency of social control, is explored in detail and attention is given to sex roles and sexual behavior in prison. Suggested solutions to these problems—conjugal visits and furloughs—are discussed. The chapter ends with an examination of the problems associated with prison violence.

11-1 Inmate Social Systems in Male Prisons

Concern over the negative effects that inmates have on one another led early penologists to separate prisoners. This was to curtail verbal and physical contact or to enforce the silent system to prohibit verbal contact. With the end of the silent system came the opportunity for inmates to interact verbally. One of the results of this interaction has been the opportunity for prisoners to create a prison subculture or community. This development has not been immune to debate or study.

11-1a Prisonization: Socialization into the Inmate Systems

In 1940, Donald Clemmer published his study of the male community at the maximum-security prison in Menard, Illinois. This study is now recognized as one of the most important works in the area of inmate socialization. Although this study was conducted in the 1940s, some of its conclusions can be applied to today's prison settings. One of Clemmer's most important contributions was the creation of the concept of prisonization. Clemmer defined prisonization as "the taking on, in greater or lesser degree, of the folkways, mores, customs, and general culture of the penitentiary." The process starts as the new inmate learns his status as a prisoner. The most influential aspects of prisonization are "the influences which breed or deepen criminality and anti-sociality and make the inmate characteristic of the criminalistic ideology in the prison community." The effectiveness of this process on a given inmate is dependent upon several factors:

- The inmate (e.g., personality, vulnerability)
- The types of relationships the inmate had outside the facility
- Whether the inmate becomes a member of a primary group in prison
- His or her placement in the prison (the specific cell, cell mate, etc.)
- The degree to which the inmate accepts the dogmas and codes of the prison culture

Clemmer contends, however, that the most important factor is the primary group[3], although that position has been questioned by later investigators.[4] Clemmer saw prisonization as the process by which new inmates become familiar with and internalize prison norms and values. He argued that once inmates become prisonized, they are immune to the influences of conventional value systems. Today, this notion is widely held by students of prisonization.[5] Recent research has also suggested that prisons help encourage inmates to adopt the prisonization process.[6]

11-1b Wheeler's Test: The U-Shaped Curve Hypothesis

In the early 1960s, Stanton Wheeler empirically tested Clemmer's concept of prisonization in a study at the Washington State Reformatory. Wheeler found strong support for Clemmer's concept of prisonization. Wheeler also discovered that the degree of prisonization varied according to the phase of an inmate's institutional career, developing along a U-shape curve. Inmates tended to be more receptive to the institutional values of the outside world during the first period of incarceration (measured at the end of the first six months) and during the last period (the final six months prior to release). They are less receptive during the middle period (more than six months remaining), also referred to as the prison career. During the last period, as the inmate is anticipating release back

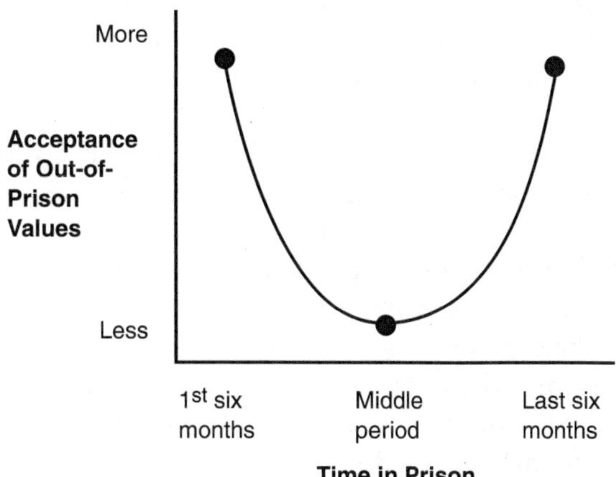

Figure 11-1
The U-Shaped Curve

into society, his main reference group shifts from the inmates within the institution to the society outside. This results in a more conventional, normative orientation similar to that characterized by inmates upon arrival and during the first six months of incarceration. Wheeler concluded that Clemmer's concept of prisonization should be reformulated to include the variable of prison career phase.[7] Figure 11-1 illustrates the U-shaped curve.

11-1c The Inmate Subculture: Three Models for Analysis

Since Wheeler's 1961 publication, numerous investigators have studied the process of prisonization and inmate subculture. Some of them have used Wheeler's methodological approach. An analysis of these studies and theoretical contributions reveals the emergence of three basic models to explain the inmate subculture. The models have been given different names, but they can be described as the **deprivation model,** the adaptive model, and the **importation model**.

Deprivation model A prisonization theory based on the concept that the inmate subculture stems from prisoners' adaptation to the physical and psychological losses created by incarceration.

Importation model A theory of prisonization based on the concept that the inmate subculture is not created from internal prison experiences but rather from external patterns of behavior that inmates bring to prison.

Deprivation Model

Sykes is the main proponent of the theory that the inmate subculture is the result of the attempt to adapt to the deprivations imposed by incarceration, or what he called pains of punishment. These include the deprivations of social acceptance, material possessions, heterosexual relationships, personal autonomy, and personal security.[8] The inmate lacks the outlets necessary to deal with the deprivation, loss of status, and degradation that are commonly found behind prison walls. Consequently, inmates have few alternatives. Since they seldom escape the realities of prison psychologically or physically, inmates often suffer from these pains of imprisonment. "But if the rigors of confinement cannot be completely removed, they can at least be mitigated by the patterns of social interaction established among the inmates themselves."[9] According to Sykes, the inmate has a choice of either uniting with his fellow captives in a spirit of cooperation or withdrawing to seek only the satisfaction of his own needs. In either case, the inmate's pattern of behavior is an adaptation to the deprivations of the prison environment.

Adaptive Model

According to the adaptive model, the social system available to inmates enables them to minimize, through cooperation, the pains of imprisonment. For example, if inmates cooperate in exchanging favors, it not only removes the opportunity for some to exploit others, but it allows them to more easily accept material deprivation. Their social system redefines the meaning of material possessions. The inmates believe that highly valued material possessions result from connections, instead of from hard work and skill, and allow them to insulate their self-conceptions. Additionally, the goods and services that are available to inmates can better be distributed and shared within a cooperative social system.

The inmate social system can also help to solve the problem of personal security, to alleviate the fear of further isolation, and to restore the inmate's sense of self-respect and independence.[10] The inmate can begin to recapture his male role in the characteristics associated with dignity, composure, courage, and the ability to "take it" and "hand it out." These traits are emphasized by the inmate's social system and are regarded to be masculine traits.

Support for the adaptation model also comes from a study conducted by Richard A. Cloward.[11] In the late 1950s, Cloward examined the structural accommodation—his term for the situation in which some inmates gain special privileges from the staff by assisting them to maintain control and the status quo. The resulting roles develop due to the inmate's need to adapt to the internal character (i.e., particular characteristics) of the prison situation. These analyses are in line with Erving Goffman's discussion of total institutions. Goffman does not deny that inmates bring various experiences, but he maintains that the institutional process of mortification and degradation essentially nullifies the impact of those experiences.[12]

It is important to note that these studies were conducted in all-male institutions. Charles R. Tittle conducted a study in an institution housing both men and women under similar conditions in the late 1960s. He found some gender differences in inmate social structures but concluded that generally "the data seem to justify the conclusion that inmate organization is largely a response to institutional conditions." This follows the adaptive model as well.[13]

A more recent study on female inmates has revealed that they have unusually high testosterone levels. This has been associated with high incidents of violence and criminal incidents. The study measured the testosterone level of eighty-seven female inmates housed in a maximum-security prison. Further, their criminal behavior was scored from a series of court records.[14]

Due to the pains of imprisonment and the associated degradation, inmates repudiate the norms of the staff, administration, and society. They join forces with each other, developing a social system that enables them to preserve their self-esteem.

Importation Model

According to John Irwin and Donald R. Cressey, the more traditional approach to an understanding of the inmate subculture is that men bring patterns of behavior with them to prison.[15] Clemmer recognized that the prison subculture depended in part on the men's conditions and experiences outside the prison, despite his theory of prisonization of new inmates.[16] Clarence Schrag, who collected pre-prison as well as in-prison data, also related prison activities to the broader community.[17]

Irwin and Cressey argued that social scientists have overused inside influences as explanations for the inmate culture. Irwin and Cressey emphasized the need to make a distinction between prison culture and criminal subculture.[18] To do this, they postulated three types of prison subcultures, only two of which are criminal.

The first type, the thief subculture, refers to the patterns of values that are characteristic of professional thieves and other career criminals (e.g., instant gratification). This type is found inside the prison setting as well as outside. This type is not restricted to criminals and is evident among police, correctional officers, college professors, students, and other categories of persons who "evaluate behavior in terms of in-group loyalties."

The second type of inmate subculture is the convict subculture. The central value is utilitarianism, in which the most "manipulative and most utilitarian individuals win the available wealth and such positions of influence as might exist." These patterns can be found anywhere people are incarcerated, and it is "characterized by deprivations and limitations of freedom and in them available wealth must be competed for by men supposedly on an equal footing." Many of the members of this category have spent a great deal of time in juvenile institutions.[19]

Finally, Irwin and Cressey discussed the legitimate subculture, which is made up of inmates who isolate themselves or are isolated by other inmates. They make up the largest portion of the inmate population and are of little or no trouble to the staff. They reject both the criminal and the thief subcultures. They are "oriented to the problems of achieving goals through means which are legitimate outside prisons."[20] Clemmer also found that most were not members of inmate groups. According to his study, 40 percent of the interviewed inmates stated that they did not consider themselves as members of any group, while another 40 percent said that they were members only of a "semi primary group."[21]

Irwin and Cressey indicated that a combination of the convict and the thief subcultures form what is referred to as the inmate subculture. Some conflicts exist between the two groups, but they also share some values. It is not known how much each or both influence the members of the legitimate subculture. Nor is it known what influence the members of the latter have on each other. But Irwin and Cressey hypothesize that all three subcultures bring to the prison patterns of behavior and attitudes from experience. The inmate culture is really an "adjustment of accommodation of these three systems within the official administrative system of deprivation and control."[22]

The research on these two models was conducted by Charles W. Thomas at a maximum-security prison in the southwest in 1970. Thomas emphasized that inmates have a past, a present, and a future, and that all are related to the process of prisonization. His research was designed to show the importance of both importation and deprivation variables. When an inmate arrives at prison, both the formal organization and the inmate society compete for his allegiance, and these two represent conflicting processes of socialization. Thomas calls the efforts of the formal organization "re-socialization" and those of the inmate society "prisonization." The success of one requires the failure of the other. The prison is not a closed system, and in explaining the inmate culture, all of these factors must be examined: pre-prison experiences, both criminal and noncriminal; expectations of prison staff and fellow inmates; quality of the inmate's contacts with persons or groups outside the walls; post-prison expectations; and the immediate problems of adjustment that the inmate faces. Thomas found that the greater the degree of similarity between pre-prison activities and prison subculture values and attitudes, "the greater the receptivity to the influences of prisonization." He also found that inmates from the lower social class are more likely to become highly prisonized and that those who have the highest degree of contact with the outside world have the lowest degree of prisonization. Finally, those with a higher degree of prisonization were among those who had the bleakest post-prison expectations.[23]

Leo Carroll, based on his 1970s study on race relations in an eastern prison, was very critical of the deprivation model, arguing that it "diverts attention from inter-relationships between the prison and the wider society . . . and hence away from issues such as racial violence."[24] Carroll's research generally supported the importation model but he concluded that the model was incomplete. He extended the importation model in his analysis of racial violence within one prison. Looking at the problem of powerlessness that all inmates face, Carroll analyzed ways in which attempts to cope with this problem might be influenced by the racial identity of the inmate. He then explored "some of the consequences of these differential adaptations in terms of maintaining and perhaps intensifying racial hostility imported into the prison from the community."[25] Recently, scholars have claimed that the importation model holds the "superior explanation for the inmate subcultures found in modern American prisons."[26] This view has been strengthened by correctional reforms and federal-court decisions that have eased some of the inmate's pains of imprisonment.[27] According to Carroll and Jacobs, inmates have been enabled to maintain close contact with the outside world by factors such as the liberalization of visitations, telephone and mail privileges, and the permission to wear street clothing.

The Integration of Importation and Deprivation Models

Although the importation model has been regarded as the superior model, some have claimed that the integration of both models is ideal. Barry Schwartz, in his study of a Pennsylvania institution for boys, concluded that pre-prison experiences must be considered, as well as the "functional point of view, which refers such behavior to the system in which it is embedded."[28]

The cross-cultural studies of Ronald Akers, Norman Hayner, and Werner Gruninger also supported both models. The functional or adaptation model was only partially supported by their data from several countries and from one jurisdiction in the United States. Their data revealed that "the inmate culture varies by whatever differences in organizational environment there are from one institution to the next." They also found support for the importation view, "because it appears that the level of nonconformity to staff norms is more a reflection of the larger culture from which the inmates are drawn than the specific environment of the prison in which they are currently confined."[29]

This integrative approach has been summarized by Thomas. "The existence of collective solutions in the inmate culture and social structure is based on the common problems of adjustment to the institution, while the content of those solutions and the tendency to become prisonized are imported from the larger society."[30]

The integrative approach has also been used in explaining drug use in prison. Akers and his colleagues found that drug use was more or less a function of the adjustment problems individuals faced in prison.[31]

Charles W. Thomas, David M. Petersen, and Rhonda M. Zingraff studied inmates in a federal maximum-security prison. They concluded that it is not reasonable to argue that either the importation or deprivation model explains the inmate subculture. Variables of each are equally important. "The more relevant issues appear to be how the rather vague propositions associated with each model can be stated more precisely and, more importantly, how they can be merged into a single theoretical framework."[32] Recently, this argument, which is based on the integration of both of these models, has been proposed as a more comprehensive view of the inmate prisonization process.[33]

TABLE **11-1** Prison Terminology

Term	Definition
Fish	New inmate
Get-back	Revenge in prison
Script	Prison money
Shank	A knife
Snitch	A prison informer
Waste	To kill someone
Bug out	To act crazy
Hack	A correctional officer
Hole	Punitive segregation
Joint	Prison
Pruno/Hooch	Prison made booze
Punk	Inmate that sexually services other inmates

11-1d Social Roles of the Inmate System

Gresham Sykes, in his study of a maximum-security prison, emphasized the social system in prison and the role of a specialized vocabulary. If prisoners were kept in their cells at all times, an aggregate, but not a society, would exist. In such an aggregate, the officials would merely have to care for the physical needs of the inmates. Inmates leave their cells, however, to eat, work, exercise, attend religious services, attend prison school, and watch television. These activities are the foundation of a prison social system. Sykes contends that this resulting social system can be mapped by observing the special language that develops.[34]

Sykes states that the special language is not developed for secrecy or to symbolize the loyalty of the inmates to each other, but rather as a distinguishing symbol. Special terms designate the social roles played by the inmates. Although these words differ from institution to institution, the roles they designate remain the same.[35]

An example of the special terminology used by inmates to designate social roles can be seen in Leo Carroll's study of a small eastern institution for males.[36] He found that whites had social types similar to those of the whites in Sykes's study but African-Americans had a different set of social roles and a different form of organization. Their focus was racial identification. They were united in a solitary group that was based on two ideological perspectives. One, which Carroll calls soul, emphasizes the historical African-American culture and affirms the importance of acceptance and perseverance. The other, black nationalism, values African culture and emphasizes revolution against racism, colonialism, and imperialism. It was reported that both were imported into the prison from the outside world. In his book, *Life Without Parole*, Victor Hassine (1999) asserted that the tenor of the prison lingo was "generally vulgar and aggressive, expressed with self-important arrogance. Yet, at the same time it exhibited an unbridled honesty that implied a certain unconditional tolerance for the opinions and beliefs of others."[37] Table 11-1 shows some commonly used prison terminology.

11-1e The Inmate System as an Agency of Social Control

The inmate social system can create problems for guards and other prison personnel. The resulting social roles can also create difficulties for inmates upon release and for society. The inmate social system, however, also serves as an agency of social control within the prison. The inmate society becomes a powerful influence over the prisoner, as it is their only reference group. This is enhanced by the inmate's need for status and susceptibility to peer-group pressure. The inmate might also find social support in the peer group instead of in authority figures.[38] Inmates will allow themselves to be controlled by the social system of their peers—a form of social control that is functional to the prison since it maintains order within the institution.

Two powerful groups seek control within the correctional facility—the correctional officers, who are mainly interested in custody and security, and the inmates, who are interested in escaping from the pains of imprisonment. One of the most cited studies is that of Richard Cloward, who examined the power struggle between these two groups.[39]

Cloward notes that in most institutions, force can be converted into authority because people recognize the legitimacy of authority and are motivated to comply. In prison, however, inmates have rejected the legitimacy of those who seek to control them and a problem of social control is the result. In many ways, the job of the custodian is a difficult one. He or she is expected to maintain control and security within the institution, but has to give up the traditional method of doing so, which is force. The liberal philosophy of treatment and rehabilitation, with its accompanying policy of granting the inmates more input into the regulation of prison life, has become less popular in recent years but continues to present problems for guards who wish to exercise more social control of inmates.

Forms of Social Control

Control is an essential component for the proper functioning of a prison facility. There is no greater asset for a correctional administrator than to keep the correctional institution secure. Many have argued that, in correctional settings, job security is provided in a controlled environment. The absence of control can end up costing many corrections professionals their careers. Consequently, it is imperative for the corrections student to study social control in prisons with specific emphasis on the types of controls that exist.

Segregation

Segregation One of the forms of social control used by various correctional institutions; based on the expulsion or separation of an individual from the group.

One of the forms of social control that is used by various correctional institutions is **segregation**—expulsion from the group—although the success of this method is questionable. The worse the behavior, the more prolonged is the inmate's stay in the institution. The inmate might be transferred to a more secure facility, which relocates him/her, but does not solve the problem. Officials must handle the problem of controlling the inmate, since he or she cannot "be expelled from the system as a whole."[40] Another form of segregation is solitary confinement, usually imposed for extreme behavior. With the present overcrowding problems, there is limited space in which to implement this method. Also, courts have placed some restrictions on the use of solitary confinement.

Incentives

If correctional officers cannot use physical force or segregation, they must have other methods to control inmates. The use of incentives, rooted in the practice of granting good time and parole, has developed. First, there is an emphasis on voluntary isolation. Correctional officers often tell inmates to watch out for other inmates, do their own time, and not get involved with others. At times, parole is recommended for those inmates who do not participate in certain primary-group activities. Recently, an incentive philosophy developed based on rehabilitation and social reintegration. Cloward describes this incentive system as a "functional equivalent of the historic separate and silent systems."[41] His thesis is that the system does not work because the goals for which inmates are told to strive are not available to them.

It has been claimed that the goal in prison is to rehabilitate the inmate by helping him or her reintegrate into society. Not all inmates cannot be forced to reform; therefore, the application of negative sanctions only antagonizes the inmate. Inmates must voluntarily participate in their own rehabilitation and the modern prison programs have been devised to secure this goal. Yet, rates of recidivism are high and prisons are characterized by pressures toward deviant, not conforming, behavior. Cloward argues that these are results of a system that promises rehabilitation and provides inmates incentives to strive toward that goal, but then returns them to a society that will not let them achieve that goal. "Thus the society itself bars access by legitimate means to socially approved goals the prisoner has been led to covet," and the presence of recidivists in prison undermines the rehabilitative goal for new inmates. The recidivists, by their presence, are making the statement that "you cannot make it legitimately on the outside."[42] This undermines the effectiveness of the incentive system for those inmates who might be inclined to cooperate.

Illegitimate Opportunities

Inmates who will not cooperate with the incentive system must be controlled. Cloward suggests that this is done by providing them with illegitimate opportunities to satisfy certain needs and desires, and he explains how this system leads to social control. Correctional officers have more power than inmates although they cannot control prisoners without inmate support. Physical force is no longer an acceptable weapon, segregation is limited, and incentives do not always work. "Limitations on power in the one system therefore compel adaptive or reciprocal adjustments between the two systems. In effect, concessions must be made by the officials to the inmates." A system of accommodation develops in which the correctional officers provide the inmates with illegitimate ways to fulfill their needs and, in return, those inmates exert social control over other prisoners. The system provides that all parties fulfill their roles. If the inmates do not perform, the correctional officers can threaten to withdraw and establish relationships with other inmates. If correctional officers do not perform, inmates can organize their peers in a way to embarrass them. "Each is captive and captor of the other," and this results in stability within the prison. As inmates become upwardly mobile, they become more conservative as they do not want to upset their positions in the system. Consequently, the accommodative system leads toward inmate passivity and docility and the inmate elites "constitute the single most important source of social control in the prison." They are against the official value system but they avoid unnecessary conflict with that system. They play an integrating role between the inmate system and the official system. "They mediate and modify the diverse pressures emanating from each system. They bring order to an otherwise strifeful situation."[43]

Social Control: An Original Approach

Although John Irwin has made recent contributions to the advancement of knowledge in corrections,[44] one of his works, "The Changing Social Structure of the Men's Prison," presents his original analysis of the inmate social structure in men's prisons in 1977.[45]

Irwin's Approach

Irwin stated that there is currently more conflict among inmates and staff members in prisons than has been observed in the past. He attributes this to the increasing conflict in our society.

Irwin traced the development of theories about the prison community, demonstrating how the general theories prevalent in sociology permeate such studies. The earlier findings about inmate social roles took place in a social system that was made up of those whose duty was to maintain order and those who had to adapt to the pains of imprisonment. The result was a system of accommodation. Some prison leaders would receive special privileges in exchange for assisting guards in maintaining order. The various social roles reflected the functions within the accommodative system.

In the 1960s, however, the climate of the prison began to change. The inmate population shifted to minorities, mainly African-Americans and Puerto Ricans, who brought with them the African-American nationalistic and militant organization from the society outside the prison. The rising development of racial pride and activism among Hispanics spread to prisons. In California, Hispanic inmates became more hostile to whites and developed closer relationships to African-American inmates. In the meantime, white inmates were developing a deep sense of the injustices of prison conditions, especially with regard to the indeterminate sentence. "In 1969 the 'political' activities in the prisons were fused with the outside radical movement, and the 'prison movement' came into being."[46]

In the 1970s, inmates began to organize and demand improvement of their living conditions. Administrators reacted with fear and hostility. They attempted to identify the revolutionaries and transfer them to other institutions. During this time, social scientists were launching their attacks on the rehabilitative ideal. Some argued that treatment had failed and was being applied in a discriminatory manner. A new ideology of community corrections was substituted, but it was also criticized.

Apparently this has not affected the inmate social code. According to Irwin, no single inmate culture, system, or code has emerged. Such a culture is precluded by the variety of ethnic, class, and criminal elements within the prison, the variety of experiences the inmates have had outside the prison, and the open hostility within the prison. Today's correctional system is over represented with African-American and Hispanic inmates, which is beginning to create a predominant inmate code that is formed along racial and ethnic lines.[47]

The Small Clique

The small clique is the main component of the prison social world. It ranges from a group of two or three, to a large organization such as the CRIPS (Common Revolution in Progress—a gang in the United States). The small cliques have little or nothing to do socially with other groups in the correctional facility. Most of these cliques form their own gangs in prison, predominantly along racial, ethnic, and demographic lines. With the emergence of gangs, prisons have become much more complex settings. Some of these gangs include the White Mafia, Black Muslims, the Mexican Mafia, and the Aryan Brotherhood. The diversity that exists in gangs intensifies power struggles within the institution and generates a "cycle of violence and vengeance."[48]

The Sub-Rosa Economic Life

According to Irwin, the prison community is also characterized by the sub-rosa economic life. In almost every prison, a legal economic system exists. Inmates may earn money on prison farms or in industries, although their wages are severely limited and they are not free to spend the money how they choose. Irwin is referring to an informal, secret economic system, which is usually illicit, although it may be tolerated.[49]

Irwin argued that this sub-rosa economic system has also undergone changes recently. Affluence has increased in prison, as it has in society. Inmates are not allowed to have cash, but many acquire it, smuggled in by friends or family. They have more contraband (e.g., illegal drugs, alcohol) than before. Gambling and distributing contraband are the main forms of economic activity. "Wheeling and dealing" is frequent and extremely important as goods are still relatively scarce in prison. To acquire contraband, inmates interact with others whom they would otherwise avoid. Rules for wheeling and dealing develop, which are violated frequently, thus increasing hostilities. Stealing and cheating are acceptable under the theory that "might makes right." An inmate has to be able to protect himself/herself if there is some contact associated with these sub-rosa economic activities. Because individuals cannot usually protect themselves on their own, gangs and cliques develop.

Effects on Correctional Officers and Administrators

These changes in the inmate prison community have affected guards and the administrative officials. Prison guards are becoming more professionalized, even developing unions. Conflicts have developed between the old and the new officers. The nature of this conflict is, at times, rooted in the fact that old correctional officers may be fixed in their ways and resist the proposed changes suggested by the new personnel. The inmates know this and use the conflict to their advantage. "These divisions are going to remain and continue to play an important role in shaping the prison social world. They must be included in any sociological examination of the contemporary prison."[50]

Finally, the violence associated with sub-rosa economic activities is easier for the administration to accept, despite the frequency. This violence does not threaten the moral values or self-concepts of the administration and is not as disturbing to them psychologically. Also, it lends itself to lock-ups and other repressive control measures. The lives of the administrators, however, are not easier. They constantly face increasing demands and organization by guards and a loss of the underlying philosophy of rehabilitation that is used to justify the practices of the institution. In addition, administrators have to face the public's demand to be tough on inmates while considering the rehabilitative potential of inmates.

The System Aspects of the Sub-Rosa Economy

Vergil Williams and Mary Fish, in their extensive discussion of the sub-rosa economic system in prisons, have argued that administrators must look at the illicit economic transactions as a network or system and not as individual acts. For example, a guard may discover that inmate John, who wanted to change his cell assignment, made a clandestine arrangement with inmate Steve, who was in a position to influence the change. John paid Steve two cartons of cigarettes for this transaction. The guards may react only to this transaction and not consider the total economic system. But if John and Steve were not caught, the transactions in the following scenario might result: Steve gives the cigarettes to Paul, to whom he owes a debt for another illicit activity. Paul has an outstanding bad debt and he uses the cigarettes to hire Roger to beat up Dick, who owes the debt. The transactions can continue, with the same two cartons of cigarettes serving as payment for each transaction. Ironically, the payment can eventually be returned to the first inmate in the series of transactions.

It is important, both to the goals of custody and treatment, that correctional officers understand the nature of these illegal economic transactions. Correctional officers must maintain peace among inmates, keep contraband out of prisons, and prevent escapes, all of which may be related to the criminal transactions. As inmates gain power through these illicit economic transactions, they may gain access to contraband, facilitate escapes, and gain power over other inmates. One or all of these activities can lead to violence within the prison. Treatment can be affected in those cases in which inmates engaging in illicit activities are motivated primarily by their rebellion against society rather than by their desire to solve an immediate economic need. For those types of inmates, success in illegal prison ventures can serve to convince them that such activities are worthwhile and should be continued in society upon release.[51]

11-1f Sexual Problems in Prison

There are two problems of extreme concern both to prison officials and to inmates—the sexual adjustment of the inmate within the institution and the maintenance of the inmate's emotional ties with family and friends outside the prison. In the past, studies have shown that "those inmates with strong family ties, and who have maintained those ties during incarceration, are more successful on release than those offenders without such ties."[52] Isolation from family and friends, and from members of the opposite sex, can be the most severe punishment an inmate faces. Absence from his/her family means a loss of responsibility, a loss of awareness of the problems of the outside world, and the lack of an opportunity to support and care for the family.

Isolation from the opposite sex implies abstinence from the satisfaction of heterosexual relationships at a time when sex drives can be quite strong. Many turn to homosexual behavior not because of a preference, but out of need for a sexual outlet.

Homosexuality

It is impossible to obtain accurate data on homosexual acts within a prison or jail due to secrecy. Additionally, some prison administrators contend that homosexuality is not a problem within their institutions. Clemmer found that 40 percent of the men in his prison study had some homosexual experiences while in prison. Sykes reported 35 percent, and Joseph Fishman, in a 1934 study, estimated the percentages to be between thirty and forty-five.[53] These estimates were discussed at a conference on prison homosexuality in the early 1970s. Peter C. Buffum wrote a synthesis of the five working papers presented at that conference and concluded that the evidence suggests that many of the beliefs about prison homosexuality are myths. Among the myths is the high incidence of homosexual rape in prisons and that rape is the main form of prison homosexuality. The belief that establishing outlets for sexual drives can solve the problem is also a myth.[54] Others have not agreed with this position since they argue it is impossible to retrieve the total number of homosexual acts that may have been diverted through the implementation of adequate sexual outlets.[55]

In a discussion of prison homosexuality, it is important to understand prisoner sexual problems before their entering prison. Correctional facilities merely present situations in which people must make a sexual adjustment.

Male Homosexuality: Findings of Earlier Studies

All sexual assaults that take place within the confinement of prisons and jails cannot be categorized as homosexual attacks.[56] Most of these attacks are made for political reasons in order to demonstrate dominance over some individuals.

Frequently, a male who is particularly vulnerable to homosexual attacks enters into a relationship with another male who agrees to protect him from the attacks of others.[57] Earlier studies found that the homosexual acts of male prisoners seemed to be a response to their sexual needs coupled with their background of socialization. Men are taught to be aggressive and it has been argued that for some, playing the male role (the wolf) in a homosexual act enables them to retain this self-concept. Such men are usually from a background in which a man's masculine self-concept is based more on sexual activity than on any other characteristic (in contrast to males who gain masculinity from job status or family or both). It is very important to his self-concept that he retain the only measure of masculinity he has. Playing the male role allows him to continue thinking that he is masculine, because he is the aggressor and the penetrator. Although he may be looking for a meaningful emotional relationship to replace those he had outside the prison, he is more likely to be looking for the release of physical tension. Many inmates see the relationship as "little more than a search for a casual, mechanical act of physical release. Unmoved by love, indifferent to the emotions of the partner he has coerced, bribed, or seduced into a liaison, the wolf is often viewed as simply masturbating with another person."[58]

Carroll's Study: Homosexuality and Race Relations

Leo Carroll's study of male inmates is consistent with prior findings that emphasize the violent and physical nature of the sexual relationships in men's prisons, as opposed to the predominant family nature of such relationships in women's prisons. Carroll also found that prostitution is the most frequent type of homosexual relationship and that it is usually an interracial relationship. However, he found that aggressive and violent sexual behavior was often explained not in terms of an attempt to prove one's masculinity, but as the result of racial problems.

Carroll reviewed the historical existence of tension regarding sexual relations between African-Americans and whites in society. White men have often had access to African-American women as well as white women but white women have been almost totally inaccessible to African-American men. If an African-American man did gain such access, even with the consent of the woman, he faced great trouble, even death by lynching. African-American men were also criticized for not being able to protect their women from white men. According to Carroll, this background influences prison sexual relationships between African-Americans and whites. Sexual assaults of African-American prisoners on whites can be partially explained by the lack of female sexual partners and the greater solidarity of African-Americans within the prison, "but the motive force behind them has its roots deep within the entire socio-historical context of black-white relations in this country. The prison is merely an arena within which blacks may direct aggression developed through 300 years of oppression against individuals perceived to be representatives of the oppressors."[59]

Carroll observed that traditionally in our society, African-Americans have been unable to prove their masculinity in the ways that white men are able. In prison, an African-American has a chance, as one inmate said, to show that he is a man "by making a white guy into a girl." Instigating a sexual assault upon a white "is to some extent an imitation rite by which black prisoners demonstrate their manhood and blackness to their peers." African-Americans rationalize this behavior as retaliation for the way the white man has treated them in society. "He's been raped—politically, economically, morally raped," said an African-American.[60] They pick victims who are better educated than they are and who lack criminal identity. They see those persons as being middle class, the class they perceive as the main oppressor. Another reason is that "their isolation precludes retaliatory responses."[61]

The African-Americans often harass and threaten their victims before the attack. In addition to heightening the activity, such harassment serves other purposes. The aggressor can find out whether the young man has friends who will come to his aid and he might use the harassment to gain the trust and confidence of the victim and thus manipulate him. Sexual assaults are called train jobs, because several inmates are involved. In most interracial assaults, the white victim is subjected to the sexual attacks of several African-Americans, although the composition of the African-American group changes from time to time.[62]

There is a reason why other white inmates do not protect the young and physically small from such attacks by African-Americans. According to Carroll, the stronger whites use the situation. After African-American inmates are through with the victim, the white inmates who want sexual relationships come along, are kind to him, and seduce him. After the treatment a white victim has received from the African-American inmates, "it ain't nothing for him to take care of me and a coupla of others; he's glad to do it."[63]

This discussion of male homosexuality and the forms it takes in prison should be considered with the previous discussion of the importation-versus-deprivation theories advanced to explain the inmate community. Prison presents the inmate with a problem of sexual deprivation, but according to Buffum (speaking of the options the inmate faces—nocturnal sex dreams, masturbation, and sexual contact with the same sex), "the meaning, amount, and character of these adjustments will be strongly dependent on the meaning that these same behaviors had for the inmate before he or she was incarcerated."[64] Although Carroll's study focused on black-on-white violence, white-on-black assaults do occur and have been the source of much attention recently.

Recent Issues Affecting Prison Homosexuality

HIV Human Immunodeficiency Virus; virus that causes AIDS.

The issues affecting prison homosexuality discussed earlier are augmented in today's correctional facilities by the presence of the **HIV** virus. This reality of today's correctional system has made matters more complex for prison administrators and guards. The safe-sex campaigns launched via mass communication have had little effect inside prisons. This is mostly because inmates do not have access to condoms and other means of protection against the HIV virus. The deprivation of heterosexual activity in addition to the lack of availability of condoms increases the chances of inmates being infected by the HIV virus. The problem is so serious that in states such as Texas, Acquired Immune Deficiency Syndrome (AIDS) was the leading cause of death among its inmates in 1994, causing 138 deaths. To address this, the Texas Department of Criminal Justice (TDCJ) uses protective custody if contact with an HIV-positive inmate poses a threat to other inmates. In addition, special housing may be used if a warden perceives an inmate's violent behavior as a threat to the safety of others. Although it is known that homosexual acts take place in today's prison facilities, their frequency and nature are unclear. The misunderstanding that exists in society concerns the occurrence of the homosexual acts. This has been augmented in recent years by the media. A sex scandal in a Georgia prison involving fourteen employees, including a deputy warden, headlined many newspapers. These individuals were indicted for having sex with female inmates—an episode of prison misconduct in which force of a psychological, rather than a physical, nature powered the abuse.[65] Another incident that received national attention involved Marion Barry, mayor of Washington, D.C., who was alleged to have engaged in oral sex in a crowded prison visiting room while serving time for possession of cocaine. In this incident, it was alleged that Barry's visitor was a prostitute.[66] These incidents are thought to occur frequently by the public. In 1993, the *New York Times* published an article titled "The Rape Crisis Behind Bars," which discussed the entrenched tradition of rape in prison and went on to regard prison as a training site for most rapists.[67] Unfortunately, these assumptions remain mostly unchallenged.

Consensual sexual activity among inmates has been examined less frequently than has coerced sex. Studies of sex between homosexuals in correctional facilities have taken the perspective that this type of sex is either a social problem or is a result of being institutionalized. Recent studies argue that inmates often improvise while in prison, as heterosexual contact is nonexistent.[68] Few researchers have examined male-to-male sexual relationships between caring partners because there is thought to be little or no violence in this situation. Consensual sex in prison is viewed by many as being less threatening than rape to the inmate or institutional security. It has been reported that this type of sexual encounter occurs more frequently than rape in today's prisons.[69]

Homosexual Rape in Prisons

Susan Brownmiller supported the importation theory of homosexual rape. Brownmiller argued that rape in prison is a power play. She analogized homosexual rape in a male prison to the rape of a female by a male in society—it is the result of a need to dominate, control, and conquer. "Prison rape . . . is an acting out of power roles within an all-male, authoritarian environment in which the younger, weaker inmate, usually a first time offender, is forced to play the role that in the outside world is assigned to women."[70]

Some studies have suggested that consensual sex in prison seldom happens and that sexual assaults are extremely rare. These studies report that the number of males admitting to being raped in prison are less than 1 percent.[71] A study was conducted in 1994 at a Delaware prison. Its purpose was to explore the nature and frequency of sexual contact between male inmates. The authors of this research administered a survey of sexual behavior to respondents who were questioned extensively about the sexual activity they engaged in, observed directly, and/or heard about "through the grapevine" before their entry into the prison treatment program. The findings of this study suggested that (1) although sexual contact is not widespread, it nevertheless takes place; (2) the preponderance of the activity is consensual instead of forced; and (3) inmates themselves perceive the myth of pervasive sex in prisons, often contradicting their own realities.[72]

Despite the finding made by the previously mentioned study, there is an increasing concern over the rights of inmates not to be the victim of sexual assaults. One approach to inmate rape is represented by the Prisoner Rape Education Project (PREP), a pioneering team effort led by survivors and professionals. This approach was issued in 1993 by the Safer Society project of the New York State Council of Churches. PREP aims at providing practical information and advice to inmates and staff on avoidance and survival; it consists of two audiotapes that are custom-made for prisoners and a manual for staff. Aside from this approach sponsored by private organizations, the courts are also rendering some attention to the issue of rape in prisons. In July 1993, the Federal Court of Appeals (Eleventh Circuit) affirmed a statewide prison training program on rape. This program was ordered in 1990 by Florida district court judge James C. Paine, who stated in *LaMarca v. Turner*, that "rape is one of the most degrading events, short of death, that can occur in prison."[73] In 1994, the U.S. Supreme Court, in

Farmer v. Brennan, reinstated an inmate's right to claim money for damages from prison officials for failing to render protection from rape.[74] It is only safe to assume that rape will continue to take place in prisons as the incarceration rate grows to unprecedented proportions.

Alternatives to Prison Homosexuality

Several suggestions have been made to decrease prison homosexuality without using solitary confinement. **Conjugal visits** in prisons and home **furloughs** are the two most frequently discussed.

Conjugal visits Visitation program that allows inmates to engage in sexual and social contact with their respective partners in a specified area of the prison facility.

Furlough An authorized temporary leave from prison during which the offender may engage in certain types of behavior (e.g., attend a funeral, visit family members, seek employment).

Conjugal Visits Administrators in some jurisdictions permit conjugal visits. This system provides prisoners with opportunities for sexual and social contacts with their spouses in a relaxed, unsupervised area of the prison community. During the visits, the couple may engage in sexual intercourse or use the time in any other way they choose. In some cases, the visit has been expanded to include the entire nuclear family, not just the spouse. Some involve an entire weekend instead of just a few hours on visiting day.

One of the first institutions in the United States to permit conjugal visits was the Mississippi State Prison at Parchman. Parchman, an old plantation converted into a penal farm, consists of 21,000 acres of land and sixteen inmate camps. Each camp had a residence building and a camp sergeant. Parchman was largely self-sufficient and the buildings and grounds were maintained by prison labor.

Parchman has no record of when or how the first conjugal visits were started, although it is said that they can be traced as far back as 1918, when African-Americans were allowed to take their wives or girlfriends to their rooms. For privacy, they hung towels up around their beds. Later, the inmates built what came to be known as the "red houses." These separate buildings were used for private visits of inmates with their wives. These visits were not guarded, and the inmate and his visitors were free to stroll anywhere on the 21,000 acres. Only married couples were permitted to use the conjugal visiting facilities, which consisted of rooms that were eight by ten feet in size, furnished with mirrors, beds, and tables. "About one-fourth of Parchman's 1,700 inmates have access to these rooms: the three-fourths who do not include disciplinary cases, condemned prisoners, unmarried men, and all women."[75]

This is one example of the conjugal visits that are presently taking place in prisons throughout the United States. Conjugal visits are allowed in only seven states despite that there is a growing number of groups that advocate the implementation of this program across the nation. One of the negative effects of conjugal visits involves the humiliation that some women have to endure from guards as they are escorted to a room to meet with their spouses. It is often reported that guards make fun of and reprimand these women while they are being searched. Most prison wives struggle with decisions concerning their sexual lives. Some of them believe that they should be celibate until their husbands are released, while others agree with their spouses that extramarital sexual encounters are acceptable until the inmate is released from prison. It is important to note that it is not sex that most prison wives miss the most, but rather they long to be held in the privacy of their home. This has led to the formation and continuing growth of support groups across the nation that advocate the creation of improved visitation conditions, including special playrooms where fathers can spend time with their children. This is particularly important as it has been estimated that 80 percent of all women and 50 percent of all men in prison have children. Statistics also show that more than 1.5 million minors have a parent behind bars. Forty-three percent of these children are under the age of seven, while 45 percent are between the ages of seven and twelve.[76] Most studies suggest that the closer the ties of the incarcerated inmate with his family, the less likely the inmate will commit crimes once released.

Furloughs Furloughs are special permits that allow inmates to leave prison temporarily in order to see family. Mississippi was the first state to allow inmates to take leaves from prison to visit their families. In 1918, ten-day holiday leaves were allowed for minimum custody inmates. In 1922, Arkansas instituted a furlough program, but for the next thirty-two years, no additional jurisdiction adopted the furlough. In the 1960s, several states and the entire federal prison system began furlough programs.[77] During the 1988 presidential elections, furloughs became a popular topic as Vice-President Bush raised the issue with regard to Willie Horton. Mr. Horton was released on furlough in Maryland, which was being governed at the time by Michael Dukakis. When on furlough, Horton raped a woman twice and then stabbed her husband. At the time, voters saw furloughs as part of Dukakis's liberal policy toward inmates—this damaged Dukakis's credibility as a presidential candidate and assisted Bush in winning his presidential bid. The publicity given to Horton affected furloughs and they declined in number in 1988. This took place despite evidence that suggests that inmates commit few crimes while they are on leave.[78] The number of furloughs increased in some areas of the country in the 1990s, as suggested by a survey conducted by the American Correctional Association (ACA). One of these states, Florida, experienced a 73 percent increase in furloughs over the previous year. In addition, several states have recently reported a success rate of 95 percent to 100 percent in their furlough programs.[79]

Today, furloughs for inmates are not being considered in some jurisdictions. This is a rather recent phenomenon but is likely to remain in place for some time due to the current struggle against terrorism. There is very little doubt that the United States is opting for a more conservative agenda that has ultimately affected the correctional field.

Advocates of furlough programs argue that they encompass conjugal visiting but eliminate the possibility of degradation and allow sexual relations to occur in normal circumstances and surroundings. Furloughs are broader than conjugal visits because they allow the inmate to leave the institution to look for a job or attend a funeral. Advocates also argue that by allowing inmates to benefit from furloughs, they are reducing the amount of violence that is likely to take place in prisons, as the potential of seeing a loved one will motivate offenders to behave well while in custody. This would serve as a behavior modification reward mechanism.

Furlough programs do involve risks. Additional children may be born, illegal offenses may be committed, and inappropriate behavior could occur. However, such risks exist anytime an inmate is released from prison. Since most inmates are eventually released, the challenge is to find ways to help them readjust to the community.

11-1g Violence in Prisons

The violence, other than homosexual rape, which occurs in the prison community is also important. Recently, the television network HBO created a program called "Oz," which depicts some of the violence that takes place inside prison.[80] The reaction by many viewers was of shock and disbelief that such incidents can occur inside a controlled facility. The most recent statistics suggest that the annual number of assaults by inmates rose 20 percent—from 21,590 in 1990 to

25,948 in 1995. Also, assaults on staff grew by one-third, from 10,731 in 1990 to 14,165 in 1995. Despite this trend, fewer inmate violations unrelated to assault were reported in 1995 than in 1990.[81]

Inmate Self-Inflicted Violence

According to Hans Toch, the most frequent form of violence in prisons is self-inflicted. Little attention is paid in the press to such violence and it is rarely reported, although these incidents can result in the death of the inmate.[82]

Self-inflicted violence is downplayed by inmates. "Inmates see it as an unmanly and weak thing to do unless it is blatantly manipulative."[83] Such violence is also ignored by staff, who may see the publicity as a negative indication that the prison is lax on security.

There are numerous violent incidents taking place daily in prison, given the nature of the offenses committed by most inmates. According to the Bureau of Justice Statistics (2000), in 1990, 570,000 inmates were in prison for violence-related charges. This is followed by 251,000 inmates for drug-related charges and 245,000 inmates for committing property offenses.[84]

Assaults, Batteries, and Prison Homicides

James B. Jacobs, in his study of the Stateville Prison, pointed out that although the "most distinctive manifestation of prison violence is homosexual rape,"[85] there are other types of violence. It is hard to define violence but it includes verbal threats (called assaults), batteries (the offensive touching of a person), and in the extreme, homicide. An inmate describes the condition of a fellow inmate who was the victim of a violent episode, referring to the fellow inmate as having "his intestines spilling out from a razor slash across his stomach. We had to keep pushing his entrails back into place as we raced the gurney down the corridor."[86] Prison violence may consist of any combination of these forms, involving inmates against guards, guards against inmates, or inmates against each other. One of the most serious crimes inside correctional facilities is prison homicide.

In 1977, Sawyer F. Sylvester, John H. Reed, and David O. Nelson published *Prison Homicide*, the result of their 1973 study on prison data from all states and federal jurisdictions. The work has been described by criminologist John C. Ball, former president of the American Society of Criminology, as the most extensive work on prison homicide.

The investigators found that there are more prison homicides in maximum-security prisons among inmates who have a history of violence, although the main factors in such homicides were not gang conflicts or racial tensions. They found that to understand the prison homicides, it was necessary to look at the relationship of the murderer to the victim. Most prison homicides, like those outside prison, involve the more violent members of society. However, a distinction must be made between those murders involving one assailant and those involving multiple assailants. Multiple assailants seem to be more rational and take more effort to plan their homicides than do single assailants, who are more emotional or episodic. For example, the latter might kill because of a homosexual relationship, whereas the former might kill those who violate the inmate code as punishment. Multiple assailants are usually younger, more intelligent, and more often from urban environments. They are more likely to have committed another homicide while in prison and they, like all assailants, have prior records of violence outside the prison, although those acts of violence were usually serious personal crimes and burglary, not homicide. Single assailants, on the other hand, "seem to have a less patterned criminal career. If not serving sentences for homicide, they are usually serving shorter sentences than assailants in multiple-assailant homicides."[87]

What explains rates of violence in prisons? Sylvester, Reed, and Nelson concluded that size, not density, of the prison is an important variable but noted that large prisons may have a selective population of persons most likely to engage in homicide. It might also be that it is more difficult to control the population in large rather than in small prisons. They found no evidence of a relationship between recreational facilities and homicide rates. They stated, however, that they had no measure of the quality or the use of these facilities and no indication of their value for reasons other than possibly preventing homicide. They found no evidence of interracial conflict when examining prisons nationwide, although there was some proof that it might be a factor in state prisons. Overall, African-Americans and whites were victims in proportion to their numbers in the general prison population.

> Given the fact that young blacks outside prison walls are twelve times as likely to be victimized by homicide, the racial parity of victimization within prison walls is striking. Anything that might be construed to be a "subculture of violence" among blacks outside prison appears to be ameliorated by conditions inside prison walls.

They warned, however, that one must be cautious in interpreting the data and that their study should not serve "as a justification for what is, but a call to further responsibility and action."[88]

Statistics show that more than 314 correctional officers at the federal, state, and local levels have been killed in the line of duty by inmates. One of the first recorded incidents involved the death of Andrew F. Turner, a correctional officer at the Leavenworth Federal Penitentiary in Kansas. He was killed by inmate Robert Stroud, with a homemade knife, because of a disciplinary report Turner filed a day earlier. As punishment, President Woodrow Wilson commuted Stroud's sentence to life imprisonment. To help fill the long days behind bars, Stroud developed a fascination with birds, and soon after his death he became known as "The Birdman of Alcatraz."

Violence is a predominant phenomenon among inmates as well. The most recent governmental publications available report that between 1990 and 1995, 410 inmates were killed by other inmates in both state and federal prison facilities.[89] This figure is not inclusive of homicides, suicides, or aggravated assaults that occurred in jails. These statistics only include reported crimes. The lack of reporting occurs because the victim fears retaliation or assumes correctional staff will not take any action to punish the offender.

Prison Riots

The historical occurrence of riots in this country is important to the sociological analysis of the causes of riots. In 1969, thirty-nine riots were reported; in 1970, fifty-nine occurred, which is an increase of 51 percent. Recently, riots at Santa Fe in 1980 and Atlanta in 1987 have received public attention. According to Michael Welch's book *Prison Violence in America*, 260 riots were reported in the United States between 1971 and 1983.[90] The primary cause of these riots was racial problems, while the second was inmate dissatisfaction with rules or privileges. It has also been reported that most of these inmate riots involved twenty-five to forty-nine inmates, while only eighteen of them involved 500 inmates or more. Most often, riots occur in a series. The Jackson, Michigan, riot of 1952 was followed by more than twenty-five riots through 1953. The 1955 riot in Walla Walla, Washington, was followed by a long series of disturbances, as was the Attica riot in

Spotlight 11-1

Stages of Prison Riots

1. Initial Explosion: The sudden (or planned) uprising in which inmates gain partial control of the institution.
2. Organization: The emergence of leadership among inmates. This takes place as correctional personnel mobilize to respond.
3. Confrontation: Inmates are confronted by force. This can vary from long discussions to the issuance of quick warnings.
4. Termination: Custodial control is regained. This is done through firepower, nonlethal force, or an agreement.
5. Explanation: The incident is investigated with the intent of identifying the cause of the disturbance while providing public assurances that all necessary remedies have been implemented.

Source: *Correctional Institutions* by Fox, © 1983. Adapted by permission of Pearson Education, Inc., Upper Saddle River, NJ.

September 1971. In contrast, studies reveal that only one outburst occurred in this country between 1884 and 1888 and that in no decade before the 1920s were there more than five riots reported.

An important feature of these earlier riots is that they were isolated incidents, unrelated to influences outside the institution. In their 1956 analysis, sociologist Frank E. Hartung and psychologist Maurice Floch classified riots as brutal or collective. Most of the early disturbances were brutal in nature, triggered mainly by complaints about harsh conditions—poor, insufficient, or contaminated food; inadequate, unsanitary, or dirty housing; sadistic brutality by prison officials; or a combination of these factors.[91] According to Hartung and Floch, prisoners would complain to officials about these conditions, officials would get defensive and resort to disciplinary measures, prisoners would complain and violate internal prison rules, assault others or themselves, and occasionally riot.

The second type, the collective riot, first took place in 1952 according to Hartung and Floch. This type differs sociologically and psychologically from the brutal type. In the 1960s, riots in American prisons took a dramatic shift, analogous to the civil rights protests and student protests of the time. Prisoners still demanded medical, recreational, and educational improvements, but it was increasingly common for inmates to question the legitimacy of their incarceration and to claim that they were political prisoners of an unjust and corrupt political system. Although all prison riots are unique, they usually take place in stages. Spotlight 11-1 explains the five stages of prison riots.

Some inmates contend that their crimes are a justifiable retaliation against a society that denies them the opportunity for social and economic gain. Denial of basic rights in prison, cruel punishment, racial prejudice, and other violations of the system make inmates one of America's most deprived minorities. There is a development of political protest in prisons. Prisoners, like members of labor unions and civil rights organizations, can be viewed as a group of individuals searching for an effective way of expressing demands and achieving results from the political system. Their attempts have gained more public reaction although that reaction has not been reflected in substantial prison reform. Prisoners have also formed unions to improve their bargaining power. Hartung and Floch theorized that the collective riot results from the combination of three sociological and social psychological components: (1) the nature of the maximum custody prison; (2) the aggregation of different types of inmates within one prison; and (3) the destruction of semiofficial, informal inmate self-government by a new administration.[92]

Most inmates, historically and at the time Hartung and Floch were writing, were incarcerated under conditions of maximum security. Most inmates do not need that type of security yet they live in confined quarters where almost every detail of their lives is monitored and ordered, leaving them with little to do except plan to escape. Hartung and Floch claimed that incarceration under such conditions leads to emotional problems. That, combined with the second reason—the mingling of different types of inmates—gives aggressive inmates an even greater advantage over the more passive prisoners. The aggressive inmates, including the predatory habitual criminals, take over the leadership of the inmate groups. With an insufficient number of guards, some of the administrative functions of the prison are given to the inmates. They then develop power over other prisoners and the administration. It is the inmates and not the officials who are in a position to maintain order and discipline within the prison. Those inmates are able to "obtain a great deal of self-expression" and are in a sense "elevated to semiofficial self-government." They are in control of those few things that make prison life tolerable and in return for this power, they regulate other inmates, which pleases the officials. Hartung and Floch contended that when such inmate control was removed during periods of reform and not replaced with other avenues for inmate self-expression, problems resulted. The aggressive inmates then became a destructive force. This is still true in today's prisons.

Recent attempts have been made to prevent prison riots although they vary from institution to institution. Studies on the lessons of prison riots have suggested that correctional institutions can help prevent the disturbances by ensuring that their emergency response teams are fully functional; by taking aims to prevent illegal drugs from entering prisons; by improving communication with inmates; by creating intensive training for prison officers; and by establishing various inmate programs. In some cases, such as that of the State Correctional Institution at Huntington, Pennsylvania, conflict-resolution programs have been implemented to reduce prison violence by teaching inmates the skills and resources to handle their own and other inmates' anger. This program also teaches correctional officers the communication skills necessary for positive interaction with prisoners.[93] However, the implementation of these programs does not guarantee a riot-free environment. Some have argued that as long as there are overcrowded prison facilities in the United States there will be an increasing numbers of riots.

Summary

In this chapter, the inmate community, or subculture, with its various social roles was discussed. Starting with Clemmer's concept of prisonization, the development of the theories and studies of inmate subculture were traced. The views of various sociologists who have argued that the inmate subculture is the result of adaptation as well as importation were examined. Inmates do make certain adjustments in prison because of the pains of imprisonment, which are the deprivations imposed by prison life. Those adjustments are also influenced by the background experiences of inmates, as well as by their current contacts with the outside world and their expectations for the future.

The specific problems associated with prison homosexuality were discussed and conjugal visits and furloughs were examined as possible solutions to this issue. If the analyses are correct, and prison homosexuality fulfills more than purely physiological needs, it is quite possible that neither conjugal visits nor furloughs will have a great impact in reducing it. If aggressive male homosexuality is the result of the aggressor's need to be dominant and to demonstrate his masculinity, or if it represents racial tension, it will not be decreased by programs aimed only at opportunity for sexual release. Finally, prison violence and the patterns of such violence, especially prison riots, were discussed and several suggestions for preventing these incidents were considered.

The discussions in this chapter make it clear that the problems that individuals face when they are incarcerated cannot be ignored. The ways in which inmates adapt to prison life have implications not only for the security of the institution and of society, but for the future of the inmates and society when the incarcerated individuals are released.

Notes

1. Trasler, Gordon, "The Social Relations of Persistent Offenders," in Robert M. Carter, Daniel Glaser, and Leslie T. Wilkins, eds., *Correctional Institutions* (Philadelphia: J.P. Lippincott and Company, 1972), p. 207.
2. Sykes, Gresham M., *The Society of Captives* (Princeton, NJ: Princeton University Press, 1958), pp. 63–83.
3. Clemmer, Donald, *The Prison Community* (1940; reprint ed., New York: Rinehart and Winston, 1958), pp. 298, 300, 301.
4. See, for example, Barry Schwartz, "Peer Versus Authority Effects in a Correctional Community," *Criminology* 11 (August, 1973), 233–257.
5. Adams, Kenneth, "Adjusting to Prison Life," in Michael Tonry, ed., *Crime and Justice: A Review of Research*, vol. 16 (Chicago: University of Chicago Press, 1993), pp. 275–359.
6. Michael, J. Lillyquist, *Understanding and Changing Criminal Behavior* (Englewood Cliffs, NJ: Prentice Hall, 1980); and C. W. Thomas and D. M. Peterson, "A Comparative Organizational Analysis of Prisonization," *Criminal Justice Review* 6 (1981): 36-43.
7. Wheeler, Stanton, "Socialization in Correctional Communities," *American Sociological Review* 26 (October, 1961), 697–712.
8. Sykes, *Society of Captives*, p. 82, emphasis deleted.
9. Sykes, *Society of Captives*, p. 82, emphasis deleted.
10. Sykes, Greshan M., and Messinger, Sheldon L., "The Inmate Social System," in Richard A. Cloward et al., eds., *Theoretical Studies in Social Organization of the Prison* (New York: Social Science Research Council, 1960), p.17.
11. Cloward, Richard A., et al., *Theoretical Studies in Social Organization of the Prison* (New York: Social Science Research Council, 1960), pp.21, 35–41.
12. Goffman, Erving, "On the Characteristics of Total Institutions," chapter 2 in Donald R. Cressey, ed., *The Prison: Studies in Institutional Organization and Change* (New York: Holt, Rinehart and Winston, 1961), pp. 22–47.
13. Tittle, Charles R. "Inmate Organization: Sex Differentiation and the Influence of Criminal Subcultures," *American Sociological Review* 34 (August, 1969), 503.
14. James Dabbs and Marian Hargrove, "Testosterone: Age and Behavior Among Female Prison Inmates", *Psychosomatic Medicine: Journal of the American Psychosomatic Society* (1997), 59: 477.
15. Irwin, John, and Cressey, Donald R., "Thieves, Convicts and the Inmate Culture," *Social Problems* 10 (Fall, 1962), 143.
16. Clemmer, *Prison Community*, pp. 229–302.
17. Schrag, Clarence C., "Social Types in a Prison Community," unpublished master's thesis, Seattle: University of Washington, 1944.
18. Irwin and Cressey, "Thieves, Convicts and the Inmate Culture," p. 142.
19. Irwin and Cressey, "Thieves, Convicts and the Inmate Culture," p. 148.
20. Irwin and Cressey, "Thieves, Convicts and the Inmate Culture," p. 148.
21. Clemmer, *Prison Community*, p. 130.
22. Irwin and Cressey, "Thieves, Convicts and the Inmate Culture," p. 153.
23. Thomas, Charles W., "Prisonization or Resocialization: A Study of External Factors Associated with the Impact of Imprisonment," *Journal of Research in Crime and Delinquency* 10 (January, 1975), 13–21.
24. Carroll, Leo, "Race and Three Forms of Prisoner Power: Confrontation, Censoriousness, and the Corruption of Authority," in C. Ronald Huff, ed., *Contemporary Corrections: Social Control and Conflict* (Beverly Hills, CA: Sage Publications, 1977), p. 40.
25. Carroll, "Race and Three Forms," in Huff, ed., p. 41.
26. Wright, Richard, A., *In Defense of Prisons* (Westport, CT: Greenwood, 1994). (For a different view, see Geoffrey Hunt, Stephanie Riegal, Tomas Morales, and Dan Waldorf, 1993, "Changes in Prison Culture: Prison Gangs and the Case of the Pepsi Generation," *Social Problems* 40: 398–410).
27. Carroll, Leo, *Hacks, Blacks, and Cons: Race Relations in Maximum Security Prison* (Prospect Heights, IL: Waveland, 1988).
28. Schwartz, Barry, "Pre-Institutional vs. Situational Influence in a Correctional Community," *The Journal of Criminal Law, Criminology and Police Science* 62 (Winter, 1971), 542.
29. Akers, Ronald L., Hayner, Norman S., and Gruninger, Werner, "Prisonization in Five Countries: Type of Prison and Inmate Characteristics," *Criminology* 14 (February, 1977), 538.
30. Quoted in Akers, Hayner, and Gruninger, "Prisonization," p. 548.
31. Akers, Ronald L., Hayner, Norman S., and Gruninger, Werner, "Homosexual and Drug Behavior in Prison: A Test of the Functional and Importation Models of the Inmate System," *Social Problems* 21 (No. 3, 1974), 410–422.
32. Thomas, Charles W., Petersen, David M., and Zingraff, Rhonda M., "Structural and Social Psychological Correlated of Prisonization," *Criminology* 16 (November, 1978), 390–391.
33. Lawson, Darren P., Segrim, Chris, and Ward, Theresa D., "The Relationship Between Prisonization and Social Skills Among Prison Inmates" (Sept. 1996), *Prison Journal*, vol. 76, no. 113, p. 293 (17).

34. Sykes, *Society of Captives*, pp. 5–6, 84.
35. For discussions of the special vocabularies utilized in men's prisons, see Clemmer, *The Prison Community*, pp. 89–90; Clarence Schrag, "A Preliminary Criminal Typology," *The Pacific Sociological Review* 4 (Spring, 1961), 11–16.
36. Carroll, Leo, *Hacks, Blacks, and Cons: Race Relations in a Maximum Security Prison* (Lexington, MA: D. C. Heath and Co., 1974).
37. Hassine, Victor, *Life Without Parole,* 2nd ed. (Los Angeles, CA: Roxbury Publishing Co., 1999).
38. Trasler, "Social Relations of Persistent Offenders."
39. Cloward, "Social Control in the Prison," p. 22.
40. Cloward, "Social Control," p. 23.
41. Cloward, "Social Control," pp. 27–28.
42. Cloward, "Social Control," p. 31
43. Cloward, "Social Control," pp. 35, 42, 48.
44. Irwin, John, and Austin, James, *It's About Time: America's Correctional Binge,* 2nd ed. (Wadsworth, 2001).
45. Irwin, John, "The Changing Social Structure of the Men's Prison," chapter 1 in David F. Greenberg, ed., *Corrections and Punishment,* vol. 8., Sage Criminal Justice System Annuals (Beverly Hills, CA: Sage Publications, 1977), pp. 21–40
46. Irwin, "The Changing Social Structure of the Men's Prison," p. 27.
47. See Theodore G. Chiricos and Charles Crawford, "Race and Imprisonment: A Contextual Assessment of the Evidence," in Darnell F. Hawkins, ed., *Ethnicity, Race and Crime: Perspectives Across Time and Place,* (Albany, NY: State University of New York Press, 1995).
48. Clarke, Harold, "Gang Problems: From the Streets to Our Prisons," *Corrections Today,* vol. 54, no. 5 (July, 1992), p. 8.
49. For a detailed discussion of the inmate sub-rosa economy, see Vergil Williams and Mary Fish, *Convicts, Codes and Contraband* (Cambridge, MA: Ballinger Publishing Company, 1974).
50. Irwin, "The Changing Social Structure of the Men's Prison," p. 37.
51. Williams, Vergil L., and Fish, Mary, *Convicts, Codes, and Contraband: The Prison Life of Men and Women* (Cambridge, MA: Ballinger, 1974), pp. 137–142.
52. Markley, Carson W., "Furlough Programs and Conjugal Visiting in Adult Correctional Institutions," *Federal Probation* 37 (March, 1973), 19–26.
53. Fishman, Joseph, *Sex in Prison* (New York: National Library Press, 1934), cited in Peter C. Buffum, *Homosexuality in Prisons* (U.S. Department of Justice, et al., Washington, D.C.: U.S. Government Printing Office, 1972), p. 13.
54. Buffum, *Homosexuality in Prisons,* p. 2.
55. For a discussion on the myths of sex in prison see "Sex in Prison: Exploring the Myths and Realities," Christine A. Saum, Hilary L. Surratt, James A. Inciardi, Rachael E. Bennett, *Prison Journal,* December, 1995, vol. 75, no. 4. p. 413 (18).
56. Eigenberg, Helen, "Homosexuality in Male Prisons: Demonstrating the Need for a Social Constructionist Approach," *Criminal Justice Review* 17: 2 (1992): 219–234.
57. For more information, see "The Deal Behind Bars," Stephen Donaldson, *Harper's Magazine,* (August, 1996), vol. 293, no. 1755, p. 17 (2).
58. Sykes, *Society of Captives,* p. 97.
59. Carroll, *Hacks, Blacks, and Cons,* p. 184.
60. Carroll, *Hacks, Blacks, and Cons,* p. 185.
61. Carroll, *Hacks, Blacks, and Cons,* p. 186.
62. Carroll, *Hacks, Blacks, and Cons,* p. 183.
63. Carroll, *Hacks, Blacks, and Cons,* p. 186.
64. Buffum, *Homosexuality in Prisons,* p. 9.
65. Curriden, M., "Prison Scandal in Georgia: Guards Traded Favors for Sex," *National Law Journal* (September 20, 1993), p. 8.
66. Nichols, B., "Barry Denies Sex-In-Prison Allegations," *USA Today* (January 6, 1992), p. A3.
67. Donaldson, S., "The Rape Crisis Behind Bars," *New York Times* (December 12, 1993), p. A11.
68. Irwin, J., *Prison in Turmoil* (Boston: Little, Brown, 1980).
69. See Nacci, P. L., and Nkane, T. R., "The Incidence of Sex and Sexual Aggression in Federal Prisons," *Federal Probation* 7 (1983), 31–36.
70. Brownmiller, Susan, *Against Our Will: Men, Women and Rape* (New York: Simon and Schuster, 1975), p. 258.
71. Lockwood, D., *Prison Sexual Violence* (New York: Elsevier, 1980); also Tewksbury, R. "Measures of Sexual Behavior in an Ohio Prison," *Sociology and Social Research* 74 (1989b), 34–39.
72. Saum, Christine A., Surratt, Hillary L., Inciardi, James A., and Bennett, Rachel E., "Sex in Prison: Experiencing the Myths and Realities," *Prison Journal* (December, 1995), vol. 75, no. 4. p. 413 (18).
73. Donaldson, Stephen, "Can We Put an End to Inmate Rape?" *USA Today Magazine* (May, 1995), vol. 123, no. 2600, p. 40(3).
74. Donaldson, "Can We Put an End to Inmate Rape?" p. 13.
75. "Only on Sunday," *Time* (August 18, 1967), 49. For a detailed study of the Parchman program of conjugal visiting, see Columbus B. Hopper.
76. Dallao, Mary, "Coping with Incarceration—From the Other Side of the Bars," *Corrections Today* (October, 1997), vol. 59, no. 6. p. 96(3).
77. Markley, "Furlough Programs," pp. 20–21.
78. "Study of 53,000 Inmates on Furlough in '87 Finds Few Did Harm," *New York Times.* (October 12, 1988), p. 12; "Tough Talk Cuts Prison Furloughs," *Tampa Tribune* (November 27, 1988), p. 12.
79. "Prison Furloughs Up 73% From Last Year," *Tallahassee Democrat* (November 12, 1990), p. 2c. For a discussion and evaluation of the Florida Community Control Program (FCCP), see Dennis Wagner and Christopher Baird, "Evaluation of the Florida Community Control Program," Bureau of Justice Statistics (Washington, DC: U.S. Department of Justice, January, 1993).
80. Silver, Marc. "This Is Not 'I Love Lucy' " (Violent Graphic Depiction of Life on the Home Box Office Series "OZ"), *U.S News and World Report* (July 14, 1997), vol.123, no. 2. p. 8 (1).
81. Chaiken, Jan M. *Census of State and Federal Correctional Facilities,* 1995 (Washington, D.C.: Bureau of Justice Statistics. U.S. Department of Justice, August, 1997).
82. Toch, Hans, *Peacekeeping: Police, Prisons, and Violence* (Lexington, MA: D.C. Heath and Company, 1976), p. 61.
83. Toch, Hans, "A Psychological View of Prison Violence," in Albert K. Cohen, George F. Cole, and Robert G. Bailey, eds., *Prison Violence* (Lexington, MA: D.C. Heath and Company, 1976), p. 49.
84. Bureau of Justice Statistics (2000), *Correctional Populations in the United States, 1997,* and *Prisoners in 2000,* U.S. Department of Justice, Washington, D.C.
85. Jacobs, James B., "Prison Violence and Formal Organization," chapter 6 in Cohen et al., eds., *Prison Violence,* p. 79.
86. Hassine, *Life Without Parole,* p. 13.
87. Sylvester, Sawyer F., Reed, John H., and Nelson, David O., *Prison Homicide* (New York: Halsted Press, 1977), p. xxii.
88. Sylvester, Reed, and Nelson, *Prison Homicide,* pp. 75, 82.
89. Bureau of Justice Statistics, *Correctional Population in the United States, 1995* (Washington, D.C.: U.S. Department of Justice, 1997), p. 18.
90. Welch, Michael, "Prison Violence in America: Past, Present, and Future," In *Visions for Change: Crime and Justice in the Twenty-First Century,* Roslyn Muraskin and Albert R. Roberts, eds.(Englewood Cliffs, NJ: Prentice Hall, 1996).
91. Hartung, Frank E., and Floch, Maurice, "A Social-Psychological Analysis of Prison Riots: An Hypothesis," *Journal of Criminal Law, Criminology, and Police Science* 47 (May-June, 1956), 51.
92. Hartung and Floch, "A Social-Psychological Analysis of Prison Riots," 52.
93. Love, Bill, "Programs Curbs Prison Violence Through Conflict Resolution," (State Correctional Institution of Huntingdon, Pennsylvania), includes related article, "Stemming the Violence," *Corrections Today* (August, 1994), vol. 56, no. 5, p. 144 (3).

Chapter 12

The Female Inmate

Outline

Until recently, the female involvement in the criminal justice system was seldom the subject of study in academic settings. Various reasons have been given for this neglect: women have constituted a much smaller percentage of total offenders, their crimes generally do not threaten society, and women arrested for violations of the law are usually first-time offenders.

In general, female offenders have not been perceived as a grave social problem. They have not been the subjects of prison violence and as inmates they have been considered easier to manage than males, resulting in less security in women's institutions. The early view on female criminality was based on the idea that police were less likely to arrest women and juries were less likely to convict them due to a general attitude of protectiveness and benevolence. This became known as the chivalry hypothesis. Women are considered to be treated better than men. This is exemplified by frequently made comments regarding correctional facilities for women as "country clubs."

Recently, some of these widely held beliefs have been challenged as scholars have begun to take a more in-depth look at the role of females in the criminal justice system. This chapter focuses on the female offender in the correctional system. A brief history of females in the correctional system and a comparison of male and female arrest rates are explored. The profile of the female offender and the discussion of institutions for female offenders is analyzed. The emergence of the separate institution for females and why so little empirical research has been conducted on these institutions and their occupants is examined. Finally, the new generation jails for female offenders are discussed.

Key Terms

chivalry hypothesis
battered woman syndrome

12-1 History

Chivalry hypothesis Early view on female criminality which held that police were less likely to arrest women and juries were less likely to convict women, due to a general attitude of protectiveness toward this gender.

Until the late nineteenth century, male and female inmates occupied dungeons, almshouses (poorhouses), and jails. Usually women and children were not segregated from men, resulting in many instances of sexual abuse. Institutions were plagued with physical and sexual violations and exploitation as well as the inevitable corruption that occurs when there is no classification of inmates.

Elizabeth Gurney Fry, a middle-class Quaker, was the first person in the United States to fight for changes in the treatment of sentenced children and women. When Fry and other fellow Quakers visited London's Newgate Prison in 1813, they were shocked by the conditions surrounding women. This so affected Fry that she began to push for separate institutions for women, to be staffed by women, while offering a domestic environment. Due to Fry's efforts, a parliamentary committee heard about the conditions in which female offenders were incarcerated and, in 1918, ordered reforms to be implemented immediately.

As prison reform began in the United States, the practice was to segregate women into corners of existing institutions, which were usually modeled after the penitentiary system. There were few women inmates, a fact that was used to justify not providing them with a matron, vocational training, or educational programs.[1] In 1873, the first prison for women, the Indiana Women's Prison, was opened. Its emphasis was on rehabilitation, obedience, and religious education. Other institutions followed—a facility in Framingham, Massachusetts, in 1877; a reformatory for women in New York in 1891; the Westfield Farm in 1901; and an institution in Clinton, New Jersey in 1913. Separate institutions for women continued to be the pattern of incarceration until the first coed prison of modern times was established in the United States in 1971. Gradually, other states built facilities for women. In 1998, an estimated 951,900 women were under the care, custody, or control of the correctional system. This translates into a rate of one out of every 109 adult women in the United States as having some kind of correctional status in a given day.[2]

As mentioned earlier, little attention has been given to the female offender until recently. Evidence of this phenomenon can be traced back to the 1967 report of the President's Crime Commission which contained no references to the female offender in its 222 pages.[3] This paucity of data is interesting considering that "women's reformatories were among the very first to involve themselves in research." The Bedford Hills Reformatory for Women in New York employed a psychologist in 1910 and, in 1912, opened a Laboratory of Social Hygiene for research. At that same time, a Massachusetts reformatory for women established a research department. These developments came well before research departments in prisons for men. Most of the early efforts were abandoned, however, because of financial problems and apathy of prison officials. When research on inmates began, it was usually conducted on male populations.[4]

In the 1960s, a significant emphasis was placed on the rights of female offenders in the United States. This was aided by the political climate of the country at the time. Soon after, with a Republican administration, the attitude toward female inmates began to change once again. The growing punitive drug-related laws of the 1980s, accompanied by a rising fear of crime, led to a no tolerance approach toward offenders in general. This approach has had a negative impact on female inmates as it has led to the existing lack of concern for their special needs. Some of these needs include the emotional trauma of weakening the ties with their children, loss of financial assets, and uncertain relationships with husbands and other loved ones. These needs, when not properly addressed, result in an unbearable prison environment in which radical measures such as suicide or escape become feasible options.

12-2 The Female in the Criminal Justice System

In an article on the female offender, Ray R. Price, after noting some of the changes the women's liberation movement created in our society, summed up the position of women in the criminal justice system:

> Probably no part of our society has been so exclusively a male domain as the criminal justice system. The criminal law has been codified by male legislators, enforced by male police officers, and interpreted by male judges. Rehabilitation programs have been administered by males. The prison system has been managed by men, primarily for men.[5]

This lack of attention to women and crime has been particularly noticeable in the literature on the female offender. Before examining the characteristics of the female offender, however, it is important to note some of the differences in the data on arrests of males and females. This brief overview outlines the differences in the correctional facilities for each, as well as the various ways in which male and female inmates react to imprisonment.

12-2a Research on Women's Prisons

Several explanations for the absence of study of women's prisons have been offered recently. First, women constitute roughly only 5 percent of the state correctional population, and at least half of that number have been found to reside in jails, not prisons. Women in jails are incarcerated for lesser offenses than those in prisons. It is reasonable to assume that researchers have paid little attention to female inmates because they do not create the serious problems created by male inmates, most of who reside in prisons as opposed to jails. Second, the relatively smaller population of women makes research difficult. Samples are not as large and it is not easy to generalize as it is with data on male inmates. It is also difficult to compare the various studies that are conducted. Third, the lack of research on women prisoners might be a function of who conducts the research. Women have conducted most of the studies on the female offender, and until recently, large numbers of women have not been trained in social science research methodology. Fourth, some past studies have indicated that administrators of correctional facilities for women are more reluctant than those in men's prisons to allow researchers to enter their institution.

It is important to note that the combination of the women's rights movement, the rise of feminist scholarship, and the noted increase in female criminality have begun to reverse the long-standing neglect of research on women's prisons. In direct response to these factors, a rich and complex literature that examines the treatment of women by criminal justice scholars has begun to emerge.[6] This trend will continue and will benefit society by educating the public about the complexities involved in incarcerating female offenders.

12-2b Data on Arrests and Offending Rates of Males and Females: A Comparison

An extensive discussion of the problems of interpreting data from the *Uniform Crime Reports,* the basic source of data on crime, cannot be undertaken here.[7] The Federal Bureau of Investigation, which compiles data, warns that one should be careful interpreting the data.

Arrest rates of males and females differ significantly. Although males constitute roughly 50 percent of the population in the United States, they account for 78 percent of all of the arrests made in the United States in 1999. Statistics from 1999 suggest that the most significant percentage of all arrests, 12 percent for

TABLE 12-1 Male and Female Offending Rates

Offending Rates: Number of Offenders per 1,000 residents			Ratio of Offending Rates
Year	*Male*	*Female*	*Male: Female*
1993	135	19	7.1
1994	140	20	7.0
1995	124	19	6.4
1996	107	19	5.7
1997	99	15	6.5

Source: Bureau of Justice Statistics, U.S. Department of Justice, "Women Offenders" (December, 1999).

males offenders, were for drug abuse violations. In contrast, the most significant percentage of all female-related arrests, 14 percent, was for larceny-theft.[8]

The offending rates (rate at which males and females commit crimes) for both males and females have changed in recent years (see Table 12-1). The ratio of male to female offending rates has been reduced recently from 7.1 in 1993 to 6.5 in 1997. In 1993, for every seven male offenders there was only one female offender. In 1997, for every six male offenders there was one female offender.[9]

If the present trend of arrest and offender rates of adult women continues to rise, the use of probation will increase, developing more opportunities for diverting offenders out of correctional facilities or increasing the capacity of correctional institutions. The increasing cost associated with the physical facilities will be compounded by the need for increased medical, psychological, and psychiatric personnel and services as well as for educational, recreational, and vocational opportunities. If trends continue, female correctional facilities may face some of the same problems witnessed in male institutions in recent years, such as overcrowding.

Interpretation of Data on Female Arrests

The dramatic increase of female offending and arrest rates may be because women are gaining equal standing with their male counterparts in society. Their role in criminal behavior has recently changed from passive to aggressive. Today more women are being sentenced for drug-related offenses (which carry longer prison terms) than in the past. The findings produced in a survey suggested that one-third of female offenders, compared to one-quarter of male inmates, used a needle to inject illegal drugs.[10] The number of female arrests is likely to continue at a faster rate than the number of male arrests due to the increasingly participatory role of women at all levels of society, including criminality.

There are still many unanswered questions. For example, when reviewing the 1999 data, why are arrests of women for property crimes significantly greater (323,118) than for violent personal crimes (71,468)?[11] In one of her earlier examinations of female criminality, Freda Adler suggested that since the latter are mainly crimes of passion involving interpersonal relationships, the lower rate of increase for women in this area may indicate that women are more interested in improving their financial status.[12]

Other explanations may be more plausible. Normally, cultural changes take place faster in economic areas than in other areas; women may be trained to restrain their emotions and violence more than are men, and that training might be easier to overcome in areas that are not domestic. It might be that men who are attacked by women are less likely to report such assaults, or if they are reported, police are less likely to arrest than in cases in which men assault women. Support for the economic reasons comes also from an analysis of crime data from other countries. According to Adler, when the economic disparity between men and women decreases, rates of female criminality increase correspondingly.

Joseph Weis emphasized that when close attention is paid to the official crime rates in the United States, the increases in rates of female criminality are not surprising. He looks at the dramatic increases in larceny, mainly shoplifting, a crime for which most arrests are women.[13] These crimes are tied to the traditional female roles "in the legal and illegal marketplaces; women move from shopper to shoplifter, from cashing good checks to passing bad ones, from taking aspirins to popping bennies and barbs, from being a welfare mother to being accused of welfare fraud, and so on." [14]

Weis's position is that the image of the new female criminal is a myth based on pop criminology and official crime data. After studying self-reports of middle-class delinquency, he argues that this data reflects gender-role opportunities. Weis concludes that the alleged relationship between female liberation and the emergence of a new type of female criminal is a social invention, not a reality. "Women are not more violent today than a decade ago and the increase in property offenses suggests that the sexism which still pervades the straight world also functions in the illegal marketplace."[15]

Another scholar who has written extensively about women and crime, Rita James Simon, states "women are committing those types of crimes that their participation in the labor force provides them with greater opportunities to commit than they had in the past." The propensities of men and women to commit crimes are not basically different; the difference has been in opportunities.[16]

Darrel J. Steffensmeier has brought many of these explanations together in his evaluation of trends in female criminality from 1960 to 1990. He indicates that much of the change in both male and female criminality is similar and reflects the social and legal forces that influence both, but that there are several differences. Using official data, confirmed by both the National Crime Victimization Survey (NCVS) and self-report data, Steffensmeier notes that women are much more likely to be involved in property crimes, especially the minor offenses of larceny-theft, fraud, forgery, embezzlement, and prostitution.

He describes several factors that he believes account for these differences. First, society has different expectations for women. Women are expected to be caregivers. They are socialized to be wives and mothers, which leaves little time for a criminal lifestyle. Even with many women choosing a career path, this socialization factor remains strong. Women also are affected by their sexual and/or physical attractiveness. Fathers and husbands tend to be protective of women and girls and create a double standard for their behavior. It is acceptable for males to be aggressive and engage in rough and wild behavior, but the expectation is not the same for females. The criminal justice system often reinforces this standard by giving more latitude to males and restricting the behavior of females. In addition, society's value on femininity makes it difficult for a female to violate this stereotype and act in nonfeminine ways that would lead her into criminal opportunities.

Second, the moral development of men and women is such that women are more likely to make choices that do not hurt others while men tend to be more aggressive. Women are less likely to engage in violence and in behaviors that affect others.

Third, physical strength and aggression are key qualities of criminal offenders. Women are either less strong and aggressive or perceived to be so and are therefore less likely to be accepted in criminal subcultures. When a woman is included in this subculture, she is included as a female, either as someone's partner or as property in the pimp-prostitute relationship.

Finally, many women lack access to criminal opportunity. Not only are they perceived as less qualified for criminal behavior, they have limited access to the types of jobs that provide an opportunity for crime. Jobs such as truck driver and laborer often provide opportunities for theft and other crimes not associated with typical female jobs.[17]

Female criminality is a complex phenomenon that deserves more attention. The studies discussed suggest several variables that might be influential. Although scholars do not agree on why male and female arrests rates are changing, the traits of female offenders may present some insight.

12-2c Profiles of Female Offenders

The typical female inmate is best portrayed in the Bureau of Justice Statistics Special Report of Women Offenders (2000). This report indicates that female inmates resemble male inmates in terms of race and ethnic background. While nearly two-thirds of female offenders serving a probation sentence are white, almost two-thirds of those who are confined to local jails or state/federal prisons are minorities. This includes blacks and/or Hispanics.[18]

Females committed to state or federal prisons are older than their counterparts confined to jails or serving probation sentences. While one in every five females serving probation sentences or confined to a local jail are under twenty-five years old, one in eight state prisoners and one in eleven federal inmates are of this same age. Among females, nearly 25 percent of federal prison inmates are at least forty-five years of age. Nearly half of all females serving a sentence in both state and local jails have never been married. Further, the majority of females involved with the justice system report having received at least a high school education. Approximately 30 percent to 40 percent of inmates that have a high school diploma also report having attended some college.[19]

Although half of female inmates have not been married, approximately seven in ten female offenders under correctional supervision report having minor children (under the age of eighteen). Of these female offenders with children, they reported having an average of 2.11 children that were under eighteen. The separation from their children augments the isolation and overall sadness female inmates experience when confined to prison.[20]

When compared to their male counterparts before entering prison, female prisoners experienced harsher economic circumstances. About four in ten female inmates serving time in state prisons reported they had been employed full-time before their arrest. However, data on their male counterparts suggests that nearly six in ten male inmates had been working full-time before being arrested. When considering incomes, females earned less before they entered prison. In 1999, about 37 percent of women and only 28 percent of men reported having monthly incomes of $600. While only less than 8 percent of males had been receiving welfare assistance before they were arrested, 30 percent of female inmates reported to have been receiving assistance preceding their arrest.[21]

In the 1990s, a different type of female offender began arriving at prisons—the battered woman. These women often find themselves in a correctional institution because they resorted to violence to end their victimization after enduring long periods of abuse by their husbands. Statistics suggest that female offenders who committed homicide were almost twice as likely as a relative, such as a par-

TABLE **12-2** **History of Physical or Sexual Abuse of Female Offenders**

	Probation	Local Jails	State Prisons
Ever Physically or Sexually Abused	41%	48%	57%
Before age 18	16	21	12
After age 18	13	11	20
Both periods	13	16	25
Ever Abused			
Physically	15%	10%	18%
Sexually	7	10	11
Both	18	27	28

Source: Bureau of Justice Statistics, U.S. Department of Justice, "Women Offenders" (December, 1999).

ent or sibling, to have killed an intimate partner (husband, ex-husband, or boyfriend).[22] Unfortunately for many of them, their action is not considered an act of self-defense because in most cases they are not being threatened at the time the offense takes place. However, due to events that have publicized the long, painful agony of these women (e.g., the O.J. Simpson criminal trial), a new line of defense based on the **battered woman syndrome** has been created. Defense attorneys now often rely on the claim that long periods of abuse result in a woman's empowerment as she takes action against her aggressor. Despite the fact that some of these abused women receive commuted sentences, many remain in prison facilities serving long sentences after a homicide conviction. Table 12-2 shows the history of physical and sexual abuse experienced by female offenders under correctional supervision in 1999. As evident, a large portion of them experienced physical or sexual abuse before entering the correctional system.

Battered woman syndrome An act of aggression on the part of a woman who has been physically abused by a man with whom she had a close relationship.

12-2d Centralization and Decentralization: A Comparison

Most of the early analyses conducted on the construction of women's prisons revealed a process of centralization by various states. From 1930 to 1959, only two or three prisons were constructed for female offenders in each decade. Most of these were built in the South and West because prison construction for women in these regions was lagging. In the 1960s, several more female prisons were built in the South and West, with seventeen more constructed in the 1970s. Two more female prisons were built in the Northeast during the 1970s. It was not until the 1980s that the biggest growth took place, with the construction of more than thirty-four new prisons for female offenders.

The process of centralization of women's facilities, however, has begun to reverse. Although one study indicated that in 1988, forty-four states housed all-female inmates in one or two facilities, several states had made arrangements for the extensive expansion of facilities for women. Some consider the expansion, or decentralization, as a positive factor for female inmates. It is clear that the potential exists for the reversal of the current trend regarding inmate isolation and inferior programs offered in female facilities. Conversely, some believe that this will only increase the potential for women to be sent to custodial institutions unnecessarily.

At the turn of a new millennium, most facilities for women are situated in rural areas of the United States. Their location creates a further hardship on female inmates as it moves them farther away from their families and familiar environments. In some cases, this isolates female inmates to such a degree that they often lack visitors for months. Many inmates who are also mothers suffer from an increasingly weak relationship with their children. This isolation is often augmented by the lack of services that female prisons provide. The remote locations of female prisons make it difficult for volunteers to travel, resulting in the lack of adequate staffing for programs and services often offered in male correctional institutions.[23]

12-2e Architecture

A Law Enforcement Assistance Administration (LEAA) survey classified the architecture of female institutions into four categories. In the first category was the complex, featuring a group of buildings, constructed around the administration building and including several living units as well as facilities for vocational and educational types of programs. Second was the single building, with all functions housed in one building. Third was the campus design, similar to a college campus. In this design, there is a large area with trees, shrubs, and a group of buildings placed throughout the grounds, each with a special function. Finally, the cottage design contains small buildings resembling multifamily homes. "Each cottage is designed to be self-sufficient and contains individual rooms, as well as kitchen facilities. This design is intended to replicate, to the extent possible, a homey atmosphere."[24] Some institutions have variations on these designs—for example, a cottage within a complex.

Of the institutions that were built between 1930 and 1966, most have followed the traditional style, which is the cottage or modified cottage. This style is the most appropriate since most female prisons have small inmate populations. These institutions have simple classification techniques. A study by Strickland in 1966 suggested that most of these female facilities were custody-oriented; the rest were either custodial, treatment-oriented, or treatment facilities. Despite the fact that the number of female prisons is increasing, the total number constitutes only a small percentage of all prisons in the United States.[25]

In contrast to institutions for adult males, institutions for adult females are generally more aesthetic and have a less secure environment. Female inmates are not regarded as high security risks since they have not proven to be as violent as male inmates. Despite some exceptions, institutions for female offenders are built and maintained with the view that the occupants are not great risks to themselves or to others. This is evidenced by the architecture of most female correctional facilities. Some of these facilities have rooms and not the open cells or dorms of the male facilities. Many facilities also allow curtains, bedspreads, and cooking areas, creating an almost home-like environment. Some even allow female inmates to wear their own clothing and to have greater latitude with commissary items (e.g., cosmetic products).

12-2f Security Levels

Currently, most women's prisons are designated as medium-security facilities. As in the past, there are few custody-graded facilities because there are fewer female inmates. Security-graded females must be housed in the same facility and all females are incarcerated either in medium or maximum-security prisons regardless of their needs.

12-2g Personnel

The administration of female correctional facilities has changed dramatically in recent years. In 1966, female correctional administrators headed only ten female institutions, whereas in 1993, 237 of the 1,653 correctional administrators were females.[26] This trend does not necessarily suggest that female inmates receive better treatment in facilities headed by female administrators. Although it does point to the fact that as women advance in our society, they have not excluded

Indiana Women's Prison is the oldest established women's prison in the nation. It began taking offenders in 1869.
Indiana Women's Prison

seeking and advancing to professional positions within the correctional system. This phenomenon is likely to continue.

12-2h Educational and Vocational Programs for Women

One of the advantages of the relatively smaller population in female prison is that inmates have a greater opportunity to interact with staff. There is also a chance for better innovation in programming. Unfortunately, the smaller number of female inmates has justified the lack of funding for educational and vocational programs, as well as the absence of research on the effectiveness of such programs.

Traditionally, female correctional institutions reflect the expected role that women play in our society. In the late nineteenth century, when reformers advocated separate institutions for women, the emphasis was on reformatories, not prisons, where women were to learn the behaviors appropriate for the female role in society. They lived in cottages that were like homes, not in large institutional-type structures characteristic of prisons for men.

For example, women prisoners were trained to milk and care for cows. Joy Eyman aptly states the situation:

> Dairymen are turning to women to help ease the labor shortage. Those dairymen who have tried women in milking operations are pleased with the results. Women are proving to be better milkers than men and understand the problems of swollen udders, mastitis, and other mammary infections.[27]

Some programs for women have been designed to reflect the same domestic role played by women in history. Many are determined by federal funding that supports the programs. At the national level, the transfer of programs from one area to another has often failed to take into account local differences that might impede such transfers. In the past, a LEAA study suggested that the criminal justice system should "focus on the female offender as a woman, and examine how her needs relate to those of other women on the outside," not on how she may differ from male offenders or on traditional concepts of causation of crime among women.[28]

Although there have been attempts in recent years to address the particular needs of some incarcerated women, many of today's vocational and technical

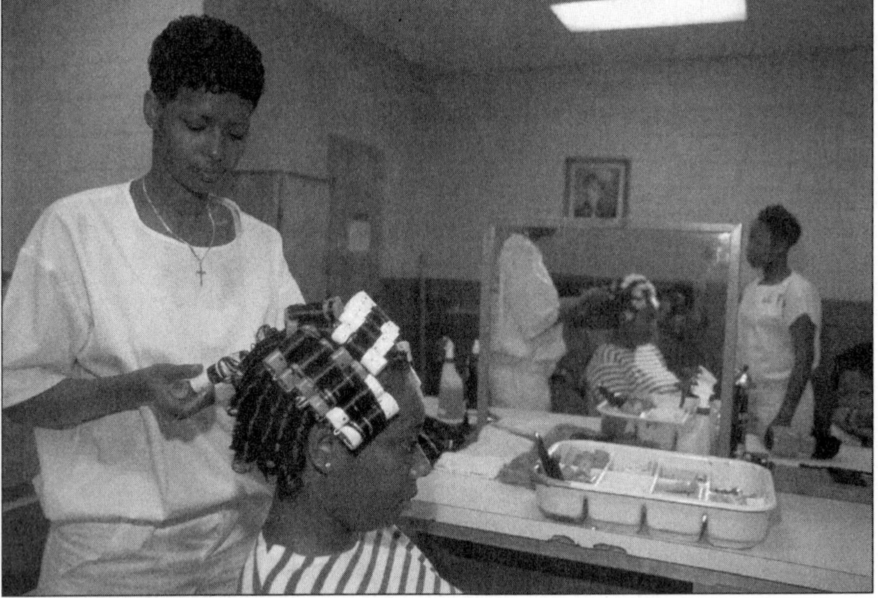

Female inmates hold jobs that allow them to learn a trade with the hope that, upon release, they will engage in a legitimate lifestyle.
A. Ramey/PhotoEdit

programs provide far less than they should. In general, programs for women fall into five major categories. These include:

1. Institutional maintenance including clerical work, food service for the institution, and general cleaning and maintenance of the grounds;
2. Education, which is mostly remedial;
3. Vocational training, most often geared toward stereotypical jobs (cosmetology, sewing, food service, and clerical skills);
4. Treatment (including Alcoholic Anonymous, Narcotics Anonymous, etc.); and
5. Medical care.[29]

Martha Wheeler, past president of the American Correctional Association (ACA), warned about designing programs for female inmates on the assumption that they will not play the traditional female role in society. She indicated that in her work, many female inmates indicate that they prefer the traditional role. When some of these inmates at the parole stage are asked about getting jobs, their response is that they want to "get a man." Wheeler raised the issue of whether the responsibility is to prepare these women for new functions in society or to meet them where they are and help them with programs that enable them to become more secure with the world in which they expect to live. Wheeler concluded by stating "at the risk of contradicting NOW (National Organization of Women), I really have to say that we should let our women say something about where they are and where they want to be and where they want to go."[30]

The point is not to force all women to assume nontraditional roles but to make educational and vocational training available that enables them to assume such roles if they so choose. Training programs in women's prisons are not as extensive as those in men's prisons and they still emphasize the traditional female roles in society and do not adequately prepare women for employment outside the home. Educational facilities are usually inferior to those in men's prisons, which is particularly distressing as female inmates want more training than is available to them and that many do expect to work and to support dependents when they are released. The variety of educational courses from which they can choose is considerably limited compared to those offered to men. The same is true of the industries that exist within prisons. "Although women are much less likely to be sent to prison than are men, once there, the opportunities afforded to women for rehabilitation and vocational training are much less than are those for men."[31]

The National Advisory Commission on Criminal Justice Standards and Goals recommended that in institutions for women:

> Appropriate vocational training programs should be implemented. Vocational programs that promote dependency and exist solely for administrative ease should be abolished. A comprehensive research effort should be initiated to determine the aptitudes and abilities of the female institutional population. This information should be coordinated with labor statistics predicting job availability. From data so obtained, creative vocational training should be developed which will provide a woman with skills necessary to allow independence.[32]

A survey conducted among state prisons for women indicated that some of the problems facing vocational programs in these institutions include aging equipment, limited funding, and lack of competent civilian staff.[33] This survey was mailed to all state prisons for women. Some of the other problems reported in this survey included inconsistent attendance (inmates enter mid-course and leave prison or are transferred to other units before completing the training program), a low inmate pay scale (female inmates are paid on a lower scale than their male counterparts, at times receiving only half the amount paid to men), and low inmate self-esteem. Survey respondents not only highlighted the problems with these programs but they also made several recommendations to improve the existing services. These include:

1. Certifying programs by the appropriate industry or state board and allowing inmates to take required exams while still incarcerated.
2. Equal pay for women and men in comparable inmate jobs.
3. New and/or updated equipment in instances where existing machines and equipment are no longer adequate (e.g., sewing machines and computers).
4. Increased interaction with employers in the community.
5. A stronger partnership between the department of corrections and the department of education or other educational suppliers.
6. Encouraging women to enroll in nontraditional programs.
7. Coordinated moves and transfers in states that have multiple facilities, enabling inmates to complete training courses.[34]

One educational training program was the subject of media attention due to its high success rate. The program, established in Oklahoma prisons, teaches female inmates the basic concepts for preventing the transmission of sexually transmitted diseases (STDs). The program is so popular among inmates that it has a continuous waiting list. In 1996, ninety-five women completed the program. Nearly 125 women completed the program by the end of 1997. The program is believed to be highly beneficial to female inmates, because, according to Melanie Spector, a health-department counselor, "women incarcerated are among the highest risk for HIV and STDs." She added that, "The same behavior and psychological issues that have put them in jail can put them at risk for HIV."[35] According to Spector, "They are a forgotten population, a disenfranchised population, and a population where the disease manifests itself . . . that's where we need to be—in the prison. I know it's not as nice as being at a university, but that's where the prevention efforts need to be."[36] The program, which started in 1995, is a collaborative effort among several institutions, including the HIV

Resource Consortium, the Oklahoma State Department of Health, Tulsa Community AIDS Partnership, Tulsa City-County Jail, Tulsa Community College, and the Oklahoma State Department of Corrections. It is worth noting that inmates who complete the sixteen-hour program also have the option of receiving one college credit through Tulsa Community College.[37]

Other programs in female correctional facilities address parenthood, specifically issues that arise when female inmates, probationers, and parolees give birth while under some form of supervision or confinement. Among the many programs developed to address this particular issue are the Program for Caring Parents at the Louisiana Correctional Institute for Women, Project HIP (Helping Incarcerated Parents) at the Maine Correctional Center, Neil J. Houston House, a substance abuse program for female nonviolent offenders in Massachusetts, and the Nursery Program at Taconic Correctional Facility in New York.[38] Although each of these programs has a unique approach, they all share the same quality of service designed to strengthen the bonds between parent and child, while improving the parenting skills of the offenders who are enrolled in the programs.[39] These programs are primarily concerned with the offenders in their role as mothers, but they also focus on the proper nurturing of a child during the first year of life. This aim is based on the findings made in various studies that link a lack of love and nurturing by a mother during the first year of a child's life with that child's inability to develop compassion and empathy for others later in life.

12-2i Medical Treatment of Female Inmates

Many of the new facilities for female inmates have begun to address the major medical and treatment programs necessary to meet the special needs of women. The small number of female inmates and their frequent, expensive medical needs have made their treatment problematic in both the state and federal systems. The two main areas of medical treatment for women are obstetrics and gynecology. Not only are some women pregnant when they enter the system, but many women's lives are threatened by their reproductive problems. In 1992, the lawyer of several female inmates who filed suit against the state of Georgia over sexual abuse discovered during his investigation several cases of women with cancerous breast lumps who had not been treated properly.

Another similar circumstance occurred in April 1995, when in federal court, female prisoners sued the two largest women's prisons in California, alleging that inmates suffer terribly from conditions such as tuberculosis (TB), AIDS, and cancer.[40] They also claimed that in some cases, inmates died due to inadequate medical care. In their twenty-one page complaint, lawyers representing the female inmates told of long delays in obtaining care for life-threatening illnesses, disruptions in administration of desperately needed medications, and frequent misdiagnoses of cancer, meningitis, and other serious illnesses. Among the cases cited is one in which an inmate had legs so swollen that she could barely walk. Despite her condition, the prison personnel required her to walk to the dining hall when she wanted to eat. The inmate was found frequently outside the prison medical clinic lying on the ground and crying in pain. It is reported that for months, she begged medical doctors for help, without success. Finally, although the doctors found she had cancer, little medication was given to her. Inevitably, this lack of care resulted in her death nine months later.

Another case cited by a women's attorneys involved an inmate with HIV at the other correctional facility in question. The inmate tested positive for TB but was taken off preventive medication because she was pregnant. She soon developed full-blown TB during her pregnancy. Despite the fact that she later contracted pneumonia, the inmate was not diagnosed until she was sent to an outside hospital to deliver her baby. According to the complaint, the inmate was sent back to prison only one day after her baby was born.[41]

Drug treatment is another weakness in female prisons. Female inmates often find these programs insufficient to meet their needs. This is especially problematic as growing numbers of female inmates are being incarcerated for drug crimes or drug-related property crimes. Current drug treatment is an adaptation of programs designed for male correctional facilities. These programs neglect the special problems of abuse and lack of self-esteem that plague many women in prison on drug-related charges.[42] Despite this, some drug-treatment programs work. In Michigan, programs address the special health-care needs of its female inmate population. Specifically, Michigan's substance-abuse program called Njideka (which means "survival is paramount") has received a great deal of attention for its alleged effectiveness.[43] The program's focus is HIV intervention and it is designed specifically for women engaged in high-risk behaviors. To fulfill this purpose, ten weekly HIV empowerment workshops are conducted. The content of the workshops is presented and discussed from a culturally relevant perspective so that women can identify with the HIV-prevention messages and effectively perceive their risk for acquiring HIV via drug use and other related behaviors.[44]

12-2j The Female Prison Community

In Chapter 11, how male offenders adjust to the pains of imprisonment was discussed and the development of the inmate community was analyzed. An inmate community develops in women's prisons, too, although its nature and purpose differ from those of the male inmate community.

Less has been written on the female inmate community and most of the literature in this area was written by prison administrators or other inmates and is not systematic or scientific. We now consider some of the few systematic studies.

Source of Female Inmate Societies

In the discussion of the male prison community, two theories concerning the source of the inmate culture—importation and deprivation—were considered. These theories have also been applied in an analysis of the source of female inmate societies. Rose Giallombardo concluded that deprivation theory alone cannot explain inmate social systems, although deprivation may precipitate its development. "The evidence reported thus far indicates that the adult male and female inmate cultures *are* a response to the deprivations of prison life, but the *nature* of the response in both prison communities is influenced by the differential participation of males and females in the external culture."[45] The latter refers to the concept of importation. Giallombardo illustrates her point by primarily reviewing gender roles within penal institutions for women and girls. Those gender roles reflect the roles that women play in our society. Roles and statuses are imported into prison, along with attitudes and values. The deprivations of prison life provide the structure in which these roles are played.

When the inmate systems of men and women are compared, the evidence suggests that the roles within those systems differ and they reflect the traditional differences in attitudes, values, and roles that have distinguished men and women in this culture.

Pains of Imprisonment

In his study of male inmates, Greshem Sykes suggested that loss of security is the greatest problem that the male inmate faces. Female offenders appear to be more concerned with the loss of liberty and autonomy. They miss their freedom and resent the restrictions on communications with family and friends. They are frustrated because they have no control over events in the outside world—their children might be neglected, a loved one might become sick or die, or their husbands might be unfaithful. In the institution, their lives are scheduled for them and the rules are strictly enforced. For example, they must walk by twos to meals and cannot be late. They may be locked in their rooms at night if they do not want to sit in the living room with the other inmates. They cannot use the telephone to call relatives and the sounding of a bell controls many of their actions. They cannot change these rules and are not allowed to voice opposition.

For some female offenders, prison is a deprivation of goods and services to which they are accustomed. As soon as they enter the institution, they are stripped of most of their worldly possessions. "In this single act, a kind of symbolic death of the individual takes place. In the performance of this stripping and mortifying process, the prisoner is brought to terms with society's rejection of the criminal."[46]

Joycelyn Pollock-Byrne has reviewed the studies that analyze the sex differences in prisonization by focusing on the influence of deprivation and importation. She concludes that these early studies are wrong in their assumption that women do not form a subculture like men do. The problem of these earlier studies is that they attempt to measure prisonization using concepts adapted to the male institution, not the female. Consequently, Pollock-Byrne argues that these studies miss the different needs of female inmates who do form a subculture.

Regarding importation factors, female inmates are characteristically different from males. For the most part, female inmates are less likely to be violent, to have a professional involvement in crime, and to have extensive criminal histories. Most female inmates, unlike the majority of males, are likely to have been the subject of exploitation and abuse. In fact, many females are likely to have committed their crimes out of economic necessity to support their dependent children.[47] Female inmates are also less likely to fight against one another on the basis of race.[48]

The deprivation factors facing women result from their inability to visit with their children and the rest of their families. Incarceration places them in a situation where they have to be around people they might never chose to associate with in the outside world and female inmates lose much of their privacy. Inevitably, this creates severe tension for those whom close, personal relationships are so critical.

Many female inmates engage in homosexual activities and create pseudo-families and friendships to deal with the pains of imprisonment.[49] Homosexuality may not be a lifestyle for many of these women but it is a response to the human need for affection and the attention they often miss. Pseudo-families evolve to replace familial relationships in the real world, most commonly the mother-daughter relationship. These family units are used in female institutions to control inmates just as the gang units are used in male facilities. These pseudo-families are not as strong today as they were a decade ago because of family programs and furloughs that alleviate some of the deprivations of imprisonment.[50]

A main reason that women experience prisonization differently than men has to do with their role as mothers. The loss of the parental role creates tension for many of these female inmates. It is estimated that between 70 percent and 80 percent of incarcerated women are mothers. It can be concluded that while the pains of imprisonment for men may seem to be a much tougher experience, the overall prison experience is believed, by leading scholars, to be more difficult for women.[51]

Social Roles of Female Inmates

Like male prisoners, female inmates develop a special language to designate social roles. Although some of the same social roles exist, the language differs among women. The differences arise from the inmate subculture, which serves as a substitute for the family. For example, the woman who plays the male role in the family is called the stud and the female is called the femme. They may refer to each other as daddy or mommy. Their family relationship takes on not only sexual dimensions, but also an economic dimension. For female inmates, the family is the basic socioeconomic unit. The members of the family share legal and illegal goods. The economic and sexual relationships are closely related. Some women become involved in homosexual relationships for economic reasons. The femme might become involved in homosexuality so that the stud will get items for her, or the latter might seduce the former with economic goods and services. Gifts are given to show fidelity, love, and concern.[52]

12-2k Parity Issue

Aside from their unique subculture and the predicaments it brings, female prisons are currently facing other challenges. One of these challenges is the parity issue. Most reform efforts for female inmates are based on the assumption that women should receive the same treatment as men do while incarcerated. To ensure this equality, litigation is often used to bring female institutions into compliance. However, such litigation has not always provided the services needed in female correctional institutions. Although the reasons the states provide for lack of equal services vary, most claim that they cannot provide equal services because females make up a smaller proportion of the total inmate population. In addition, some claim that they do not have the necessary resources to provide equal services for both male and female inmates. The courts have stated that this is not justifiable reason but many states still have yet to comply.[53]

The parity of treatment issue is not so simple. Equality of service delivery is not what equal treatment means when one understands the differences in prisonization for males and females. As mentioned previously, females have radically different needs than their male counterparts. A male correctional officer working in a female facility makes it very clear how important it is to understand these differences. Men are more concerned with their macho images, power, and control, while women are more concerned with their children, their relationships, and their economic situation.[54]

There is a need to understand these differences and use this knowledge to influence policy. Providing parity for women does not mean giving equal treatment but treatment based on the needs of female offenders.[55] Many women end up over-incarcerated because state departments of corrections over-restrict low-risk inmates. They have a small number of females so it is easier to restrict them in existing facilities than to provide appropriate ones.

An understanding of the needs of female offenders is necessary. Correctional administrators must understand the problems that motherhood places on female inmates and must direct prison policy to meet the programming needs of females in today's society.

12-2l The New-Generation Jails

Due to the fast-growing number of inmates, facilities are being built in all regions of the country to house female offenders. Some of the new-generation jails attempt to offer the same services to women that are available to their male counterparts. It is important to study these new facilities as statistics show us that a large number of female offenders either serve their time or await trial in jails as opposed to prisons.

Today, more than 100 facilities in the United States are podular direct or new-generation jails. Most of these have emerged during the past decade. One of the many reasons why these facilities have increased in number is because they offer a different relationship between inmates and their keepers. The podular direct facilities "substitute the coercion represented by steel bars, environmental irritants, intermittent supervision, and violence of older jails with individual rooms, carpeting, and a relatively safer, quieter, and directly supervised situation."[56]

A study was recently conducted to explore how male and female prisoners adapted to these new facilities.[57] The findings of this study suggested that female inmates experienced the conditions of confinement at the podular direct supervision in a very different way than did their male counterparts. As male offenders become satisfied with podular units, female offenders expressed their dissatisfaction. The authors of this study were careful to conclude that the findings of this study were not final and stated a need to conduct research on these new facilities and their impact on female offenders.[58] The continuance of this type of research is necessary if a great majority of female offenders are to be housed in these new-generation jails.

Summary

This chapter analyzed adult female offenders in corrections. For most of our history, female offenders were simply ignored. Scholars concentrated their attention on males and juveniles. With the increasing crime rates among women, scholars have turned their attention to the subject, although they are not in agreement on the causes of these increased female-offender rates. Increased opportunities in the marketplace compete with women's liberation as main explanations.

In addition, the interpretation of data on female offenders while studying the profile of female offenders was discussed. The centralization and decentralization of women's prisons, the architecture of female correctional facilities, security levels of these institutions, the personnel and location of female prisons, educational and vocational programs offered to female offenders, and the pains of imprisonment that are often part of the female experience behind bars were examined. A brief look at the new-generation jails, which are aimed at offering the same services for both male and female offenders, was explored.

One of the main challenges for corrections is recognizing that equal treatment for women does not mean receiving the same treatment that men receive. The needs of female inmates are unique and the outcomes envisioned for these women cannot take place if their needs are not met. As a result, rehabilitation cannot work, recidivism will continue, and other victims (primarily the children of these women) will continue to suffer.

Notes

1. Ross, J.G. et al., National Evaluation Program, Phase 1 Report, Assessment of Coeducational Corrections, National Institute of Law Enforcement and Criminal Justice (Washington, D.C.: U.S. Government Printing Office, 1978).
2. A Bureau of Justice Statistics Special Report, U.S. Department of Justice, "Women Offenders," December, 1999, Washington, D.C.
3. President's Commission on Law Enforcement and Administration of Justice, *Task Force Report: Corrections* (Washington, DC: U.S. Government Printing Office, 1967).
4. Rasche, Christine E., "The Female Offender as an Object of Criminological Research," in Brodsky, Annette M., *The Female Offender* (Beverly Hills, CA: Sage Publications, 1975), p. 10.
5. Price, Ray R., "The Forgotten Female Offender," *Crime and Delinquency* 23 (April, 1977), 101–102.
6. Nagel, Ilene H., and Johnson, Barry L., "The Role of Gender in a Structured Sentencing System: Equal Treatment Policy Choices and the Sentencing of Female Offenders Under the U.S. Sentencing Guidelines," *Journal of Criminal Law and Criminology*, (Summer, 1994), 85, no. 1, pp. 181–221.
7. For a discussion of the criticisms of this source of data on crimes, see Sue Titus Reid, *Criminal Justice*, 6th ed. (Cincinnati, OH: Atomic Dog Publishing, 2001).
8. Bureau of Justice Statistics, U.S. Department of Justice, "Sourcebook of Criminal Justice Statistics," 2000, Washington, D.C.
9. Bureau of Justice Statistics Special Report, U.S. Department of Justice, "Women Offenders." December, 1999, Washington, D.C.
10. U.S. Department of Justice. Bureau of Justice Statistics. "Women in Prison." (March 1994).
11. Bureau of Justice Statistics Special Report, U.S. Department of Justice, "Women Offenders," December, 1999, Washington, D.C.
12. Adler, Freda, *Sisters in Crime: The Rise of the New Female Criminal* (New York: McGraw-Hill, 1975), p. 16.
13. Weis, Joseph G., "Liberation and Crime: The Invention of the New Female Criminal," *Crime and Social Justice* 6 (Fall-Winter, 1976), 19.
14. Weis, "Liberation and Crime."
15. Weis, "Liberation and Crime," p.24; see also Gary J. Jensen and Raymond Eve, "Sex Differences in Delinquency: An Examination of Popular Sociological Explanations," *Criminology* 13 (February, 1976), 427–449.
16. Simon, Rita James, *Women and Crime* (Lexington, MA; D.C. Heath, 1975).
17. Steffensmeier, Darrel, "National Trends in Female Arrests, 1960–1990; Assessment and Recommendations for Research," *Journal of Quantitative Criminology*, 1993, 9:413–441.
18. Steffensmeier, Darrel, "National Trends."
19. Steffensmeier, Darrel, "National Trends."
20. Steffensmeier, Darrel, "National Trends."
21. Steffensmeier, Darrel, "National Trends."
22. Snell, Tracy, "Women in Prison." U.S. Department of Justice. Bureau of Justice Statistics. (March, 1994).
23. Church, George, "The View from behind Bars," *Time* (Fall, 1990), pp. 20–21.
24. Glick, Ruth M., and Neto, Virginia V., *National Study of Women's Correctional Programs* (Washington, D.C.: Department of Justice, Law Enforcement Assistance Administration National Institute of Law Enforcement and Criminal Justice, 1977), p. 20.
25. American Correctional Association, *ACA Directory 1993* (Laurel, MD: American Correctional Association, 1993), p.xvii.
26. American Correctional Association, *ACA Directory*.
27. Eyman, Joy, *Prisons for Women* (Springfield, IL: Charles C. Thomas, 1971), p.60, quoted in Glick and Neto, *National Study*, p.xxliv.
28. Glick and Neto, *National Study*, p.xxv.
29. Wilson, Christine Ennulat, "Women Offenders: A Population Overlooked." In Miriam Williford, ed., *Higher Education in Prison: A Contradiction in Terms?* (Phoenix, AZ: American Council on Education and the Oryx Press, 1994).
30. Wheeler, Martha, "The Current Status of Women in Prisons," in Brodsky, *The Female Offender*, p. 85. 1977.
31. Simon, Rita James, *The Contemporary Woman and Crime* (Rockville, MD: National Institute of Mental Health, 1975), p. 76.
32. The National Advisory Commission on Criminal Justice Standards and Goals, *Corrections* (Washington, D.C.: U.S. Government Printing Office, 1963), p. 378, emphasis deleted.
33. Winifred, Mary, "Vocational and Technical Training Programs for Women in Prison," *Corrections Today* (August, 1996), vol. 58, no. 5, p. 168(3).
34. Winifred, "Vocational and Technical Training," p. 168.
35. "Inmate Program Chosen for National Recognition," (for teaching the prevention of sexually transmitted diseases among female inmates) *AIDS Weekly Plus* (June 30, 1997), no. 9, p. 26(1).
36. "Inmate Program Chosen," p. 26.
37. "Inmate Program Chosen," p. 26.
38. Scheridan, John J., "Inmates May Be Parents, Too," *Corrections Today* (August, 1996), vol. 58, no. 5, p. 100(3).
39. Scheridan, "Inmates May Be Parents,Too," p. 101.
40. "Female Inmates Sue California Prisons, Neglect of TB, AIDS, Cancer Care Cited" (Tuberculosis), *AIDS Weekly* (April, 1995), p. 16(2).
41. "Female Inmates Sue," p. 17.
42. Church, George, "The View from behind Bars," *Time* (Fall, 1990), pp. 20–21.
43. Epp, Jann, "Exploring Health Care Needs of Adult Female Offenders," *Corrections Today* (October, 1996), vol. 58, no. 6, p. 96(4).
44. Epp, "Exploring Health Care," p. 99.
45. Giallombardo, Rose, *The Social World of Imprisoned Girls: A Comparative Study of Institutions for Juvenile Delinquents* (New York: John Wiley and Sons, 1974).
46. Giallombardo, Rose, *Society of Women: A Study of a Woman's Prison* (New York: John Wiley and Sons, 1966), p. 96.
47. Pollock-Byrne, Joycelyn, *Women, Prison, and Crime* (Pacific Grove, CA: Brooks/Cole Publishing, 1990), pp.129–160.
48. Church, George, "The View from behind Bars," *Time* (Fall, 1990), pp. 20–21.
49. Church, "The View from behind Bars."
50. Pollock-Byrne, *Women, Prison, and Crime*, pp. 129–160.
51. Harris, Jean, "Comparison of Stressors Among Female versus Male Inmates," *Journal of Offender Rehabilitation* 19 (1993), pp. 43–56.
52. Williams, Vergil L., and Fish, Mary, *Convicts, Codes, and Contraband: The Prison Life of Men and Women* (Cambridge, MA: Ballinger Publishing Co., 1974), pp. 99–122.
53. Muraskin, Roslyn, and Alleman, Ted, "Disparate Treatment in Correctional Facilities," *It's a Crime: Women and Justice* (Englewood Cliffs, NJ, Regents/Prentice-Hall, 1993), pp. 211–225.
54. Whittaker, Richard, "Working in Women's Prisons—A Male Perspective," *Corrections Today* 52 (1990), pp. 58–159.
55. Chesney-Lind, Meda, "Patriarchy, Prisons, and Jails: A Critical Look at Trends," *Prison Journal LXXI* (Spring-Summer, 1991), pp. 51–67.
56. Jackson, Patrick G., and Stearns, Cindy A., "Gender Issues in the New Generation Jail," *Prison Journal* (June, 1995), vol. 75, no. 2, p. 203(19).
57. Jackson and Stearns, "Gender Issues," p. 213.
58. Jackson and Stearns, "Gender Issues," p. 213.

Chapter 13

Inmates' Legal Rights

Outline

Although they are incarcerated, inmates deserve the protection of the U.S. Constitution and have rights. The history of inmate rights is reviewed in this chapter and an overview of the First, Fourth, Eighth, and Fourteenth Amendments is provided. Prison programs, legal rights, and prison overcrowding are examined.

Recognition of inmates' legal rights has a short history. The earlier position of the courts on inmates' rights was expressed in an 1871 case in which a federal court declared bluntly that the convicted felon:

Key Terms

conditions of confinement
hands-off doctrine
inquisitory system
habeas corpus
cruel and unusual punishment
deliberate indifference
double celling
ex post facto

> **Has as a consequence of his crime, not only forfeited his liberty, but all his personal rights except those which the law in its humanity accords to him. He is for the time being the slave of the state.[1]**

In the 1970s, the U.S. Supreme Court took another view on inmates' rights, as expressed by this 1974 statement:

> **But though his rights may be diminished by the needs and exigencies of the institutional environment, a prisoner is not wholly stripped of constitutional protections when he is imprisoned for crime. There is no iron curtain drawn between the Constitution and the prisons of this country.[2]**

Before 1974, lower federal courts began looking into prisoners' claims that they were being denied basic constitutional rights during confinement. By the 1980s, numerous lawsuits had been filed by inmates and federal courts scrutinized prison conditions, particularly regarding overcrowding. Entire prison systems were placed under federal court orders to reduce populations and make other changes in their conditions. By the 1990s, there was an explosion of federal lawsuits concerning circumstances of incarceration.

It is important to understand that the decisions of courts in one jurisdiction do not apply to courts in other jurisdictions. Courts faced with similar facts may, and often do, decide issues differently. Only

when the U.S. Supreme Court decides the issue is the case binding on all courts, although the Supreme Court has not decided many inmates' rights cases.

The law of inmates' rights is changing rapidly and some of the cases discussed in this chapter will be altered or overruled while this book is in production. Many of the cited cases are recent decisions, although there are exceptions. The Supreme Court cases are important regardless of their date of decision (if they have not been changed by later Supreme Court cases) and lower federal court cases are important for historical reasons or because they are critical in a particular area and are still good law. All cases are checked prior to the printing of this text and whether changes have occurred will be ascertained, such as a higher appellate court's decision to alter or overrule a cited case.[3]

13-1 Historical Overview

In the United States, administration of state prisons has historically been considered off limits to federal courts. Federal courts would not hear cases from state courts because no federal rights were involved. Federal courts observed a hands-off doctrine toward federal prisons, reasoning that prison administration is a part of the executive, not the judicial, branch of government.

State courts traditionally have not heard complaints from inmates concerning conditions within state prisons. State courts have heard cases involving postconviction remedies that attacked the confinement itself, as opposed to the **conditions of confinement.** Conditions were considered to be within the realm of prison administration and were not a proper sphere for judicial interference.

Conditions of confinement Circumstances that surround the incarceration experience of the offender.

Hands-off doctrine A policy used by federal courts to justify a nonintervention approach in the administration of correctional facilities.

This unwillingness of federal courts to interfere with the daily administration of prisons is called the **hands-off doctrine** and is seen in federal court decisions. In 1950, the Seventh Circuit stated that "The Government of the United States is not concerned with, nor has it the power to control or regulate the internal discipline of the penal institutions of its constituent states. All such powers are reserved to the individual states."[4]

In 1979, in *Bell v. Wolfish*, the Supreme Court emphasized that prison administrators should be accorded wide-ranging deference in the adoption and execution of policies and practices that in their judgement are needed to preserve internal order and discipline and to maintain institutional security.[5]

If federal courts defer to prison officials for the daily administration of prisons, on what basis are those courts involved today? What brought inmates to their attention? The civil rights activism of the 1960s included the treatment of inmates and during that period federal courts began to explore what was happening inside prisons. Many of the earlier cases involved allegations of physical brutality as well as questionable living conditions.

One of the most publicized of the earlier accounts of corporal punishment within a modern prison came from two Arkansas facilities. Among other punishments was the inflicting of electric shock through a device wired to the genitals and one of the big toes of the inmates. Arkansas prisoners alleged that inmates had been murdered at the prison and buried in the prison yard. In 1967, the Arkansas governor released a prison report that had been ordered and then suppressed by the former governor. That report

> Painted a picture of hell in Arkansas. To maintain discipline, prisoners were beaten with leather straps, blackjacks, hoses. Needles were shoved under their fingernails, and cigarettes were applied to their bodies."[6]

In January 1968, Thomas O. Murton, Arkansas prison system superintendent appointed by the governor, exhumed the bodies of three inmates who allegedly had been murdered by inmates or prison officials. The national attention caused the governor to fire Murton. A movie, *Brubaker*, portrayed the attempts of Murton to reform the Arkansas prison system. His own accounts are found in the book *The Dilemma of Prison Reform*.[7]

The federal district court heard evidence on the Arkansas prison and concluded that inmates were living under degrading and disgusting conditions. The court found the prison system unconstitutional. The need for judicial intervention in the administration of prisons was stated emphatically by the federal court. "If Arkansas is going to operate a Penitentiary System, it is going to have to be a system that is countenanced by the Constitution of the United States."[8]

13-2 Litigation Affecting Inmates

13-2a An Introduction

Since the 1970s, federal courts have heard many cases on prison conditions. Federal intervention has been extended to jails as well. Some prison officials have been ordered to close facilities until conditions are corrected while others have been ordered to change specific conditions. Officials who have defied these orders have been held in contempt of court. Judges continue to defer to prison authorities concerning day-to-day prison operations but they intervene when federal constitutional rights are violated.

In analyzing inmates' rights historically, prison officials spoke of the difference between rights and privileges. Rights require constitutional protection; privileges are there by the grace of prison officials and may be withdrawn at their discretion. In 1971, the Supreme Court rejected the position that "constitutional rights turn upon whether a governmental benefit is characterized as a 'right' or a 'privilege.'"[9]

A hierarchy of rights is recognized, although some are considered to be more important than others and therefore require more extensive due process. An inmate's right to be released from illegal confinement is more important than the right to canteen privileges. Some of the other rights that are top-ranked in the hierarchy are the right to protection against willful injury, access to courts, freedom of religious belief, freedom of communication, and the right to be free of cruel and unusual punishment.

The recognition of inmates' rights and of the hierarchy of rights does not mean that the government (or prison officials acting as government agents) may not restrict those rights. Rights may be restricted if prison officials can show that the restriction is necessary for security or for other recognized penological purposes such as discipline and order.[10]

When analyzing whether prison officials have shown one or more of these purposes, the Court uses a reasonableness test. "When a prison regulation impinges on inmates' constitutional rights, the regulation is valid if it is reasonably related to legitimate penological interests."[11] The reasonableness test is not as strict as the closer analysis that the Court applies to basic constitutional rights. A less stringent test is used in prison because the Court recognizes that "limitations on the exercise of constitutional rights arise both from the fact of incarceration and from valid penological objectives—including deterrence of crime, rehabilitation of offenders, and institutional security."[12]

In *Turner v. Safley*, the Supreme Court suggested several factors that should be considered when analyzing whether infringements on individual rights are appropriate within a prison:

1. Whether there is a logical connection between the regulation and the legitimate interest it is designed to protect;
2. Whether inmates have other means of exercising that right;

3. The impact that accommodating the right in question would have on other inmates, correctional officers, and prison administration and staff; and
4. The absence of readily available alternatives that fully accommodate the prisoner's rights at little or no cost to valid penological interests.[13]

13-2b Substantive Legal Rights

The Bill of Rights provides for our individual constitutional rights, as applied to the states through the Fourteenth Amendment. Those rights, known as substantive legal rights, include the right to counsel, the right to be free of unreasonable searches and seizures, the right to a public trial by a jury of one's peers, and the right to be confronted by witnesses. Courts have held that some, but not all, of these rights apply to inmates. The First Amendment is the basis for considerable litigation on prison issues and includes freedom of speech, assembly, the press, and religion, and the right to address the government when rights are violated. Another important source of rights is the Eighth Amendment, the right to be free of unreasonable searches and seizures.

The Fourteenth Amendment right to due process and equal protection is crucial to the understanding of inmates' rights. Certain elements of due process must accompany disciplinary decisions, such as rescinding an inmate's acquired good time or placing inmates in solitary confinement. Equal protection becomes an issue in the discussion of the differences in treatment, work opportunities, and medical care provided for male inmates, as compared to females. Due process and equal protection are the foundations for enforcing all rights.

13-2c Due Process and Equal Protection

Inquisitory system System in which the accused is presumed to be guilty and must prove his or her innocence.

The criminal justice systems in the United States are adversary, in contrast to the **inquisitory system** characteristic of some other countries. The two approaches are distinguishable in several ways. The adversary approach assumes that the accused is innocent until proven guilty. The accused does not have to prove his or her innocence; that burden lies with the state (or the federal government in a federal trial). In contrast, the inquisitory system assumes guilt and the accused must prove that he or she is innocent. This difference between the two approaches is related to another basic contrast—the inquisitory approach places a greater emphasis on conviction than on the process by which that conviction is secured. The adversary approach, however, requires that proper procedures be followed which are designed to protect the rights of the accused.

In the United States, the adversary system embodies the basic concepts of equal protection and due process. These concepts are considered necessary to create a system in which the accused has a fair chance against the tremendous powers of the prosecutor and the resources of the state. Theoretically, the protections prevent the prosecutor from obtaining a guilty verdict of an innocent defendant. In reality, justice does not always prevail.

The difficulty of defining due process is illustrated by this comment of a former U.S. Supreme Court justice:

> "Due Process" . . . cannot be imprisoned within the treacherous limits of any formula. Representing a profound attitude of fairness between man and man, and more particularly between the individual and government, "due process" is compounded of history, reason, the past course of decisions, and stout confidence in the strength of the democratic faith we possess. "Due process" is not a mechanical instrument. It is not a yardstick. It is a process.[14]

In a 1994 case, the Second Circuit defined substantive due process as a method that "protects individuals against government action that is arbitrary, conscience-shocking, or oppressive in a constitutional sense, but not against government action that is 'incorrect or ill-advised.'"[15]

Case Study 13-1

Liberta v. Kelly

Mario Liberta and Denise Liberta were separated and Denise had obtained two protective orders that required Mario to live apart from Denise and their young son but that granted him visiting privileges with the child. Mario had a history of abusing his wife physically. On the occasion in question, he persuaded her to let him see the child in her presence, indicating that he would bring a friend with him. The friend left quickly, however, and Mario forced Denise to perform oral sex on him while the child watched, after which he raped Denise. After a long discussion of other issues in this case, the court focused on the defendant's argument that he had been denied equal protection of the law because the New York sodomy and rape statutes included only men as defendants.

Women and men are not similarly situated with regard to rape. Rape is unquestionably a crime that requires male participation as a practical matter and only male rape of a female can impose on the victim an unwanted pregnancy. These facts provide an "exceedingly persuasive justification" for a statute that provides heightened sanctions for rapes committed by men. Moreover, it cannot be contended that a rape statute punishing only men "demean[s] the ability or social status" of either men or women, particularly in the context of a penal code that prohibits coercive sexual conduct by women. The exclusion of women from [the New York statute] therefore, does not deny men equal protection of the laws.

The basis for the right to due process and equal protection comes from the Fourteenth Amendment to the Constitution, which guarantees that U.S. citizens shall not be deprived "of life, liberty, or property, without due process of law" or denied "the equal protection of the laws."

The concept of due process means that those who are accused of crimes and are processed through a criminal justice system must be given the basic rights guaranteed by the Constitution. For example, defendants may not be subjected to unreasonable searches and seizures by the police. When questioned about acts that, upon conviction, may involve a jail or prison term, defendants do not have to answer questions by the police until they have an attorney present. If they do not wish to talk even with an attorney present, they may remain silent. If defendants cannot afford an attorney, the state must provide one for them. They do not have to testify against themselves at trial and certain rules of evidence must be observed during the trial.

Defendants may not be tried twice for the same offense. Once a judge or jury has decided that a defendant is innocent, the state may not bring those same charges again. The state must conduct the criminal trial and the processes preceding and following that trial by the rules embodied in the Constitution, as interpreted by the Supreme Court of the United States, and according to established procedural statutes.

The equal protection clause of the Fourteenth Amendment is the focus of frequent lawsuits. The clause declares that the state may not attempt to enforce statutes against persons solely based on specific characteristics such as race, age, or gender. The state or federal government, however, may enact statutes that distinguish between men and women if there are legitimate reasons for doing so, and this may become a key matter in prison issues.

The brief excerpt in Case Study 13-1 from *Liberta v. Kelly* indicates the reasons why the federal court upheld New York's exclusion of women as defendants from its rape and sodomy statutes. According to the federal court, the New York statute did not violate the equal protection clause of the federal Constitution.[16]

In recent years, several states have changed their rape and sodomy statutes to include women as perpetrators. However, the point of this case is that it is not necessarily a violation of equal protection to define these offenses as crimes that may be committed only by men.

The equal protection clause, like the due process clause, must be examined in the context of the facts of a given case. This is why it is impossible to state the law on most issues. Such elasticity of American constitutional provisions is important, but at times frustrating, as there may not be an immediate, definitive answer.

13-2d Procedural Issues

The enforcement of inmates' legal rights requires an understanding of the difference between criminal and civil cases. Not all constitutional rights that exist at the pretrial, trial, and appellate stages of criminal cases apply to civil cases and some of the rules of evidence differ. Criminal cases are considered to carry a heavier burden of responsibility than civil cases since the accused may face death as punishment. The distinction between criminal and civil cases is important for another reason. The number of civil cases filed in the past two decades has increased more dramatically than the number of criminal cases. Inmates have accounted for many of these filings. The resulting backlog in civil courts means that inmates (and others) may face a long wait before a case is decided. It is also argued that many of the cases that inmates file are frivolous and should not be consuming the time of already overcrowded courts.

Habeas Corpus

Habeas corpus A written court order requiring that the accused be present before the court in order to determine the legality of custody and confinement.

Most civil actions brought by inmates are over confinement conditions or prison officials' actions. They involve one of two types of legal actions: ***habeas corpus*** or a Section 1983 action. *Habeas corpus* translated literally means "you should have the body." There are numerous types of *habeas corpus* actions, but the most relevant to this chapter is the action brought by the correctional client who is requesting that the court grant a writ of *habeas corpus*, directing prison officials to release a particular individual.

When inmates request a writ of *habeas corpus*, they argue that they are illegally confined. Inmates make this argument because prison conditions are alleged to be unconstitutional or because they may have been disciplined without observance of proper procedures. The *habeas corpus* action holds that "I am being held illegally in this prison because my rights have been violated. Therefore, I should be released." Historically, only a few inmates have been successful in their *habeas corpus* petitions, but multiple petitions are filed by numerous inmates.

Supreme Court Chief Justice William Rehnquist, a committee Rehnquist appointed to study the issue of *habeas corpus*, and the Bush administration sought measures to curb abuse of this process. Congress has considered legislation to limit *habeas corpus* petitions, but at the time of this writing, the legislation has not passed. Proponents of these efforts argue that finality in the law is important and that in capital cases, the delays created by subsequent *habeas corpus* petitions are too long. Continuous appeals cost the government money and question the legitimacy of the justice procedure. Opponents argue that as long as inmates have a legal issue, especially if they are under death sentences, a court should hear their arguments.

The April 1991 Supreme Court decision in *McCleskey v. Zant* imposed new limits on death-row inmates' filings of *habeas corpus* petitions. The Court had recognized previously that *habeas corpus* petitions may be denied for inmates who have abused the process. For example, an inmate might have several issues to appeal, but may bring only one. If that one is denied, the inmate might try to file another petition for a writ of *habeas corpus* and that subsequent petition may be denied if it could have been filed with the earlier writ. In *McCleskey*, the Court admitted, however, that it had not clearly defined the criteria to base that an inmate had abused this appeals process. In this case, the Court said that "a petitioner may abuse the writ by failing to raise a claim through inexcusable neglect."[17]

In his second *habeas corpus* petition, McCleskey claimed that he was convicted of murder as a result of evidence obtained in violation of his constitutional rights when the government planted an informant in the jail to get information from him. McCleskey showed that for almost a decade, the government had concealed the evidence that the inmate was an informant. McCleskey argued that he could not have included this in his first petition for *habeas corpus* because the information was not available to him at that time. The Court disagreed and held that he should have brought up this ground for appeal in his first petition. Since he did not do so, he was not entitled to a second chance.

McCleskey's first petition concerned the argument that he was convicted unfairly because of racial discrimination. He cited evidence that he and other African-American men whose alleged victims were white were four times more likely to be convicted of murder than African-American men convicted of murdering nonwhite victims. The Court questioned the evidence and upheld the conviction. McCleskey was executed in the fall of 1991. In May 1992, the Court limited *habeas corpus* proceedings further by stating that federal courts are no longer required to conduct hearings on the petitions of state inmates challenging their convictions. This is true even if those inmates can show that their attorneys had not presented facts properly or those crucial to their cases at their trials.[18]

In 1995, the U.S. Supreme Court facilitated the possibility that inmates may win new trials on some *habeas corpus* writs. In *O'Neal v. McAninch*, the Court concluded that offenders deserve the benefit of the doubt if the federal courts are not certain if mistakes committed by the trial court were harmless. This made it harder for judges to dismiss the mistakes made by the trial courts.[19]

Section 1983 Actions

A second and more frequently used method by inmates in their petitions to federal courts is a Section 1983 action. This is usually filed for monetary damages to compensate for illegal actions taken by prison (or police) officials against inmates. The name is derived from the section number of the federal statute under which the action may be brought. As a section of the Civil Rights Act, it is provided that:

> Every person who, under color of any statute, ordinance, regulation, custom, or usage, of any State or Territory, subjects or causes to be subjected, any citizen of the United States or the person within the jurisdiction thereof to the deprivation of any rights, privileges, or immunities secured by the Constitution and laws, shall be liable to the party injured in an action at law, suit in equity, or other proper proceeding for redress.[20]

In order to come under the jurisdiction of this statute, inmates must show that prison officials deprived them of their rights as protected by the U.S. Constitution or by a federal statute. Section 1983 claims may encompass any aspect of an inmate's life.

If an inmate succeeds in a Section 1983 action, he or she may be awarded damages for the deprivations, as described in Spotlight 13-1. The federal court can mandate prison officials to modify the prison conditions that led to the constitutional violation. In cases of extreme violations, courts have closed jails or

Spotlight 13-1

Enforcing Inmate Rights through Civil Cases

In 1989, a New York court awarded $1.3 million in seven lawsuits brought by inmates for damages caused by the actions of police in the 1971 Attica prison riots. These awards were granted to those who did not participate in the riots but who were victimized by excessive force of authorities attempting to regain control of the prison. Police efforts during that uprising were described by a state investigating committee as constituting the "bloodiest encounter between Americans since the Civil War." Individual damage awards ranged from $35,000 to $473,000.[1]

Larger damage awards have been made in cases in which individuals have sued police for violating their civil rights. Rodney King, who suffered permanent injuries as a result of force used on him by Los Angeles police officers, was awarded $3.8 million in damages by a jury that heard his case against the Los Angeles Police Department. However, a jury refused to award King punitive damages from individual officers. Two of the officers were convicted of violating King's civil rights and were sentenced to serve time in prison.[2]

1 "Court Awards $1.3 Million to Inmates Injured at Attica," *New York Times* (October 26, 1989), p. 14.

2 "Rodney King Gets $4 Million in Compensation for Beating," *New York Times* (April 20, 1994), p. 1; "Rodney King Jury Refuses to Award Punitive Damages," *New York Times* (June 29, 1994), p. 1.

prisons until conditions were corrected. In cases of overcrowded facilities, judges can order prison officials to reduce the inmate population.[21]

Tests of Civil Liability

Cruel and unusual punishment Punishment prohibited by the Eighth Amendment of the U.S. Constitution. The interpretation of what constitutes cruel and unusual punishment is left to the courts' discretion.

Deliberate indifference Criteria used when considering the failure of a prison official to address the needs of an inmate properly.

The Supreme Court has developed tests for determining whether and inmate's constitutional right to be free of the Eighth Amendment's ban against **cruel and unusual punishment** has been violated. The tests are stated broadly and are open to interpretation. In its first case on the issue concerning prison conditions, the Court held that an inmate may bring a successful Section 1983 action against prison officials who deny him or her adequate medical care for a serious medical problem only if it can be shown that the officials acted with **deliberate indifference** to the inmate's needs. In *Estelle v. Gamble*, the Court stated that allegations of "inadvertent failure to provide adequate medical care," or of a "negligent . . . diagnos[is]" do not establish the requisite state of mind for a violation of the cruel and unusual punishment clause.[22]

In subsequent years, the Court analyzed the cruel and unusual punishment issue further. In June 1991, the Court decided *Wilson v. Seiter*, which involved a felon who was incarcerated at the Hocking Correctional Facility (HCF) in Nelsonville, Ohio. The inmate, Pearly L. Wilson, argued that his confinement constituted cruel and unusual punishment. He sought to distinguish *Estelle v. Gamble* on the grounds that the case involved a one-time act or violation. The majority rejected that distinction, stating that the mental element is implicit in the ban against cruel and unusual punishment. Case Study 13-2 gives more details.[23]

The Supreme Court sent the case back to the lower court because it could not determine the standard that the court had applied. The significance of the case is that the Court interpreted the Constitution to require that when inmates question prison conditions, they must show a negative state of mind of officials in order to win their cases. Specifically, they must prove that prison officials harbor deliberate indifference. Dissenters noted that in many cases, this standard will be difficult or impossible to prove.

Case Study 13-2

Wilson v. Seiter

The complaint alleges overcrowding, excessive noise, insufficient locker storage space, inadequate heating and cooling, improper ventilation, unclean and inadequate restrooms, unsanitary dining facilities and food preparation, and housing with mentally and physically ill inmates. Petitioner sought declaratory and injunctive relief, as well as $900,000 in compensatory and punitive damages....

Petitioners...charged that the authorities, after notification, had failed to take remedial action. Respondents...denied that some of the alleged conditions existed, and described efforts by prison officials to improve the others....

[The Court reviewed prior cases, concluding the following:]

These cases mandate inquiry into a prison official's state of mind when it is claimed that the official has inflicted cruel and unusual punishment. Petitioner concedes that this is so with respect to some claims of cruel and unusual prison conditions....Petitioner...suggests that we should draw a distinction between "short-term" or "one-time" conditions (in which a state of mind requirement would apply) and "continuing" or "systemic" conditions (where official state of mind would be irrelevant). We perceive neither a logical nor a practical basis for that distinction. The source of the intent requirement is not the predilictions of this Court, but the Eighth Amendment itself, which bans only cruel and unusual punishment. If the pain inflicted is not formally meted out as punishment by the statute or the sentencing judge, some mental element must be attributed to the inflicting officer before it can qualify.

Inhumane prison conditions are often the result of cumulative actions and idleness by numerous officials inside and outside a prison, sometimes over a long period of time. In those circumstances, it is not clear whose intent should be examined and the majority offers no real guidance on this issue. Intent is not very meaningful when considering a challenge to an institution, such as a prison system.[24]

In June 1994, the Court applied a subjective rather than an objective standard in determining whether prison officials have the required state of mind to constitute deliberate indifference. *Farmer v. Brennan* involved an inmate who is biologically male but has some characteristics of a woman. He alleged that he was raped by another inmate after he was incarcerated in an all-male prison. He argued that placing a transsexual in an all-male population constituted deliberate indifference to his safety. Officials knew or should have known of the risks involved. The Court rejected that objective standard, stating that prison officials may be held liable for unsafe prison conditions only if they "know that inmates face a substantial risk of serious harm and disregard that risk by failing to take reasonable measures to abate it."[25]

Finally, the Court has held that it is not necessary for inmates to suffer significant injuries in order to prevail in a case alleging physical brutality in violation of the prohibition against cruel and unusual punishment. More attention is given to that issue later in the chapter's discussion of *Hudson v. McMillian.*[26]

13-3 Prison Conditions Total View

Although the various constitutional rights of inmates are considered separately, it is important to understand that courts do not look at these rights in isolation. The concern is with overall incarceration conditions. For example, in two cases, the Supreme Court has held that **double celling**, or double bunking (i.e., more than one person per cell), of inmates is not unconstitutional. That does not mean, however, that the Court would consider double celling constitutional under any circumstances.

Double celling The practice of housing two (or more) offenders in a room that was originally designed for one.

The first case, *Bell v. Wolfish*, involved the housing of two inmates in the same cell in a modern jail facility. The Court noted that the inmates were not required to remain in their cells for long periods of time and double celling was not expected to have the negative effect that it could have under more restrictive circumstances. In 1981, in *Rhodes v. Chapman*, the Court considered double celling in an Ohio prison. Again, the Court was reviewing a relatively new facility. The Southern Ohio Correctional Facility has several workshops, gymnasiums, schoolrooms, day rooms, two chapels, a hospital ward, a commissary, a barbershop, a library, a recreation field, a visitation area, and a garden. Cells were reasonably comfortable, with sixty-three square feet of space and bunk beds, a wall-mounted sink, a toilet, a cabinet, a shelf, a high nightstand, and a radio. Cells were ventilated and well heated and many had windows that could be opened. Noise had not been a serious problem, and, as in the *Bell v. Wolfish* case, most inmates were allowed considerable time outside their cells.[27]

It is also necessary to distinguish types of facilities when analyzing whether certain prison conditions are unconstitutional. Most prisons are classified as maximum-, medium-, or minimum-security. Conditions that might be justified for security in a maximum-security prison may not be permitted in those designed for inmates who need only limited supervision. Likewise, conditions considered constitutional for convicted persons serving sentences in prison or jail may not be appropriate for pretrial detainees.

13-3a First Amendment Rights

One of the most important rights in the United States is the right to self-expression and to communicate with other people. The First Amendment of the U.S. Constitution establishes that Congress cannot make any laws that prohibit the free exercise of religion, speech, or the press. These rights are important to inmates as well. The difficult adjustment problems in prison may be eased by communication with family and friends. Injustices within prisons are eliminated primarily by courts and the right of inmates to petition the courts is critical. Freedom of religion involves not only the right to think and believe but also the right to engage in religious practices.

Mail

Inmate correspondence has produced considerable litigation partly because of the importance of contact with the outside world and partly because this right involves persons outside the prison. In the past, prison officials refused to mail or give letters to inmates, censored mail, deleted comments from outgoing and incoming letters, removed articles considered to be detrimental to the inmate, and decided who could correspond with particular inmates. Prison officials claimed that these actions were necessary to maintain prison security.

The Supreme Court considered prison censorship of personal mail in a case involving inmates who were not permitted to write letters in which they complained unduly or magnified grievances. They were forbidden to express any inflammatory views, whether political, racial, or religious, or to send letters that pertained to criminal activity. Letters that were lewd, obscene, defamatory, or contained foreign matter were forbidden. All incoming and outgoing mail was screened for violations of these regulations. When an official found a violation of these rules, the letter was returned to the inmate, who received a disciplinary report and punishment. In *Procunier v. Martinez*, the Court held that censorship of an inmate's mail is constitutional "if that is necessary to maintain security, order, rehabilitation. Even then, the censorship may be no greater than is necessary to protect those legitimate governmental interests."[28]

Spotlight 13-2

Federal Regulations Concerning Incoming Mail

In its 1989 decision, *Thornburgh v. Abbott*, the U.S. Supreme Court summarized the federal regulations concerning publications that an inmate might receive without prior administrative approval.[1] Some of these points are:

I. A publication may be rejected by prison officials "only if it is determined detrimental to the security, good order, or discipline of the institution or if it might facilitate criminal activity." Prison officials may not reject a publication "solely because its content is religious, philosophical, political, social, or sexual, or because its content is unpopular or repugnant."

II. Publications may be rejected by prison officials if they meet any of the following criteria, which are specified by statute:

a. It depicts or describes procedures for the construction or use of weapons, ammunitions, bombs, or incendiary devices.

b. It depicts, encourages, or describes methods of escape from correctional facilities, or contains blueprints, drawings, or similar descriptions of Bureau of Prisons institutions.

c. It depicts or describes procedures for the brewing of alcoholic beverages, or the manufacture of drugs.

d. It is written in code.

e. It depicts, describes, or encourages activities that may lead to the use of physical violence or group disruption.

f. It encourages or instructs in the commission of criminal activity.

g. It is sexually explicit material that by its nature or content poses a threat to the security, good order, or discipline of the institution, or facilitates criminal activity.[2]

III. Prison officials may not establish an excluded list of publications but, rather, must examine each issue in every publication. To determine whether a publication is acceptable, the statute provides the following categories, which may be excluded:

a. Homosexual (of the same sex as the institution population)

b. Sado-masochistic

c. Bestiality

d. Involving children[3]

IV. Material in the first three categories may be admitted if officials determine it "not to pose a threat at the local institution." Ordinarily explicit heterosexual material will be admitted, and other material may be admitted if it has scholarly, literary, or general social value. Homosexual material that is not sexually explicit is admitted; material discussing the activities of gay-rights groups or gay religious groups, as well as literary publications with homosexual references or themes, is to be admitted.

V. Prison officials may exclude materials only by following stated procedures, such as advising the inmate promptly in writing of the exclusion and the reasons. The inmate may appeal, and an independent review may be called for by the publisher. The Court notes that there is little doubt that this kind of censorship "would raise grave First Amendment concerns outside the prison context." But the Court recognizes also that exceptions to First Amendment rights may be made in prisons "with due regard for the 'inordinately' difficult undertaking that is modern prison administration."[3]

1. *Thornburgh v. Abbott*, 490 U.S. 401 (1989).
2. Code of Federal Regulations, Chapter 28, Section 540.70 (b) (1988).
3. Code of Federal Regulations, Chapter 28, Section 540.71 (b) (7).

In 1989, in *Thornburgh v. Abbott*, the Court overruled *Martinez* to the extent that *Martinez* covered incoming mail. Regulations concerning incoming mail must be analyzed under the four criteria set forth in *Turner v. Safley*, discussed earlier, and are valid if they are "reasonably related to legitimate penological interests." The result is that the Court has approved more stringent rules for the regulation of incoming prison mail, which poses a greater threat to security than does outgoing mail. Spotlight 13-2 contains further information from *Abbott* and federal regulations concerning incoming publications that may be excluded from prison facilities.[29]

An example of the type of censorship that was not permitted by a federal court is found in *McNamara v. Moody*, in which prison officials refused to mail a letter written by an inmate to his girlfriend. The letter was returned to the inmate with a note indicating that:

> It was in poor taste and absolutely unacceptable for mailing from this institution. . . . The next time you write a letter such as the one attached, you may be sure that you will meet with the disciplinary team.[30]

The letter in question alleged that the censors lead such "blah" lives that they "must masturbate themselves while they read other people's mail." The letter alleged also that another inmate told the writer that the censor "has a cat and that he is suspected of having relations of some sort with his cat."

Prison officials argued that it was necessary to censor this mail for security reasons and that censorship was permissible because the words were obscene. The Court disagreed, holding that the words were not obscene ("Vulgar it is; obscene it is not") and that prison officials had not demonstrated that censorship was necessary for prison security and discipline. The Supreme Court refused to hear the case, thus allowing the lower court decision to stand.[31]

Disciplinary action against an inmate who wrote a letter to his brother, referring to various prison personnel as "punks" and "bitches," concluding with the comment, "I hope they all read this letter and get their kicks off of it," was a violation of that inmate's free speech rights.[32] Prison officials may not censor mail solely for the purpose of eliminating comments that may be unflattering to prison officials.[33]

In another case, the court held that a prison regulation requiring that all outgoing mail directed to the media and to the clergy be sent to the prison mailroom unsealed (in contrast to mail addressed to attorneys, which may not be inspected) does not violate an inmate's First Amendment rights. Prison officials may censor such mail only if it contains threats or escape plans.[34]

Limitations that prison officials may place on the right of inmates to communicate by mail with the outside world vary according to the type of mail. In federal prisons, mail falls into two categories: privileged (or special), and general. General mail is mail between an inmate and anyone not in the privileged category. General mail "is subject to being opened by prison officials, checked for contraband, read for plans to perform illegal acts, and then re-closed and delivered to the prisoner." Privileged or special mail is mail between an inmate and attorneys or other persons connected with the courts or treatment of the inmate, legislative officials, and other public officials. Privileged mail "enjoys more protection than general mail in that it cannot be read by prison officials and can be opened to check for contraband only in the presence of the inmate to whom it is addressed."[35] States have similar regulations for prison mail.

Packages may be categorized as privileged or general mail. The Supreme Court has upheld the right of prison officials to prohibit the receipt of hardcover books by inmates unless they are mailed directly from publishers, book clubs, or bookstores. The Court considers the regulation to be a security measure. Correspondents might send contraband such as money, drugs, or weapons into prison inside the hardback books. Officials may open packages to determine whether there is contraband but prisons are given discretion in limiting, or in some cases prohibiting, receipt of packages because of the time required for these checks.[36]

The correspondence that causes the greatest concern for prison officials is correspondence between inmates in different prisons. In *Turner v. Safley*, the Supreme Court upheld a ban on such mail under the circumstances that existed in that case. The provisions in question permitted mail between "immediate family members who are inmates in other correctional institutions" and correspondence between inmates "concerning legal matters." Any other correspondence between inmates was permitted only if "the classification/treatment team of each inmate deems it in the best interest of the parties involved."[37]

Publishing Rights

The right of inmates to record and publish their thoughts should not be confused with the right to earn royalties on the sale of those publications. Many jurisdictions have Son of Sam statutes, which prohibit convicted persons from receiving profits from the sale of books written about their crimes. The name Son of Sam comes from the New York statute enacted because of public concern that Sam Berkowitz, who murdered six young people in New York in the late 1970s, would make millions from his writings about the killings.

The statute, which became the model for many of the subsequently enacted state statutes, provides that any proceeds from "the accused or convicted person's thoughts, feelings, opinions, or emotions regarding [the] crime" must be turned over to the Victim Compensation Board. The statute covers reenactment "by way of a movie, book, magazine, article, tape recording, phonograph, radio, or television presentation," and requires that the person contracting with the criminal must turn over proceeds to the Victim Compensation Board.[38] The New York statute contains provisions for victims to bring civil actions against their perpetrators and to recover from the victim's compensation fund.

The constitutionality of the New York statute was upheld by a New York court in 1979.[39] In 1987, the New York Crime Victim Compensation Board ruled that convicted murderer Jean Harris, author of *Stranger in Two Worlds*, must turn over her $45,000 advance for the book. If she did not have that money, the publisher was to pay the same amount to the board. Any profits above that advance were to be turned over to the family of the man whom Harris murdered. Harris planned to give the royalties, which were over $100,000, to charity, but the New York Court of Appeals upheld the statute. The court rejected arguments that the statute interferes with First Amendment rights. The inmate is free to exercise those rights, but he or she may not profit financially from the crime. This decision was vacated in early 1992 and sent back to the New York Court of Appeals for consideration in light of *Simon & Schuster, Inc., v. New York State Crime Victims Board*.[40]

In *Simon & Schuster, Inc.*, the book at issue was *Wiseguy: Life in a Mafia Family*, an account of the life of Henry Hill, a career criminal who became an informant. The lower federal court upheld the statute but the Supreme Court reversed it, holding that the Son of Sam statute is inconsistent with the First Amendment right to free speech. In order to infringe on that right, the state must show "that its regulation is necessary to serve a compelling state interest and is narrowly drawn to achieve that end." Although the state has an interest in preventing crime, in preventing criminals from profiting from their crimes, and in compensating victims, the Court said the state could not show a compelling reason for targeting a criminal's assets from writing about the crime. The court also stated that the statute is too broad and that had it been in effect when Malcolm X wrote his autobiography, that work would have been included within the statute since it included comments of his crimes before he became a civil rights leader.[41]

New York enacted another Son of Sam statute in 1992. This statute permits state authorities to seize some assets of criminals and hold them for a period of seven years to cover any civil damages that victims might be awarded. The statute permits judges to award restitution to crime victims if they ask for it and if the award is in the interest of justice. The new statute may cover money that criminals received from talk shows as well as books, for it defines profits of crime as "any assets or income obtained through the use of unique knowledge obtained during the commission of . . . the crime." Presumably, the new statute avoids the defect of the previous one, which targeted speech.[42]

In May 1993, a Florida circuit judge ruled that Danny Rolling would not be permitted to profit financially from the crimes for which he was accused: the murders of five University of Florida students. Subsequently, Rolling pleaded guilty to those murders and was sentenced to death.[43]

Visitations

Professional treatment personnel, scholars, and courts recognize the importance of visits for inmates as well as for their families and friends. The National Conference of Commissioners on Uniform State Laws emphasizes that confinement without visitation:

> Brings alienation, and the longer the confinement, the greater the alienation. . . . Visitation has demonstrated positive effects on a confined person's ability to adjust to life while confined as well as his ability to adjust to life upon release.[44]

Prison visitation creates security problems and requires careful planning and supervision. Prison policies require that inmates submit lists of visitors for prior approval. Some persons on those lists may be denied visiting privileges for security or other reasons. Visits may be regulated by hours, days, and frequency by prison officials as the regulations are reasonably related to legitimate prison goals. Prison officials may not be arbitrary and capricious in denying visitation privileges. For example, they may not deny an inmate visits with a person of another race solely because the two are of different races.[45] Nor may prison officials deny visitations to a gay or lesbian friend of an inmate solely because they are involved romantically. There is no reasonable connection between maintaining prison security and safety and the denial of such visits.[46]

Contact visits may be denied to inmates who are dangerous to themselves or others or when the risk of smuggling contraband is high. Contact visits are to be distinguished from conjugal visits, in which sexual relationships are permitted. In contact visits, inmates may be permitted to hug and embrace a family member or friend. In some institutions, that is the extent of contact permitted and correctional officers monitor the visits. In other institutions, inmates may have limited contact with visitors. This may be important particularly when children are involved.

Inmates who are denied contact visits for security reasons may be permitted noncontact visits. For example, the inmate and his or her visitor may be separated by glass. They may talk over a phone or through a screened hole in the glass, but they may not touch each other. Another arrangement permits a dangerous inmate to be in the same room with a visitor but the inmate is restrained with handcuffs, body chains, or both.

Visits with Family and Friends

The Supreme Court has recognized the importance of permitting inmates to see their families and friends, suggesting that such visits might be "a factor contributing to the ultimate reintegration of the detainees into society." That statement, however, comes from a case involving pretrial detainees in detention in the largest jail in the country, the Los Angeles County Central Jail, which has a capacity of 5,000 inmates. In *Block v. Rutherford*, the Court upheld the total prohibition against visitations in that jail. The Court emphasized that security is a critical problem in a large population and that even small children may be used by family and friends to smuggle contraband into the jail.[47]

The position taken by the Supreme Court in *Block v. Rutherford* must be limited to the facts of the case. The Court emphasized that pretrial detainees, who are incarcerated because they have been denied bail or were unable to make bail, are likely to be charged with serious offenses. The Court also cited as additional reasons for denying visits: the large size of the population, which would create tremendous administrative problems if visits were permitted, the danger of drugs being brought into the jail, and the short period of confinement. In other situations, the Court might not uphold a total prohibition on contact visits and some lower courts have taken that position. Some prison officials maintain that prison contact visits reduce tensions and aid in inmates' rehabilitation.

Visitation is important for the inmates' spouses as well. Studies of inmates' wives indicate that they suffer more than just the denial of companionship and sexual relations when their husbands are incarcerated. They are socially ostracized and rejected, despite their lack of involvement in the criminal activity that led to the incarceration. They face problems coping with their children, financial difficulties, and problems of self-esteem.[48]

The importance of family has led some institutions to permit inmates to marry while they are incarcerated and such marriages have been increasing in number. In Florida, hundreds of marriages have been conducted since 1985, when a federal court held that the state could not prohibit inmate marriages unless it could show a security risk or a threat to inmate rehabilitation. Before that decision, Florida permitted inmate marriages only if the inmate was near the end of his or her term or if marriage was necessary to legitimatize children.[49]

In 1989, a federal court in New York declared a policy forbidding inmates to marry unless they were ready for parole unconstitutional. The court said the prohibition was not reasonably related to the goal of punishment.[50]

Permitting inmate marriages does not mean that conjugal visits are tolerated. Conjugal visiting is common in many European prisons although it is rarely allowed in the United States. U.S. courts have refused to hold that inmates have a constitutional right to marry and engage in conjugal relations.[51] In *Turner v. Safley*, the Supreme Court held that states may place substantial restrictions on inmate marriages, but those restrictions must be "reasonably related to legitimate penological objectives," one of which is institutional security.[52]

It has been held that prison officials may deny an incarcerated inmate and his spouse the opportunity to attempt conception through artificial insemination. Numerous reasons are cited for denial of such requests. If proper procedures for artificial insemination are not followed, the procedures may be ineffective or result in the birth of a defective child. Proper procedures are expensive and would require additional prison facilities and personnel. The inmate may be permitted to leave the facility, which creates a security risk. Providing the services for indigent inmates increases the costs. For these reasons, the Bureau of Prisons has adopted a policy prohibiting artificial insemination for inmates in federal prisons and courts have upheld this policy.[53]

Visits with the Press

Another type of visit that is important to inmates is the right to visit with the press. In *Pell v. Procunier*, the Supreme Court upheld a California statute providing that "press and other media interviews with specific individual inmates will not be permitted." The Court said internal security required that some restrictions be made upon face-to-face contacts with outsiders. The restriction on visits with the media must be viewed in perspective with alternatives. Inmates may communicate with the press through prison-approved visits and through the mail. The Court concluded that as long as reasonable and effective means of communications are available and there is no discrimination in the content of those communications, the prison must be given great latitude in regulating visits with the press.[54]

The Supreme Court has held that there is no right of access to government information or sources of information within the government's control, and the news media has no constitutional right of access to a county jail, over and above that of other persons, to interview inmates and make sound recordings, films, and photographs for publication and broadcasting by newspapers, radio, and television.[55]

Religious Worship

Some studies indicate that religion reduces discipline problems in prison.[56] Freedom of religion is a First Amendment right and numerous court cases argue this important right to freedom and what it means in a prison setting. The U.S. Supreme Court announced the general rule in 1972 in *Cruz v. Beto*. An inmate must be given "a reasonable opportunity of pursuing his faith comparable to the opportunity afforded fellow prisoners who adhere to conventional religious precepts." This does not mean that all religious sects or groups must have identical facilities or personnel. "But reasonable opportunities must be afforded to all prisoners to exercise the religious freedom guaranteed by the First and Fourteenth Amendments without fear of penalty."[57] The word reasonable is included in this statement since prison officials at times find themselves denying individuals religious practices that may pose a security risk to the institution. Conversely, security is a reason for denying certain religious practices, such as the use of peyote by Native American inmates.[58]

An inmate may claim a right to practice religious beliefs only if the religion is a recognized one. Deciding whether a claimed religion is a legitimate religion may be a problem, as Spotlight 13-3 indicates. A second issue is whether the inmate is a sincere believer in that religion. If the religion is found to be a recognized one and the inmate is a committed follower, questions may arise over whether the inmate should be permitted to practice all aspects of the religious belief. It is clear that some observances may not be permitted for security reasons or because of the time and personnel required to secure the prison during those observances.[59]

Other issues may involve diet, grooming, and dress. Some inmates' requests for special food and diet compatible with their religious beliefs have been recognized. For example, some courts have upheld the request of Jewish inmates for kosher food, although some courts have refused. Generally, requests by Muslims to have a diet free of pork are upheld.[60] But a request from an inmate to be served a vegetarian diet because of his religious beliefs was denied. The court

Spotlight 13-3

Real or Imaginary Religions: The Prison Dilemma

One of the most litigated examples of inmate-claimed religions is that of the Church of the New Song (CONS), which was organized in the early 1970s by Harry William Theriault, a federal inmate. Theriault claimed himself the Bishop of Tellyus, obtained a mail-order divinity degree, and deemed his cell the Fountainhead Seminary. He converted other inmates to his Eclatarian Faith until prison authorities transferred him to solitary confinement. Previously, Theriault had been involved in litigation concerning his conviction and sentence, as well as prison conditions. He sued prison officials for deprivation of his constitutional right to the free exercise of religion. In spite of Theriault's admission that CONS was started as a game, the court said CONS was to be considered a bona fide religion under the First Amendment.[1]

Shortly after *Theriault v. Carlson* was decided, a sect within the church made a formal request to the Federal Bureau of Prisons to provide 700 porterhouse steaks for the inmates to celebrate the sect's rituals. Theriault announced that he had no affiliation with that sect and that the request was not sanctioned.[2] The Court of Appeals remanded the case to the lower court to determine the validity of the alleged religion against the suspect background of Theriault and the dubious formation of the sect. On remand, the district court found that CONS was not a religion.[3]

Theriault appealed again and the Court of Appeals sent the case back to the district court as it had not indicated its basis for finding that CONS was not a religion.[4] On remand, the district court found that CONS was a "masquerade designed to obtain First Amendment protection for acts which otherwise would be unlawful and or reasonably disallowed by the various prison authorities but for the attempts which have been and are being made to classify them as 'religious' and, therefore, presumably protected by the First Amendment." The court noted that even if CONS were a religion, the prison could exercise reasonable controls over the practice of the religion. "To give a prisoner who is an admitted escape artist and who has been convicted of assault and battery on corrections officers the unrestricted freedom which he demands would make a mockery of the corrections system and would afford him privileges not available to other inmates, unless they joined his union."[5]

Theriault's appeal of this decision was dismissed because his petition contained vile and insulting references to the trial judge.[6] The issue of whether CONS is a religion is not settled. In Iowa, it was held to be a religion.[7] In Illinois, a court ruled that CONS was not a religion for First Amendment purposes.[8]

The question of what constitutes a religion arose in the case of the Metropolitan Community Church (MCC), frequently referred to as the homosexual or gay church, although membership does include heterosexuals. The State of California denied requests by inmates to practice this religion in prison. The state contended that the MCC was not a bona fide religion. The court rejected that contention. The court ruled that in order to maintain the ban, the state would have to show that if the ban were removed, there would be a clear and present danger of a breach of prison security. At that point, California allowed the religion to be practiced within the prisons.[9]

1. *Theriault v. Carlson*, 339 F. Supp. 375 (N.D. Ga. 1972), vacated and remanded, 495 F. 2d 390 (5th Cir. 1974), cert. denied, 419 U.S. 1003 (1974).
2. Cited in comment, "The Religious Rights of the Incarcerated," *University of Pennsylvania Law Review* 125 (April, 1977): 818.
3. *Theriault v. Silber*, 391 F. Supp. 578 (W.D. Tex. 1975).
4. *Theriault v. Silber*, 547 F. 2d 1279 (5th Cir. 1977), cert. denied, 434 U.S. 943 (1977).
5. *Theriault v. Silber*, 453 F. Supp. 254, 260, 262 (W.D. Tex. 1978).
6. *Theriault v. Silber*, 569 F. 2d 301 (5th Cir. 1978).
7. See *Remmers v. Brewer*, 361 F. Supp. 537 (S.D. Iowa 1973), Aff'd. per Curiam, 494 F. 2d 1277 (8th Cir. 1974), cert. denied, 419 U.S. 1012 (1974).
8. *Hundley v. Sielaff*, 407 F. Supp. 543 (N.D. Ill. 1973).
9. *Lipp v. Procunier*, 395 F. Supp. 871 (N.D. Cal. 1975).

Case Study 13-3

Jones v. North Carolina Prisoner's Union, Inc.

First Amendment associational rights, while perhaps more directly implicated by the regulatory prohibitions, likewise must give way to the reasonable considerations of penal management...[N]umerous associational rights are necessarily curtailed by the realities of confinement. They may be curtailed whenever the institution's officials, in the exercise of their informed discretion, reasonably conclude that such associations, whether through group meetings or otherwise, possess the likelihood of disruption to prison order or stability, or otherwise interfere with the legitimate penological objectives of the prison environment.

recognized the institutional concern with the inmate's health in justifying refusal of this request.[61]

In 1992, a court ruled against an inmate who claimed that cutting hair was against his religious beliefs and thus he should not be required to comply with the prison regulation concerning hair length. The court did not question the sincerity of the inmate but deferred to prison authorities concerning the rationale for this rule. The court concluded that the "loss of absolute freedom of religious expression is but one sacrifice required by their incarceration."[62]

It has been held reasonable for prison authorities to refuse to permit an inmate to wear a rosary with an attached hard plastic crucifix because the crucifix could be used to remove handcuffs.[63] In May 1994, a court granted preliminary permission to inmates who were adherents of the Santeria religion to wear multicolored beads. Prison officials argued that some inmates wear these beads as a sign of gang membership. The court said that might not be a reason to prohibit all inmates from wearing them for religious reasons. This case, however, followed the passage of the 1993 Religious Freedom Restoration Act, which reversed two Supreme Court decisions. The act requires that freedom of religion may not be restricted except under circumstances that constitute a "compelling state interest" and is accomplished by the "least restrictive means" available. Prison officials lobbied unsuccessfully for exemptions, arguing that the act would have devastating results in prisons.[64]

Freedom of Assembly and Self-Government

The First Amendment guarantees the right of persons to assemble freely. Inmates have argued that this freedom, along with the right to engage in self-government, applies also to them. In 1977, in *Jones v. North Carolina Prisoner's Union, Inc.*, the Supreme Court upheld the right of prison officials in North Carolina to restrict the activities of prison unions, a decision described by two dissenting justices as a "giant step backward" in inmates' rights. In *Jones*, the Court contemplated the right of inmates to associate with each other and the restrictions that officials could place on this right, as the brief excerpt in Case Study 13-3 indicates.[65]

Access to Courts

The right of access to courts, recognized by the Supreme Court in *Ex Parte Hull* in 1941, is an inmate's most important right.[66] Without access to courts, most other rights have limited meaning. In 1969, in *Johnson v. Avery*, the Supreme Court invalidated a Tennessee prison regulation that forbade inmates to assist one another in preparing legal cases. Because many institutions do not provide

Case Study 13-4

Bounds v. Smith

[This] fundamental constitutional right of access to the courts requires prison authorities to assist inmates in the preparation and filing of meaningful legal papers by providing prisonsers with adequate law libraries or adequate assistance from persons trained in the law...

Among the alternatives are the training of inmates as paralegal assistants to work under lawyers' supervision, the use of paraprofessionals and law students, either as volunteers or in formal clinical programs, the organization of volunteer attorneys through bar associations and other groups, the hiring of lawyers on a part-time consultant basis, and the use of full-time staff attorneys, working in either new prison legal assistance organizations or as part of public defender or legal services offices.

legal services, the effect of that regulation was to deny some inmates access to courts. *Johnson* recognized the right of an inmate to the services of a jailhouse lawyer but the Court restricted the use of such services to inmates in institutions that provided no reasonable alternative.[67] Some jailhouse lawyers are highly recognized for their legal services while they are inmates.[68] The individuals have a fairly good understanding of case law. They use their skills to assist some of their peers in their effort to petition the courts for a review of their cases.

In 1977, in *Bounds v. Smith* (see Case Study 13-4), the Court presented some guidelines concerning the meaning of the right of access to courts.[69] The meaning of *Bounds* has been litigated. It has been held that the case does not require that the assistance of attorneys be made available to inmates and the requirement of adequate access to courts may be met through providing adequate law libraries.[70] Conversely, not permitting inmates (such as those on death row or in administrative segregation) to go to the law library and browse may be unconstitutional, depending on the facts. Some courts have upheld these restrictions because of the threat to security posed by death-row inmates but some recent cases have held to the contrary. In 1992, a federal court in Arizona held that prison officials denied inmates access to courts by restricting their access to the prison law library and by restricting inmates' opportunities to engage in confidential phone calls to their attorneys. The court stated:

> The vast majority of adult prisoners incarcerated by [the Arizona Department of Corrections] have no adequate means to research the law, crystalize their issues, present their papers in a meaningful fashion, and get them filed in court.[71]

The court noted that some inmates are not permitted to go to the library and that policy denies them an opportunity to browse, a privilege that is necessary for those who do not know which materials they need. For those who do not speak or read English, a law library is not adequate access to courts.

In upholding a policy of permitting death-row inmates access to the law library only through a paging system in which requested books are delivered to them in their cells, a federal court in Pennsylvania emphasized that court decisions "like the decisions of the prison administrators, must not be made in a vacuum, but rather must give due consideration to the depraved nature of the crimes committed and the 'character of the inmates.'"[72]

Security might be a sufficient reason for denying an inmate the opportunity to go to the library although some courts hold that legal assistance must be provided. Further, indigent inmates must be provided sufficient papers, pens, and other materials to make it possible for them to do research and law libraries must be staffed with persons trained in legal research.[73] This does not mean that those persons must be attorneys or even trained paralegals.[74]

One court stated that it is sufficient that they be "intelligent lay people who can write coherent English and who have had some modicum of exposure to legal research and to the rudiments of prisoner-rights law." In addition, there must be a sufficient number of persons to assist the inmate population.[75] Harassment of inmate paralegals by prison officials may deny other inmates adequate access to courts.[76] Adequate access to courts extends to pretrial jail detainees who are proceeding *pro se* (on their own, without attorneys).[77]

The right of inmates to access the courts does not include the right to appointed counsel for all appeals. An indigent defendant is entitled "as a matter of right to counsel for an initial appeal from the judgment and sentence of the trial court," but is not necessarily appointed counsel for all subsequent appeals.[78]

Inmates do not have a right to appointed counsel for civil cases. One court has held, however, that female inmates may have greater rights than male inmates. It was found unconstitutional for Michigan to cut back on its policies to provide legal assistance to female inmates in civil parental rights cases, as parenthood is part of the liberty guaranteed by the Fourteenth Amendment.[79] Female inmates may need more legal assistance than do male inmates (and require the assistance of paralegals or attorneys) because "female prisoners lack their male counterparts' history of 'self-help' in the law, . . . [and] equal protection considerations may require that library facilities be supplemented by assistance from a lawyer."[80]

In addition to the right to access legal materials, inmates have the right to reasonable and confidential communication with their retained attorneys. Prisons must provide visitation policies and adequate facilities for inmate visits with attorneys and must allow communication by mail with counsel. The Supreme Court allows prison officials to open letters from attorneys to inmates and to search for contraband as long as it is done in the presence of the inmates to whom the letters are addressed. This action is not censorship because the mail is not read. Prisons may require attorneys to indicate on the outside of the envelope that the mail is from a legal office.[81]

Inmates who retain attorneys for their legal actions against prison officials may be entitled to attorney fees upon winning their cases. In 1989, a federal judge ordered Michigan state correctional officials to pay $1.48 million in attorney fees to compensate inmates' attorneys for their time and legal services. The compensation included an award for the "stress, frustration and outrage" the inmates' attorneys suffered from the misconduct of state attorneys. In the case, the judge ruled that inmates were denied adequate access to courts, endured excessive restrictions on their legal mail, were deprived of adequate warm clothing and adequate access to toilets, and that officials failed to deter correctional staff from subjecting African-American inmates to racial slurs.[82] The legal fees are one of the largest awards in a prison lawsuit.[83]

Adequate access to courts is also used to file frivolous suits. A recent article noted a few examples. One inmate filed a suit claiming he was the victim of cruel and unusual punishment because he was served melted ice cream. Another alleged that he was served creamy peanut butter after ordering chunky, while another inmate who had an ulcer claimed he should be provided with lamb, veal, and oysters. His physician said these foods were permitted, but not required, for his health. Since the 1960s, when only a few hundred inmate suits were filed each year, the number grew to 33,000 in 1993. Those lawsuits constituted 15 percent of

Case Study 13-5

Hudson v. Palmer

[T]he Fourth Amendment proscription against unreasonable searches does not apply within the confines of the prison cell. The recognition of privacy rights for prisoners in their individual cells simply cannot be reconciled with the concept of incarceration and the needs and objectives of penal institutions.

Prisons, by definition, are places of involuntary confinement of persons who have a demonstrated proclivity for antisocial criminal, and often violent, conduct...

Within this volatile "community," prison administrators are to take all necessary steps to ensure the safety of not only the prison staffs and administrative personnel, but visitors. They are under an obligation to take reasonable measures to guarantee the safety of the inmates themselves. They must be ever alert to attempts to introduce drugs and other contraband into the premises...

Virtually the only place inmates can conceal weapons, drugs, and other contraband is in their cells. Unfettered access to these cells by prison officials, thus, is imperative if drugs and contraband are to be ferreted out and sanitary surroundings are to be maintained.

the total number of civil lawsuits filed in federal courts that year.[84] This is because restrictions on the ability of inmates to file lawsuits have been lifted since the 1960s. Attempts are currently underway to reintroduce restrictions to limit the number of inmate lawsuits. This is permissible to eliminate frivolous lawsuits only. It is not permissible if it denies inmates adequate access to courts for legitimate claims.

13-3b Fourth Amendment Rights

The Fourth Amendment prohibits unreasonable searches and seizures, with the dispute resting on the definition of "unreasonable." In the prison setting, the need for security has highest priority as it enables prison officials to conduct searches and seizures that are not permissible in other settings. In 1984, in *Hudson v. Palmer* (see Case Study 13-5), the Supreme Court considered the application of the Fourth Amendment to prison cell searches. With an emphasis on the difficult problems of maintaining security in a prison setting, the Court reviewed the recent history of violence in prisons and in that context issued its opinion.[85]

Hudson was decided by a five to four vote by the Court. Justice John Paul Stevens, who wrote an opinion in which he concurred in part and dissented in part, took the unusual step of reading his opinion from the bench when the decision was announced:

> By telling prisoners that no aspect of their individuality, from a photo of a child to a letter from a wife, is entitled to constitutional protection, the Court breaks with the ethical tradition that I had thought was enshrined forever in our jurisprudence.

Hudson v. Palmer was brought by an inmate who alleged that the officer who searched his cell did so out of malice and not for security. He claimed the officer destroyed his personal property. Justice Stevens agreed with the Court that random searches are necessary and permissible but he disagreed with the Court's conclusion that no matter how malicious, destructive, or arbitrary a cell search and seizure may be, it cannot constitute an unreasonable invasion of any privacy or possessory interest that society is prepared to recognize as reasonable.

According to Justice Stevens, the small amount of possessions and limited privacy that an inmate might have in a cell are little compared to what the rest of society has, but "that trivial residuum may mark the difference between slavery

Case Study 13-6

State v. Palmer

All twelve inmates, including appellant, in appellant's "pod" of Cell Block Six were to undergo body cavity searches. The intelligence officer testified that he authorized an initial digital rectal search and, if that search revealed the presence of an object, the inmate would be X-rayed. Finally, if the inmate did not voluntarily give up or excrete the object, it would be removed. A correctional medical assistant performed an initial digital rectal search on appellant. Appellant was then escorted to a medical examining room where a medical doctor performed a second digital search. During the search, the doctor felt the presence of an object and ordered an X-ray of the appellant's pelvic area. The X-ray revealed the presence of a foreign object believed to be a shotgun shell.

Following the X-ray, appellant was transported to the central unit hospital's emergency room. A second doctor, trained in sigmoidoscopy examinations, first performed a rectal examination that consisted of the insertion of a small scope to determine the nature of the foreign object. Appellant refused to submit to that examination and, eventually, was forced to lay on the table by corrections officers. Appellant finally agreed to position himself on the table so that the item could be removed, and the doctor removed the shotgun shell, which had been wrapped in tissue paper in a condom. During the procedure, appellant testified that he suffered severe pain and discomfort and, following the removal, he suffered some bleeding.

Searches of other inmates revealed balloons filled with gunpowder and a detonation cord, and subsequent searches led to the discovery of blasting caps and a homemade rip gun capable of shooting a shotgun shell. Other inmates had consented to voluntarily pass or remove the contraband they possessed. One other inmate, who did not immediately excrete his contraband, was placed in an isolation cell and eventually passed a balloon filled with gunpowder.

[The appellate court discusses the dispute between the appellant and the prison officials over the method in which these searches occurred; the appellate court sees no reason to disturb the trial court's findings that the procedures were appropriate under the circumstances.]

Many factors must be considered in determining whether a search is reasonable. They include the crime allegedly being committed, society's interest in punishing the act, and the reliability of the means employed to conduct the search. They also include the strength of law enforcement suspicions that evidence of crime will be revealed, the importance of the evidence sought, and the possibility that the evidence may be recovered by less intrusive means...We acknowledge that the search and removal probably resulted in discomfort, pain, and humiliation, however, the removal resulted from the method by which appellant chose to hide the contraband and by appellant's refusal to voluntarily pass it...

The immediate methods employed in this case were reasonable...In view of all the facts and circumstances surrounding this case, we do not find that the search and seizure violated appellant's Fourth Amendment right.

and humanity." In *Block v. Rutherford*, the Supreme Court upheld routine searches of cells while inmates were absent.[86]

Searches of a person are more intrusive, although there are degrees of intrusiveness. Searches by means of mechanical devices may be conducted at any time without prior authorization of a supervisor. A casual search of a person or frisk of an inmate may be conducted at any time and is routine before and after the inmate has contact visits with family and friends.

The most intrusive search is the body search, which may involve a strip search or a manual search of body cavities. The Supreme Court has upheld body cavity searches after inmates have had contact visits.[87] The U.S. Court of Appeals for the Second Circuit has upheld random visual inspections of inmates' body cavities even without suspicion of contraband. In a 1992 decision, the court said this is permitted because of the high percentage of inmates who engage in substance abuse and violent behavior.[88]

Permitting strip searches of inmates because of the practice of storing contraband inside the body is illustrated by the excerpt from *State v. Palmer* in Case Study 13-6. *Palmer* illustrates some of the issues associated with strip searches—the manner and place in which they occur and who conducts the search.[89]

Although it may be argued that pretrial detainees have a greater expectation of privacy than offenders who have been convicted and incarcerated in prisons, courts have upheld some types of body searches, such as visual body cavity searches.[90]

Strip searches have been held unconstitutional when conducted on a person who visits an inmate, unless the prison official has reasonable cause to think that visitor is attempting to smuggle contraband into the jail or prison. In other words, strip searches of visitors are permitted only when it is reasonable to think that is necessary for security reasons.[91] It is unreasonable to search a visitor who is leaving the prison, as that visitor is no longer in a position to introduce contraband into the prison.[92] Some courts have held that it is unconstitutional to have a policy of strip searching all persons brought to jail, even those charged with minor offenses.[93]

Male and female inmates have questioned searches by, or in the presence of, correctional officers of the opposite gender. Generally, pat-down searches have been upheld as meeting the requirements of *Turner v. Safley*.[94] Searches are necessary to satisfy the security need of prisons and opposite-gender searches (along with permitting opposite-gender officers to supervise showers and other inmate activities) may be necessary to satisfy another legitimate institutional goal, that of equal opportunity employment.[95]

Not all judges and justices agree with permitting opposite-gender pat-down searches. In a 1990 case upholding these searches, one dissenting judge said:

> To treat men and women as equals does not require that courts ignore that differences exist. Even prisoners are entitled to a modicum of privacy and are entitled not to be embarrassed by needlessly requiring that they expose their nakedness and private parts to guards of the opposite sex. My colleagues have stripped the prisoners of their limited privacy rights . . .[96]

13-3c Eighth Amendment Rights

Physical Abuse

The Eighth Amendment prohibits cruel and unusual punishment. This phrase has been interpreted to include various activities within prisons. For example, it is not permissible for inmates to attack other inmates physically. Corporal punishment of inmates may constitute cruel and unusual punishment. Correctional officers and administrators may use reasonable force to maintain security, but they may be liable to inmates who bring civil suits against them, claiming that their Eighth Amendment rights have been violated.

In February 1992, the Supreme Court considered physical abuse of inmates by correctional officers. In *Hudson v. McMillian*, the Court held that inmates may bring actions for cruel and unusual punishment against prison officials who use physical force that may result in injuries, even if the injuries are not significant. This case involved an inmate who got into an argument with a correctional officer. Other officers intervened and the inmate was placed in restraints and walked from his cell to a lockdown area. During this excursion, the officers kicked and punched the inmate, who suffered minor bruises, loosened teeth, and a cracked dental plate. The inmate brought a civil suit against the officers and won a modest damage award, which was overturned on appeal to a federal circuit court. The U.S. Supreme Court reversed it, holding that the inmate was entitled to damages even though he did not suffer significant injuries.

Although all of the justices did not agree on the reasons, seven joined the affirmative in this case, which extends inmates' rights. Clarence Thomas was the most recently appointed justice at that time. His dissenting opinion, in which

Justice Scalia joined, may provide significant insight into Justice Thomas's impact on the future of the Court. Thomas argued that an inmate must show a serious injury in order to bring a successful suit for injuries against a prison official, and he also attacked the Court's modern interpretations of the Eighth Amendment's cruel and unusual punishment clause. The result is that in only a short time on the bench, Justice Thomas aroused considerable debate about his judicial positions, far more so than did Justice David Souter, who was appointed the previous year.[97]

In December 1993, the Eighth Circuit held that the use of a stun gun on an inmate who refused to sweep his cell when ordered to do so constituted the kind of "torment without marks" that the Supreme Court prohibited in *Hudson v. McMillian.* According to the court, prison officials do not have the legal right to use force anytime an inmate disobeys an order.[98]

Courts have held that the cruel and unusual punishment clause of the Eighth Amendment extends to general prison conditions. Courts look to the totality of conditions within prisons to determine whether they are bad enough to constitute cruel and unusual punishment. Those conditions may include overcrowding, unsanitary areas, methods of discipline, and /or food that is not prepared properly or nutritiously or that contains foreign matter.

Medical Care

Prison officials have broad discretion in determining the medical care that inmates should receive. It is difficult for courts to make such determinations. The Supreme Court has articulated a standard for care, stating in 1976 in *Estelle v. Gamble,* "deliberate indifference to serious medical needs of prisoners constitutes the kind of cruel and unusual punishment that is prohibited by the Eighth Amendment."[99] A decade later, the Court stated that to be actionable, delay in providing medical care for inmates must be prompted by "obduracy and wantonness, not inadvertence or error in good faith."[100]

In 1982, in *Ruiz v. Estelle,* a lower federal court looked at the Texas prison system (TDC) and concluded that the Eighth Amendment was being violated. The court found a "continuous pattern of harmful, inadequate medical treatment" that led to "anguish and inexpedient medical treatment to inmates on a large scale."[101]

In *Ruiz,* the court ordered substantial changes including more qualified medical staff, elimination of inmate labor in medical and pharmacological functions, improvement of physical facilities, establishment of diagnostic and sick-call procedures and work classification procedures, and a complete overhaul of the record-keeping system. Improvements were made in the Texas system, and court monitoring ended in December 1992.[102]

It is important to distinguish cases in which inmates argue that they are subjected to cruel and unusual punishment because of inadequate medical care as opposed to other conditions, such as prison physical conditions. With regard to medical care, since *Estelle v. Gamble* (decided in 1976), the Court has required that to prevail in such cases, inmates must prove that officials' deprivation of medical services indicates a deliberate indifference to inmates. This stricter test has not been applied to prison physical conditions. In 1991, however, the Court imposed the deliberate indifference standard to other prison cases, making it much more difficult for inmates to prevail in cases involving prison conditions.[103]

AIDS: A Special Prison Medical Problem

AIDS (Acquired Immune Deficiency Syndrome) has become a household word in the United States, as educational efforts to alert people to the deadly and rapidly spreading disease have had some success. Thousands of people have died of AIDS and there is no known cure. There is evidence that AIDS is spread primarily through sexual contact and intravenous drug use. Jails and prisons face acute problems concerning the spread of this disease and the prevalence of AIDS raises numerous legal issues in prisons.

One of those issues concerns whether prison officials may isolate or segregate persons with the HIV virus or AIDS. In 1991, the Eleventh Circuit upheld a segregation policy in the Alabama prisons. The court noted that this policy is a reasonable means of limiting behavior that might cause the spread of the disease. The lawsuit was brought by 150 inmates with HIV or AIDS who sought to have the policy eliminated. The court held, however, that the lower court should reassess the plaintiffs' argument. By being segregated, they were denied equal access to educational and recreational programs, as well as legal assistance.[104]

The following year, the Fifth Circuit upheld a Mississippi State Penitentiary policy of identifying and segregating HIV-positive inmates.[105] A federal district court in New York ruled that a policy of naming and isolating a HIV-positive inmate violated her privacy and due process rights. Louise Nolley, who was confined for three months at the Erie County Holding Center, was incarcerated in a cellblock reserved for mentally ill inmates and those with contagious diseases. Special red identifying marks were placed on her files, her transportation documents, and her clothing bag. The court held that the red sticker served no purpose other than to publicize Nolley's condition to prison officials as well as inmates serving in custodial positions and constituted an overreaction to AIDS hysteria; that Nolley did not constitute a threat to the general population; and that she was in greater danger by being placed in a cell block with persons who have contagious diseases.[106]

A report released in 1994 indicates that only Alabama and Mississippi segregate all inmates known to be HIV-positive. The trend in U.S. prisons and jails is to consider these inmates on a case-by-case basis.[107] Some prison systems are looking more closely into general conditions under which HIV-positive inmates are confined. California inmates protested their conditions and won some concessions, such as enhanced programs, improved medical care, and training of correctional officers to handle the problems of HIV-positive inmates.[108] Some other restrictions on HIV-positive inmates, however, may be upheld. In 1993, the Ninth Circuit agreed with the policy of prohibiting contact visits between such inmates and their attorneys.[109]

Another issue concerning AIDS in prisons is contact visits between inmates and their families. In 1987, New York's highest court upheld prison officials' decision to prohibit conjugal visits between an inmate infected with AIDS and his wife. The court held that this refusal was not an unreasonable interference with the rights of the inmate or of his spouse.[110]

Right to a Smoke-Free Environment: A Recent Challenge

For many years, society has been faced with medical evidence of the harmful effects of smoking, including secondhand smoke. Many states have enacted legislation providing smoke-free environments or restricted smoking areas within establishments such as restaurants and public buildings. Administrative officials within some jails and prisons have instituted smoking restrictions or bans. In some facilities that do not have restrictions on smoking, inmates have filed suits arguing that the lack of a smoke-free environment exposes them to health risks and constitutes cruel and unusual punishment. These demands pose a serious dilemma as one court noted, "Nowhere is the practice of smoking a more imbedded institution than in the nation's prisons and jails, where the proportion of smokers to nonsmokers is many times higher than that of society in general." That court, however, refused to rule in favor of the inmate's demand for a smoke-free environment, suggesting that it was unworkable. The U.S. Supreme Court refused to review the case.[111]

Before 1993, lower federal courts issued conflicting rulings on the issue of whether the failure to provide inmates with a smoke-free environment constituted cruel and unusual punishment. The U.S. Supreme Court had refused to hear some of these cases[112] until 1993, when the Court agreed to review *Helling v. McKinney*, from the Ninth Circuit. In this case, the Court recognized the right of a Nevada inmate to offer proof that celling him with another inmate who smoked five packs of cigarettes a day subjected him to short-term as well as long-term health hazards. At the time the Supreme Court heard the case, however, the inmate had been moved to another institution and was not celled with the five-pack-a-day smoker. On remand, the inmate would have to prove that he was subjected to unreasonably high levels of environmental tobacco smoke (ETS), an objective factor.

13-3d Fourteenth Amendment Rights

The Fourteenth Amendment prohibits the denial of life, liberty, or property without due process or equal protection, which are basic concepts of U.S. criminal justice systems.

The due process clause may be invoked in inmate discipline cases. Such claims involve decisions regarding good-time credits, deprivation of freedom and privileges within the prison environment, segregated housing or solitary confinement, and transfers for disciplinary reasons. The focus in due process claims is on the procedures by which these decisions are made.

Inmates' due process claims must pass a two-part test. First, the claim must involve a liberty or property interest within the Fourteenth Amendment. If it does, the test is to determine what process is due in that situation. If there is no liberty or property right, decisions maybe made without giving reasons to inmates. Further, the Court has held that inmates' freedom does not fall within the meaning of liberty. That right is extinguished when they are convicted. Thus, an inmate sentenced to ten years in prison has no liberty interest in being released sooner. States may create liberty interests by statute; if they do, due process must be provided when that liberty is denied.

Olim v. Wakinekona illustrates the due process issue regarding transfer. Wakinekona was serving several sentences, including a life sentence without possibility of parole, in the Hawaii State Prison. When problems erupted in the maximum-security control unit to which Wakinekona had been assigned, a committee held hearings to determine who caused the disturbance. Testimony was taken from other inmates and the discipline committee concluded that Wakinekona and another inmate were the instigators.

Wakinekona was notified of a hearing to determine whether he should be reclassified within the prison and whether he should be transferred. The hearing was held by the same committee that found him to be the troublemaker. Wakinekona attended the hearing with his counsel. He was told that despite his progress and his desire to continue in the vocational training in that prison, he was a security risk and a threat to the staff. Since Hawaii had no other maximum-security facilities, he was transferred 4,000 miles away to Folsom State Prison in California.

Wakinekona sued, alleging that his right to due process was denied because the same committee that labeled him a troublemaker decided to transfer him. He claimed he was entitled to an unbiased tribunal in the latter decision. The Supreme Court held that Wakinekona did not have a liberty interest in remaining in Hawaii and therefore was not entitled to an unbiased tribunal. Wakinekona would not have been freed if he had remained in Hawaii and the possibility of being released would not have been affected by his transfer. Consequently, the Court emphasized that often it is necessary to transfer inmates from one prison to another, even from one state to another, and that they have no liberty interest against such transfers.[113]

Even if the inmate can show that there is a liberty interest, the due process requirements are limited. In *Hewitt v. Helms*, inmate Helms, serving a term in a state correctional institution in Pennsylvania, sued prison officials on the claim that he was placed in administrative segregation without due process. Helms had been given a misconduct report for his alleged part in a riot in which correctional officers were injured. The Court agreed that he had a liberty interest in remaining in the general population. That interest derived from the state statutes and therefore does not necessarily apply in other cases. But, said the Court, that liberty interest does not entitle the inmate to more than a nonadversary and informal hearing.[114]

The Court's holding in *Helms* illustrates why it is so important to read the facts of cases and the reasoning of judges and justices carefully. The Supreme Court heard and decided *Wolff v. McDonnell*, a case involving reducing the good-time credits of an inmate (mentioned earlier in this chapter). In *Wolff*, the Court required that inmates who faced disciplinary charges for misconduct must be given twenty-four hours advance written notice of the charges against them; a right to call witnesses and present documentary evidence in defense, unless doing so would jeopardize institutional safety or correctional goals; the aid of a staff member or inmate in presenting a defense, provided the inmate is illiterate or the issue complex; an impartial tribunal; and a written statement of reasons relied on by the tribunal. *Wolff* did not require all elements of due process. The Court did not require that inmates be provided with an attorney at disciplinary hearings and it limited the right to call and cross-examine witnesses. Prison officials may reduce the number of witnesses without giving reasons.[115]

In *Helms*, the Court emphasized that its holding in *Wolff* involved procedures that affected the length of time the inmate would be incarcerated. *Wolff* involved good-time credits, which cut the prison time served. Prison officials had revoked those credits. The Court said that is different from changing the status of an inmate within a prison or transferring an inmate to another prison. Subsequently, the Court held that when states provide for good-time credits, revocation of those credits may occur only when sufficient evidence has been presented for revocation.[116] In addition, the Court has held that due process requires that when prison officials refuse to call witnesses requested by an inmate at a disciplinary hearing, the officials must give reasons for their refusal, although they do not have to give written reasons.[117]

Another requirement of the Fourteenth Amendment is that all persons are guaranteed equal protection of the law. Equal protection claims in prisons are brought primarily by female inmates who allege that they do not have the same access as male inmates have to medical care, vocational training, and educational opportunities. An earlier study disclosed that, in most cases, this allegation was correct even in those instances in which female and male inmates occupied the same general facilities. In addition, it is argued that female inmates have additional needs, such as maternity care. Women have unique problems that may not be met within jail and prison facilities.[118]

Women are more likely, however, to have private rooms, which in some institutions are more like dormitory rooms than cells. Women may have greater freedom of movement within the prison. Male inmates may allege that these differences violate their equal protection rights. Prison officials may argue that generally, female inmates do not engage in the serious violence that is characteristic of many maximum-security prisons for men.

The critical issue is to determine at what point females, when compared to males, are denied equal protection in prison (or vice versa). The Supreme Court has not ruled on whether women are being discriminated against as a class and the cases in the lower courts must be analyzed carefully. The issue is not whether a particular service such as educational programs must be provided, but whether it is provided for equally between genders.[119]

A recent case, *Klinger v. Nebraska Department of Correctional Services*, analyzed the equal protection claims of female inmates and held that programs for female and male inmates must be "substantially equivalent." Equal protection requires parity of treatment. There is no justification for paying women less per hour than men are paid, nor is there justification for providing female inmates inferior medical services and dental care, less access to the law library, and fewer educational opportunities. Prison officials are also liable for damages because they knew of the differences, refused to do anything to alleviate them, and thus exhibited deliberate indifference to the rights of female inmates.[120]

13-4 Prison Programs and Legal Rights

The rights discussed thus far are guaranteed by the Constitution but there are also activities and programs that are not required by that document. The question is whether inmates have a constitutional right to an education, vocational training, and work opportunities.

There is evidence that education and work opportunities are therapeutic for inmates.[121] Courts have not ruled that inmates have a right to any educational opportunities they may choose although some courts have ruled that inmates do not have a right to a free college education.[122] In the past, the lack of educational or work opportunities, combined with an absence of other programs, has been cited by courts as evidence that the overall prison system does not meet minimum constitutional requirements. In 1991, however, the Court ruled that to prevail on allegations of unconstitutional conditions within the prison, inmates must show deliberate indifference on the part of prison officials.

Inmates may be paid for their work but compensation is not mandatory. A 1990 federal court noted that compelling an inmate to work without pay is not unconstitutional. The Thirteenth Amendment specifically allows involuntary servitude as punishment after conviction of a crime and this court held that "compensating prisoners for work is not a constitutional requirement but, rather, 'is by the grace of the state.'"[123]

13-5 Analysis of Prison Reform

Despite changes in conditions, many jails and prisons remain under federal court orders until specified changes are made. The problems of jail and prison overcrowding and inmate violence are of particular concern and are related to all of the other issues discussed in this chapter.

Case Study 13-7

Ruiz v. Estelle

The overcrowding at TDC exercises a malignant effect on all aspects of inmate life. Personal living space allotted to inmates is severely restricted. Inmates are in the constant presence of others. Although some degree of regimentation and loss of privacy is a normal aspect of life in any prison, the high population density at TDC leaves prisoners with virtually no privacy at any time of the day or night. Crowded two or three to a cell or in closely packed dormitories, inmates sleep with the knowledge that they may be molested or assaulted by their fellows at any time. Their incremental exposure to disease and infection from other inmates in such narrow confinement cannot be avoided. They must urinate and defecate, unscreened, in the presence of others. Inmates in cells must live and sleep inches away from toilets; many in dormitories face the same situation. There is little respite from these conditions, for the salient fact of existence in TDC prisons is that inmates have wholly inadequate opportunities to escape the overcrowding in their living quarters.

Even when they are away from the housing areas, inmates are confronted with the inescapable reality that overcrowding is omnipresent within the prison confines...

13-5a Overcrowding

Today, overcrowding is the main problem faced by prisons and jails. Part of jail overcrowding results from holding those sentenced to prison until space is available. State and federal prison populations rose to a record high 7.4 percent in 1993, or 948,881 inmates. It was estimated that between 18 percent and 29 percent of the nation's facilities were overcrowded at the end of 1993. These figures represent a 12 percent increase in the number of federal inmates.[124] One of the main reasons for the increase in prison inmates in recent years is the increase in persons convicted of drug offenses.[125] In February 1994, thirty-nine states plus the District of Columbia, the Virgin Islands, and Puerto Rico were under federal court orders to reduce prison populations or to remedy other unconstitutional conditions.[126] This trend has continued in recent years.

Research on the effects of overcrowding has been conducted for some years but only recently has attention been given to the serious effects it has on inmates.[127] Federal courts have accepted the position that overcrowding has negative effects on those incarcerated. The excerpt in Case Study 13-7 from the 1980 federal court case involving the Texas prison system (TDC) is an example. In *Ruiz v. Estelle*, nearly every aspect of the TDC operation was found to be unconstitutional and the prison was placed under court order to develop plans for bringing the system into compliance with constitutional standards. Living conditions in Texas prisons have improved in recent years and the system has been removed from monitoring, although overcrowding remains a daily concern. As the case citation indicates, *Ruiz* has a long history.[128]

In the fall of 1990, a federal court ruled that prison overcrowding was so severe that it constituted cruel and unusual punishment at the Pennsylvania State Correctional Institution at Pittsburgh. Inmates were double-bunked in cells built for one person, resulting in such closeness that both could not stand up at the same time and one had to lie on his bed. Inmates were confined to their cells for sixteen to twenty-two hours a day. When they were out they faced violence from other inmates, such as rape. The prison needed plumbing repairs and it housed mice, lice, birds, and bedbugs. The state was told bluntly to clean up its prison.[129]

Most jail and prison problems are related to overcrowding.[130] The most serious consequence is violence, a challenge correctional administrators will continue to face.

13-5b New Court Challenges

Recently, the United States Supreme Court has heard few cases related directly to the rights of inmates. For example, in a case decided on February 26, 2002, *Porter et al. v. Nussle,* the Supreme Court held that the Prison Litigation Reform Act (PLRA) which directs that "no action shall be brought with respect to prison conditions under Section 1983, or any other Federal law, by a prisoner until such administrative remedies as are available are exhausted" applies to all inmate suits. In this case, the Court indicated that it did not matter whether the case involved a procedural issue or a charge of officer brutality, when considering the application of the PLRA. Consequently, Mr. Nussle, a state prison inmate, had to exhaust all internal remedies before seeking the relief of the courts.[131]

In another recent case, *Johnson v. United States,* the United States Supreme Court held that the Sentencing Reform Act of 1984, which replaced most forms of parole with supervised release overseen by the sentencing court, was not applied retroactively. The case involved the court's decision to sentence Mr. Johnson to prison in March, 1994, after he violated two conditions of his release. The court further sentenced Johnson to a twelve month supervised release. Attorneys representing the plaintiff argued that the courts did not cite any authority when ordering Johnson to an additional twelve months of supervised release and in their view, the sentence was being applied in an ***ex post facto*** manner, violating the Ex Post Facto Clause. Despite this, the United States Supreme Court did not accept this argument and declared that the sentence issued to Johnson was not in direct violation of the Ex Post Facto Clause and therefore would stand.[132]

Ex post facto After the fact.

Additional legal issues have recently affected the correctional system and the justice system. International outrage has been expressed as a result of alleged Al-Queda members being held in the United States base in Guantanamo Bay, Cuba. The United States government has not been clear in the status of these suspects, which has led to international protests alleging violations of international laws. This public scrutiny has increased as months have passed since the detainees were originally captured. To this day, no decision has been reached in how to legally process them, giving rise to critics' comments which allege that the United States government is contradicting its tradition of fairness and the process involving well-balanced justice. They claim the detainees have not been offered the basic Constitutional rights afforded to all individuals residing the United States.

Summary

Inmates must retain reasonable opportunities to exercise basic human rights while they are incarcerated. According to the U.S. Supreme Court:

> The continuing guarantee of these substantial rights to prison inmates is testimony to a belief that the way a society treats those who have transgressed against it is evidence of the essential character of that society.[133]

The preceding quote came from a 1984 Supreme Court decision. As noted earlier in this chapter, in 1991 the Court ruled that in order to prevail in lawsuits concerning prison conditions, inmates must prove that prison officials are indifferent to their plight. This new approach makes it more difficult for inmates.

The Supreme Court has made it clear that some rights are forfeited by inmates and that security needs may permit restrictions normally recognized while incarcerated. This chapter surveyed the historical and current approaches to the legal rights of inmates, beginning with a look at the traditional hands-off doctrine, in which federal courts refused to become involved in the daily administration and maintenance of prisons. As a result of recognized abuse of prisoners and the civil rights movement, courts began to abandon the hands-off policy. Courts still defer to prison officials but they no longer tolerate violations of basic rights.

This chapter examined the procedures for filing lawsuits, followed by an overview of the First, Fourth, Eighth, and Fourteenth Amendments of the Constitution. The First Amendment rights of inmates, including the importance of mail and other communication, was discussed. Visitation, religious worship, freedom of assembly and self-government, and access to courts—all rights within the First Amendment—were examined. The chapter discussed the Fourth Amendment right to be free from unreasonable searches and seizures, the Eighth Amendment right to be free from cruel and unusual punishment, and the Fourteenth Amendment rights to due process and equal protection. All of these rights may be restricted if prison officials show it is necessary to maintain a legitimate prison goal such as security and safety.

Many of the problems of incarceration are related to overcrowding and there are two basic ways to solve this problem. More facilities can be built although if they are built and filled, the absence of prison space remains. The second solution is to reduce prison populations. This has been done in some states by enacting statutes that permit governors to declare an emergency situation when notified that the prison population has reached 95 percent (or some other pre-determined figure) of legal capacity. Problems can occur, however, when those released inmates commit new crimes.

This chapter focused on the rights of inmates, but these rights must be viewed in the context of society's needs. One problem with the recognition of inmates' rights is that there is not always public support for the approach, nor is there public support for spending more money on facilities. Inmates who file frivolous lawsuits are finding strong reactions not only from prison officials and the public, but also from judges and Supreme Court justices who are devising ways to reduce these unnecessary appeals. The courts, the public, inmates, and prison officials may all be expected to find a reasonable balance that will permit society to be protected and to exercise its right to punish those who offend without demeaning or degrading inmates.

Notes

1. *Ruffin v. Commonwealth*, 62 Va. 790, 796 (1871).
2. *Wolff v. McDonnell*, 418 U.S. 539 (1974).
3. For a discussion on the law of prisoners' rights, see John W. Palmer, *Constitutional Rights of Prisoners*, 6th ed. (Cincinnati, OH: Anderson, 1999).
4. *Siegel v. Ragen*, 180 F.2d 785, 788 (7th Cir. 1950), cert. denied, 339 U.S. 990 (1950), reh'g denied, 340 U.S. 847 (1950).
5. *Bell v. Wolfish*, 441 U.S. 520 (1979).
6. *Time* (February 9, 1968), p. 14.
7. Murton, Thomas O., *The Dilemma of Prison Reform* (New York: Holt, Rinehart and Winston, 1976).
8. *Holt v. Sarver*, 309 F. Supp. 362 (E.D. Ark. 1970). This case has a long history of remands and reversals leading to the Supreme Court case *Hutto v. Finey*, 437 U.S. 678 (1978), reh'g denied, 439 U.S. 1122 (1979).
9. *Graham v. Richardson*, 313 F. Supp. 34 (D. Ariz. 1970), aff.,d., 403 U.S. 365, 375 (1971).
10. See *O'Lone v. Estate of Shabazz*, 482 U.S. 342 (1987), on remand, 829 F. 2d 32 (3rd Cir. 1987), and on remand, 829 F. 2d 31 (3rd Cir. 1998), superceded by statute as stated in *Allah v. Menei*, 844 F. Supp. 1056 (E.D. pa. 1994).
11. *Turner v. Safley*, 482 U.S. 78 (1987), superceded by statute as stated in *Campos v. Coughlin*, 1994 U.S. Dist LEXIS 5721 (S.D.N.Y. 3 May 1994).
12. *Turner v. Safley.*
13. *Turner v. Safley.*
14. *Joint Anti-Fascist Refugee Committee v. McGrath*, 341 U.S. 123, 162-163 (1951), Justice Frankfurter, concurring.
15. *Lowrane v. Achtyl*, 20 F. 3d 529, 537 (2nd Cir. 1994).

16. *Liberta v. Kelly*, 839 F2d 77, 93 (2nd Cir. 1988), cert. denied, 488 U.S. 832 (1988), citations omitted.
17. *McCleskey v. Zant*, 499 U.S. 467 (1991), reh'g. denied, 501 U.S. 1224 (1991), and stay denied sub. nom., 112 S. Ct. 37 (1991), cert. denied sub. nom., 112 S. Ct. 38 (1991).
18. "A Window on the Court," *New York Times*, (May 6, 1992), p.1, referring to the Court's decision in *Keeney v. Tamayo-Reyes*, 112 S. Ct. 1715 (May 1992). The federal statute at issue is codified in the U.S. Code, Title 28, Section 2254 (1994).
19. *O'Neal v. McAninch*, 513 U.S. 432 (1995).
20. U.S. Code, Title 42, Section 1983 (1994).
21. For an extensive analysis of 1983 actions, see H.E. Barrineau III, *Civil Liability in Criminal Justice*, (Cincinnati, OH: Anderson, 1987). For a discussion of the possibilities for suing prison officials in their personal capacities for violation of Section 1983 rights, see David L. Abney and Lynne W. Abney, "Corrections Law: The Fate of Prisoner Damages Actions after *Will v. Michigan Department of State Police*," *Criminal Law Bulletin* 26 (March-April, 1990): 167–171. For a contrary opinion, see Robert Bartels, "Corrections Law: Why Will Won't Destroy Section 1983 Damages Actions," *Criminal Law Bulletin* 27 (January-February, 1991): 59–66. The case in question is *Will v. Michigan Department of State Police*, 491 U.S. 58 (1989).
22. *Estelle v. Gamble*, 429 U.S. 97, 106 (1976), reh'g. denied, 429 U.S. 1066 (1977), and on remand, 554 F. 2d 653 (5th Cir. 1977), reh'g. denied, 59 F. 2d 1217 (5th Cir. 1977), cert. denied, 434 U.S. 974 (1977), citations omitted.
23. *Wilson v. Seiter*, 501 U.S. 294 (1991), footnotes and citations omitted, remanded, 940 F. 2d. 664 (6th Cir. 1991).
24. *Wilson v. Seiter*, 501 U.S. 294 (1991), Justice White, dissenting, remanded, 940 F.2d. 664 (6th Cir. 1991).
25. *Farmer v. Brennan*, 1994 U.S. LEXIS 4274 (1994).
26. *Hudson v. McMillian*, 112 S. Ct. 995 (1992), on remand. 962 F. 2d. 522 (5th Cir. 1992).
27. *Bell v. Wolfish*, 441 U.S. 520, 545 (1979); *Rhodes v. Chapman*, 452 U.S. 337 (1981).
28. *Procunier v. Martinez*, 416 U.S. 396, 413 (1974), overruled in part by *Thornburgh v. Abbott*, 490 U.S. 401 (1989), superceded by statute as stated in *Lawson v. Dugger*, 844 F. Supp. 1538 (S.D. Fla. 1994).
29. *Thornburgh v. Abbott*, 490 U.S. 401 (1989), superceded by statute as stated in *Lawson v. Dugger*, 844 F. Supp. 1538 (S.D. Fla. 1994).
30. *McNamara v. Moody*, 606 F. 2d. 621 (5th Cir. 1979), cert. denied, 447 U.S. 929 (1980).
31. *McNamara v. Moody.*
32. *Bressman v. Farrier*, 825 F. Supp. 231 (N.D. Iowa, 1993).
33. *Travis v. Norris*, 805 F. 2d. 806, 808 (8th Cir. 1986).
34. *Smith v. Delo*, 995 F. ed 827 (1993).
35. *United States v. Stotts*, 925 F. 2d. 83, 85 (4th Cir. 1991), later proceeding sub. nom., 1991 U.S. Dist. LEXIS 15643 (E.D.N.C. 1991).
36. *Bell v. Wolfish*, 441 U.S. 520 (1979).
37. *Turner v. Safley*, 482 U.S. 78 (1987), superceded by statute as stated in *Campos v. Coughlin*, 1994 U.S. Dist. LEXIS 5721 (S.D.N.Y. 3 May 1994).
38. N.Y. CLS Exec., Section 632-a (1994).
39. *In re Berkowitz*, 430 N.Y.S. 2d. 904 (N.Y. Sup. Ct. 1979).
40. *Children of Bedford, Inc. v. Petromelis*, 573 N.E. 2d. 541 (N.Y. 1991), vacated, 112 S. Ct. 859 (1992), and different results reached on reh'g., 79 N.Y. 2d 972 (N.Y. 1992).
41. *Simon and Schuster, Inc. v. Members of the New York State Crime Victims Board*, 724 F. Supp. 170 (S.D.N.Y. 1989), aff'd. sub. nom., 916 F. 2d 777 (2nd Cir. 1990), reversed, 112 S. Ct. 501 (1991).
42. New York CLS Exec. 632-a (1994).
43. "Rolling and Fiancee Can't Profit from Story," *Tallahassee Democrat* (May 19, 1993), p. 2c. The case is *Rolling v. State*, 619 So. 2d. 20 (Fla. Dist. Ct. App. 5th Dist. 1993), corrected, 18 Fla. L. Weekly D 1294 (Fla. Dist. Ct. App. 5th Dist. 1993).
44. National Conference of Commissioners on Uniform State Laws (NCCUSL), Model Sentencing and Corrections Act, Section 40115. Comment (1979) citations omitted.
45. *Martin v. Wainwright*, 525 F. 2d. 983 (5th Cir. 1976).
46. *Doe v. Sparks*, 733 F. Supp. 227 (W.D. Pa. 1990).
47. *Block v. Rutherford*, 468 U.S. 576 (1984).
48. See Laura T. Fishman, *Women at the Wall: A Study of Prisoners' Wives Doing Time on the Outside* (New York: State University of New York Press, 1990); Fishman, "Prisoners and Their Wives: Marital and Domestic Effects of Telephone Contacts and Home Visits," *International Journal of Offender Therapy and Comparative Criminology* 32 (April, 1988): 55–65.
49. "Prisoner Marriages Setting Records," *Tallahassee Democrat* (December 11, 1989), p. 5.
50. *Langone v. Coughlin*, 712 F. Supp. 1061 (N.D.N.Y. 1989).
51. See *McCray v. Sullivan*, 509 F. 2d 1332 (5th Cir. 1975), remanded, 399 F. Supp. 271 (S.D. Ala. 1975), cert. denied, 423 U.S. 859 (1975).
52. *Turner v. Safley*, 482 U.S. 78 (1987), superceded by statute as stated in *Campos v. Coughlin*, 1994, U.S. Dist. LEXIS 5721 (S.D.N.Y. 3 May 1994).
53. See *Goodwin v. Turner*, 908 F. 2d. 1395 (8th Cir. 1990), reh'g. denied in banc, 1990 U.S. App. LEXIS 17169 (8th Cir. 1990).
54. *Pell v. Procunier*, 417 U.S. 817 (1974).
55. *Houchins v. KQED, Inc.*, 438 U.S. 1 (1978).
56. See, for example, a report by the National Council on Crime and Delinquency, "Does Involvement in Religion Help Prisoners Adjust to Prison?" It is available from the Council, 685 Market Street, Suite 620, San Francisco, CA, 94105.
57. *Cruz v. Beto*, 405 U.S. 319, 322, text and n. 2 (1972), appeal after remand, *Cruz v. Estelle*, 497 F. 2d. 496 (5th Cir. 1974).
58. See *Employment Division of Oregon v. Smith*, 494 U.S. 872 (1990), reh'g. denied, 496 U.S. 913 (1990), remanded, 799 p. 2d. 148 (Ore. 1991).
59. See, for example, *O'Lone v. Estate of Shabazz*, 482 U.S. 342 (1987), and on remand, sub. nom., 829 F. 2d. 32 (3rd Cir. 1987), and on remand, sub. nom., 839 F.2d. 32 (3rd Cir. 1987), superceded by statute as stated in *Allah v. Menei*, 844 F. Supp. 1056 (E.D. pa. 1994).
60. See David L. Abney, "Our Daily Bread—Prisoners' Rights to a Religious Diet," *Case and Comment* 90 (March-April, 1985): 28–38.
61. *LaFevers v. Saffle*, 936 F. 2d. 1117 (10th Cir. 1991).
62. *Scott v. Mississippi Department of Corrections*, 961 F. 2d 77 (5th Cir. 1992).
63. *Mark v. Nix*, 983 F. 2d. 138 (8th Cir. 1993), reh'g. denied, 1993 U.S. LEXIS 2409 (8th Cir. 15 February, 1993).
64. See "Religious Freedom Act Worries AGs," *American Bar Association* 80 (February, 1994): 20. The Act is codified at U.S. Code, Title 42, Sections 200bb et seq. (1994).
65. *Jones v. North Carolina Prisoner's Union, Inc.*, 433 U.S. 119, 132 (1977).
66. *Ex Parte Hull*, 312 U.S. 546 (1941), reh'g. denied, 312 U.S. 716 (1941).
67. *Johnson v. Avery*, 393 U.S. 483 (1969). For a discussion of jailhouse lawyers, see Dragan Milovanovic, "Jailhouse Lawyers and Jailhouse Lawyering," *International Journal of the Sociology of Law* 16 (November, 1988): 455–475.
68. See, for example, "His Own Case Was Futile, So He Now Works for Others," *The Miami Herald*, (November 19, 1989), p.4B.
69. *Bounds v. Smith*, 430 U.S. 817, 821, 828, 831 (1977), citations omitted.
70. See *Blake v. Berman*, 877 F. 2d 145 (1st Cir. 1989).
71. *Casey v. Lewis*, 834 F. Supp. 1553 (D. Ariz. 1992), later proceedings, 834 F. Supp. 1553 (D. Ariz. 1993), 834 F. Supp. 1569 (1993), 834 F. Supp. 1009 (D. Ariz. 1993).
72. *Peterkin v. Jeffes*, 661 F. Supp. 895 (E.D. Pa. 1987), aff'd. in part and vacated in part, 855 F. 2d. 1021 (3rd Cir. 1988), on remand, 1989 U.S. Dist. LEXIS 13828 (E.D. Pa. 1989), later proceedings, 953 F. 2d 1380 (3rd Cir. 1992).
73. See *Casey v. Lewis*, 834 F. Supp. 1553 (D. Ariz. 1992); later proceedings, 834 F. Supp. 1477 (D. Ariz. 1993); 834 F. Supp. 1569 (D. Ariz. 1993); 837 F. Supp. 1009 (D. Ariz. 1993).

74. See *Knop v. Johnson,* 977 F. 2d 996 (6th Cir. 1992), cert. denied sub. nom., 113 S. Ct. 1415 (1993), and cost/fees proceeding sub. nom., 1994 U.S. Dist. LEXIS 867 (W.D. Mich. 7 Jan. 1994), reversing a lower court holding that prison officials must provide either attorneys or paralegals for inmates.
75. *Knop v. Johnson,* 977 F. 2d 966 (6th Cir. 1992), cert. denied sub. nom., 113 S. Ct. 1415 (1993).
76. *Prisoners' Legal Association v. Roberson,* 822 F. Supp. 185 (D.N.J. 1993).
77. *Kaiser v. Sacramento County,* 780 F. Supp. 1309 (E.D. Cal. 1991).
78. *Murray v. Giarratano,* 492 U.S. 1 (1989). See also *Douglas v. California,* 372 U.S. 353 (1963), reh'g. denied, 373 U.S. 905 (1963); and *Griffin v. Illinois,* 351 U.S. 12 (1956), reh'g. denied, 351 U.S. 958 (1956).
79. *Glover v. Johnson,* 1994 U.S. Dist. LEXIS 5999 (E.D. Mich. 1994). The Supreme Court case concerning the right of parenthood is *Meyer v. Nebraska,* 262 U.S. 390 (1923).
80. *Knop v. Johnson,* 977 F. 2d. 996 (6th Cir. 1992), cert. denied sub. nom., 113 S. Ct. 1415 (1993).
81. *Wolff v. McDonnell,* 418 U.S. 539 (1974).
82. *Knop v. Johnson,* 685 F. Supp. 636 (W.D. Mich. 1988), cert. denied sub. com., 713 S. Ct. 1415 (1993).
83. "Judge Awards $1.48 Million to Lawyers in Michigan Prison Case," *Criminal Justice Newsletter* 20, (April 17, 1989): 6.
84. "Flood of Prisoner Rights Suits Brings Effort to Limit Filings," *New York Times,* (March 21, 1994), p. 1.
85. *Hudson v. Palmer,* 468 U.S. 517 (1984), citation omitted, remanded, *Palmer v. Hudson,* 744 F. 2d. 22 (4th Cir. 1984).
86. *Block v. Rutherford,* 468 U.S. 576 (1984).
87. *Bell v. Wolfish,* 441 U.S. 520 (1979).
88. See *Covino v. Patrissi,* 967 F. 2d. 73 (2nd. Cir. 1992).
89. *State v. Palmer,* 751 P.2d. 975, 976, 977 (Ariz, App. 1987), footnotes and citations omitted.
90. See, for example, *Covino v. Patrissi,* 967 F. 2d. 73 (2nd Cir. 1992).
91. See *Hunter v. Auger,* 672 F. 2d. 668 (8th Cir. 1982); and *Marriot v. Smith,* 931 F. 2d. 517, reh'g en banc denied, 1991 U.S. App. LEXIS 13199 (8th Cir. 1991).
92. See *Marriott v. Smith,* 931 F. 2d. 517 (8th Cir. 1991), reh'g. en banc denied, 1991 U.S. App. LEXIS 13199 (8th Cir. 1991).
93. *Giles v. Ackerman,* 746 F. 2d. 614 (9th Cir. 1984), cert. denied, 471 U.S. 1053 (1985).
94. *Turner v. Safley,* 482 U.S. 78 (1987).
95. See *Tim v. Gunter,* 917 F. 2d. 1093 (8th Cir. 1990). cert. denied, 501 U.S. 1209 (1991) (permissible for female officers to conduct pat-down search on male inmates).
96. *Tim v. Gunter,* 917 F. 2d. 1093 (8th Cir. 1990), cert. denied, 501 U.S. 1209 (1991), Judge Bright dissenting.
97. For a discussion of the case, see the following: Doretha M. Van Slyke, Note. "*Hudson v. McMillian,* and Prisoners' Rights: The Court Giveth and the Court Taketh Away," *American University Law Review* 42 (1993):1727–1760; Dale E. Butler, Comment. "Cruel and Unusual Punishment Takes One Step Forward, Two Steps Back," *Denver University Law Review* 70 (1993): 393–412; and Donald H. Wallace, "The Eighth Amendment and Prison Deprivations: Historical Revisions," *Criminal Law Bulletin* 30 (January-February, 1994): 5–29.
98. *Hickey v. Reeder,* 12 F. 3d. 754 (8th Cir. 1993), reh'g. denied, 1994 U.S. App. LEXIS 1614 (8th Cir. 1 Feb. 1994).
99. *Estelle v. Gamble,* 429 U.S. 97 (1976), reh'g. denied, 429 U.S. 1066 (1977), remanded, 554 F 2d. 653 (5th Cir. 1977), cert. denied, 434 U.S. 974 (1977).
100. *Whitley v. Albers,* 475 U.S. 312, 313 (1986), appeal after remand, 788 F. 2d. 650 (9th Cir. 1986). See also *Ruark v. Drury,* 21 F. 3d 213 (8th Cir. 1994).
101. *Ruiz v. Estelle,* 679 F. 2d. 1115 (5th Cir. 1982), amended in part, vacated in part, reh'g. denied in part, 688 F. 2d 266 (5th Cir. 1982), cert. denied, 460 U.S. 1042 (1983), appeal after remand sub. nom., 724 F. 2d. 1149 (5th Cir. 1984), later proceedings sub. nom., 661 F. Supp. 112 (S. D. Tex. 1986); 981 F. 2d. 1256 (5th Cir. 1992).
102. "Settlement Ends Federal Control of Texas Prisons," *New York Times,* (December 13, 1992), p. 17. For an analysis of the Texas prison system, see Steve J. Martin and Sheldon Ekland-Olson, *Texas Prisons: The Walls Came Tumbling Down* (Austin: Texas Monthly Press, 1987).
103. *Estelle v. Gamble,* 429 U.S. 97 (1976), reh'g. denied, 429 U.S. 1066 (1977), remanded, 554 F. 2d 653 (5th Cir. 1977). The 1991 case is *Wilson v. Seiter,* 501 U.S. 294 (1991), remanded, 940 F. 2d. 664 (6th Cir. 1991).
104. "Court Backs Policy to Separate Inmates with the AIDS virus," *The New York Times,* (September 20, 1991), p. 4. See *Harris v. Thigpen,* 941 F. 2d. 1495 (11th Cir. 1991).
105. *Moore v. Mabus,* 976 F. 2d 268 (5th Cir. 1992).
106. *Nolley v. County* of Erie, 776 F. Supp. 715 (W.D.N.Y. 1991), supplemental opinion, 802 F. Supp. 898 (W.D.N.Y. 1992), set aside, on reconsideration, remanded, 798 F. Supp. 123 (W.D.N.Y. 1992).
107. "Prisons and Jails Integrating More HIV-Positive Inmates," *Criminal Justice Newsletter,* 25 (March 1, 1994): 6.
108. For a discussion see "California Inmates Win Better Prison AIDS Care," *The New York Times,* (January 25, 1993), p. 7.
109. *Casey v. Lewis,* 834 F. Supp. 1553 (D.Ariz. 1992), later proceedings, 834 F. Supp. 1477 (D. Ariz. 1993), 834 F. Supp. 1569 (D. Ariz. 1993), 837 F. Supp. 1009 (D. Ariz. 1993). For a discussion of female inmates and AIDS, see David K Marcus and Roger Bibace, "A Developmental Analysis of Female Prisoners' Conceptions of AIDS," *Criminal Justice and Behavior* 20 (September, 1993): 249–253.
110. *Doe v. Coughlin,* 523 N.Y.S. 2d. 782 (N.Y.Ct. App. 1987), reargument denied, 70 N.Y. 2d. 1002 (1988), cert. denied, 488 U.S. 879 (1988).
111. *Doughty v. Board of County Commissioners for the County of Weld,* 731 F. Supp. 423 (D. Colo., 1989).
112. See, for example, *McKinney v. Anderson,* 959 F. 2d. 853 (9th Cir. 1992), on remand of 924 F. 2d. 1500 (9th Cir. 1991), aff'd., remanded, 113 S. Ct. 2475 (1993), on remand, remanded, 5 F. 3d. 365 (9th Cir. 1993), holding that under some circumstances smoke within a prison may constitute cruel and unusual punishment.
113. *Olim v. Wakinekona,* 461 U.S. 238 (1983), remanded, 716 F. 2d. 1279 (9th Cir. 1983).
114. *Hewitt v. Helms,* 459 U.S. 460 (1983), remanded, 712 F. 2d. 48 (3rd Cir. 1983).
115. *Wolff v. McDonnell,* 418 U.S. 539 (1974).
116. *Superintendent, Massachusetts Correctional Institution v. Hill,* 472 U.S. 445 (1985).
117. *Ponte v. Real,* 471 U.S. 491 (1985), remanded sub. nom., 482 N.E. 2d, 1188 (Mass. 1985).
118. *Jails in America: An Overview of Issues* (Laurel, MD: American Correctional Association in Cooperation with the National Coalition for Jail Reform, 1985), p. 24.
119. For a general discussion, see Charlotte A. Nesbitt, "Female Offenders: A Changing Population, *Corrections Today* 48 (February, 1986): 76–80.
120. *Klinger v. Nebraska Dept. of Correctional Services,* 824 F. Supp. 1374 (D. Neb. 1993).
121. See Hans Toch, "Regenerating Prisoners Through Education," *Federal Probation* 51 (September, 1987): 61–66.
122. See *Hernandez v. Johnston,* 833 F. 2d. 1316 (9th Cir. 1987).
123. *Murray v. Mississippi Department of Corrections,* 911 F. 2d. 1167 (5th Cir. 1990), cert. denied, 111 S. Ct. 760 (1991).
124. Bureau of Justice Statistics, *Prisoners in 1993* (Washington, DC: U.S. Department of Justice, 1994), p. 1.
125. See "Drug Crimes Push Record Prison Population," *The New York Times,* (May 10, 1993), p. 16.
126. *Status Report: The Courts and the Prisons* (Washington, DC: National Prison Project, 1994), as cited in "Status Report on Prison Lawsuits," Criminal Justice Newsletter 25 (February 15, 1994): 8.
127. For more information on the effects of jail and prison overcrowding, see Michael S. Vaughn, "Listening to the Experts: A National Study of Correctional Administrators' Responses to Prison Overcrowding," *Criminal Justice Review* 18 (Spring, 1993): 12–25.

128. *Ruiz v. Estelle,* 503 F. Supp. 1265 (S.D. Tex. 1980), aff'd. in part, and vacated in part, modified in part, appeal dismissed in part, 679 F. 2d 1115 (5th Cir. 1982), amended in part, vacated in part, 688 F. 2d. 266 (5th Cir. 1982), cert. denied, 460 U.S. 1042 (1983), appeal after remand, sub. nom, 724 F 2d 1149 (5th Cir. 1984), later proceedings sub. nom., 661 F. Supp. 112 (S.D. Tex. 1986); 981 F. 2d 1256 (5th Cir. 1992).
129. *Tillery v. Owens,* 719 F. Supp. 1256 (W.D. Pa. 1989), aff'd., 907 F. 2d. 418 (3rd Cir. 1990), cert. denied sub. nom., 112 S.Ct. 343 (1991), and aff'd. w/o opinion, 993 F. 2d. 879 (3rd Cir. 1993).
130. For more detailed analyses of jail and prison overcrowding and their effects, see Paul B. Paulus, *Prison Crowding: A Psychological Perspective* (New York: Springer-Verlag, 1988).
131. *Porter et al. v. Nussle,* No. 00853, Argued January 14, 2002—Decided February 26, 2002.
132. *Johnson v. United States,* No. 99-5153, Argued February 22, 2000—Decided May 15, 2000.
133. *Hudson v. Palmer,* 468 U.S. 517, 523, 525, (1984), on remand, 744 F. 2d. 22 (4th Cir. 1984).

Chapter 14

The Juvenile Offender

Outline

Key Terms

status offenders
parens patriae
beyond a reasonable doubt
double jeopardy
gangs
obedience/conformity model
reeducation/development model
treatment model

For the past several years, the images of school children running for their lives in the presence of a gunman has been a popular image in the media. In Jonesboro, Arkansas, two adolescents, ages eleven and thirteen, pulled the school fire alarm and began shooting at classmates and teachers as they exited the school. Several individuals, including a schoolteacher, died. A few days later, in Springfield, Oregon, a young man began shooting at random in his school cafeteria. This incident left two students dead and a few others wounded. In 1999, two students opened fire on their peers at Columbine High School in Littleton, Colorado. The death toll reached fifteen, including the two offenders who committed suicide after the incident.[1]

The year 1979 was officially designated the "International Year of the Child," focusing on the needs and rights of children. The year was also characterized by continually rising rates of crime among juveniles and the involvement of children in violent crimes. Data made available in the late 1970s led a popular magazine writer to conclude, "It would appear we have met the enemy—and he is our child."[2] Many people at that time explained juvenile crime by criticizing the juvenile court system, called by some the "failed system." According to one article, the juvenile justice system, a sieve through which most of these kids come and go with neither punishment nor rehabilitation, has become a big part of the problem.[3]

Today, the juvenile courts are under attack by conservatives who argue that juveniles must be punished as adults. Texas, who leads the nation in the number of juvenile offenders currently on death row, has been at the center of this debate. If the state of Texas "were a nation it would lead the world in executions of those convicted of crimes committed when they were younger than eighteen years old".[4] Many have claimed that recent changes in the juvenile justice system have been caused by the nature and extent of the juvenile crime problem.

The discussions in this chapter focus on juveniles who are considered delinquent or criminal, as it has been alleged that they have violated the criminal law or were engaged in noncriminal behaviors considered serious enough for juvenile court adjudication. Juvenile courts today have jurisdiction over those who run away from home, are considered incorrigible by their parents, and are truant from school. Such acts may bring juveniles under the jurisdiction of the juvenile court and are called status offenses. The juveniles who engage in these offenses are called status offenders. The term status offender includes juveniles who are brought under the jurisdiction of the juvenile court due to their neglect or dependency. These juveniles are not the focus of this chapter.

Status offenders
A juvenile who commits an offense that would not be considered a crime if it had been committed by an adult.

In earlier chapters, the elements of due process as they apply to criminal trials were discussed. The role of the police, and prosecuting and defense attorneys, as well as the function of the criminal courts, were analyzed. All of those procedures and structures were developed to protect the rights of adult defendants and to provide them with the opportunity for a fair trial. In the late 1800s, this system of criminal justice was considered too harsh for some special cases, especially those of juveniles.[5] As a result, a special system was created for these cases. The following section focuses on the system designed for the special handling of juveniles.

14-1 Background and History

The first recorded discussion of juvenile problems dates back 3,700 years,[6] but the first juvenile code was the Biblical code. It stated that stubborn and rebellious children could be taken by their parents into the city to be stoned to death by the city's elders. Other provisions allowed the death sentence for children who cursed or killed their parents. The philosophy of punishment was "an eye for an eye, tooth for tooth, hand for hand, foot for foot, burning for burning, wound for wound, stripe for stripe."[7] No distinctions were made between punishment for acts committed by children and those committed by adults.

In England, under the common law, a child under seven was considered incapable of committing a crime. A child between seven and fourteen years was presumed incapable, but that was a rebuttable presumption. At the age of seven, a child could be found guilty of a felony and punished as an adult. A child over age fourteen was treated as an adult. A 1961 study noted that during the prior 100 years in England, children were hanged for offenses that would now be considered trivial. "And at a somewhat earlier period, there were 200 capital offenses with the law making little or no distinction between child and adult offenders."[8]

In colonial America, children were treated like adults. In the nineteenth century, a thirteen year-old boy was hanged in New Jersey for an alleged homicide he had committed. Children who escaped the death penalty often faced corporal punishment and deprivation. In the United States before 1899, "boys and girls were sadistically punished by private and public floggings, deprived food, lodged in dungeons and cells along with adults, forced to do cruelly hard labor, and otherwise abused and neglected."[9]

The first attempt at specialized treatment for children occurred in the English court of chancery. It applied the doctrine of ***parens patriae***, in which the sovereign had the power to oversee any children in his kingdom who might be neglected or abused by their parents. The court exercised this duty only when it was thought necessary for the welfare of the child, and that rarely occurred. Protection of society and punishment of parents were not considered sufficient reasons to invoke the power. Both in the English system and the system adopted during the early period of American history, the doctrine applied only to chil-

Parens patriae
The historical doctrine of the states' power to serve as the ultimate parent of the child.

dren who were in need of supervision or help because of the actions of their parents or guardians—not because the children themselves were delinquent. The extension to the juvenile court of jurisdiction over delinquent children was an innovation adopted in Illinois in 1899.[10]

Before 1899, special institutions existed that were developed to segregate juvenile delinquents from other criminals. The New York House of Refuge, established in 1824, was the first of these juvenile institutions and served as a model for others. These institutions were an improvement over the previous conditions, but they handled children after they committed crimes and placed little emphasis on prevention and rehabilitation. They represented society's desire to remove the delinquents from sight, for they were prisons that emphasized hard work and discipline. They did, however, eliminate some of the evils of imprisoning children with adult criminals.

By the middle 1800s, the United States established probation for juveniles and built separate detention facilities for them. The 1800s also saw the evolution of progressive ideas in the care and treatment of dependent and neglected children. The creation of protective societies, such as the Society for the Prevention of Cruelty to Children developed in New York in 1875, paved the way for the juvenile court. Illinois established the first juvenile court in 1899. Other states quickly followed and by 1925, all but two states had a juvenile court system. All states had a juvenile code in place by 1945.

The growing dissatisfaction with the treatment of juveniles and the increasing emphasis on humanitarianism encouraged reformers to press their advocacy of a system that would emphasize rehabilitation rather than punishment. Their focus was on individualized handling and treatment of the offender. Although in theory, the treatment of offenders seems to be the goal of today's juvenile courts, in practice, the advocacy for punishment is increasing.

14-2 The Juvenile Court

Before a court can dispense individualized treatment, it must acquire jurisdiction over the child. The philosophy of the juvenile court is based on the doctrine of *parens patriae.* Under this doctrine, the state delegates the care of children to the parents. If parents violate that trust in their guardianship, the state may take custody of the child.

14-2a Doctrine of *Parens Patriae*

The doctrine of *parens patriae* became firmly established in early case law. A Pennsylvania court ruled that although parents are usually the best guardians of their children, their right to rear them could be surrendered. If parents neglect their responsibility, the public has an interest in protecting their children.

The establishment of the juvenile court in 1899 extended the doctrine of *parens patriae* to delinquent children. The doctrine assumes that the state is "the ultimate parent of the child," and the proceeding of the juvenile court was to be one in which the state "reaches out its arm in a kindly way and provides for the protection of its children."[11] Figure 14-1 illustrates today's procedures for the handling of a juvenile offender case.

14-2b Contrast with Criminal Court

The juvenile court, with its emphasis on individualized treatment, was originally designed as a social agency or clinic. It was to be a social institution designed to protect and rehabilitate the child, not a court designed to determine the child's guilt. The purpose of the juvenile court was to protect the child from the stigma associated with the proceedings in a criminal court. Even the vocabulary of the courts differed. Children would not be arrested, but summoned. They would not

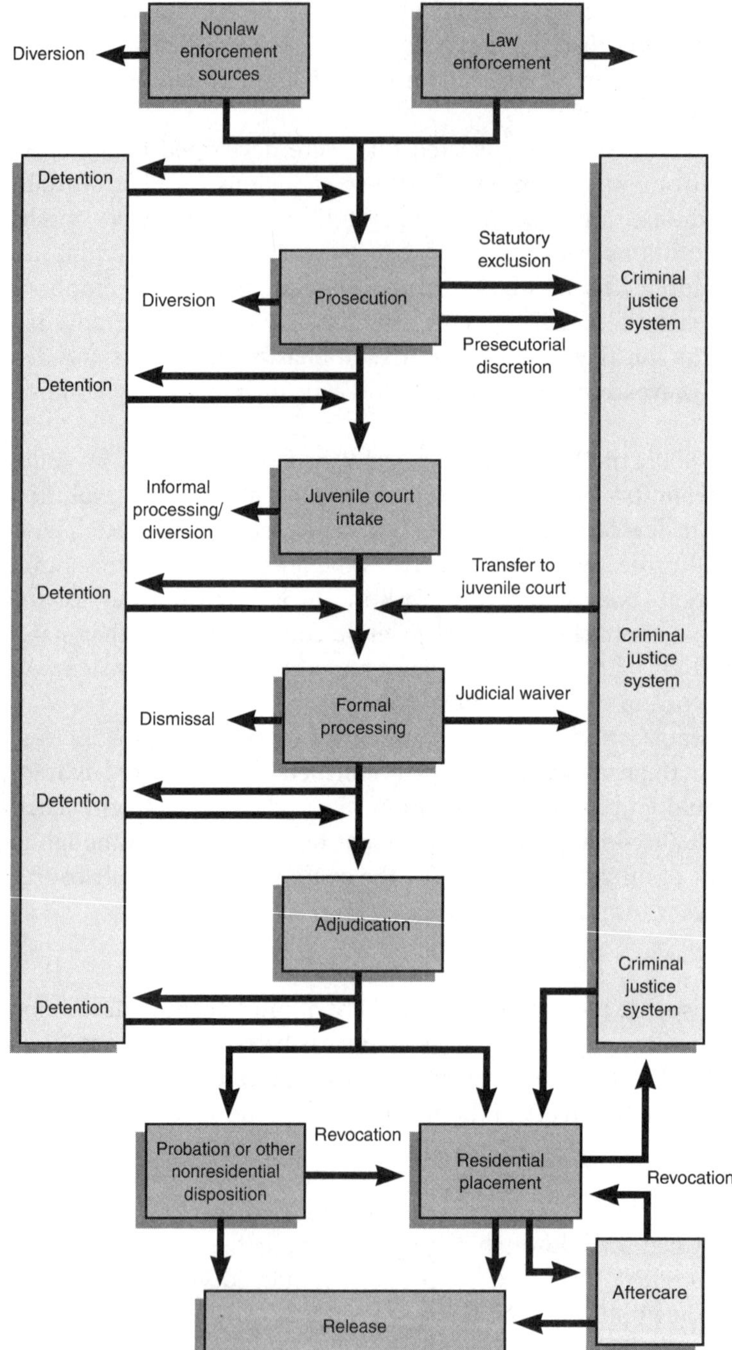

Figure 14-1
The Stages of Delinquency Case Processing in the American Juvenile Justice System

Note: This chart gives a simplified view of case-flow through the juvenile justice system. Procedures vary among jurisdictions. The weights of the lines are not intended to show the actual size of caseloads.

Source: Howard Snyder et al., *Juvenile Offenders and Victims: 1996 Update on Violence* (Washington, D.C.: U.S. Department of Justice, 1996), p. 76.

be indicted, but a petition would be filed on their behalf. If detention was necessary, children would be detained in facilities separate from adults but not in jails. They would not have a trial, but a hearing, which would be private and in which juries, defense counsel, and prosecuting attorneys would rarely be used. The hearing would be informal and judges would act as parents disciplining their children with love and affection.

Juveniles would not be sentenced in the criminal court. After the hearing they would be adjudicated. A disposition would be made only after a careful study of the juvenile's background and potential, and the decision would reflect the best interests of the child. The relationship between the child and the judge was seen as that of a counselor-patient or doctor-patient relationship.

The juvenile court hearing differed from the criminal court in theory as well. Rules of evidence that characterize the criminal court were not applied to the juvenile court. For example, the juvenile did not have the right to cross-examine his or her accusers. There was no need for that safeguard since everyone was assumed to be acting in the best interests of the child. Hearsay evidence, which would be excluded from the criminal court, would be admitted in the juvenile court. Judges needed all the information they could attain for an adequate disposition of the case and it was not thought that the information might be false. The emphasis in the juvenile court was not on what the child did but on what the child was. The court was concerned with a diagnosis that would enable the judge to save the child through proper treatment.

The juvenile court was to be treatment, not punishment, oriented. The purpose of the court was to prevent children from becoming criminals by catching them in the budding stages and giving them the love and protection that would be provided by parents who believed their children are salvageable.

The early advocates of the juvenile court believed that law and humanitarianism were not sufficient for treatment of the juvenile. They expected the court to rely heavily on the findings of the physical and social sciences. Research findings were to be applied scientifically in the adjudication and disposition of juveniles. This was the first attempt to utilize the social sciences in law. The failure of the social sciences to develop sufficient research to implement this philosophy adequately, the failure of the legal profession to recognize and accept those findings that would be of assistance, and the abuse of discretion by correctional officials are perhaps responsible for the tensions that have developed over the lack of procedural safeguards in the juvenile court.

14-2c Procedural Safeguards

Because the juvenile court acted as a wise parent, "the historic leaders of the juvenile court movement firmly believed that formal procedure . . . [would be] at best, excess baggage and, at worse, positively harmful."[12] The procedural safeguards of the criminal court were not applied. The founders believed that justice is cold and often cruel. It is based on the concept of punishment and the founders wanted more for the juvenile offender. They believed that the system they devised would go beyond justice and not give children what they deserved, but what was best for them in the way of treatment and rehabilitation. The benevolent attitude has been questioned by some social scientists. Anthony Platt, who refers to the early proponents of the juvenile court as the child savers, takes the position that the juvenile court diminished the civil liberties and privacy of juveniles and that the child-saving movement was promoted by the middle class to support its own interests.[13] Some scholars claimed that this approach was meant to safeguard supraconstitutional rights and children were given more rights than those given to adults in criminal court. The juvenile court did not take away rights, it added to them. It gave greater protection to children than they could get in the criminal court.[14]

A. W. Pisciotta notes the less than benevolent attitude of the court toward females and African-Americans. In the early 1800s, African-American youths were often held in adult facilities while white youths were sent to juvenile residential institutions. These African-American children received little education or other specialized programming. Females were deprived as well. Their programming was directed at reforming their religious and moral values and their domestic skills.[15]

Case Study 14-1

Commonwealth v. Fisher[16]

[The juvenile court]...is not for the punishment of offenders but for the salvation of children...No child under the age of 16 is excluded from its beneficent provisions. Its protecting arm is for all who have not attained that age and who may need its protection. It is for all children of the same class...

To save a child from becoming a criminal, or from continuing in a career of crime, to end in maturer years in public punishment and disgrace, the Legislature surely may provide for the salvation of such a child, if its parents or guardian be unable or unwilling to do so, by bringing it into one of the courts of the state without any process at all, for the purpose of subjecting it to the state's guardianship and protection...

It is for their welfare and that of the community at large...Every statute that is designed to give protection, care, and training to children, as a needed substitute for parental duty, is but a recognition of the duty of the state, as the legitimate guardian and protector of children where other guardianship fails.

The courts emphasized that the procedural safeguards of the criminal court were set aside in the interest of treatment and the welfare of the child because they were incompatible with those interests. Since the state, in recognizing its duty as parent, was helping and not punishing the child, no constitutional rights were violated. The child is legally a ward of the state and has no constitutional rights that the courts must respect. This philosophy of the juvenile court was summed up in an early court decision, part of which appears in Case Study 14-1. Note the clear indication that the juvenile court was perceived as an institution far more humane than the adult criminal court, always acting in the best interests of the child.

14-2d The Reality of the Juvenile Court System

The dream of the rehabilitative ideal of the founders of the juvenile court has not been realized. Although "the rhetoric of the juvenile court movements speaks of assistance, treatment, friendly concern; the reality reflects the hardness of the criminal process."[17] In the frank words of former Supreme Court Justice Abe Fortas, "There may be grounds for concern that the child received the worst of both worlds: that he gets neither the protections accorded to adults nor the solicitous care and regenerative treatment postulated for children."[18]

In reality, the juvenile often receives punishment, not treatment. Being processed through the juvenile court rather than the criminal court does not remove the stigma of being labeled a criminal. "Despite all protestations to the contrary, the adjudication of delinquency carries with it a social stigma. This court can take judicial notice that in common parlance 'juvenile delinquent' is a term of opprobrium and it is not society's accolade bestowed on the successfully rehabilitated."[19] The delinquent label that is often given to juvenile offenders is most prevalent in instances when the former offender is attempting a new or different lifestyle. When the juvenile tries to seek employment, he or she often encounters questions pertaining to past behavior (e.g., number of times arrested, convicted, and/or sentenced). It is often difficult to find a job when the offender answers positively to the questions mentioned. This labeling also extends to loan applications and organization membership requests.[20]

Adjudication as a juvenile delinquent may destroy a child's reputation in his or her community and "the stigma of conviction will reflect upon him for life."[21] That label is particularly tragic since the juveniles may have been adjudicated for a relatively minor offense such as truancy or insubordination. But for a child,

"Any brush with the law can leave indelible blots on. . .[his] record and life course, and cannot be treated lightly."[22]

In reality, the juvenile did not receive "more than justice," as the juvenile court founders promised. In many cases, the state failed to act in the best interests of the child with the result that "American juveniles . . . exchanged the precious heritage of individual freedom under law for the tyranny of state intervention whenever the state considers that its interests are affected."[23]

In 1967, the U.S. Supreme Court declared that changes had to take place in the juvenile court system. Other cases followed that historic decision and extended to juveniles many of the constitutional protections already recognized for adults.

In re Gault

In re Gault was the first juvenile case from a state court to be heard by the United States Supreme Court. The events that led to *Gault* began on June 8, 1964, when fifteen-year-old Gerald Gault and a friend were taken into custody in Arizona. A Mrs. Cook had complained that the boys were making lewd phone calls to her. Gault's parents were not notified that their son had been arrested. When they returned home from work that evening and found that Gerald was not there, they sent his brother to look for him and eventually discovered that he was in custody. The parents were never shown the petition that was filed the next day. At the first hearing, attended by Gerald and his mother, Mrs. Cook did not testify and no written record was made of the proceedings. At the second hearing, Mrs. Gault asked for Mrs. Cook to appear but the judge said that would not be necessary. The judge's decision was to commit Gerald to the State Industrial School until his age of majority (i.e., eighteen years old).

When the judge was asked on what basis he adjudicated Gerald delinquent, he said he was not sure of the exact section of the code. The section of the Arizona Criminal Code that escaped his memory defined a misdemeanant as a person who "in the presence or hearing of any woman or child. . . uses vulgar, abusive, or obscene language." For this offense, a fifteen year-old boy was committed to a state institution until his majority. The maximum legal penalty for an adult was a fine of $5 to $50 or imprisonment for a maximum of two months. An adult would be afforded due process at his trial but a juvenile was not so entitled.

The judge also said, based on his recollection, that Gerald had been before the juvenile court in the past, that Gerald was "habitually involved in immoral matters." He had once stolen a baseball glove and then refused to tell the police department the truth about the incident. He had also admitted to making nuisance phone calls although there had been no adjudication of delinquency in those incidents.

The case was appealed to the U.S. Supreme Court, which reversed the decision. Justice Fortas delivered the opinion for the majority. Counsel had raised six basic rights: notice of charges, right to counsel, right to confrontation and cross-examination, privilege against self-incrimination, right to a transcript, and right to appellate review. The Supreme Court ruled only on the first four of these issues. The court limited the extension of procedural safeguards in the juvenile court to those proceedings which might result in the commitment of youths to an institution in which their freedom would be curtailed.

Justice Fortas reviewed the philosophy of the juvenile court, noting that the founders were acting in what they thought to be a humanitarian and benevolent fashion. But, he said, the reality of the juvenile court is that the dream has not materialized. Lack of procedural safeguards has in many instances resulted in an adjudication of delinquency based on inaccurate facts. What was designed to be a court that would always act in the best interests of the child had become an institution that was often arbitrary and unfair. It was therefore necessary to inject some procedural safeguards into the juvenile court. The Supreme Court in *Gault* did not answer many questions regarding elements of due process and juveniles. Lower courts have considered most of these issues.

Kent v. United States

The *Kent* case was decided a year before *Gault.* Although it was decided by the U.S. Supreme Court and carried some weight with other courts, it dealt with the interpretation of a Washington, D.C., statute and not a federal constitutional issue.

Kent, a sixteen year old, was arrested and charged with rape, housebreaking, and robbery. In accordance with a Washington, D.C. statute, jurisdiction over Kent was waived from the juvenile to the criminal court. Kent's requests to see his social service file and to have a hearing on the waiver issue were denied despite the fact that the statute required a full investigation prior to waiver. In denying Kent's requests, the judge did not offer any findings of fact or state any reasons for the transfer.

Kent was indicted by a grand jury and tried in criminal court. He was found not guilty by reason of insanity on the rape charge but guilty of the other charges. He received a total of thirty to ninety years in prison. His case was affirmed on its first appeal, but the U.S. Supreme Court reversed the decision. The Court acknowledged the doctrine of *parens patriae* and the need for flexibility in juvenile court proceedings, but emphasized the need for procedural protections when acts with such serious consequences are made. The Court concluded that "there may be grounds for concern that the child receives the worst of both worlds, that he gets neither the protection accorded to adults nor the solicitous care and regenerative treatment postulated for children."[24]

14-2e Other Supreme Court Decisions

Not all aspects of procedural process have been extended to juveniles by the Court but a few decisions have extended some of the basic rights of juvenile defendants. In *In re Winship,* the Court extended the standard of proof of **beyond a reasonable doubt** to juvenile court cases.[25] The Court has refused to extend the right to a trial by jury to juveniles, reasoning that to do so might put an end to "what has been the idealistic prospect of an intimate, informal protective proceeding."[26] The Court recognized the freedom of states to provide jury trials for juveniles and some have done so. As of 1987, twelve states granted the right to trial by jury for juveniles.[27]

Beyond a reasonable doubt Part of jury instructions in trials, in which the jurors are told that they can only find the defendant guilty if they are convinced "beyond a reasonable doubt" of his or her guilt. Thus, a juror (or judge sitting without a jury) must be convinced of guilt of a crime (or the degree of crime, as murder instead of manslaughter).

Double jeopardy Prosecuting an individual twice for the same offense; prohibited by the Fifth Amendment of the U.S. Constitution.

In 1974, the Supreme Court considered the issue of **double jeopardy**, which is a second prosecution after a first trial ends in an acquittal for the same offense. The Court ruled that there could not be an adult criminal trial after a juvenile court hearing in which an offender was found to be delinquent. The juvenile has a right to a transfer hearing to determine whether he or she should be tried in adult court before any delinquency hearing is held.[28]

In 1984, the Supreme Court reiterated its commitment to the *parens patriae* doctrine in the juvenile court and refused to rule the New York preventive detention statute for juveniles as invalid. The Court reasoned that preventive detention protects society from dangerous juveniles in addition to protecting those juveniles from themselves. The Court upheld the statute in *Schall v. Martin* because the juveniles were apprehended for serious crimes. They were detained briefly and their detention followed proper procedural safeguards.[29]

Perhaps the most controversial area of concern regarding juveniles is whether they should be subjected to capital punishment. The Supreme Court has considered the issue. In *Eddings v. Oklahoma,* the Court considered the death sentence for Monty Lee Eddings, who was sixteen when he killed an Oklahoma highway patrol officer. The issue was not decided in this case, however. The Court remanded the case for resentencing, noting that mitigating factors had not been considered in the original sentencing. Those factors were considered and Eddings was again sentenced to capital punishment. Before his case reached the U.S. Supreme Court again, however, the Oklahoma Court of Criminal Appeals changed the sentence to life imprisonment.[30]

In *Thomson v. Oklahoma,* the Court reversed the capital sentence of William Wayne Thomson who was fifteen when he committed a heinous capital crime.[31] In 1989, the Court upheld the capital sentences of two youths, ages sixteen and seventeen years. In *Stanford v. Kentucky,* the Court emphasized that whether a punishment is cruel and unusual and thus forbidden by the Eighth Amendment is determined in part by the attitude of society. The Court concluded,

> We discern neither a historical nor a modern societal consensus forbidding the imposition of capital punishment on any person who murders at 16 or 17 years of age. Accordingly, we conclude that such punishment does not offend the Eighth Amendment's prohibition against cruel and unusual punishment.[32]

14-2f Legislative Changes in the Juvenile Court Philosophy

It is clear from some of the Supreme Court decisions that the court does not consider that all elements of due process are constitutionally required in juvenile court hearings. This does not, however, preclude states from passing statutes that require, for example, a trial by jury in juvenile hearings. Some states have enacted statutes changing the sentencing of juveniles. The trend in sentencing juveniles involves the removal of status offenders from the jurisdiction of the juvenile court, harsher sentences for violent and persistent juveniles, and proportionality. A greater emphasis is on tailoring the punishment of the juvenile to the seriousness of the offense committed. The changes have led some to refer to the second revolution in juvenile justice.[33]

The first change, removing status offenders from the jurisdiction of the juvenile court, received impetus from the Juvenile Justice and Delinquency Prevention Act, passed by Congress in 1974 and subsequently amended.[34] The main goad of the act is finding alternatives to incarceration for juveniles, especially status offenders. Before states can receive federal funds, they must meet several requirements, one of which is to "provide within three years after submission of the initial plan that juveniles who are charged with or who have committed offenses that would not be criminal if committed by an adult, or such nonoffenders as dependent or neglected children, shall not be placed in juvenile detention or correctional facilities." States must also provide that neither status offenders nor "juveniles alleged to be or found to be delinquent" may be confined or detained "in any institution in which they have regular contact with adult persons incarcerated because they have been convicted of a crime or are awaiting trial or criminal charges."[35] The proposed juvenile justice standards would remove noncriminal behavior from the jurisdiction of the juvenile court and it is this proposal that has been the most controversial.[36]

One of the most comprehensive legislative changes of the state statutes regarding juveniles took place in the state of Washington in 1977, when the Juvenile Justice Act became effective.[37] That act defines juvenile, youth, and child as "any individual who is under the chronological age of eighteen years and who has not been previously transferred to adult court, or who is over the age of eighteen years but remaining under the jurisdiction of the court as provided [in another section of the Act]." A juvenile offender is "any juvenile who has been found by the juvenile court to have committed an offense." An offense is defined as "an act designated a crime if committed by an adult under the law of this state, under any ordinance of any city or county of this state, under any federal law, or under the law of another state if the act occurred in that state."[38]

14-3 Violent Juveniles and Society's Reaction

According to the Office of Juvenile Justice and Delinquent Prevention, during the period from 1973 through 1988, the number of juvenile arrests for Violent Crime Index offenses (including murder and non-negligent manslaughter, forcible rape, robbery, and aggravated assault) varied with the changing size of the juvenile population. However, in 1989, the juvenile violent crime arrest rate broke out of this historic range. The years between 1988 and 1991 experienced a 38 percent increase in the rate of juvenile arrests for violent crimes. The rate then diminished, with the juvenile arrest rate increasing very little between 1991 and 1992. This rapid growth over a short period moved the juvenile arrest rate for violent crimes in 1992 far above the rate for any other year since the mid-1960s.[39]

In 1997, an estimated 2,838,300 juveniles were arrested in the United States. Of these, the majority were white (71 percent) males (74 percent) between sixteen and seventeen years of age (48 percent). Most juveniles (701,500) were arrested in 1997 for property crimes. Of these, larceny-theft appeared to be the crime that led to most (493,900) arrests. In contrast, in 1997, 123,400 juveniles were arrested for violent crimes.[40]

As the number of violent juveniles has increased and the media and politicians have sensitized the American people to the nature of their crimes, public fear and public policy have developed at an alarming rate. The main reaction has been a get-tough stance regarding juvenile crime.

This reaction directly opposes the tradition of the juvenile court to treat the juvenile's problems using the philosophy of *parens patriae.* The public has increasingly argued against the permissiveness of the juvenile justice system. Many feel that violent juveniles should be treated as adults, as the national commissions on violence and crime of the 1960s and the presidential commissions of the 1980s documented.

A great deal of the existing research indicates that most of the violent crime is committed by a small portion of juvenile offenders although the public still feels that the system should be changed to react to their violence.[41] These juveniles have been regarded as "the violent few." Such juveniles are believed to be the ones most in need of a response from the system. The system's current failure to stifle growing juvenile violence is the result of its failure to provide that response. It can only be asserted that once the system responds, the faith of the public can be restored.

This response should be more comprehensive than originally envisioned by the founders of the juvenile justice system. Instead of continuing to utilize the resources of the juvenile system for the purpose of handling this growing problem, there should be a range of options available, including options in the juvenile justice system, the criminal justice system, a combination of the two, and the use of specialized components from both the juvenile and criminal justice systems. If this is not accomplished, violent juveniles will continue to be handled by the juvenile system, which means they will be processed much like nonviolent offenders or they will be sent to the criminal justice system where they usually receive more lenient treatment due to age.

Some have suggested that the resources of both systems be expanded to respond to the violent juvenile problem. In the past, specialized components, such as programs designed for the sole purpose of dealing with violent juveniles, have been rare. Donna Hamparian makes several suggestions for the components that each of these programs should contain. Law-abiding and safe programming, staff-intensive security programming, close ties to the community, contracting with private community agencies, juvenile involvement in choice and decision making, and group therapeutic programs illustrate a systematic, comprehensive approach in dealing with violent juvenile offenders.[42]

14-3a Juvenile Gangs

Gangs
Groups of individuals who create an allegiance toward a common goal. In prison, these gangs often engage in unlawful or criminal behavior.

The problems that are caused by gang activity in adult correctional institutions have been well documented,[43] although little is known about the difficulties posed by **gangs** in juvenile correctional institutions. In a national study conducted in 1990 of 155 state juvenile institutions, it was estimated that gang-related affiliation in juvenile correctional facilities ranged from 0 percent to 22 percent[44]—one out of every four inmates was identified as a gang member in approximately 30 percent of the institutions surveyed. The rate was 50 percent or higher in 12 percent of the institutions.

The study also showed that the number of female gang members in these institutions was lower than that of males. Over half of the institutions surveyed did not identify any female gang members. Race also played a role in juvenile gang activity. Twenty-two percent of the institutions reported having a separate white gang. Gangs formed along racist and ethnic lines are more likely to engage in behavior that oppresses individuals that belong to another racial or ethnic group.

One of the greatest problems for juvenile correctional institutions is growing gang violence. The study mentioned previously showed that 28 percent of the institutions reported an assault on a correctional official by a gang member during the period of one year. One-third of these assaults resulted in hospitalization. Over 50 percent of the institutions reported that gangs were responsible for damage to government property. In addition, juvenile prison gangs are responsible for most of the drug consumption and distribution within the correctional institution. This represents a security nightmare to prison administrators.

The methods for dealing with gang violence demonstrate the growing need to address and correct the problem. The institutions reported the use of transfers, informers, segregation, isolation of leaders, lockdown, prosecution, interruption of communications, dealing with gang members on a case-by-case basis, ignoring their existence, infiltration, displacement of members to different institutions, cooption of prisoners to control gangs, meeting with gang leaders on as-needed basis, and joint meetings between various gang leaders.

The study also asked administrators for their recommendations concerning gang control within the institution. Many of the administrators felt that staffing and education were weak in the gang area and they suggested more formal training and the hiring of specialized staff. Staff members who reflect the cultural backgrounds of the juveniles and who specialize in youth problems, social issues, and counseling were believed to be the most beneficial additions in confronting the gang problem. The primary issue was less hiring of security staff and more recruitment of counseling staff, or, more rehabilitation and less punishment and social control.

Of the administrators surveyed, most stated that there needed to be a consistent effort to define gang activity and to identify gang members. This effort would require the involvement of the staff members, who would be encouraged to increase their understanding of gangs.

Administrators also cited the prevention and elimination of gangs as a goal. It was sustained that if juvenile detention facilities provided more counseling, they could increase the self-esteem necessary to stop gang involvement. They recommended a speaker bureau of ex-gang members as a method for deterring potential gang members.

Procedural recommendations were also made and aimed at a get-tough policy with juvenile gang members. One method suggested the separation of members. More extensive measures involved the development of statutory law, making it a violation to engage in gang-related activities within the detention facility. A final measure involved the transfer of juveniles identified as gang members to adult institutions. The bottom line was not to tolerate gang activity within the correctional institution.[45]

It is important to note that the gang problem is not only prison-based. Most juvenile gangs have their roots in the streets. The 1997 National Youth Gang Survey suggested that almost 72 percent of large cities surveyed reported active youth gangs in their jurisdictions. This was followed by 33 percent of small cities and 24 percent of rural counties.[46]

14-3b Gender Differences

Traditionally, female juvenile offenders have been committed to juvenile facilities less frequently than males. Data on children in custody in 1989 revealed that males accounted for 88 percent of commitments and 81 percent of detentions, while females made up 48 percent of all voluntary commitments. Recent data (1995) on arrests shows a change in this trend. Reports state that between 1985 and 1994, the percentage of growth in female arrests was greater than the increase in male arrests for most offense categories.[47] This later trend is in direct contradiction to the prior literature that shows the juvenile system was unwilling to deal with female offenders. Some have explained the latest rise of arrests among female juvenile offenders as a reflection of the changing social roles in our society. The face of the juvenile offender is changing to one that the system may not be ready to host. Despite this, administrators are addressing the frequent violent incidents that take place in juvenile institutions.

14-3c Waiver to Criminal Court

With the increasing juvenile violence in correctional facilities, one option that has emerged has been to transfer violent youth offenders out of the juvenile system altogether. In one of the few national studies of juvenile waivers to date, Hamparian and her colleagues describe the main reasons for judicial waiver—minors being waived their right to be treated as juvenile offenders and consequently sent to adult courts. One reason is media and community reaction. The crimes committed by some juveniles are so violent that public sentiment pushes the system to find a more severe alternative for such children. Since the adult system is based on punishment and not benevolence, the better choice appears to be the adult system. This is illustrated in the publicized cases in which juveniles, who have killed fellow classmates, have been immediately treated as adult offenders by the criminal justice system.

A second reason for sending juveniles to adult courts is to find a viable option for chronic violent offenders. At times, the juvenile court no longer has resources to treat the offenders and they are then subject to the laws of adults.

Another reason is to remove those youths who act like adults in their commission of a crime from the rest of the juvenile inmate population. The rationale for doing this is based on the assumption that "removing the bad apples" will prevent further contamination. Some affirm that these juveniles are so violent and street-smart that no amount of remediation from the juvenile court can work.

Lastly, many believe that by waiving the juvenile to adult court, the juvenile has a better chance of receiving a longer sentence. Such people believe that violent juveniles are too far gone for any assistance by the juvenile court.[48]

The primary purpose in considering a juvenile an adult before the courts is that the youth will receive a more severe sentence.[49] As the number of violent offenders increases, the use of waivers should become a primary tool for dealing with a system that does not have the options for dealing with violent juvenile offenders. Many have suggested that judicial waivers should be used more for violent offenses and not property offenses.[50]

14-3d Harsher Legislative Sentences for Violent Juveniles

Some jurisdictions have enacted harsher sentences for juveniles who commit violent offenses, while others have looked at the overall issue of whether the punishment for juvenile offenses is appropriate or at the type of offense committed.

Using juvenile justice records from ten states on their handling of violent offenders between 1985 and 1989, and adult court data from fourteen states, the juvenile court's handling of violent offense cases involving sixteen and seventeen year-olds was compared with violent case dispositions in the criminal (adult) courts.[51] Despite the fact that adult court defendants were expected to have lengthier criminal records, the study showed that violent juvenile offenders were more likely to receive more severe punishments in juvenile court than were adult violent offenders in criminal court. This study found that criminal courts were more likely (32 percent) than juvenile courts (24 percent) to incarcerate violent offenders. The findings of the study further suggested that juvenile courts made greater use of formal probation than did criminal courts (25 percent compared to 9 percent).

One of the states that has responded to the growing juvenile crime rate is Texas. In 1987, Texas enacted a law that allows the court to transfer cases to adult court when the juvenile is thirteen or fourteen years of age—below the minimum of fifteen years old. The law affects juveniles thirteen or fourteen years of age who have committed either capital murder, murder, aggravated sexual assault, aggravated kidnapping, deadly assault of a law enforcement officer, correctional officer, or a court participant, and attempted murder. The juvenile can be sentenced up to thirty years. The first phase of the sentence is served in a Texas juvenile facility. If the child is not paroled by age eighteen, he or she will be moved to the adult system for the balance of the sentence.[52] Other states have enacted similar laws.

14-4 Juvenile Corrections

In the 1700s and early 1800s, it was thought that the family, the church, and other social institutions should handle juvenile delinquents. Jail was the only form of incarceration and that was for the purpose of detention pending trial. From 1790 to 1830, the traditional forms of social control began to break down as mobility and town sizes increased. Belief in sin as the cause of delinquency was replaced by a belief in community disorganization. Some method was needed whereby juveniles could be placed back into an orderly life. It was decided that

A juvenile holding center in Champaign, Illinois. It appears as if it is a school or some other form of educational facility.
Andy Rhodes

the institution known as the House of Refuge or the "well-ordered asylum," was the answer. The model was patterned after the family structure and was used for juveniles, adult criminals, the aged, the mentally ill, orphans, unwed mothers, and vagrants. By institutionalizing these persons, their lives again had order as they were removed from the corruption of society. Life in the institution was characterized by routine.

By the 1850s, many admitted that custody was all the institutions offered. Overcrowding, lack of adequate staff, and heterogeneous populations all led to the realization that institutionalization was not accomplishing its purpose. The next concept for juveniles was the training school, which was often built around a cottage system. It was thought that cottage parents would create a home-like atmosphere. Hard work, especially farm work, was emphasized. In the past seventy years, few changes have occurred, although the number of institutions has increased and some new types have evolved. Honor farms, vocational and educational training schools, and forestry and honor camps now exist, as well as a number of treatment techniques.

14-4a Short-Term Incarceration

The overall number of juveniles in jails has increased significantly. In 2000, there was an average of 7,615 jail inmates. This is a substantial increase as there were only 1,736 juveniles confined to jail in 1983.[53] The use of jail for juveniles is called detention and is described as the temporary care and maintenance of children, held for the court, who are pending adjudication of their cases.

Not all children who are arrested end up in detention. Whether detention is necessary can be determined by the seriousness of the charge, prior record, failure to appear, and availability of adult supervision. In 1984, the case of *Schall v. Martin* was upheld by the Supreme Court. This case supports the use of preventive detention in cases when it is believed the child is likely to commit another crime before the next court date and that it is serious enough to be considered an adult offense.[54]

The low number of jail facilities for juveniles has meant that some juvenile offenders are sent to adult jails. In these adult facilities, they may not be separated from the view or sound of adult inmates. This is still true although the Federal Juvenile Justice and Delinquent Prevention Act, which was amended in 1980, requires all states to remove youths from the adult jail system. In some facilities where juveniles are separated, correctional officers have been known to await the eighteenth birthday of a particular unruly juvenile with the gift of being immediately escorted to a jail cell housing adult offenders.

Many of the detained juvenile offenders are not held on delinquency charges, but for status offenses, because they are victims of abuse and neglect and because they need foster care. The number of detained juveniles is over-represented by low-income and minority children.[55]

14-4b Types of Correctional Facilities for Juveniles

Most of the correctional facilities for juveniles may be classified as one of three types. The first, the training school, houses the majority of confined juveniles—generally, this is the largest type of facility. It was the first type of facility widely accepted for the confinement of juveniles, and it is the most secure. Some jurisdictions operate other types of facilities that are less secure, such as ranches, forestry camps, or farms. These are generally located in rural areas and permit greater contact with the community than is the case with the training school. The least physically secure facilities are halfway houses and group homes.

Generally, halfway houses and group homes for juveniles are less secure than those for adults, have been more recently constructed, and are designed to accommodate a much smaller population. Like many of the adult facilities, however, they are often located in rural environments. In many institutions, an attempt has been made to make the facility as home-like as possible. Campus-like environments or cottage-type settings are not uncommon, with a small number of juveniles housed in each building along with cottage or house parents.

Despite these efforts, the architecture of many of the facilities for juveniles reflects the premise that all who are confined must face the same type of security as those few who actually need the secure environment. Security is important but needs vary. According to the juvenile corrections mandate, institutions should "seek the least restrictive alternative type of institution for each of its inmates." This reflects the public's concern for enhancing the juvenile's contact with the outside world.

Community and facility security are also important. The goal is to develop alternatives that are nonrestrictive but at the same time protect the community.[56] The American Correctional Association (ACA) acknowledges the individual rights of the juvenile but feels these rights should be balanced with facility security.

According to the ACA, this balance can be achieved by focusing on size, organization, and location of juvenile facilities. Smaller facilities increase staff contact with juveniles and the personal needs of the juveniles are more likely to be met. Organizational procedures designed to meet the needs of the inmate, the institution, and the public are more likely to benefit all. Location is perhaps the most critical factor. If contact with the outside is to be maintained, then juvenile facilities must be located near community resources that can be used to assist the juvenile.[57]

14-4c Administration and Operation of Juvenile Correctional Facilities

The administration and operation of juvenile correctional facilities differ in various aspects from the administration of adult facilities. It is best to discuss administration and operation in terms of institutional models, the executive who heads the institution, the staff, and the programs in juvenile corrections.

Institutional Models

Juvenile correctional institutions can be analyzed according to their two basic goals—treatment and custody. In an analysis of six institutions, investigators

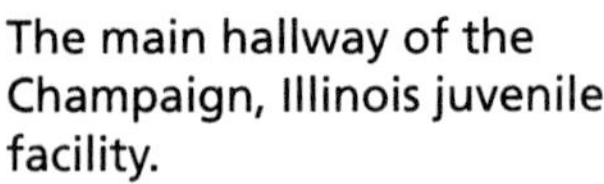

The main hallway of the Champaign, Illinois juvenile facility.
Andy Rhodes

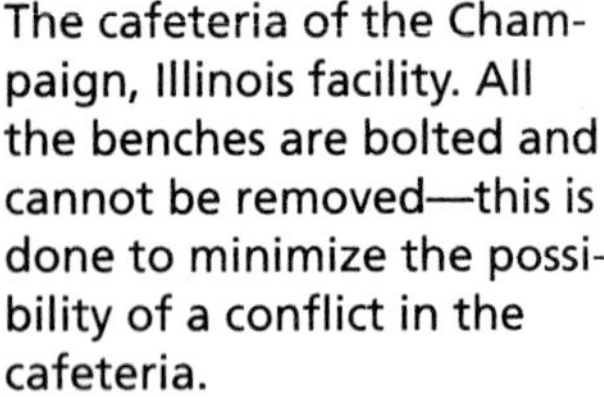

The cafeteria of the Champaign, Illinois facility. All the benches are bolted and cannot be removed—this is done to minimize the possibility of a conflict in the cafeteria.
Andy Rhodes

Obedience/conformity model
Model that emphasizes habits, respect for authority, and training in conformity.

Reeducation/development model
Model that place emphasis on changing inmates through training. It is characterized by close inmate-staff relations, emphasis on changes in attitudes and social behavior, the acquisition of skills, and the development of personal resources.

Treatment model
Model that promotes the idea that offenders should be treated and consequently released back to the community.

developed three organizational models on the treatment-custody-treatment continuum: obedience/conformity, reeducation/development, and treatment.

The **obedience/conformity model** emphasizes habits, respect for authority, and training in conformity. Conditioning is the main technique used in this model. All inmates are expected to conform to external controls immediately. This process is pursued with strong staff control and many negative sanctions. Today, this model represents most of the custodial-type institutions for juveniles.

The **reeducation/development model** places emphasis on changing inmates via training. Characterized by closer inmate-staff relations than that of the obedience/conformity model, this approach emphasizes changes in attitudes and social behaviors, the acquisition of skills, and the development of personal resources.

Compared to the other two models, the **treatment model** seeks greater personality changes in inmates. The focus in the treatment institution is on the psychological reconstitution of the inmate. Punishments are seldom utilized and are not severe. Varied activities and gratifications are stressed while emphasis is placed on self-insight and the development of self-esteem. "In the milieu treatment-variant, attention is paid to both individual *and* social controls, the aim being not only to help the inmate resolve his personal problems but also to prepare him for community living."[58]

Why are these models important? The goals of an institution affect the organization in many ways. They influence the way that staff members perceive and execute their responsibilities, the perceptions of the inmates, and the day-to-day operation of the institution. The goals are attained through the executive who translates these goals into realistic programs. The structure of power and authority, the nature of programs offered, the level of conflict in the organization, the interaction of staff and inmates, and the interaction among inmates are all affected by the organizational type, and the executive plays a key role in the organization.

The Executive

The executive of the juvenile correctional institution "formulates specific goals and policies that give meaning and direction to the enterprise," "is the link between the organization and its environment," and "establishes the structure of roles and responsibilities within the organization that enable it to pursue its goals."[59] The role is an extremely important one and requires well-qualified personnel. This individual, called a superintendent, has the difficult task of providing leadership to those overseeing juvenile offenders while assuring the public that punishment is being carried out. The executive of a juvenile facility must also face the challenges of limited funding which restricts the implementation of rehabilitative programs in the juvenile correctional institution. The job of the executive can be both frustrating and challenging.

Staff

In addition to the executive, there are several other levels of staff in juvenile correctional institutions. These levels include other top administrators, treatment personnel, academic and vocational teachers, custodial staff, and persons who provide indirect services. The executive often has an assistant or deputy superintendent, or several persons at that level. For example, an assistant superintendent in charge of indirect services, of social services, and of residential environment, depending on the total size of the institutional staff. Likewise, the number of teachers, both academic and vocational, as well as the number of treatment personnel, varies according to the size and funding of the institution.

Nonprofessional personnel are also employed at juvenile institutions. In the past, parents, usually a husband and wife team, lived in small cottages with the youths. In today's correctional facilities, however, it is common to find individuals who work eight-hour shifts and live in the community. These individuals have different titles: youth counselors, group counselors, group supervisors, and cottage supervisors. Individuals occupying such positions as business director, superintendent of buildings and grounds, and secretary provide indirect services.

Individuals occupying these various positions in juvenile correctional facilities, when compared with those who occupy comparable positions in adult institutions, are better educated. They are predominantly male, young, white, and married, and have served in juvenile corrections for several years. Those who are employed in residential institutions, however, tend to be older and less educated. A sincere interest in the welfare of children but a lack of resources for hiring the most qualified persons has been a problem, as well as the insufficient number of employees, especially in the areas of psychological and psychiatric treatment.[60]

Staff is an essential element in all juvenile institutions. In a study of male juveniles in an Ohio residential institution, investigators found that staff members frequently use their power to their own advantage and may victimize the inmates. They found that staff members' reactions to the boys depend in part on their previous work experience and on the length of time they have worked with juveniles. During their careers, staff members go through plateaus, or stages, and their relationships with inmates vary. There was some evidence of physical brutality and sexual exploitation against inmates, staff members aiding in escapes, staff members neglecting their responsibilities, and various forms of deception of inmates. Administrators were reported as having the need to keep more violent youths under control and to develop a punishment-centered and repressive atmosphere. This atmosphere affected staff and inmate morale, with the result that "[r]elationships among staff members are characterized by high intraorganization conflict. Organizational processing of boys, in addition, creates an environment which is antitherapeutic at best and only a step from the chain gang at worst."[61]

14-4d Programs and Treatment

Special facilities for juveniles were originally established to isolate them from the harmful effects of society and from incarcerated adults. Later, with the development of the juvenile court, the philosophy of salvaging the juvenile became predominant. Various commissions during the past century have, however, pointed out the failure of juvenile corrections to provide adequate services and programs to enable the implementation of this treatment philosophy. During the last two decades, courts have required elements of due process in the adjudication of juveniles, but also changes in the disciplinary handling of institutionalized juveniles, as well as in the degree and kinds of services provided in those institutions.

Today, numerous programs are in place throughout the many juvenile facilities in the United States and some have made recent claims of being highly successful. The first of these programs is called Youth as Resources (YAR). This program, which is implemented in the Indiana Department of Corrections, has been regarded as highly successful in its efforts to give juveniles a sense of belonging, self-worth, responsibility, and community connection.[62] YAR was created by the National Crime Prevention Council in 1986 with funding from the Lilly Endowment. It is based on the assumption that youths are resources and when treated as such, can make a difference in local communities. As part of the program, more than 1,500 young people in state and regional Indiana youth correctional facilities have designed and implemented a variety of projects, ranging from violence prevention to educating children about the harmful effects of drugs and gangs. In 1995, YAR was evaluated and the following findings were made:

- Many of the participants grew excited about the possibility of building communities.
- Adult leaders claimed that 78 percent of youth participants in the program learned about working together.
- Many of the young people in correctional settings stated that YAR gave them a sense of belonging.[63]

Due to the high success claimed by participants of this program, other states are being encouraged to implement similar programs in their juvenile facilities. This campaign is being aided by the creation of a document that highlights the work of the Indiana program, which will serve as the framework for implementing YAR in any juvenile correctional setting nationwide.

Another program established in Delafield, Wisconsin, aims at developing juvenile sex offenders into responsible individuals equipped to meet life's challenges.[64] The program, Stout Serious Offender Treatment Program (SSOP), claims that less than 50 percent of its participants have returned to an institution. Currently, SSOP staff includes two full-time social workers, a group facilitator, seven youth counselors, six teachers, and a section manager. The program is based on an intensive six-phase group-therapy approach aimed at addressing juvenile sex offender dynamics.

SSOP also uses a behavioral level system through which each offender is expected to progress. Level I indicates minimal cooperation with rules and responsibilities and level IV represents the maximum level of adherence to rules.[65] It is expected that SSOP will be replicated in other jurisdictions, much like YAR.

Unfortunately, some of these programs, such as YAR and SSOP, do not last due to budgetary constraints or bad publicity about their alleged failure to rehabilitate youth offenders. It is expected, however, that new programs will be implemented as innovative ideas are put into practice.

14-4e Juvenile Inmate Social System

In earlier chapters, male and female inmate social systems were discussed. The theories concerning the origin of inmate social systems, considering whether they are imported into prison or whether they represent an adaptation to the pains of imprisonment, were explored. The differences in the inmate social system of women was compared to that of male inmates. It can be concluded that the development of the inmate culture might be a reaction to the deprivations of prison life, but that the nature of that response—the differences in the social systems of male and female offenders—is strongly influenced by the cultural differences that the genders experience outside prison. Female offenders develop a system that simulates the family while men develop one that allows them to be aggressive and domineering. The differences are even seen in the nature of homosexual relationships.

Studies have revealed that inmate social systems develop among institutionalized juveniles as well, although there are not many of these studies. A survey of juvenile correctional facilities studied the differences between veterans (juveniles who had been at the institutions the longest periods of time), and newcomers. It was revealed that a core of veterans tended to emerge, that they reinforced each other, and that reinforcement set the tone for the entire program. They were also extremely influential on those new to the system. A social climate, controlled and dominated by the veterans, developed and had a far greater influence than the staff.[66]

A study of male juvenile offenders in a public training school found an informal inmate code that served to legitimize the stronger inmates' exploitation of the weaker ones. The code was functional for some of the aggressive inmates and provided them with a sense of dignity, confidence in their achievements, and a way to develop self-esteem. It was also a reason to avoid the "people-changing" techniques of the correctional staff. The code victimized the weak and the white, who were in the minority. Those inmates were considered "losers" in the inmate social system and were further ostracized by their peers. "Therefore, the code clearly works to the disadvantage of the weak by increasing both their exploitation by peers and their isolation from staff." The investigators concluded that the inmate social code was the result of the importation of norms from the outside as well as of attempts to adjust to the deprivations of institutional life.[67]

Another study examined the inmate social system of a private training school. This study also revealed the presence of a strong inmate social system in which boys gained power and status through interaction with their peers. Violence, scapegoating, ranking, and manipulation were found to be the "underlying mechanisms of social control" and they were "patterned into roles which intermesh in a stable pecking order." The deviant values of the inmates were sustained by relationships with their peers within the cottage. Weaker inmates were exploited by the stronger; the social exchanges of peers were "institutionalized and taught to new members as the 'law' of the cottage." The negative values of the boys were far more powerful in the socialization process than were the values of the correctional staff.[68]

An analysis of the female juvenile inmate social system of three institutions found that all of the facilities simulated the family life of women outside of institutions. The inmates referred to their relationships as marriages, with the traditional roles of mothers, fathers, and children. Even divorce was mentioned. In this study, it was determined that the "informal social system is functional in that it provides substitute relationships for the community ties that were severed, and it enables the inmates to experiment in new social roles." The problem, however, is that the female juvenile inmates tend to view the new roles as reality. The extent to which these adaptations affect the ability of the offender to adjust to, establish, and maintain meaningful heterosexual relationships after release from confinement is not known.[69]

14-4f Deinstitutionalization

Dissatisfaction with the closed institution (highly guarded and isolated facilities) in the twentieth century has led to several movements—diversion (divert the juvenile offender away from prison), community corrections, and deinstitutionalization. The latter began with an emphasis on probation, foster homes, and community treatment centers for juveniles. The California Youth Authority established in the early 1960s and the closing of the institution for juveniles in Massachusetts in 1970 and 1971 have given impetus to the movement.[70]

Some claim the movement toward deinstitutionalization for juveniles began in the early 1960s when the government began granting money to localities to improve conditions in the field of delinquency. Others contend it began when social scientists began to assume roles that clinicians had been playing and became involved in policy decision making at the local and federal levels. Still others point to the interest of lawyers in reforming the juvenile court in the 1960s and 1970s. Some have argued that the movement toward decarceration was motivated primarily by a desire to save the cost of constructing new facilities and repairing existing institutions.[71]

Whatever the reasons, it is clear that the movement toward deinstitutionalization is unlike most others in the field. It involves a major change: abandoning large institutions and replacing them with a different concept of corrections. The process has been described as follows:

> [T]he penal institution has been dissected like a cadaver in a morgue. No organ, no angle, no aspect has defied scrutiny and commentary. The net result of these analyses has been a literature which has hardened attitudes toward the institution as a snake pit; as a demonic invention conceived with the best of intentions but which, like so many other innovations grounded in the blind zeal of reformers, turn out to be as bad as or worse than the practices they replace. The pendulum has swung to the point that modern reformers—both lay and professional—would demolish the institution stone by stone.[72]

Jerome G. Miller advocated deinstitutionalization in Massachusetts. In 1969, he took charge of the state's Department of Youth Services. He first attempted reform of the system, but "after fifteen months of bureaucratic blockades, open warfare with state legislators, and sabotage by entrenched employees, Miller abandoned reform and elected revolution."[73] Between 1969 and 1973, Miller closed the state institutions for juveniles, placing the juveniles in community-based facilities. It is significant that this radical approach first occurred in this state as it was the same place that built the first training school for boys in 1846, and the first for girls in 1854.

When Miller decided to close the oldest training school for boys, he decided to move all of the youths on the same day. They were screened carefully and those who qualified were sent home. The rest were taken to the University of Massachusetts. The program there involved four factors: placement, advocacy, group leaders, and a national conference on delinquency prevention and treatment programs.

1. In terms of placement, the university was seen only as a buffer. The goal was to place individuals back in the community as soon as possible, in a viable living situation with job and education opportunities and a method for follow-up study of the youths while they were in the community.
2. Each boy from the institution had an advocate, a student who was responsible for daily and hourly supervision during the month and for assisting the boy in integrating back into the community.
3. Group leaders, selected from the staff of one of the detention centers, led group discussions of juveniles and advocates.
4. The themes of social problems, education and employment, and family and alternative placement models were discussed at the national conference, which featured discussion groups and nationally known speakers and leaders.[74]

The Massachusetts experiment with deinstitutionalization has been evaluated by a team of social scientists from Harvard University. In the early stages of evaluation, they concluded, guardedly, that the experiment was a success. In 1977, however, this conclusion was questioned. Although the recidivism rates of the youths had not increased or decreased, and it might be concluded that deinstitutionalization, although no better, was no worse than institutionalization and certainly was more humane, the evaluators pointed out that there was a crisis in the reaction of the public, the courts, and the police. The concern was over the need for more secure facilities. A task force was appointed to consider the issue. At the same time, the evaluators conducted their final survey of staff connected with the programs for youth in that state. They concluded, "we are left with a picture of the reformed agency showing clear signs of difficulty and crisis in the political structure that supports it, and some suggestions of difficulty in its actual operations." The evaluators were looking specifically at the effects of the use of extreme tactics in affecting reform.[75]

Miller left the Massachusetts Department of Youth Services in 1973 for a similar position in Illinois. He has been attacked as a poor administrator who spent money without legislative approval:

> Hubbub follows him like a swarm of hornets. When he left Massachusetts to head the Illinois department of child welfare, he soon alienated the state's social workers, put the child welfare system into a swivel and was forced to resign. But Pennsylvania

quickly hired him.[76] Subsequently Miller became president of the National Center for Action on Institutions and Alternatives.

Another critic of Miller's actions in Massachusetts stated that, "with quiet reformist satisfaction, he left the state to its own devices and went elsewhere . . . Massachusetts is sending so many youthful offenders to training schools in nearby states that its neighbors are beginning to complain."[77]

The deinstitutionalization efforts in Massachusetts have been criticized because Miller closed the juvenile institutions without first providing reasonable alternatives for handling the confined juveniles. "More generally, the massive expansion of the population on probation and parole has not been accompanied by extensions in the degree and scope of outside supervision," with the result that probation and parole supervision were meaningless in many cases.[78]

In evaluating deinstitutionalization, it is important to consider the issue of whether the negative effects of institutionalization will occur also in community treatment centers or other forms of handling juveniles. Large institutions for juveniles primarily house those offenders who were in smaller institutions previously. The smaller institutions or those involved primarily in community corrections must take responsibility for at least part of the failure of the correctional system to rehabilitate juveniles. Replacing large institutions with smaller facilities may not have a significant impact on juvenile offenders.[79] If juveniles who already have a strong orientation toward crime are confined together, they may continue to infect and teach each other, as well as the new inmates.

The movement toward deinstitutionalization or decarceration might encourage some youths to commit crimes or to continue committing crimes, as they believe that they will not be punished. The movement toward removing status offenders from the juvenile justice system should not be confused with a continued need to confine more serious offenders.

A recent study on the effects of deinstitutionalization confirms the results of the Massachusetts study on deinstitutionalization. It was found that those juveniles assigned to alternatives other than training school had higher rates of recidivism than those who completed the training school experience. The results of this study contrast with those of another study conducted in 1990 that claimed that community alternatives were at least as effective as institutionalization.

The conclusion drawn from this inconsistency is that "neither institutional programs nor community-based programs are uniformly effective or ineffective."[80] It appears that the design of the program is the critical factor. For the design of the program to be effective, it must be related to a plausible theory of delinquency, it must be implemented correctly, and it must be carefully evaluated.

Deinstitutionalization is not the sole answer. Arguments on either side of the debate are not so simple. Reduction in recidivism among juveniles will involve a more informed policy concerning what works.[81]

Summary

The study of the handling of juveniles in the United States is perhaps one of the most discouraging of all phases of the criminal justice system, for it has been in this area that rehabilitation, reformation, and reintegration have become unattainable goals. It is clear from the discussion at the beginning of this chapter that the juvenile justice system based its philosophy on the concept of *parens patriae* since its creation in Cook County, Illinois.

Various aspects of juvenile offenders including the major Supreme Court cases affecting juvenile offenders, society's reaction to the juvenile crime problem, the nature and type of juvenile offender, juvenile gangs, the rendering of harsher sentences to juvenile offenders, and the institutional models in existence today were studied. The examination of these topics was aimed at developing and achieving a better understanding of the complexities involving the incarceration of juvenile offenders in the United States today.

Recent juvenile crimes in school settings have made a substantial impact on the public, leaving many with the fear that they can no longer regard schools as safe. The number of juveniles held in state prisons increased from 2,300 in 1985 to 5,400 in 1997,[82] and this has resulted in a frenzy that has been greatly influenced by the media. Many issues concerning the existing juvenile offender policies have been raised. The existing juvenile crime policies will become more punitive as Americans demand a safer environment for their children, particularly during a time when most Americans feel the price of safety can never be too high.

Notes

1. CNN, April 28, 1999.
2. Cronley, Connie, "Blackboard Jungle Updated," *TWA Ambassador* (September, 1978), 25; See also R. J. Rubel, *Violence in Schools—Implications for Schools and School Districts* (College Park, MD: Institute for Reduction of Crime, Inc., 1978).
3. *Time* (July 11, 1977), p. 25, 27.
4. World Socialist Web Site, www.wsws.org, "Texas to Execute Three for Crimes Committed as Juveniles," By Kate Randall (May 25, 2002).
5. Flicker, Barbara, "History of Jurisdiction Over Juveniles and Family Matters," in Francis X. Hartmann, ed., *From Children to Citizens*, (New York: Springer-Verlag, 1987), p. 237.
6. Kramer, S., *History Begins at Sumer* (Toronto: Doubleday, 1959), p. 12.
7. See Deut, 2:18–21; Prov. 20:20; Exod. 21:15–16, 24–35, and Lev. 21:9.
8. Nicholas, F., "History, Philosophy, and Procedures of Juvenile Courts," *Journal of Family Law* 1 (Fall, 1961), 158–159.
9. Reed, A., "Gault and the Juvenile Training School," *Indiana Law Journal* 43 (Spring, 1968), 641.
10. Ketchman, Orman, "The Unfulfilled Promise of the American Juvenile Courts," in Margaret Keeny Rosenheim, ed., *Justice for the Child* (New York: Free Press, 1962), p. 24.
11. *Statr v. Scholl*, 167 N.W. 830, 831 (1918).
12. Paulsen, Monrad, "The Constitutional Domestication of the Juvenile Courts," in Philip B. Kurland, ed., *Supreme Court Review*. (Chicago: University of Chicago Press, 1967), p. 239.
13. See Anthony Platt, *The Child Savers* (Chicago: University of Chicago Press, 1969).
14. Alexander, P., "Constitutional Rights in the Juvenile Court," in Rosenheim, Margaret K., ed. *Pursuing Justice for the Child* (Chicago: The University of Chicago Press, 1978), pp. 89–92 (emphasis added).
15. Pisciotta, A. W., "Race, Sex and Rehabilitation: A Study of Differential Treatment in the Juvenile Reformatory, 1825–1900," *Crime and Delinquency* 29 (1983), 254–269.
16. *Commonwealth v. Fisher*, 62 At. 198, 199, 200 (S. Ct. Pa. 1905).
17. Paulsen, Monrad, "Role of Juvenile Courts," *Current History* 53 (August, 1967), 240.
18. *Kent v. United States*, 383 U.S. 541, 556 (1966).
19. *Winburn v. State*, 32 Wis. 2d 152, 162 (1966).
20. For a discussion on labeling theory, see Vold, George, B., Bernard, Thomas, J., and Snipes, B. Jeffrey, *Theoretical Criminology*, 5th ed. (New York: Oxford University Press, 2002).
21. *Jones v. Commonwealth*, 38 S.E. 2d 444, 447 (1946).
22. Fisher, B. C., "Juvenile Court: Purpose, Promise, and Problems," *Social Service Review* 34 (March, 1960), 78.
23. Ketchman, "The Unfulfilled Promise of the Juvenile Court," p. 38.
24. *Kent v. United States*, 383 U.S. 541, 554-555 (1967).
25. *In re Winship*, 397 U.S. 358 (1970).
26. *McKeiver v. Pennsylvania*, 403 U.S. 528, 543 (1971).
27. Rossum, R. A., Koller, B. J., and Manfredi, C. P., *Juvenile Justice Reform: A Model for the States* (Claremont, CA: Rose Institute of State and Local Government and the American Legislative Exchange Council, 1987).
28. *Breed v. Jones*, 421 U.S. 519 (1974), remanded, 519 F. 2d 1314 (9th Cir. 1975).
29. *Schall v. Martin*, 467 U.S. 253 (1984).
30. *Eddings v. Oklahoma*, 455 U.S. 104 (1982).
31. *Thomson v. Oklahoma*, 470 U.S. 830 (1988).
32. *Stanford v. Kentucky*, 492 U.S. 361 (1989).
33. Hellum, Frank, "Juvenile Justice: The Second Revolution," *Crime and Delinquency* 25 (July 9, 1979), 299–317.
34. U.S. Code, Title 42, Section 5601 et. seq. See also Barbara Flicker, "History of Jurisdiction over Juvenile and Family Matters" in Francis Hartmann, ed., *From Children to Citizens*. (New York: Springer-Verlag, 1987), pp. 232–233.
35. 42 U.S. Code & 5633 (12) (A), (13).
36. See *The New York Times* (February 5, 1980), p. A18, col. 1.
37. Wash. Rev. Code Ann. & 13.40.020 (10), (11), (14).
38. Wash. Rev. Code Ann. & 13.40.020 (10), (11), (14).
39. Snyder, Howard N., and Sickmund, Melissa, Office of Juvenile Justice and Delinquency Prevention. *Juvenile Offenders and Victims: A Focus on Violence* (May, 1995), p. 6.
40. U.S. Department of Justice, "Juvenile Offenders and Victims: 1999 National Report" Howard N. Snyder and Melissa Sickmund, National Center for Juvenile Justice, September 1999, Washington, D.C.

41. Fagan, Jeffery, "Treatment and Reintegration of Violent Juvenile Offenders: Experimental Results," *Justice Quarterly* 7 (1990): 233–263.
42. Hamparian, Donna, "Violent Juvenile Offenders," in Francis X. Hartmann, ed., *From Children to Citizens,* (New York: Springer-Verlag, 1987), pp. 128–142.
43. Crouch, Ben, and Marquart, James, *An Appeal to Justice* (Austin, TX: University of Texas Press, 1989).
44. Knox, George W., "Gangs and Juvenile Correctional Institutions," in *An Introduction to Gangs* (Berrien Springs, MI: Vande Vere Publishing, 1991), pp. 301-309.
45. Knox, *Introduction to Gangs.* p. 301.
46. U.S. Department of Justice, "1997 National Youth Gang Survey," National Youth Gang Center, Washington, D.C., December, 1999.
47. Snyder and Sickmund, *Juvenile Offenders and Victims,* p. 14.
48. Hamparian, Donna et al., *Major Issues in Juvenile Justice Information and Training: Youth in Adult Courts: Between Two Worlds* (Columbus, OH: Academy for Contemporary Problems, 1982), p. 12.
49. Champion, Dean, and Mays, Larry, *Transferring Juveniles to Criminal Courts: Trends and Implications for Criminal Justice* (New York: Praeger, 1991).
50. Fagan, Jeffery, and Deschenes, E. P., "Determinants of Judicial Waiver Decisions for Violent Juvenile Offenders," *Journal of Criminal Law and Criminology* (1981), 314–347.
51. Snyder and Sickmund, *Juvenile Offenders and Victims,* p. 14.
52. Act of 17 June 1987, Ch. 385, Tex. Sess. Law Serv. 3764 (Vernon) (effective 1 September 1987). For a detailed discussion of the legislative history of this statute and the implications of the statute, see Robert O. Dawson, "The Third Justice System: The New Juvenile Criminal System of Determinant Sentencing for the Youthful Offender in Texas," *St. Mary's Law Journal* 19, no. 4 (1988): 943–1016.
53. *Bureau of Justice Statistics Sourcebook,* 2000, Table 6.20, p. 501.
54. *Schall v. Martin,* 467 U.S. 253 (1984).
55. Schall, Ellen, "Principles for Juvenile Detention," in Hartmann, ed., *From Children to Citizens,* pp. 349–361.
56. Cook, Phillip, "Notes on an Accounting Scheme for a Juvenile Correctional Association," in Hartmann, ed., *From Children to Citizens,* pp. 365, 367.
57. American Correctional Association, *Standards for Small Juvenile Detention Facilities* (Laurel, MD: American Correctional Association, 1991), pp. 31, 43, 58.
58. Street, David, Vinter, Robert and Perrow, Charles, *Organization for Treatment,* (New York: Free Press, 1966), p. 21, emphasis in the original.
59. Street, *Organization for Treatment,* p. 45.
60. Sarri, Rosemary C., and Vinter, Robert D., "Justice for Whom: Varieties of Juvenile Correctional Approaches," in Malcolm W. Klein, ed., *The Juvenile Justice System,* (Beverly Hills, CA: Sage, 1976), pp. 181–183.
61. Bartollas, Clemens et al., *Juvenile Victimization: The Institutional Paradox* (New York: John Wiley & Sons, 1976), p. 232.
62. Nagorski, Maria, "Volunteer Program Empowers Youths," *Corrections Today* (August, 1996), vol. 58, no. 5, p. 171(2).
63. Nagorski, "Volunteer Program," p. 171.
64. "Workshop Tackles Tough Issues," ACA 1996 Winter Conference, *Corrections Today* (April, 1996), vol. 58, no. 2, p. 60(1).
65. "Workshop Tackles Tough Issues," p. 60.
66. Vinter, Robert D., ed., with Theodore M. Newcomb and Rhea Kish, *Time Out: A National Study of Juvenile Correctional Programs,* National Assessment of Juvenile Corrections (Ann Arbor: University of Michigan Press, 1976).
67. Bartollas et al., *Juvenile Victimization,* p. 69.
68. Polsky, Howard W., *Cottage Six: The Social System of Delinquent Boys in Residential Treatment* (New York: John Wiley & Sons, 1967), pp. 168–169.
69. Pollock-Byrne, Joycelyn, *Women, Prison, & Crime* (Pacific Grove, CA: Brooks/Cole Publishing Company, 1990), pp. 145–147.
70. Bartollas et al., *Juvenile Victimization,* pp. 7–8.
71. Scull, Andrew T., *Decarceration: Community Treatment and the Deviant: A Radical View* (Englewood Cliffs, NJ: Prentice-Hall, 1977), pp. 140–141.
72. Bartollas et al., *Juvenile Victimization,* pp. 262–263.
73. *Time* (August 30, 1976), p. 63.
74. Dye, Lary L., "The University's Role in Public Service to the Department of Youth Services," in *Closing Correctional Institutions: New Strategies for Youth Services* (Lexington, MA: D.C. Heath, 1973), pp. 120–121.
75. Miller, Alden D. et al., "The Aftermath of Extreme Tactics in Juvenile Justice Reform: A Crisis Four Years Later," in David F. Greenberg, ed., *Corrections and Punishment,* (Beverly Hills, CA: Sage, 1977), p. 245. See also R.B. Coates et al., *Diversity in a Youth Correctional System—Handling Delinquents in Massachusetts* (Cambridge, MA: Ballinger Publishing, 1978); and "The Legacy of Jerome Miller," *Corrections Magazine* 3 (September, 1978): 12–18.
76. *Time* (August 30, 1976), p. 63.
77. Miller, Harry L., "The 'Right to Treatment': Can the Courts Rehabilitate and Cure?" *Public Interest* 46 (Winter, 1977): 97.
78. Scull, *Decarceration,* pp. 101–102.
79. Erickson, Maynard L., "Schools for Crime?" *Journal of Research in Crime and Delinquency* 15 (January, 1978): 32–33.
80. Gottredson, Denie, and Barton, William, "Deinstitutionalization of Juvenile Offenders," *Criminology* 31 (1993), 591–611. See also William Barton and Jeffery Butts, "Viable Options: Intensive Supervision Programs for Juvenile Delinquents," *Crime and Delinquency* 36 (1990), 238–255.
81. Gottredson and Barton, "Deinstitutionalization."
82. Bureau of Justice Statistics, Special Report (February, 2000), "Profile of State Prisoners Under Age 18, 1985-97," U.S. Department of Justice, Washington, D.C.

Chapter 15

The Death Penalty

No other topic in the field of corrections receives more attention than the death penalty. The current practices carry the same century-old arguments that both justify and deny its overall aim. This chapter offers an in-depth discussion on historical and contemporary death penalty practices and it presents current statistical information on which states are most active in issuing and carrying out death penalty convictions. Finally, it explores the most commonly used arguments for and against death penalty practices in the United States.

Key Terms

Massachusetts Code of 1864
capital punishment
Benjamin Rush
guillotine

Outline

15-1 The Historical Perspective

Although now abolished in England, the death penalty was historically a significant form of punishment. Henry VIII executed an estimated 72,000 thieves and vagabonds during his reign. In the year 1500, England had only eight capital crimes: treason, petty treason (killing of husband by wife), murder, larceny, robbery, burglary, rape, and arson. However, by the year 1800, there were over 200 capital crimes, including crimes against the public peace.

Even though American colonists did not observe most of the English laws concerning capital crimes, those laws greatly influenced them. This influence was strong in an environment where religious principles established by the Bible were very important. It was not uncommon to find criminal codes that punished individuals for engaging in behavior that was considered illegal and highly immoral. For example, in the **Massachusetts Code of 1648, capital punishment** was provided for idolatry, witchcraft, blasphemy, sodomy, adultery, rape, man stealing, treason, false witness with intent to take life, cursing or smiting of a parent, stubbornness on the part of a son against his parents, and homicide committed with malice, by guile or poisoning, or "suddenly in…anger or cruelty of passion." Each one of these provisions, "with the exception of that relating to rape, was annotated to some chapter and verse of the Pentateuch, and several exactly reproduced its language."[1]

Massachusetts Code of 1864 Legal code which established capital punishment for idolatry witchcraft, blasphemy, sadomy and adultery.

Capital Punishment Another name given to the death penalty. The punishment which results in the death of the person convicted of a heinous crime.

It is important to note that executions in the Colonies took place long before laws were passed declaring capital punishment legal. The first known execution on American soil took place in 1622, in the colony of Virginia. Daniel Frank was executed for having committed theft. Those who witnessed the execution of Daniel Frank could never have predicted its impact on the capital punishment practices of the following three centuries.[2]

15-1a Historical Justification

For centuries, the death penalty was used without thought for justification. It was accepted as an efficient method for handling difficult problems. According to Marc Ancel, author of *Capital Punishment,* this was initially due to lack of respect for human life, and later, because of the power given to the state. The sovereign was appropriated with power to keep peace, while being held responsible for dispensing justice. Such actions were meant to replace private wars and vengeance. The sovereign was also given power to take the life of a citizen if necessary to protect society.[3] Although some philosophers called for the elimination of the death penalty, the abolitionist movement started with Beccaria in the 1700s. The general reform movement of that period assisted the capital punishment abolitionists. The increasing emphasis on humanitarianism resulted in the mitigation of harsh punishments, the liberal current that limited the power of the state, and the utilitarian concept that punishment should be "no more than just, not more than necessary." This led the populous to question the need for capital punishment practices, and the death penalty was gradually eliminated in most European countries during the last half of the nineteenth century.

By the twentieth century, however, a countermovement began. Crimes were increasing and people initially began addressing the problem with a conservative spirit. The academic community also paralleled the attitude of the citizenry, with Lombroso writing about the born criminal, Garofalo writing about the socially dangerous criminal, and Darwin writing about human evolution. These ideas led some to conclude that capital punishment was a necessary eugenic measure. At the same time, "Europe experienced a strong authoritarian current of thought of which German nationalism and Italian fascism were only the most blatant examples." One of the results was an increasing emphasis on maintaining the new social order at all costs.[4]

15-1b The Abolitionist Movement in the United States

Benjamin Rush Presented the first argument against capital punishment in the United States in the home of Benjamin Franklin.

Benjamin Rush presented the first reasoned argument against capital punishment in the United States in 1787, at the home of Benjamin Franklin, although the reform movement did not begin until later. In 1821, Edward Livington prepared a report that contained a systematic rebuttal of all the arguments in favor of the death penalty. Because of the official nature of the report (Livington had been appointed to revise the criminal code of Louisiana) and its thoroughness, it gained wide publicity. Although it led to law reform in some South American countries, the report was not adopted in Louisiana.

Late in the 1800s, other reform movements emerged, and the drive to abolish the death penalty gained momentum. In 1834, Pennsylvania terminated public executions. Michigan became the first state to eliminate capital punishment in 1847, followed by Rhode Island in 1852 and Wisconsin in 1853. Other states followed, but by the end of World War I, some states had reinstated the death penalty. The abolition movement again gained momentum in the 1960s. In 1972, the U.S. Supreme Court handed down a decision in *Furman vs. Georgia* that affirmed that capital punishment laws are unconstitutional if they are discriminatory in their application. The justices stated, "in recognizing the humanity of our fellow beings, we pay ourselves the highest tribute. We...join the approximately seventy other jurisdictions in the world which celebrate their regard for civilization and humanity by shunning capital punishment."[5]

The case was based on an appeal to the Supreme Court entered by three defendants who claimed that the imposition of the death penalty constituted cruel and unusual punishment and was therefore in violation of the U.S. Constitution. In a response to this appeal, the Court ruled that capital punishment was unconstitutional in these particular cases because the imposition of the sentence involved unconstitutional discrimination. But the Court did not rule that capital punishment per se was cruel and unusual punishment and therefore unconstitutional. As a result, opportunities arose for new capital punishment legislation if applied uniformly. This placed a temporary moratorium on death penalty practices until 1976.

In 1976, thirty-five states responded to the moratorium with new legislation on capital punishment. Some of these statutes were challenged, and in 1976, the Supreme Court decided several capital punishment cases.[6] The Court lifted the moratorium and cleared the way for the first execution to take place in ten years. On January 17, 1977, Gary Gilmore was executed in Utah. His death by firing squad was the first of many since the death penalty was reinstated. In the same year, Oklahoma became the first state to adopt lethal injection as a means of execution, though it would be five more years until Charles Brooks was executed by lethal injection in the state of Texas.[7]

15-2 Data on Capital Punishment

Between 1930 and 1966, 3,857 persons were executed in the United States. The peak was reached in 1935, when 199 inmates were executed. In 1999, ninety-eight inmates were executed, which constitutes the highest number of inmates executed in any other year since the early 1950s. Eighty-five inmates were executed in 2000 and sixty-six in 2001,[8] which may suggest a slight tapering in the number of people executed per year. Experts caution, however, that predictions cannot be based on a two year trend. Between 1976 (when the moratorium on executions was lifted) and 2001, 749 individuals have been executed.[9] This figure includes the sixty-six inmates who were executed in the United States in 2001.[10]

According to recent demographic data produced by the Bureau of Justice Statistics in 2001, sixty-six persons were executed in fifteen states and by the federal government. This represents a 22 percent decrease from the eighty-five executed in 2000.[11] Although Texas has been the leader in number of executions, Oklahoma executed one more individual (18) in 2001 than Texas (17). This is the largest number of inmates executed in Oklahoma in a given year since the federal government started to track executions on a yearly basis. In 2001, the federal government executed two inmates, the highest number of executions in a year since 1957.[12] A review of the 2001 statistics shows that some states, including Oklahoma, Texas, Missouri, North Carolina, and Georgia, were the most active in executing inmates.[13]

The number of minorities on death row has been the subject of controversy in recent years. Some scholars and interest groups argue that the existing capital punishment practices in the United States are racist and biased against minorities. According to Michael Paris (2000), "multiple studies (Aguirre and Baker; Gross and Mauro) have shown that the death penalty is continuously imposed capriciously on blacks".[14] This argument has gained momentum by the publication of "Killing with Prejudice: Race and the Death Penalty in the USA." This twenty-one page report published by Amnesty International cites statistics, case summaries, and other facts in an attempt to validate the argument that racial disparity takes place in the sentencing and execution practices in the United States.[15]

In addition, independent statistical sources, such as the Bureau of Justice Statistics, report that although whites are executed the most often, African-Americans are over-represented among those executed. In 1999 and 2000, of those executed in the United States, forty-nine were white and thirty-five were black.[16]

15-3 Methods of Execution: Historical and Contemporary

Execution has been a common form of punishment throughout the world. The crimes punishable by this method have varied from one generation to the next. The form of execution has also varied from one historical era to another. In eighteenth-century England, most death sentences involved the wheel, the guillotine, hanging, or burning at the stake. These severe punishments began to disappear, however, when a democratic political philosophy started emerging.

15-3a Burning at the Stake

Burning at the stake was a popular punishment used primarily for heretics, witches, and "suspicious women." Of these, witches were by far the preferred population for this particular form of execution. The common persecution of women labeled witches resulted in millions being burned at the stake. Records indicate "the first major witch-hunt occurred in Switzerland in 1427."[17] It was not until the 1500s and 1600s, however, when witch trials gained popularity in Germany, Austria, Switzerland, England, Scotland, and Spain, that burning at the stake gained momentum.

The popularity of burning at the stake as a form of capital punishment was not limited to Europe. In the late 1600s, this form of execution crossed the ocean to North America. In 1692, the famous Salem witch trials played a significant role in the adoption of this execution method. As is evident with most forms of execution, burning at the stake did not remain popular for very long. The last legal execution by burning at the stake took place in 1834—at the end of the Spanish Inquisition.

15-3b The Wheel

The wheel was also a common method of execution and could be used in different ways. A person could be "attached to the outer rim of the wheel and then rolled over sharp spikes, or down a hill, to their death."[18] Another method of using the wheel involved laying it on its side with an individual tied to it. The wheel then turned while people took turns beating and eventually killing the accused with iron bars. This method of execution was used mostly in European countries during the Middle Ages.

This photo depicts the use of the guillotine at a public execution in Prevost at Place de la Roquette, Paris, France in 1857.
Library of Congress
Prints and Photographs Division
LC-USZ62-124552

15-3c The Guillotine

Guillotine Proposed by Dr. Joseph Guillotine of France. This form of execution is provided through the use of a machine which decapitates condemned individuals.

In 1789, Dr. Joseph Guillotine of France proposed that all criminals should be executed in the same way and that torture should be kept to a minimum. He suggested building a machine to decapitate condemned individuals. The **guillotine** was tested first on animals and then on human corpses. Through trial and error, the guillotine blade was perfected and used for the first time in 1792. Soon after, it became popular and was widely used throughout the French Revolution. The last public usage of the guillotine was in France in June 1939, although the French employed this technique until 1977.

Although today decapitation is viewed as a cruel form of punishment, at the time, it was believed to be more humane than other methods used.

15-3d Hanging

Throughout history, hanging has been a popular method of executing people. In a typical hanging, the noose fractured the individual's neck. However, if torture was to be part of the individual's punishment, several devices were available to the executioner. In cases where treason had taken place, the individual would be carved into pieces while still alive and before the hanging took place.[19] Hanging is still practiced in some nations.

15-3e Current Methods of Execution

Of all these forms of executions, hanging and beheading have survived and are still being used throughout the world, along with firing squad, stoning, lethal injection, lethal gas, and electrocution. Table 15-1 shows the specific breakdown of these methods.

In the United States, methods of execution have shifted from one era to the next, with some surviving the violent changes of American history. Today, the methods of execution used in the United States include lethal injection, electrocution, lethal gas, hanging, and the firing squad. Of these, the most frequently used is lethal injection.[20] Lethal injection was first adopted in Oklahoma in 1977 and was legislatively adopted in Texas only one day later. Other states approved of this method almost immediately, although it was not implemented without challenges. In 1978, the Texas statute that legitimized the use of lethal injection was upheld, despite the claims of a defendant that the statute was too vague and that death by injection constituted cruel and unusual punishment.[21] Figure 15-1 presents the methods of execution present in each state where capital punishment was a legal form of punishment in 2000. Additionally, the method of execution used by the federal government is lethal injection. This is pursuant to 28 CFR, Part 26.

This triple hanging was conducted in a public setting in London circa 1809. Notice the crowd which appears to cheer on to the executioners.

TABLE **15-1** Execution Methods

Method of Execution	Number of Countries Where Practiced
Firing squad	73 (sole method in 45 countries)
Hanging	58 (sole method in 33 countries)
Stoning	6
Lethal injection	5 (sole method in 1 country)
Beheading	3 countries
Electrocution	1 (United States)
Lethal gas	1 (United States)

Source: Information was obtained from Amnesty International, AIUSA Program to Abolish the Death Penalty: Methods of Execution Worldwide, 1999.

Some of the states listed in Figure 15-1 seldom utilize capital punishment although they have a legalized method of execution. The statistics presented earlier suggest most executions occur in a small minority of states that have legalized capital punishment. This trend may be more evident in the future as more states join Illinois, which placed a moratorium on the death penalty on January 31, 2000.

The most executions are carried out, in a given year, through lethal injection. Some argue, however, that the popularity associated with the use of the lethal injection is due to the public perception that it constitutes a less painful experience for the accused, while others argue that it is a swift and politically correct punishment. In spite of differing opinions, lethal injection is becoming so popular that some states, such as Florida, are considering eliminating electrocution.

15-4 Executing Minors and the Mentally Retarded

An extremely controversial topic in capital punishment is the execution of minors and/or the mentally retarded. In 2000, seven jurisdictions did not state a minimum age for an individual to be considered eligible for the death penalty, while some states have reduced their "age bar" to fourteen. If an individual at least fourteen years of age commits an act that, according to statutes, is considered a capital crime, he/she will automatically be eligible to receive the death

Lethal Injection		Electrocution	Lethal Gas	Hanging	Firing Squad
Arizona	Nevada	Alabama	Arizona	Delaware	Idaho
Arkansas	New Hampshire	Arkansas	California	New Hampshire	Oklahoma
California	New Jersey	Florida	Missouri	Washington	Utah
Colorado	New Mexico	Georgia	Wyoming		
Connecticut	New York	Kentucky			
Delaware	North Carolina	Nebraska			
Florida	Ohio	Ohio			
Georgia	Oklahoma	Oklahoma			
Idaho	Oregon	South Carolina			
Illinois	Pennsylvania	Tennessee			
Indiana	South Carolina	Virginia			
Kansas	South Dakota				
Kentucky	Tennessee				
Louisiana	Texas				
Maryland	Utah				
Mississippi	Virginia				
Missouri	Washington				
Montana	Wyoming				

Source: U.S. Department of Justice (2001), Bureau of Justice Statistics, "Capital Punishment 2000," Washington, D.C.

Figure 15-1
Methods of Execution by State, 2000

penalty if convicted. Critics argue that at the age of fourteen, very few children understand the full scope of their actions and that punishing them with death constitutes a violation of the constitutional protection against cruel and unusual punishment. Figure 15-2 illustrates the minimum age requirement for capital punishment in individual states.

National and international human rights watch groups have recently raised concerns regarding some states' practices of issuing death sentences to individuals who are legally and clinically found to be mentally retarded. At the core of this debate is whether these individuals were fully aware that their respective acts of violence were morally and legally wrong and whether they were conscious and had the maturity to understand the consequences of their actions. Despite the public pressure, the courts have been reluctant to consider the issue. This

Age 16 or less	Agïe Ï17	Age 18	None Specified
Alabama (16)	Georgia	California	Arizona
Arkansas (14)	New Hampshire	Colorado	Idaho
Delaware (16)	North Carolina	Connecticut	Louisiana
Florida (16)	Texas	Federal System	Montana
Indiana (16)		Illinois	Pennsylvania
Kentucky (16)		Kansas	South Carolina
Mississippi (16)		Maryland	South Dakota
Missouri (16)		Nebraska	
Nevada (16)		New Jersey	
Oklahoma (16)		New Mexico	
Utah (14)		New York	
Virginia (14)		Ohio	
Wyoming (16)		Oregon	
		Tennessee	
		Washington	

Source: U.S. Department of Justice (2001), Bureau of Justice Statistics, "Capital Punishment 2000," Washington, D.C.

Figure 15-2
Minimum Age Requirement for Capital Punishment Sentence, 2000

changed recently as the United States Supreme Court declared, after hearing *Atkins v. Virginia* (2002) that the execution of mentally retarded individuals constituted cruel and unusual punishment as stated in the Eight Amendment to the U.S. Constitution.[22] The implications of this decision are monumental for all individuals that have been sentenced to death despite their mental impairment. The Court also gave specific instructions that states re-try or reconsider the death sentences already issued to mentally retarded inmates.

15-5 The Death Penalty Debate

15-5a Cost

Debates over the death penalty have not changed dramatically in the past and basic arguments for and against have remained the same. Some proponents have argued that capital punishment is less expensive than keeping a person in prison for life and for that reason should be used for serious crimes. If capital punishment were applied immediately after a person received a sentence, the argument would be valid although that is almost never the case in the United States. The imposition of the death sentence is only the beginning of a long process of court appeals, collateral attacks, and petitions to the governor to commute the sentence to life or to grant a pardon.[23]

As a result, capital punishment may actually cost more than life imprisonment. Murder trials are expensive and lengthy. Even when the prosecution's case is strong, the defendant might plead not guilty because of the threat of capital punishment. In highly publicized first-degree murder cases, prosecutors are not likely to accept a guilty plea to a lesser charge, such as second-degree murder. Selecting a jury in a capital case is often a long and expensive process. Finally, the cost of incarcerating an individual on death row is greater than the cost of incarcerating other inmates. Some also argue that there is a need for better security on death row to ensure that an individual does not take his or her own life or harm others.

This was illustrated in the case of Gary Gilmore. Gilmore was scheduled to be executed on January 17, 1977, and wanted his mother and the American Civil Liberties Union (ACLU) to discontinue appealing his case, saying he wanted to die "like a man." He twice attempted suicide in prison. The state of Utah paid over $60,000 to keep Gilmore alive after those attempts. This particular figure, which was an estimated cost between November 1, 1976, and January 17, 1977, did not include the cost of food or clothing. It included $18,330 for the time Gilmore spent in the hospital after his suicide attempts, $725 for the cost of the six-man firing squad, and $19,000 for the cost of overtime work of deputies and secretaries who began working at 3:00 A.M. the day of the execution, as well as $513 "for an airplane flight to Denver where a last-minute stay of execution was overturned."[24]

15-5b Protection of the Criminal Justice System

Critics have argued that capital punishment hinders the criminal justice system by causing appellate courts in capital cases to strain the evidence or the law to avoid imposing the death penalty. The early modern history of capital punishment in the United States suggests that capital punishment had a negative impact on America's system of justice. Organizations such as the President's Crime Commission argued that it was difficult to select a jury for capital punishment cases. Once selected, it was a complex task for jury members to find the accused guilty, due to the finality of the death penalty. The possibility of the death penalty may sensationalize the entire trial and sentencing process.

Another consequence of the existence of the death penalty is panic legislation to include spectacular crimes not already covered by capital punishment.

For example, public reaction to kidnapping for political reasons, sex crimes, or skyjacking could lead to quick legislation to provide the death penalty for such offenses. Public emotions may be so high that rational debate on the issue is impossible.

According to Ramsey Clark, author of *Crime in America,* the use of capital punishment also hinders the rehabilitative efforts of prison personnel, especially chaplains, who work with those on death row. Clark also notes the depressing experiences of wardens who must attend to the last details of executions: "They know the inhumanity of the death penalty and the effect of executions on the other men in their custody." Finally, Clark cites a classic study conducted in 1961 by the American Bar Foundation, which found that long delays in capital cases "weaken public confidence in the law. This is an understatement born of self-interest. Such cases have disgusted millions."[25]

One of the most frequent arguments by those in favor of the death penalty is that the system of criminal justice will be endangered without capital punishment because of the increased murders of prison officials, inmates, and police officers. It is assumed that prisoners sentenced to life have nothing to lose and are more likely to kill prison officials. Thorsten Sellin surveyed prison officials concerning fatal and nonfatal assaults within their institutions in 1965. He received responses from forty-five states, the District of Columbia, and the Federal Bureau of Prisons. The study revealed fifty-nine assailants serving terms for crimes ranging from murder to delinquency. Only twenty of the fifty-nine had received a death sentence. Twenty additional assailants were serving terms for which they could have received the death sentence. Sellin's point, which has remained a classic perspective that is still applicable today, was that no court or jury could know which of the many persons convicted of a capital crime would commit assault or murder in prison. Nor would sentencing all people convicted of a capital crime have prevented assaults and murder in prison, since some of the assailants were convicted of crimes for which they could not receive the death penalty. Sellin concluded that immediate execution of all those convicted for capital crimes would certainly have eliminated some of the assaults and deaths. To imagine that the hazards of prison life could be "completely removed is visionary, but it is equally visionary to believe that the threat of the death penalty could play any role in reducing them."[26]

15-5c Public Opinion

Before 1936, executions were usually public and the large gatherings at these events indicated public approval. Women and children attended and refreshments were often available. These public executions legitimized the power of the monarchy. The symbolism attached to the execution (for example, the officials reading the death sentence, the presence of guards) was a reminder to the captive audience that the monarchs had the power of life and death. If anyone sought to challenge the legitimacy of the monarchy, then death was imminent. Further, public executions were thought to have a deterrent effect:

> Every contortion of the limbs was hailed with a cheer or a groan, according as the sufferer was popular or not: appalling curses and execrations rent the air and rendered the last moments of the unfortunate criminal more odious: hawkers boldly sang the praises of their wares the [sic] while a fellow creature was being doomed to death. Rich and poor, thief and lord, gentle and simple, attended to see "the hanging" and cracked jokes at the sufferer's expense... [A]s late as 1849 an execution scene which horrified Dickens delighted a crowd of over thirty thousand persons who paid exorbitant prices for the most improvised of seats.[27]

As recently as 1973, 10,000 people watched a public execution by a six-man firing squad in Uganda. The last public execution in the United States took place on August 14, 1936, in Owensboro, Kentucky, when 20,000 people viewed the hanging of Rainey Bethea. In 1977, a federal judge in Texas ruled that executions are acts of the state and therefore news professionals have a constitutional right to cover them. Despite this, the media has opted not to show the executions via television. More recently, personalities such as Phil Donahue have tried to show executions live through television outlets. They have failed, however, in their attempt to demonstrate the legality of providing this experience to the American public. Some argue that doing so will change the opinion of the American public toward the death penalty, alleging that most Americans who currently support the death penalty would change their opinions about it once they saw the barbaric details of an execution. Others argue that showing an execution on live television would legitimize the role of violence and would send the message to the public that "life is cheap." Despite the ongoing debate, executions will soon be televised or shown over the Internet, although the ramifications this will have on the American public are still unclear.

Summary

In this chapter, the issue of capital punishment from a philosophical, legal, and empirical point of view was examined. The basic issue remains: If capital punishment is working, why are homicides and other serious crimes still occurring?

Different perspectives govern the ongoing debate about whether capital punishment is a necessary and efficient method of punishment. In spite of all the debate, death sentences in the United States are being issued almost daily and it will not be long before the United States is the industrialized nation with the most death sentences and executions in the world.

Texas, which is the most active state in executions per year, is an interesting case study for future execution trends in the United States. A recent report stated that many Texans acknowledged that they would not be surprised if an innocent person had been executed in their state. Yet, 76 percent of Texans support the death penalty in its current form.[28] These results demonstrate disregard for the due process rights of the minority for the sake of punishing the majority. The majority of Texans polled in this particular study felt that they could live with the fact that a few innocent individuals were executed as the majority of the guilty were experiencing the same fate.

Although many scholars argue that Texas, with its current death penalty practices, is unique, many counter this argument by implying that it is only a matter of time before other states find themselves in the same situation. Some argue that the death penalty practices for adult offenders will slow down or end in the near future. Those who make this argument cite the recent moratorium on the death penalty implemented in the state of Illinois as a sign of trends to come. Recently, this argument has received a great deal of momentum from the decisions made by the courts—not only those mentioned earlier with respect to the execution of mentally retarded inmates, but also a decision by a U.S. District Court Judge in New York, who declared the current federal death penalty practices as unconstitutional. In his words, Judge Rakoff stated that "on the one hand, innocent people are sentenced to death with materially greater frequency than was previously supposed and that, on the other hand, convincing proof of their innocence often does not emerge until long after their convictions."[29] Supporters of the death penalty argue that in the near future, the death penalty will grow in popularity as crime rates increase, although it is in the hands of the American public to continue or change the future of the system of justice.

Notes

1. Haskins, George, "A Rule to Walk By," In *Crime and Justice in Society,* edited by Richard Quinney, 37 (Boston: Little, Brown and Company, 1969).
2. "Focus on the Death Penalty: History and Recent Developments," Anchorage, Alaska: University of Alaska Anchorage Justice Center website, 2001. www.uaa.Alaska.edu/just/death/history.html
3. Ancel, Marc, "The Problem of the Death Penalty," In *Capital Punishment,* edited by Thorsten Sellin (New York: Harper and Row, 1967), pp. 4-5.
4. Ancel, "The Problem of the Death Penalty," pp. 7-8.
5. *Furman v. Georgia,* 408 U.S. 238, 371 (1972). Justice Marshall concurring.
6. *Roberts v. Louisiana,* 428 U.S. 325 (1976) (convicted of murder in the course of armed robbery); *Woodson v. North Carolina,* 428 U.S. 280 (1976) (convicted of murder in course of armed robbery); *Profitt v. Florida,* 428 U.S. 242 (1976) (convicted for murder in course of robbery); *Jurek v. Texas,* 429 U.S. 262 (1976) (convicted of murder in course of kidnapping and forcible rape); *Gregg v. Georgia,* 428 U.S. 153 (1976) (convicted of murder in course of armed robbery).
7. Michigan State University and Death Penalty Information Center (2001). www.deathpenaltyinfo.msu.edu/c/about/methods/methods.PDF
8. U.S. Department of Justice. Bureau of Justice Statistics (2001), "Capital Punishment 2000," By Tracy L. Snell.
9. U.S. Department of Justice. Bureau of Justice Statistics (2001), "Capital Punishment 2000," By Tracy L. Snell.
10. "Executions in the U.S., 2001," Washington, D.C.: Death Penalty Information Center (DPIC), 2001. www.deathpenaltyinfo.org/dpicexec01.html
11. "Executions in the U.S., 2001."
12. "Executions in the U.S., 2001."
13. "Executions in the U.S., 2001."
14. Paris, Michael (2000), "Are We All Really Equal: Discrimination in the Courts," Unpublished paper; and Aguirre A., and Baker, D.V. (1990), "Empirical Research on Racial Discrimination in the Imposition of the Death Penalty," *Criminal Justice Abstracts* 22 (1), 135-153; and Gross, S.R., and Mauro, R. (1989), *Death and Discrimination: Racial Disparities in Capital Sentencing,* Northeastern University Press, Boston, MA.
15. "Killing with Prejudice: Race and the Death Penalty in the USA," New York: Amnesty International, 1999. www.web.amnesty.org
16. Supreme Court of the United States, *Atkins v. Virginia* No. 00-8452, Argued February 20, 2002—Decided June 20, 2002.
17. Bobit, Bonnie, *Death Row* (Torrance, CA: Bobit Publishing Company, 1999), 15–20.
18. Bobit, 15–20.
19. Bobit, 15–20.
20. Bobit, 15–20.
21. *Ex parte Kenneth Granviel,* 561 S.W. 2d 503 (1978). (For a discussion of the method of execution by lethal injection, see www.theelectricchair.com/lethal_injection_protocol.htm).
22. Paris, Michael (2000), "Are We All Really Equal: Discrimination in the Courts," Unpublished paper; and Aguirre A., and Baker, D.V. (1990), "Empirical Research on Racial Discrimination in the Imposition of the Death Penalty," *Criminal Justice Abstracts,* 22 (1), 135-153; and Gross, S.R., and Mauro, R. (1989), *Death and Discrimination: Racial Disparities in Capital Sentencing,* Northeastern University Press, Boston, MA.
23. Nakeel, Barry, "The Cost of the Death Penalty," *Criminal Law Bulletin* 14 (January–February 1978), 69–80.
24. "The Cost of Gilmore's Execution," *New York Times,* 31 January 1977, 12C.
25. Clark, Ramsey, *Crime in America* (New York: Simon and Schuster, 1970), 333–334.
26. Sellin, *Capital Punishment.*
27. John Laurence, quoted in Hall, Jerome, *Theft, Law, and Society* (Boston: Little, Brown and Company, 1935) 85.
28. The *Fort Worth Star Telegram,* 1 March 2001, 2A.
29. CNN.com Law Center, "Federal Death Penalty Overturned," July 1, 2002, from Terry Frieden, CCN Washington Bureau.

Chapter 16

The Future of Corrections

In earlier chapters, the various options for handling criminal offenders were examined. Punishment has been administered in such unique ways that it sometimes seems as if all new ideas have been exhausted, without discovering the causes of high recidivism and incarceration rates. This chapter explores the decline of an emphasis on the rehabilitative ideal, noting the return to a punishment philosophy of retribution. It also explores various perspectives on the future of corrections, including the aging of the inmate population. The existing correctional trends as they have been influenced by the war on terrorism and their impact on the future of corrections will also be examined.

Key Terms

Advanced Vehicle Notification System (AVIAN)
privatization

Outline

16-1 Decline of the Rehabilitative Ideal

In 1959, law professor Francis A. Allen coined the term "rehabilitative ideal."[1] This ideal was characterized by the juvenile court, probation, parole, and individualized sentencing and treatment. The rehabilitative ideal was based on the premise that human behavior is the result of antecedent causes that may become known by objective analysis, thus permitting the scientific control of human behavior. The assumption was that the offender could and should be treated, not punished.

The rehabilitative ideal has come under strong attack in recent years. In 1977, Allen admitted that the "case against the rehabilitative ideal has achieved spectacular success. Rarely has there been so precipitous and complete a reversal of professional opinion . . . The concept of deserved punishment is to be refurbished and pressed into service."[2] The result has been a nationwide attack on the indeterminate sentence and parole and a decrease in the support of a treatment/rehabilitation rationale for imprisonment.

The main reason for the decline in popularity of the rehabilitative ideal is that many perceive the treatment approach as unsuccessful. Several years ago, David L. Bazelon, Chief Judge of the United States Court of Appeals in Washington, D.C., concluded that the basic problem with rehabilitation as a justification for punishment was that it "should never have been sold on the promise that it would reduce crime."[3] Nevertheless, it was promised that treatment would be effective in reducing the rates of recidivism when offenders are released from prison. As crime rates continued to soar, the public became disillusioned with the rehabilitative approach.

The attack on the effectiveness of treatment came in 1974 when Robert Martinson published his article entitled, "What Works?—Questions and Answers About Prison Reform,"[4] in which he reported the results of his survey of the literature on corrections programs published between 1945 and 1967. Martinson concluded that treatment has been ineffective in reducing rates of recidivism.

Many who criticized Martinson's work alleged that he had little to do with the original report on the effectiveness of treatment. The original report was criticized as only treatment studies before 1967 were selected for analysis. He was also criticized for his failure to include all types of treatment programs. He did not focus on the differential value and the degree of effectiveness of the method. Critics argued that the conclusions in his article were inconsistent with the information reported in his book. Ted Palmer attacked Martinson for asking "What works?" instead of "Which methods work best for which types of offenders, and under what conditions or in what types of settings?"[5]

It was further argued that Martinson ignored the possibility that the characteristics of the researcher are important in analyzing the results. Martinson's study failed to consider the possibility that treatment might be effective immediately but then fade after the inmate is released from the correctional facility. Martinson did not design his study to permit quantitative and objective analysis of the partial effects of treatment programs. Finally, critics alleged that treatment in correctional institutions has been as ineffective as have efforts to combat other social problems.

It seems to have made little difference whether Martinson was correct in his initial assessment of the failure of treatment methods. He reported what many people wanted to hear and gained considerable exposure among professionals as well as the public. His work is among the most frequently cited evidence that treatment has not been effective and that society should return to a philosophy of retribution as a justification for punishment.

16-1a The Return to Retribution

For centuries, philosophers have debated justifications for punishment. This text has traced the movement from an emphasis on retribution and deterrence to the embodiment of the rehabilitative ideal, and most recently, back to a form of retribution.

Historically, the concept of retribution meant revenge, often manifested in the doctrine of "an eye for an eye and a tooth for a tooth." Under the doctrine of revenge, an offender should be treated by society in the same way that the offender treated his or her victim. Thus, the hands of a thief would be removed and the eye of the spy gouged. The extreme form of the doctrine was manifested in the use of capital punishment in the cases of those who murdered.

More recently, the doctrine of retribution has come back into favor, but this time the emphasis is on just deserts, which does not mean an "eye for an eye and a tooth for a tooth," although in some cases that would be considered appropriate. Just deserts means that the offender receives the punishment he or she deserves and no more. According to the proponents of this model, deterrence of others, protection of society, or rehabilitation of the offender may result from punishment, but they should not be the reason for punishment.

16-1b The Justice Model

One of the persons most responsible for the popularity of the justice model is David Fogel, who expressed his views in his book, "*. . . We Are the Living Proof . . .": The Justice Model for Corrections.*[6] Fogel argued that punishment is necessary for implementation of the criminal law, which is based on the theory that people act as a result of their own free will. His approach is similar to that of the classical writers, who took the position that criminal behavior is rational and based on hedonism—people choose to behave in a certain way because they gain pleasure from that behavior. However, if the pain or punishment that results from the behavior is greater than the pleasure to be gained, people will refrain from the act.

According to Fogel, offenders act on the basis of free will and they should be held responsible for their acts. They become the focal point of the criminal justice system. Fogel emphasized that all the agencies of the criminal justice system should be carried out in a milieu of justice, meaning justice for the offender does not stop with the due process accorded at trial—it continues through all stages of the system. Justice for offenders means that once they are incarcerated, the state will not attempt to force them to change, reform, or be rehabilitated.

16-1c The Aging Prison Population

There is a current trend to demonize (i.e., label as evil) all offenders found guilty for a drug-related offense. These individuals are presently facing longer punitive sentences, some of which were enacted during the Reagan administration in the 1980s. Inevitably, these longer sentences have precipitated the rising trend of the prison population. As baby boomers approach their retirement age, prisons find themselves dealing with more mature inmates, who were incarcerated at an older age or sentenced to prison for life when they were young. Most of these individuals occupy trustworthy jobs in prisons. They are viewed as inmates who pose little risk of escaping. In fact, some correctional staff members have sympathy for them. Most of the elderly offenders have been in prison for long terms and have become dependent on the system. When such dependent prisoners are released, they find themselves lost in a world in which independence is not only valued but is also a means of survival.

Specifically, the "Three Strikes and You're Out" law has been instrumental in the incarceration of inmates who, after committing a third, similar violent crime, are sentenced to life without parole. As other states adopt this law, more and more inmates are expected to die from natural causes while in prison. As a result, the citizenry should expect to pay not only for more prisons, but also for the special needs of older inmates. These include long-term medical treatment, special housing, and appropriate facilities to accommodate wheelchairs and walkers. It is likely that older inmates will have other needs, such as special diets, prescription drugs, and eyeglasses. Additionally, staff will need special training to accommodate the older inmates.

Another concern is the older inmate's vulnerability to younger inmates. Since the prison environment reflects Darwin's survival of the fittest, older inmates are likely to be victimized by the younger, more agile inmates. If a particular facility were to separate the older and younger inmates (which may be a plausible solution to the problem), the citizens in that particular jurisdiction would have to pay higher taxes to build these special units.

16-2 Lessons Learned from the Past

The National Institute of Corrections (NIC) sponsored a national conference in 1996 to discuss what was working and what was not working in planning for the future of corrections.[7] The NIC asserted that programs designed for the specific needs of offenders were effective. These programs ranged from boot camps for young street offenders to dormitories for illiterate substance abusers. These programs are designed for sex offenders, high school dropouts, the mentally ill and retarded, and the elderly. Conference attendees recommended that these programs continue to be part of the correctional system.

Conference attendees also regarded community corrections as successful in that it allows the state to effectively impose local sanctions on nonviolent offenders. They argued that although many new laws call for longer, more definite sentences for recidivists, some also contain a "presumption for local punishment." The states can administer their own punishment, especially for nonviolent offenders. This trend allows states to have more control and should continue as a part of the correctional system.

One of the last points made by those who attended the NIC conference was that technology has been and will continue to be part of corrections.[8] Many states are now implementing telemedicine—a program that allows inmates to participate in medical conferences with doctors electronically instead of being transported to a medical facility for a consultation. This technology, although expensive to implement, is reportedly highly effective in reducing the costs associated with the transportation and supervision of inmates during medical visits outside the prison facility. NIC conference attendees also concluded that computers and databases are highly effective in the proper management and operation of prison facilities around the United States. Technology will continue to serve the custodial and operational needs of American corrections.

16-2a Today's Trends and Their Impact on the Future of Corrections

Prison populations were relatively stable in the 1960s. Since that time, however, the United States has experienced an unprecedented increase in incarceration rates. Although this text has attempted to explain the reasons for this increase, it is unclear what this means for the future of corrections.

There is no universal consensus on predictions about the future of American corrections. Criminologist James Fox predicted that the rising violence of juveniles is the leading edge of a "blood bath" that is bound to take place in the future. Professor James Austin, executive director of the National Council on Crime and Delinquency, disputed this view. For some, increases in violent crime demand even more extensive incarceration sentences. Others feel incarceration fails to deter crime and furthers the plight of already disadvantaged minorities. Ben Crouch has recently examined some aspects of society and corrections that, in his opinion, point toward the future.[9] Specifically, Crouch contended that the existing social, demographic, economic, and political conditions in the United States account for a great proportion of the correctional status quo.

Crouch begins his assessment by stating that demographic shifts in the United States have influenced crime and imprisonment rates. He points out that as the baby boomers entered their late teens (in the late 1960s), crime increased rapidly.[10] However, it was not until the mid-1970s that a higher crime rate affected the incarceration rate. One reason for this delay is the fact that criminal justice systems in the 1960s may have been hesitant to incarcerate young offenders, who were instead given probation. Crouch explains that it did not take long for the system to run out of patience, resulting in the more frequent incarceration of offenders.

Economic and occupational structure shifts also led to the increase of crime and incarceration rates. Many argue that as America moved from a unionized, manufacturing economy to a more competitive and less unionized economy, the urban poor and minorities were severely affected.[11] Of all the minorities, African-Americans are reportedly one of the most affected groups, although Hispanics are becoming more affected as their population grows.

It is clear that these changes created an environment suitable for violence, drug addiction, and other vices. The growing incarceration rate and the increase in juvenile violence has led many to predict a future full of chaos and disparity.

According to Crouch, the shifts mentioned earlier provide information about the future of American corrections. Crouch argues that the economy will increasingly demand skills and attitudes that large, poor, and urban populations have a very small opportunity to acquire. Thus, members of these populations will be unable to compete in the conventional economy. Out of their inability, Crouch argues, they will likely turn to crime and, at times, even high-profile acts of violence or collective violence. This will continue to prompt public demand for tougher sanctions.[12]

Although some disagree, Crouch sustains that crime rates will fall over the next few decades because there will be a decrease in the number of young people and an increase in the number of older persons. This may lower the incarceration rate. However, Crouch warns that this may not occur if prison officials find it easy to fill the newly built prisons and if the existing conservative agenda continues its influence over the legislative and political processes. If these two trends continue, prisons in the twenty-first century will likely be large enterprises that house high numbers of unskilled, poor, powerless, and angry minorities.[13] In other words, as many critical criminologists contend, prisons will continue their legacy of serving as houses for the oppressed.

Hispanics

According to the U.S. Census Bureau, Hispanics will make up 18.9 percent of the total U.S. population by the year 2030.[14] Today's correctional system is already over-represented by Hispanics and this trend will continue, presenting more serious challenges to prison administrators.

Most problems occur because today's prison systems are ill-equipped to handle the cultural differences that surround the Hispanic inmate. Aside from the language barrier, other differences exist in the areas of religion, politics, and regard for law and authority. The lack of planning by correctional administrators and policy-makers alike can and will result in a major predicament to the correctional system of the twenty-first century.

Technology

Although most U.S. households enjoy the benefit of a personal computer, most correctional facilities lack the resources and political support to make computers available to inmates. The lack of access to computers further limits their marketability in the job place (which expresses the need for computer-literate individuals) upon release.

Despite the limited availability of computers to the inmate population, correctional staff relies increasingly upon the use of computers in the everyday operation of correctional facilities. As correctional websites are being developed, it is likely that computers will continue to play an important role in the operation of correctional facilities.

Aside from computers, prison administrators are currently benefiting from several technological advances. California is one of the states currently using the latest technology. Prison administrators in California, upon hearing rumors of a potential inmate outbreak via an underground tunnel, sought the help of Special Technologies Laboratories (STL). The STL team, using a "ground penetrating radar" (GPR), was able to locate the underground tunnel and therefore prevent the escape.[15]

Advanced Vehicle Notification System (AVIAN) Detects the heartbeat of an individual who may be hidden inside a vehicle.

Another technological advance involves the use of the **Advanced Vehicle Notification System (AVIAN)**, which detects the heartbeat of a person who may be hidden inside a vehicle. This is particularly useful to correctional staff in their daily inspections of service vehicles leaving the correctional institution.[16] Corrections, much like society, is increasing its dependency on technology and the use of intelligent computer systems.

Privatization

Privatization Trend in the correctional field in which the private sector is becoming increasingly involved in the operation of correctional institutions.

A recent phenomenon—the **privatization** of correctional facilities—has taken place. This phenomenon serves as evidence that the private sector has responded to the growing need of warehousing offenders. As the prison population continues to grow, the need for the creation of these private facilities will grow as well. Despite this, the birth of privately owned correctional facilities has been the subject of much controversy. Some of this concern is a result of reported inmate abuse and substandard accreditation requirements. Although some feel pessimistic about the future of private prisons, others argue that they will improve their record by virtue of their vulnerability to public opinion. Privatization will continue to have a significant impact on the correctional system.

The War on Terrorism

Although the war on terrorism has affected most of the United States citizenry, the criminal justice system has been particularly affected by the actions from the current administration to create, modify, and expand existing criminal justice agencies. First, the Federal Bureau of Investigation (FBI) will have a new role to play in the fight against terrorism. This, added to the division of the Immigration and Naturalization Service (INS) and the creation of a new Homeland Security Office, will expand the size and role of government in unprecedented proportions.

Corrections, like many other components of the criminal justice system, is likely to be affected by the existing governmental expansion in order to fight terrorism. The U.S. military may ask the Department of Corrections to become involved. This may only be in the advisory capacity as the federal government builds appropriate holding facilities for individuals convicted of terrorism. Issues relevant to funding are likely to have an impact on the correctional system almost immediately. As long as the U.S. fights terrorism, federal funding is likely to be prioritized in that direction while other governmental agencies, such as corrections, will receive limited money. This trend is likely to start at the federal level but will continue to the state level as well.

Summary

It is very difficult to pinpoint what has gone wrong in the U.S. system of corrections. First, our society tends to make decisions without carefully analyzing possible consequences. The public demands solutions and corrections officials take stopgap measures, which may or may not solve the growing crime problem.

Second, too much is promised. Samuel Walker, a nationally recognized criminologist, concluded that a "decline in faith in the idea of rehabilitation . . . rehabilitation has become an unpopular goal. . . The war on crime, like the Johnsonian War on Poverty, promised too much, and the backlash resulting from the failure has been costly . . ."[17]

A significant reduction in the crime rate might be an unrealistic goal for the American reform proposals. Changing only one area of the criminal justice system may not have a significant, positive effect on all other areas. For example, the public believes the return to a philosophy of retribution, or of just deserts, will reduce crime. If criminals get what they deserve, others will be deterred from crime. If convicted offenders are incarcerated for long enough, they will be deterred from committing crimes upon release. Unfortunately, the more likely effect is that a return to the retribution philosophy will exacerbate the problems in corrections. It will increase the numbers of inmates, leading to greater problems of overcrowding in the already inadequate prison facilities. This new get-tough approach may lead to a lessening of any attempts at rehabilitation, even on a voluntary basis. The programs and the personnel will not be available for the increasing numbers of inmates and the public will be unwilling to appropriate the necessary funds for expansion of treatment programs.

Third, treatment efforts should not be abandoned if the just deserts approach is adopted. It is one thing to argue against forced treatment and quite another to eliminate opportunities for inmates to participate in treatment programs voluntarily. Likewise, treatment should not be confused with humanitarianism. Efforts to make prisons more humane have led some to believe that inmates have been involved in treatment. Don Gibbons stated the difference between treatment and humanitarianism: "Humanitarian reform designates those changes that have been introduced into corrections in recent decades which serve to lessen the harshness or severity of punishment."[18] The humanitarian movement is based on the early philosophy that deprivation of liberty is the punishment. It would be excessive punishment, and therefore inhumane, to force a person to live in filth, among rats, in damp, cold, dark cells, to eat poorly prepared food constituting an unbalanced diet, and to suffer corporal punishment. Gibbons pointed out that actions, such as an increase in the number of visits, may decrease tensions in prison and may have positive effects on the inmates who receive the visitors. They may also, however, have negative effects. The visits are not treatment and should not be considered therapeutic in nature. Increased visits, classification, education, and vocational training might be referred to as adjuncts to treatment. Other adjuncts are religious activities, recreational participation, and prerelease planning. These programs are not aimed at particular therapy problems of inmates and therefore are not treatment per se.

Treatment, said Gibbons, consists of "explicit tactics or procedures deliberately undertaken to change those conditions thought to be responsible for the violator's misbehavior."[19] We should continue providing the opportunities by which those inmates who wish to change their behavior might be able to do so. As Chief Justice Warren E. Burger of the United States Supreme Court said, "We take on a burden when we put a man behind walls, and that burden is to give him a chance to change. If we deny him that, we deny his status as a human being, and to deny that is to diminish our own humanity and plant the seeds of future anguish for ourselves."[20]

Fourth, economic and political problems will need to be properly handled if change is to take place. In attempts to locate places for community-based corrections, there will be opposition. Therefore, citizens should be educated on the need for such facilities. The public will also resist the costs associated and must be convinced that the cost is greater if needed reforms do not occur.

Fifth, the need for research and evaluation of all attempted programs and reforms should be emphasized. Improvements in research methodology as well as in the development of theories must receive a high priority in corrections. Specifically, it must be ensured that the evaluators of correctional programs are independent from those providing the funding or overseeing the institutions. Furthermore, research in the area of corrections should include discussions on the history of correctional programs in order to provide a better sense of initiatives that do or do not work.

Sixth, diversion in the criminal justice system should be emphasized, especially in the case of juveniles. Unfortunately, since the President's Crime Commission first popularized the term "diversion" in the late 1960s, it has been used in too many cases to "widen the net" and draw in juveniles who never should have been involved in official processing. The process of diversion needs to be decriminalized and the number of offenses covered by criminal law reduced. Some juvenile offenders with alcohol and/or drug dependency problems should not be funneled into the criminal justice system unless they have violated other laws.

Finally, the need for the law and social sciences to work together in the area of corrections should be emphasized. Although corrections is a component of the criminal justice system, changes might have repercussions in other areas of the system of justice.

Although some of the answers to the problems in corrections are still unknown, it is clear that action must be taken. Any action that results in significant rehabilitation of those who serve time in our institutions will involve positive changes in the structure of society. No prison program can be successful if the inmate returns to a society determined to reject those who have been convicted of crimes and have served time in correctional institutions. Most inmates do eventually return to society. If the individual and society do not adequately prepare for that return, recidivism will continue to be a problem in the twenty-first century.

Notes

1. This term is credited to Francis A. Allen in "Criminal Justice, Legal Values and the Rehabilitative Ideal," *Journal of Criminal Law, Criminology, and Police Science* 50 (September-October, 1959), 226–232.
2. Allen, Francis A., "Central Problems of American Criminal Justice," *Michigan Law Review* 75 (April-May, 1977), 813–822. Quotation is on p. 821.
3. Bazelon, David L., "Street Crime and Correctional Potholes," *Federal Probation* 41 (March, 1977), 3.
4. Martinson, Robert, "What Works?—Questions and Answers about Prison Reform," *The Public Interest* No. 35 (Spring, 1974), 22–54. For a more recent assessment on programs that work, see Reginald A. Wilkinson, "What Works? (Correctional Practice)," *Corrections Today* (August, 1996), vol. 58, no. 5, 6(2).
5. Palmer, Ted, "Martinson Revisited," chapter 2 in Robert Martinson, Ted Palmer, and Stuart Adams, *Rehabilitation, Recidivism, and Research* (Hackensack, NJ: National Council on Crime and Delinquency, 1976), pp. 41–152.
6. Fogel, David, "*. . . We Are the Living Proof . . .": The Justice Model for Corrections* (Cincinnati, OH: W. H. Anderson, 1975).
7. Wilkinson, "What Works?" 6(2).
8. Wilkinson, "What Works?" 6(2).
9. Crouch, Ben M., "Looking Back to See the Future of Corrections," *Prison Journal* (December, 1996), vol. 76, no. 4, 468(7).
10. Crouch, "Looking Back," 468(7).
11. Crouch, "Looking Back," 468(7).
12. Crouch, "Looking Back," 468(7).
13. Crouch, "Looking Back," 468(7).
14. For the latest census figures, go to http://www.Census.gov/
15. deGroot, Gabrielle, "Hot New Technologies," *Corrections Today* (July, 1997), vol. 59, no. 4, 60–61; and "Ionscan Drug Detection Devices Will Be Installed in New California Prison," *Corrections Digest* (Feb. 17, 1995), vol. 26, no. 7, 7.
16. deGroot, "Hot New Technologies," pp. 60–61.
17. Walker, Samuel, "Reexamining the President's Crime Commission: The Challenge of Crime in a Free Society after Ten Years," *Crime and Delinquency* 24 (January, 1978), pp. 1, 12.
18. Gibbons, Don, *Changing the Law Breaker: The Treatment of Delinquents and Criminals* (Englewood Cliffs, NJ: Prentice-Hall, 1965), pp. 130–131.
19. Gibbons, *Changing the Law Breaker,* p. 130.
20. Burger, Warren E., "No Man Is an Island," *American Bar Association Journal* 56 (April, 1970), 328.

Glossary

A

Advanced Vehicle Notification System (AVIAN): Detects the heartbeat of an individual who may be hidden inside a vehicle.

Auburn, or congregate, system: Prison system that espoused congregate work during the day with an enforced rule of silence; also demanded that the prisoners be housed in isolation at night.

B

Bail: A system of posting bond to secure a defendant's presence at trial while allowing the accused to be released until the individual faces a trial.

Battered woman syndrome: An act of aggression on the part of a woman who has been physically abused by a man with whom she had a close relationship.

Behavior modification: Method based on learning theory; applied to change behavior by rewarding appropriate behaviors and removing reinforcements for negative actions.

Benjamin Rush: Presented the first argument against caputal punishment in the United States in the home of Benjamin Franklin.

Beyond a reasonable doubt: Part of jury instructions in trials in which the jurors are told that they can only find the defendant guilty if they are convinced "beyond a reasonable doubt" of his or her guilt. Thus, a juror (or judge sitting without a jury) must be convinced of guilt of a crime (or the degree of crime, as murder instead of manslaughter).

Boot camps: A correctional program modeled after military boot camps and aimed at reforming first-time juvenile offenders.

Bureaucratic management style: Form of management which specifies that a manager has little, if any, personal contract with those who work below him or her; it is felt that personal contact will lessen the bureaucrat's authority.

C

Capital punishment: Another name given to the death penalty. The punishment which results in the death of the person convicted of a henious crime.

Certiorari: An appeal to a higher court to review a case.

Chivalry hypothesis: Early view on female criminality; held that police were less likely to arrest women and juries were less likely to convict women, due to a general attitude of protectiveness toward this gender.

Classical school of criminology: A school of thought that held that the punishment should fit the crime.

Classical theorists: Writers and philosophers who promoted the principles set forth by the classical school of criminology.

Classification clinic: Location where an individual was classified according to security and rehabilitative programs. This concept failed because it was independent from the institution that incarcerated the offender.

Community-based corrections: An approach to punishment that emphasizes reintegration of the offender into the community through the use of local facilities.

Conditions of confinement: Circumstances that surround the incarceration experience of the offender.

Conjugal visits: Visitation program that allows inmates to engage in sexual and social contact with their respective partners in a specified area of the prison facility.

Continuing custody theory: Theory that holds that the parolee remains in the custody of the granting authority. The subject is under the same rules and regulations that governed the daily conduct of the offender before release from prison.

Contract system: System under which the state maintained inmates but sold their labor to a contractor, who in turn, supervised them while providing the necessary work equipment.

Contract theory: Theory that holds that the parolee agrees to assume the conditions of release when parole is offered. If those conditions are violated, the contract has been broken, and parole may be revoked.

Correctional officer: Individual in charge of the custody of inmates in a correctional facility.

Corrections: The component of the criminal justice system concerned with the investigation, confinement, supervision, and treatment of offenders.

Corruption through default: The form of corruption that takes place because of the indifference, laziness, or naiveté on the officer's part. As a result, the officer's job is gradually taken over by others.

Corruption through friendship: The corruption of correctional personnel that results from the absence of traditional devices that separate the ruler from the ruled. The officer cannot withdraw physically, act through intermediaries, or fall back on dignity.

Corruption through reciprocity: Correctional personnel ignore minor infractions. This takes place because of the pressure experienced by officers who realize that their merit rating depends on the cooperation they receive from those they control.

Criminal law: The norms and statutes that, if violated, subject the accused individual to governmental prosecution.

Criminologists: Professionals who engage in the scientific study of crime, criminals, and criminal behavior.

Cruel and unusual punishment: Punishment prohibited by the Eighth Amendment of the U.S. Constitution. The interpretation of what constitutes cruel and unusual punishment is left to the courts' discretion.

Cultural consistency: Theory that suggests that methods and severity of punishment will be consistent with other developments within the culture at a given time.

D

Deinstitutionalization: The process of institutional incarceration with community-based correctional facilities and programs.

Deliberate indifference: Criteria used when considering the failure of a prison official to address the needs of an inmate properly.

Deprivation model: A prisonization theory based on the concept that the inmate subculture stems from prisoners' adaptation to the physical and psychological losses created by incarceration.

Deterrence: A justification frequently used for punishing individuals. It is based on the concept that the punishment will prevent or discourage an individual from engaging in criminal behavior.

Diagnostic/reception center: Correctional units in which professional staff determine which treatment program and correctional facility are appropriate for the individual offender.

Direct supervision: Prisonization theory based on the notion that podular units create an environment that is normative; civilized behavior of inmates housed is expected. Each living area is designed to enhance the observation of and communication between inmates and staff members.

Double jeopardy: Prosecuting an individual twice for the same offense; prohibited by the Fifth Amendment of the U.S. Constitution.

Double celling: The practice of housing two (or more) offenders in a room that was originally designed for one.

Due process theory: Theory based on the concept that parole is an important phase in the process of rehabilitation.

E

Elmira Reformatory: The first true reformatory, built in 1876. It advocated the rehabilitation and reformation of offenders.

Ex Post Facto: After the fact.

F

FBI Crime Index Offenses: Classification of offenses found in the Uniform Crime Report. These include homicide, arson, forcible rape, robbery, aggravated assault, burglary, larceny/theft, and auto theft.

Federal Bureau of Prisons: Institution created in 1929 by the House Special Committee on Federal Penal and Reformatory Institutions.

Furlough: An authorized temporary leave from prison during which the offender may engage in certain types of behavior (e.g., attend a funeral, visit family members, seek employment).

G

Gangs: A groups of individuals who create an allegiance toward a common goal. In prison, these gangs often engage in unlawful or criminal behavior.

General deterrence: A punitive philosophy based on the belief that punishment in a specific case will inhibit others from committing the same offense.

Group psychotherapy: A type of psychotherapy aimed at an individual within a group setting.

Guillotine: Proposed by Dr. Joseph Guillotine of France. This form of execution is provided through the use of a machine which decapitates condemned individuals.

H

Habeas corpus: A written court order requiring that the accused be present before the court in order to determine the legality of custody and confinement.

Halfway house: A prerelease center that helps the offender engage in an adequate transition from prison to community life. Also, a facility that addresses particular problems experienced by some inmates (i.e., alcohol and drug abuse).

Hands-off doctrine: A policy used by federal courts to justify a nonintervention approach in the administration of correctional facilities.

Hanging: Historically, the most popular method of execution. In a typical hanging, the noose fractured the individual's neck.

HIV: Human Immunodeficiency Virus; virus that causes AIDS.

I

Idiosyncratic management style: This management style is referred to as being part of the "big brother" approach where the administrator tries to manage by stimulating and encouraging others to carry out their roles. This type of manager may also manipulate individuals personally.

Importation model: A theory of prisonization based on the concept that the inmate subculture is not created from internal prison experiences but rather on external patterns of behavior that inmates bring to prison.

Incapacitation: A punitive theory based on the concept that an individual offender is incarcerated to prevent the commission of any other crimes.

Indeterminate sanctions: Penalties considered to be note as harsh as prison but more stringent than probation. These include, but are not limited to, fines, parole, house monitoring, halfway houses, day treatment cnters, boot camps, and intensive supervision probation (ISP).

Indeterminate sentence: A sentence whose length is not determined by legislators or the courts, but by professionals at an institution who determine when an offender is ready to return to society.

Individual deterrence: A philosophy of punishment based on the idea that the threat of punishment may prevent a specific individual from engaging in criminal activity.

Individual psychotherapy: A form of psychotherapy aimed at addressing the specific needs of an individual. The success of this type of therapy in a controlled environment such as prison is highly questionable.

Inmate conditioning: A form of controlling inmates. Inmates are often permitted to hold a degree of power over other inmates, and in some cases are allowed infractions of the rules without penalty. In return for this treatment, inmates keep order within the correctional institution.

Inquisitory system: System in which the accused is presumed to be guilty and must prove his or her innocence.

Integrated classification system: Inmate classification system in which a classification committee, usually chaired by the warden or superintendent of the institution, was formed. The decisions of this committee were binding on the administration, and any changes in the treatment program of the inmate had to be approved by the committee.

Interaction space: This concept offers architectural designs aimed at controlling inmate interaction in the prison environment.

Intermediate sanctions: Penalties considered to be not as harsh as prison but more stringent than probation. These include fines, parole, house monitoring, halfway houses, day treatment centers, boot camps, and intensive supervision probation (ISP).

Intermittent incarceration: Type of incarceration that allows the offender who was sentenced to probation to spend weekends or nights in a local jail. The offender is part of the community while still being supervised in a controlled correctional facility.

J

Jail: A locally administered confinement facility used to detain individuals awaiting trial or serving sentences of less than one year.

Jail confinement: One of the three types of sentences that comprises most of the sentences imposed in federal and state courts for felony convictions. This type of confinement usually involves less that one year in a jail facility.

James B. Jacobs: Performed a classic correctional study on the role of wardens in correctional institutions. Further, he analyzed the involvement of the administration of the penitentiary in Stateville, Illinois.

Joseph E. Ragen: Served as the warden at Stateville, Illinois for thirty years. A former sheriff of a small Illinois town, Ragen had only a ninth-grade education and became the Stateville warden in 1936 after serving as warden of another institution in Illinois, where he had the reputation of being a strict disciplinarian.

Juries: In a criminal case, a number of individuals summoned to court and sworn to hear a trial, determine certain facts, and issue a verdict of guilty or not guilty. In some jurisdictions, juries determine the offender's sentence.

Just deserts: A principle based on the concept that an individual who commits a crime deserves to suffer for it.

Justice model: A philosophy based on the notion that justice is achieved when offenders receive punishments based on what is deserved for their offenses as specified in the law; the crime determines the punishment.

L

Law Enforcement Assistance Administration (LEAA): This administration grew out of the President's Crime Commission between 1965 and 1967. Although it was created to provide resources and coordination to state and local law enforcement agencies, it was short-lived; it was terminated in the late 1970s.

Lease system: System whereby the prison labor force was placed in the hands of a lessee for a previously agreed-upon fee.

M

Mandatory sentence: A sentence determined by statutes that requires that a specific penalty is imposed for certain convicted offenders.

Manhattan Bail Project: An experiment in the reform of bail that introduced the concept of release on one's own recognizance.

Massachusetts Code of 1864: Legal code which established capital punishment for idolatry witchcraft, blasphemy, sodomy and adultery.

Maximum-security prison: Correctional institution that holds inmates requiring the highest degree of custody and control.

Medium-security prison: Correctional institutional system in which inmates are allowed to engage in recreational activities.

Minimum-security prison: Correctional institution in which inmates are allowed extensive freedoms under limited correctional supervision.

Modification of sentence: The adjustment of an offender's sentence based on a number of factors, including the individual's good behavior in prison.

N

Neoclassical theorist: Individual who holds that situations or circumstances that make it impossible to exercise free will are reasons to exempt the accused from being convicted.

O

Obedience/conformity model: Model that emphasizes habits, respect for authority, and training in conformity.

P

Parens patriae: The historical doctrine of the states' power to serve as the ultimate parent of the child.

Parole: The continued custody and supervision, at the state and federal levels, of a released offender in the community.

Participative management style: This management style sustains that a manger should maintain an informal and friendly relationship with subordinates and may even sacrifice work requirements of the organization at times in order to keep harmony with the staff.

Penitentiary: A state or federal prison that confines offenders convicted of serious crimes and sentenced for terms longer than one year.

Pennsylvania System: Prison system based on solitary confinement whereby inmates were isolated at all times.

Personal space: The design of the new generation jail is based on the philosophy that podular units create an environment that is normative; civilized behavior of inmates housed is expected. It is believed that personal space should be encouraged to attain the previously mentioned goals.

Piece-price system: System in which a contractor pays a fixed price for each finished piece of work done by inmates.

Podular design: This design proposes living areas designed to enhance the observation of and communication (i.e., interaction) between inmates and staff members.

Positive school of criminology: A school of thought that emphasizes the individual scientific treatment of the criminal.

Positivists: Theorists who believe in the positive school of thought and who hold that the punishment should fit the criminal and not the crime.

Prerelease centers: Centers where individuals would be housed as a last step before being released from correctional supervision. These have been suggested to help alleviate the problem of overcrowding.

Principle of least eligibility: The idea that inmates should be the least eligible of all citizens to receive any social benefits beyond those required by the law.

Prison confinement: One of the three types of sentences that, comprises most of the sentences imposed in federal and state courts for felony convictions. Prison confinement usually entails a sentence of one year or more in prison.

Prison overcrowding: Condition facing prisons today. This condition has been due mostly to the creation of longer and more punitive sentences.

Privatization: Trend in the correctional field in which the private sector is becoming increasingly involved in the operation of correctional institutions.

Probation: A type of sentence in which the offender is subjected to conditioned supervision in the community.

Probation officer: An official employed by a probation agency who is mostly responsible for preparing presentence investigation reports, supervising offenders on probation, and helping to incorporate offenders back into society as lawful citizens.

Professional staff: Typically individuals who hold a college degree and work in a correctional setting conducting some form of service (e.g., counselors).

Progressives: A group of individuals who espoused social reforms, including individualized treatment of criminals to achieve their rehabilitation. They believed that treating criminals as individuals, each with a different set of needs and problems, would achieve rehabilitation and prepare criminals for mainstream society.

Public (state) account system: A system that brought the entire prison labor system under the control of the state.

PSI (Presentence Investigation Report): A report that is filed by probation or parole officers. It provides background information about the offender for the purpose of influencing the sentence imposed by the judge or parole board.

R

Reality therapy: Therapy that operates on the principle that the past is significant in an individual's behavior only to the extent that he or she so permits; the focus is therefore on the present.

Reception program: First element of a classification program; new inmates should be segregated for purposes of medical tests and for orientation.

Reeducation/development model: Model that places emphasis on changing inmates through training. It is characterized by close inmate-staff relations, emphasis on changes in attitudes and social behavior, the acquisition of skills, and the development of personal resources.

Reformation: A way in which the "prevention of crime" can be analyzed using Herbert Packer's conceptualization of behavioral prevention. In corrections, this term often refers to the idea that offenders can be changed or transformed into law-abiding citizens.

Reintegration: A punitive philosophy that emphasizes the return of the offender to the community with restored educational, employment, and family ties.

Restitution: The compensation to victims for the physical, financial, and emotional loss suffered as a result of a criminal incident. This compensation can be monetary or in the form of service to the community.

Retribution: A theory of punishment based on the premise that an offender should be punished for the crimes committed because he or she deserves it.

Revenge: A doctrine based on the concept that an individual who violates the law is punished in a way that replicates the victim's suffering.

S

Scientific method: When applied to corrections, a positivist theory that holds that social scientists should decide the punishment and treatment of offenders (rather than allowing judges or juries to decide).

Segregation: One of the forms of social control used by various correctional institutions; based on the expulsion or separation of an individual from the group.

Sentencing disparity: The variations that take place when defendants convicted of the same crime receive sentences of different types or lengths.

Shock incarceration: The process of incarcerating an individual for a brief period of time and then releasing him or her on probation.

Social contract: Doctrine that held that an individual was bound to society only by his or her consent and therefore society was responsible for the individual, and the individual was responsible for society.

Social-structural theory: A theory that relates the methods and severity of punishment to the organization and traits of the social structure; includes the division of labor in a society at a given time.

Social therapies: Social therapies promote the idea that the client is not to be rehabilitated in isolation from the environment. The two major social therapies are group therapy and mileu management. Also known as environmental therapies.

Solitary confinement: A type of confinement whereby inmates are isolated at all times; originated in the Walnut Street Jail in Philadelphia, Pennsylvania, in the late 1700s.

Split sentence: A type of sentence whereby a judge renders a sentence involving incarceration for a specific period of time followed closely by a probationary period for a fixed period of time.

State-use system: A system whereby inmates were allowed to sell their goods to state-run institutions.

Status offenders: A juvenile who commits an offense that would not be considered a crime if it had been committed by an adult.

Supermax prisons: Often referred to as "maxi-max," these institutions are built to house the most violent and aggressive individuals in the correctional system.

T

Technocratic management style: Style of management which suggests that manager may react personally with others in the organization but sees himself or herself as the outstanding expert in the organization, the chief technocrat, who directs change as necessary.

The wheel: A common form of execution which could be used in different ways. The most common was to tie a person to the outer rim of a wheel and then spike them down a hill to their death.

"Three Strikes and You're Out" law: A crime prevention tactic based on the notion that offenders who commit and are convicted of the same three serious violent offenses will be sentenced to life in prison without parole. The goal is to incarcerate repeat offenders while reducing the crime rate.

Transactional analysis: Theory based on the belief that each person has three persons within–a parent, an adult, and a child. Games, psychodrama, and script analysis help the individual to understand how these three persons control his or her behavior. The goal is to understand and develop spontaneity and a capacity for intimacy.

Treatment model: Model that promotes the idea that offenders should be treated and consequently released back to the community.

Trustee: An entrusted inmate who, due to his loyalty to correctional officers, receives extra benefits.

U

Utilitarianism: A theory that makes the happiness of the individual or society the criterion of the morally good and right.

W

Warden: The chief administrator of a correctional facility.

Writ of habeas corpus: A suit typically filed by inmates in order to challenge the legality of their imprisonment.

Case Index

Name Index

Q

R

S

T

V

W

Y

Z

General Index

D

E

F

K

L

M

N

O

P

T

U

V

W

Y